Re-Inventing Africa's Development

"Written by a Korean diplomat and Africanist, this book offers a unique perspective on the development problems of the sub-Sahara Africa (SSA), and it also suggests effective solutions for SSA to take off economically, basically through the two-step approach of *building-block and building-bridge*."

—Keun Lee, *Professor of Economics at Seoul National University, South Korea*

"The potency of this book lies in the unique qualification of the author with vast experiences richly encompassing both the Korean and African aspects and policy expertise guided by strong academic credentials. His work embodies keen insights, and is a welcome addition to the African development discourse; I highly recommend it to all those interested in meeting the African development challenges head-on."

—Augustin K. Fosu, *Professor of Economics (ISSER) at University of Ghana, Ghana*

"On the strength of a life-long front-row experience of the continent and a deep command of the literature, facts and debates, Jong-Dae Park offers an intriguing cultural argument about African development. Inspired by the experience of South Korea, it is provocative (despite its gentle tone) and likely to prove controversial. Yet, it is also hopeful and well worth reading, both for African and non-African students, scholar and practitioners of development."

—Pierre Englebert, *Professor of Political Science at Pomona College, USA*

"A perspective from an Asian with profound experience in Africa and who is keenly aware of Korea's achievements is a welcome addition for tackling Africa's development challenges and opportunities. Jong-Dae Park weaves together so immaculately his personal observations, careful reading of available literature, and insights into the Korean experience; the book forces the reader to navigate peculiar idiosyncrasy and generalities in Africa and South Korea's development so as to draw some crucial lessons."

—Siphamandla Zondi, *Professor of Political Science at University of Pretoria, South Africa*

"Jong-Dae Park is uniquely qualified to comment on the contrast between Africa and South Korea due to his background. Park's critique is not an armchair academic exercise; he is passionate about development because, as a Korean, he has witnessed first-hand the transformation of his country, while in Africa he sees the vast potential not yet realized."

—Dr. Ian Clarke, *Chairman of Clarke Group, Uganda*

Jong-Dae Park

Re-Inventing Africa's Development

Linking Africa to the Korean Development Model

Jong-Dae Park
Embassy of the Republic of Korea
Pretoria, South Africa

ISBN 978-3-030-03945-5 ISBN 978-3-030-03946-2 (eBook)
https://doi.org/10.1007/978-3-030-03946-2

Library of Congress Control Number: 2018960761

This Palgrave Macmillan imprint is published by the registered company Springer Nature Switzerland AG
The registered company address is: Gewerbestrasse 11, 6330 Cham, Switzerland

To my father, my wife Mi-Sung and daughter Han-Seo

Preface

Writing a book on Africa seems never easy, as I have realized. I think it becomes even more difficult when one is writing about Africa's development. First, your peers will remind you that the African region is made of up diverse countries, so caution is in order when making generalizations. Second, there is the inevitability, when taking serious issues with the current state of Africa's development, of being critical of many of its aspects. Furthermore, the central theme of this book is 'mindset change', and the approaches that I propose are, in essence, breaking away from the status quo. So, basically, a critical and a form of activist overtone is maintained. Critical views are taken not for the sake of criticising, but to enhance awareness for positive changes.

Hence, I may sound blunt or judgemental, but it should not be construed in any way as demeaning, because the purpose here is to critique in a professional manner. I have a special attachment to Africa, having lived here when I was a teenager, and over the years befriended many Africans. Rather, it is as a result of my belief that Sub-Saharan African nations can indeed overcome the predicament that has plagued them for so long through change that I have decided to put down my ideas in a straightforward fashion in order to contribute to the discourse and actions on Africa's development. I was heavily engaged in development cooperation for the past seven years, and the discourses and collaboration I had with various interlocutors and stakeholders produced much positive feedback.

The caveat of discussing Africa as a whole is heeded, but I believe there is a great usefulness at this juncture in discussing the Sub-Saharan African region. While Uganda is mentioned frequently and has been often examined as a case study, I have tried to bring the full picture of the region while not losing focus on the key topics. Without being prejudiced, I can say that Sub-Saharan African countries indeed have many common traits and cross-cutting issues, as experts and observers attest.

My journey to Africa started in 1973, when I landed in East Africa at the age of 13. And now, as I gaze out of my office in Pretoria to see the Union Buildings, I sense that so much time has passed since then, yet there are so many things and issues in this region that remain unchanged despite the passage of time.

When you are in Africa—and it does not matter where you are located—the issue of development cannot be avoided. I have thought about what development is and have concluded that it is the 'way of life'. Unless the way of life of the people, including its leaders, changes, the economic development that everyone is striving for cannot come about. Africa is a land blessed with so many things and has great potential for growth, but I couldn't help thinking that something of its true essence was missing.

Asian developing economies had other neighbouring countries in the region to use as a benchmark for economic development, but I am told that Sub-Saharan African countries do not have one on their continent to act as a 'catch-up' model. The countries are seen to have been exposed to, and to have reacted to, the trends and fickleness of the times, without properly formulating and consolidating national strategy that can effectively push them forward towards transformation. My work is an attempt to identify the 'missing links' to Africa's development and to suggest a new approach in the context of reinventing and reinvigorating the development of Sub-Saharan African countries.

A contribution of this book may be that it makes a forceful case that in spite of wide variations in terms of the traits, situation, level of development, etc. of different countries, the basic rule of economics and industrialization that is applicable is the same for all of them. Fundamental progress will come about when the most fundamental conditions are satisfied. But both the African countries and the international development community alike have 'skipped' many fundamentals, hence we see the continuing underperformance of African countries.

A drawback in Africa's development may be that the existing approaches have become too technical and shallow. At this juncture, mindful of Africa's complexities, it would be useful to keep matters ridiculously simple. In the simplest terms, development can be defined using just two variables—the extent of change over time—so the question can be how much and how fast change could be made.

It is no secret that things often stall, break down and fail in Sub-Saharan Africa, and the impression we get of the region is one that has been submerged for too long in poverty and a host of other troubles. It is as if there is a certain formidable obstacle that prevents Africa from moving forward. The more we learn about Africa and try to figure out what would be the best practical solutions to resolve its challenges, the more we seem to be at a lost and do not know where to start.

While Africa's situation should not be taken lightly, it must not be exaggerated either, and we should guard against being biased and superficial. If there had been any lapse in our endeavour, it may be that the real root causes were not recognized as such, and the fundamentals were ignored. Africa is made up of 54 countries, of which 49 are Sub-Saharan. In the region, except for a handful of countries branded as 'conflict zones', the majority of countries enjoy peace and stability, and they are by no means fettered from pursuing economic prosperity. To think that Africa is surrounded by insurmountable forces impeding its development is simply wrong.

If anything, in essence, Africa's chronic poverty is not due to a lack of resources or means, but to what can be cursorily described as a 'management problem'. If this is not tackled, the prospect of a major turnaround happening soon in the region remains dim. At the dawn of this millennium, Africa was painted as 'The Hopeless Continent' on the cover of *The Economist*.[1] About a decade later, in 2011, the headline turned into 'Africa Rising'.[2] Then, an article 'Africa Rising? "Africa Reeling" May Be More Fitting Now' appeared in the *New York Times* in 2016.[3]

Who knows what is in store for Africa next, but the phrase 'Africa Rising' tells us a lot about the state of Africa and how it is perceived by the world. But it appeared that the international business community was more excited by the 'Africa Rising' narrative than the Africans were, perhaps reflecting a difference in their level of interest or expectations. Obviously, there would be a large number of foreign firms interested in the 'frontier markets' of Sub-Saharan Africa.[4] Meanwhile, the mood of the development community working on the ground at that time was much more measured or largely indifferent. Thus, one might even ask: 'For whom is Africa rising?'[5]

There also seems to be a perception gap between foreigners and the locals on what constitutes opportunity and challenge. For example, outsiders look at Africa's youth population explosion as an opportunity for business—future consumers and a potentially huge labour force—while many Africans, including political leaders and intellectuals, see this as a growing burden and a challenge for social and political stability and security.[6]

Sub-Saharan African nations have largely adapted to the trend of the times, but what counts is not the short-term economic trends or the question of whether the current situation of Africa warrants optimism or pessimism, because there will always be a mixed bag of both. The potential of Africa was always there to begin with. Instead, the key question lies in what African countries actually need to do in order to achieve development. Private enterprises alone cannot drive the sustainable and inclusive growth of a nation—it will take far more than that, like a strong social fabric, well-functioning institutions, civic values and education, sound economic planning and management, industrial policy, good governance, accountability, political stability, security, etc.

As for the regions' political landscape, armed conflicts and coups over the past two decades have decreased in number, but the stability is relative and fragile, and the risks are still high. Regarding governance, institutional quality remains low and corruption continues to be a major hindrance in the region.[7] The past few years have seen a series of peaceful transition of power taking place in the region through elections and other means. In Ghana's presidential election held in December 2016, the ruling political party was changed, which is a rarity in the region. At any rate, there is a noticeable variance in the political scorecard across the countries and sub-regions in Sub-Saharan Africa.

Besides the economic and political trends, what has not been given due attention is the task of nation-building, which seems to have been long forgotten. Nation-building is about laying the core foundations of statehood, and without them firmly in place, states will invariably be limited in terms of their performance; the unity, stability and growth of a nation will be held back as well. A sign of deficiency in nation-building is playing itself out for everyone to see. For example, executive branch leaders openly and inordinately promote their ruling party, even in public functions that should be politically neutral in tenor.

A danger of drifting away in a wave of trends looms for African countries when they do not have strong institutions and governing mechanisms in place. The peril becomes more nuanced when we accept that the world today is faced with the 'trilemma' where 'we cannot have hyper globalization, democracy, and national self-determination all at once. We can have at most two out of three'.[8] This calls for African nations to become more cognizant of the situation they are in and exert greater ownership and control over their lives and destiny.

There has been no lack of articulations, debates and studies on Africa's development, but the challenge seems as complicated as ever. However, we should heed the saying that 'the more things get complicated, the better it is to return to the basics'.[9] The task here is to break down and make sense of what seems complex, while reviving the significance of the basics that were forgotten or considered banal.

The subjects covered in this book may seem quite extensive. The intention is to navigate the issue of Africa's development by identifying, putting in context or linking together various topics, fields and elements that are deemed relevant. A two-pronged 'building-block' and 'building-bridge' approach is employed. In the grand scheme of 'building-bridge', the Korean development model is brought to the fore and reviewed so that it can be used as a meaningful reference so that lessons for Africa can be drawn from it. By 'model', I mean a 'conceptual scheme' that illustrates a set of ideas on the elements, structure and process of development rather than a kind of scientific model or mathematical formula that is meant to be precise and strictly applied.[10]

Linking up the Sub-Saharan African with the Korean model of development offers many benefits. First of all, South Korea, an aid recipient turned donor, is a prominent example of successful economic and political transformation, and the Korean contemporaries are the living proof of this experience. This makes the 'evidence' and implications of the Korean model all the more authoritative. Irma Adelman notes that: 'Its achievement is frequently referred as "the Korean Miracle" and is widely considered as the most successful process of economic development in the twentieth century.'[11]

In addition, bringing Korea into the picture will help 'crystallize' the status and characteristics of African countries' development, as well as refresh our thinking on the role of foreign aid, government, economic policies, etc. This kind of application, in turn, can also shed some new light on Korea's model, so that in the end we have a better understanding of both Africa and Korea, and about development in general. And in the context of highlighting the relevance of nation-building in development, I have retraced Africa's colonial past and legacies, and Korea's historical path.

The book starts with an introductory part in which Africa's paradox and the issue of foreign aids are outlined, followed by a review on the causes of Africa's underdevelopment and concluding that the main root cause is the mindset. The discussion then moves on to the 'missing links' in Africa's development: a sense of nation, 'development-mindedness' and the strong role of state. This development-mindedness, which I have termed 'KPOP' (which stands for 'knowing', 'practising', 'owning', and 'passion'), is introduced as a key component of the mindset that is conducive to development.

Then, Korea's path of economic development and the essence of Korea's development model are examined. The relevant features are basically in conformity with the fundamentals of the industrialization process that the frontrunners of industrialization have followed.

What stands out is that Korea achieved a highly compressed industrialization and economic growth by virtue of a strong role played by the government, the active entrepreneurship of corporations and the extraordinary level of the people's work ethic. 'Application of the Korean Development Model to Africa', and 'Africa on the New Path to Development' constitute, respectively, the main and concluding body.

All things considered, the South Korean economic model is not a 'deviation' from the mainstream rule of economics and industrialization, but can be considered as 'reinforced capitalism'. From the perspective of developing nations, it only makes sense to keep their economy dynamic and structurally transitioning if they are to catch up with the more advanced economies. In this vein, the ideas of economists who stress the importance of industrialization and dynamic economic policies are duly recognized. In particular, concepts like the 'holy trinity of economics' and 'economic discrimination' proposed by Sung-Hee Jwa are considered to be valuable tools for understanding economic development.[12]

Anyone who has insights into Sub-Saharan Africa will understand that the rural-agricultural sector assumes special importance in every aspect—be it economic, social or political—for the countries of the region. Hence, many African countries have prioritized this sector, yet they continue to struggle in terms of delivering results. Under the circumstances, Korea's *Saemaul Undong*, the New Village Movement, that was launched aggressively with success during its period of rapid economic growth, offers a meaningful 'action model' for Africa in light of its value and uniqueness as a community-driven self-help movement. How this can be applied to Africa is explained.

Out of all this, 'a new development formula for Africa' is deduced. This underscores the importance of fostering the 'missing links', putting into practice 'economic discrimination (ED)', pursuing positive industrial policy and forcefully launching initiatives for the mindset change aimed at empowering the people.

The book concludes with an emphasis on the need to reset the African development approach by prioritizing attitudinal change and enacting a bold but 'harmonious' process of change. Here, a modification to Arthur Lewis' development model of economic dualism in the form of a 'medium-bridging approach' is proposed.[13]

The 'medium-bridging' approach has the merit of making economic transitions more practical and harmonious, in a 'going with the grain' fashion.[14] The pro-poor, pro-rural policies that some of Southeast Asian countries employed can similarly be taken as a medium-bridging approach.[15] In Rwanda, they call it 'home-grown solutions' that resemble Korea's mindset change and social mobilization campaigns.[16]

Pretoria, South Africa Jong-Dae Park

Notes

1. *The Economist*, 13 May 2000. See also Jonathan Berman, *Success in Africa—CEO Insights from a Continent of the Rise* (Brookline: Bibliomotion Inc., 2013), pp. 17–20.
2. *The Economist*, 3 December 2011.
3. *New York Times*, 17 October 2016. The article sites the retracting democracy and economic dynamism of African countries.
4. David Mataen explains that there is a prevailing positive economic and business case for Africa, which he calls Africa's *megatrends*: population growth and demographic shifts; cultural revolution; regionalization of markets and the consolidation and evolution of intra-African markets; rapid urbanization; commercialization of essential services; deregulation and liberalization; the growth of credit; and capital market development. See David Mataen, *Africa the Ultimate Frontier Market: a guide to the business and investment opportunities in emerging Africa* (Hampshire: Harriman House Ltd. 2012).
5. African state leaders often express optimism for Africa, saying that 'Africa is rising' at diplomatic functions and international conferences. But this is basically in contrast to African intellectuals and the general public, who frequently rebuke or mock the 'Africa rising' claim through the media (in opinions and articles).
6. In Sub-Saharan African countries, especially among political leaders and elites, there is a growing concern over the youth unemployment problem as the population continues to increase at a fast rate. There is a general sense that the time bomb is ticking and something akin to the 'Arab Spring' could happen in Sub-Saharan Africa, which could

destabilize the whole region if appropriate measures at not taken soon to address this.

7. Alexandra Dumitru and Raphie Hayat, 'Sub-Saharan Africa: Politically more stable, but still fragile', *Rabobank*, 3 December 2015, https://economics.rabobank.com/publications/2015/december/sub-saharan-africa-politically-more-stable-but-still-fragile.
8. Dani Rodrik, *The Globalization Paradox: Democracy and the Future of the World Economy* (New York: Norton & Company, 2011), p. 200.
9. This is a Korean proverb.
10. *Dictionary.com* defines 'model' as 'a simplified representation of a system or phenomenon, as in the sciences or economics, with any hypotheses required to describe the system or explain the phenomenon, often mathematic'. See http://www.dictionary.com/browse/model?s=t.
11. Irma Adelman, 'From Aid Dependence to Aid Independence: South Korea', http://www.un.org/esa/ffd/wp-content/uploads/2007/11/20071116_IrmaAdelman.pdf.
12. Sung-Hee Jwa, *A General Theory of Economic Development: Towards a Capitalist Manifesto* (Cheltenham: Edward Elgar, 2017). See also Sung-Hee Jwa, and *The Rise and Fall of Korea's Economic Development* (Cheltenham: Edward Elgar, 2017) were published in the latter half of 2017.
13. Arthur Lewis, in his article 'Economic Development with Unlimited Supplies of Labour' (1954), introduced the 'dual-sector model', which later became known as the dual-economy theory. He pointed out that the structure of most developing economies was split into a capitalist-based manufacturing sector and a labour-intensive agricultural sector with low productivity. According to him, developing countries can achieve high economic growth by moving labour input from the latter to the former.
14. See also Brian Levy, *Working with the Grain: Integrating Governance and Growth in Development Strategies* (New York: Oxford University Press, 2014). Levy explores what kind of governance enhances economic growth and argues that incremental, momentum-sustaining, 'with the grain' institutional reform is the most realistic and pragmatic way to succeed for developing countries.
15. See David Henley's, *Asia-Pacific Development Divergence: A Question of Intent* (London: Zed Books, 2015) for Southeast Asian countries'

pro-poor, pro-rural policies that differed from the policies pursued in African countries.

16. Rwanda's *Umuganda* is quite similar to Korea's *Saemaul Undong*. *Umuganda*, meaning 'coming together', is a communal self-help activity where on the last Saturday of each month, people close their shops and businesses to participate in a 'mandatory' community service like street cleaning, repairing roads and ditches, building infrastructure and environment protection works, etc. The traditional *Umuganda* is said to have taken place more frequently, like one a week.

Contents

List of Figures

List of Tables

Part I

The Paradox of Sub-Saharan Africa

1
Disillusionment and Dilemma

My Encounters with Africa

There is a famous saying in Korea that with the passage of a decade, even rivers and mountains change. Over time, things are expected to change, and for the better. Sub-Saharan Africa is so blessed with abundant natural resources, fertile soils and beautiful weather, and it attracts so many foreign visitors who come and marvel at the unexpected. You can see a lot of dynamism in the capitals, but the vast majority of the ordinary people remain poor, to the bewilderment and disappointment of many. With globalization and business opportunities, international development assistance, advances in technology, etc., one would think that the 'great convergence' would also apply in Africa.

My early encounter with Africa was a story of fascination and disillusion, and to this day Sub-Saharan Africa largely remains a land of mystification and paradox. I still remember how surprised we were when we first came to Africa. As a teenager, when I placed my first step on African soil in 1973, I was charmed by the unexpected. My father, who was a diplomat at that time, was posted to Uganda and our family stopped over Nairobi, Kenya, for a couple of days before heading

J.-D. Park, *Re-Inventing Africa's Development*,
https://doi.org/10.1007/978-3-030-03946-2_1

to Uganda. We were struck by the orderliness, cleanliness and level of development of Nairobi compared to Seoul.

This was not what we had imagined Africa to be. Kampala, which was rather modest compared to Nairobi, was nonetheless very attractive. It was a beautiful city full of gardens and greenery, sitting on the rolling hills under the fabulous blue sky, and it had a number of good hotels like the International Hotel (now called the Sheraton Kampala Hotel), which is famous for its swimming pool, which was frequented by then President Idi Amin. A scene in the Hollywood film *The Last King of Scotland* (2006), which tells a tale of a Scottish doctor who arrives in Uganda in the early 1970s to serve as Idi Amin's personal physician, was also filmed at this swimming pool.

Just before we departed Korea, I and my older brothers were scared of going to Africa and watched, of our own accord, the film *Mondo Cane* in a downtown Seoul cinema. This was to mentally 'prepare' ourselves for the worst in Africa. The movie is a documentary of all the horrible things like cannibalism that happen in Africa and elsewhere in the world, but to our relief, we did not come across anything like that. At the time, there was not much difference in the per capital income of South Korea, Uganda and Kenya ($278, $133 and $142 respectively in 1970).[1] Economic indicators aside, the actual quality of life and even some facilities and infrastructure in these African capitals looked better than that of Korea. Politically, however, in Uganda, needless to say it was trying times under the infamous Idi Amin.

The advantage of being a teenager is that you can be carefree in respect of many things, including politics, which can be left to adults to worry about. The best thing about Uganda was its beautiful weather all year round. The weather then was clearly better than now, being more moderate and predictable, without the climate change effect that we are currently seeing. I enjoyed the natural environment and the kindness of the natives, and the merry moments with my family and friends, like when we even went on a safari tour to Murchison Falls National Park and fishing on the Victoria Lake.

What was also unexpected was the level of education in Uganda. When I entered Aga Khan Middle School, I could see the marked difference between this school and the school I went to back in Korea.

We were taught with Oxford University Press and Cambridge University Press textbooks, and the science classes—physics, chemistry and biology—were all conducted in laboratory rooms. My English teacher was native Irish and the French teacher was native French. Just a few hundred metres away from my school towered the Makerere University, at that time one of the most prestigious universities in Africa.

That was my early life in Africa. A couple of years later, we departed for Turkey, but the time I spent in Uganda left a profound and lasting imprint on me. Much later, I entered the Korean Foreign Service and the first time that I engaged in work on Africa was when I was stationed at Washington, DC as a political section officer. Besides the Korean Peninsula and East Asia, I covered the Middle East and Africa.

It was in 2001 that I returned to Africa, this time to Côte d'Ivoire. For the first time in its history since independence, a military coup was launched in the country in 1999 by General Robert Guéï and political unrest ensued. Laurent Gbagbo defeated General Guéï in the presidential election held in October 2000 and it looked as if peace would be restored. As I approached Abidjan, the capital, and saw its skyline unfold before my eyes, I could see why it was called the 'Paris of Africa' or 'little Manhattan'. But in September 2002, a mutiny by disgruntled soldiers sparked a civil war, engulfing the country in chaos and uncertainty. I witnessed how a country that was long regarded as a beacon of stability and prosperity in Africa with comparatively good institutions, infrastructures and sound economy could crumble so easily. All this was a good learning experience for me to understand the fragility of African states and the dynamics of external influence in the region.

In 2006, I was working on the President's African tour to Egypt, Nigeria and Algeria in the office of the President. It was during this tour, when we were in Nigeria, that 'Korea's Initiative for Africa's Development' was announced, the first of its kind for Korea. The visit to Algeria in particular was extraordinary and unforgettable, and it inspired me to seriously contemplate Korea's soft power.

Then in 2010, when I was in Rome, I applied for the position of the head of our mission to be re-established in Uganda. My government decided to reopen the embassy in Kampala that had been closed down in 1994 and I took a once-in-a-lifetime opportunity: to become the head of the diplomatic mission to the country that you have always reminisced about, but never thought you would return to. When I first heard that the position was open, I still needed some time to think about it and to consult with my family. Obviously, physically setting up an embassy is a really challenging task, especially in places like Uganda, a landlocked country of Sub-Saharan Africa. But the more I thought about it, the more I felt that it would be a wise choice. I made the decision to return to Uganda and there was no turning back.

On 18 May 2011, I returned to Uganda for the first time in 36 years. As the British Airways plane was hovering over Lake Victoria, approaching Entebbe Airport, my heart started to beat faster. I was anxiously staring out the window. It was a dream come true and I couldn't wait to see what Uganda looked like after all those years. Coming out of the airport, moving to Kampala, I saw that there were so many more vehicles, but that the road has not been widened at all, and its condition had deteriorated significantly, with potholes and torn-off edges that I didn't see back in the 1970s.

Then there was an unbelievable traffic bottleneck of about 10 kilometres into central Kampala. It was Monday morning, making matters worse. *Boda-boda* motorcycle taxis and *Matatu* public taxis, along with other passenger cars and trucks, flooded and converged on roundabouts and crossroads as we were approaching the city. I don't know how long we were stuck in the traffic just a few kilometres away from downtown Kampala. I have not seen such chaos in my life. The total disorderliness on the outskirts of the city made me wonder whether this was the main gateway to the centre of the capital.

I sensed that something must have been going wrong for a long time for the situation to have come to this. When our car finally mounted the hills of Nakasero, things got a lot better, but still I couldn't quite catch a glimpse of the clean and orderly downtown that I used to see 36 years ago. By the time we arrived at the hotel, we were so exhausted. Apparently, population growth and concentration, deterioration of the physical infrastructure, environmental degradation in urban areas, etc. are common phenomena in the developing world. But it was not what I had expected to see. Koreans are used to fast improvement and development, and we tend to take it for granted that with the passing of time, things gets better. What I felt this day was a sober reminder that in Sub-Saharan Africa, some kind of deep-seated problems persist and that they needed to be identified and addressed.

But other than the terrible traffic situation and poorly maintained roads, the nature of Uganda is most attractive and visitors soon get to understand why Winston Churchill named Uganda 'the Pearl of Africa'. Outside the central urban district, the beautiful, lush greenery unfolds wherever you go. I couldn't forget when I travelled for the first time to western Uganda. On the way through the Mbarara District, I saw so many wonderfully manicured plantations and rich livestock farms, and densely planted vegetables and fruits growing in red and black fertile soils. It made you wonder whether this is really Africa and not somewhere in Europe.

Each way you look at it, you sense that for whatever reason, huge opportunities have been lost, but still there is great potential for growth and prosperity. Someone said that living in perennial poverty amid such an abundance and riches of natural gifts, when you have just about everything you need, is tantamount to a sin.

Afterwards, to add a little more to our adventure, we drove deep into the southwestern end of Uganda bordering Rwanda and, from there, ventured into Rwanda in order to arrive at Kigali. How the city infrastructure was managed was so impressive, and what I saw there was really an eye opener and renewed my hope for Africa. On the contrary, my visits to South Sudan after the infighting broke out there has reminded me that still in some parts of Sub-Saharan Africa, even the most basic political, social and economic conditions required to run a state are seriously deficient.

Fast forward to 2018, as if almost seven years of my assignment in Uganda was not enough, I am still working in Africa, of course with great pleasure, having moved to South Africa in February to begin another tour of duty in the continent. I have arrived at a very interesting time when South Africa's new President Ramaphosa is trying to navigate through tough political and economic challenges in the wake of Zuma's downfall. While the fight against the legacy of apartheid and the campaign to redress historical 'injustices' continues to be waged explicitly in South Africa, from a developmental point of view, South Africa nonetheless poses another dilemma. In a sense, South Africa offers an epitome of Africa's great irony.

A Glimpse Back at Colonization and Its Legacies

Colonial history and legacies, whether one likes it or not, has relevance to the nations that have experienced colonialism and is an unavoidable subject of conversation on the development processes of the nations concerned. Almost all developing countries of the world today have gone through colonialism in one form or another, and the impact it has had on Africa is considered to be especially far-reaching. But how the colonial experience is perceived by the peoples and how this has shaped their relationship with their former colonizers will depend on the nature of the colonial rule and how it was pursued, along with many other factors. Regardless, for any developing nation, understanding its historical path and status in the nation-building process is an obvious necessity.

Sub-Saharan Africa's urban centres are rapidly becoming globalized, but the tendency to view things in terms of their historical connectivity to a colonial past evidently persists in the region. And many African leaders are not shy to speak out on colonial legacies, neo-imperialism, the 'arrogance of the West', the 'conspiracy of the West', the 'political agenda of the West' and so on, whenever they feel challenged by the Western world. It could be political gesturing, rationalization or a way of expressing African solidarity. Normally, the rhetoric is not literally antagonistic, but rather political or conventional.

A typical case is when African leaders express their displeasure over 'political pressures' from Western countries on such issues as violations of human rights, the rule of law and democracy. Generally, people in the region are very receptive to Westerners and other foreigners, are pragmatic and non-ideological, and espouse 'global civilization', which is predominantly Western in its composition. Based on historical ties and geographical proximity, European nations maintain special ties with Africa, and they continue to play 'principal' roles in the region as major partners.

The influence of the major Western powers was truly far-reaching. By 1921, the British Empire, at its peak, was covering about one-quarter of both the world's population and territory: about 4.6 billion people and 37 million km^2 respectively.[2] France, another former colossal power, boasts over 56 member states in La Francophonie on a par with the Commonwealth of Nations membership of 53. Interestingly enough, those who have lived both in the Commonwealth and the Francophonie world would be able to tell there are some differences between them, reflecting respective colonial legacies. Most Latin American countries were formerly Spanish colonies, and many other colonial powers existed in the nineteenth and twentieth centuries.

The vast majority of developing countries have experienced colonialism in some form or another. The influence of the West in terms of political, economic and social institutions, as well as popular cultures and the 'modern' way of life, has been dominant in the rest of the world, and this continues under globalization, although now there are more players in the region. Africa was the object of an all-out exploitation by the Western powers in the nineteenth century. Continuous population growth and concentration in Europe from around the early fifteenth century required an increasing supply of farmland, foods and energy, but there were also widespread epidemic diseases, wars and exploitation by rulers and landlords. Power struggles, frequent wars among Europeans powers and the difficulty in extracting resources from their own boundaries led European states to seek wealth overseas.[3]

The fragmentation of the European political systems actually started much earlier, with the fall of the Roman Empire in the late sixth century and the expansion of Islamic powers in the eighth century. The nobility built fortresses against potential invaders and looters, while exploiting the serfs and mobilizing troops to put down rebellions by the serfs, and to counter attacks from outside and within. The frequency of wars was on the rise and never-ending, and new armouries like cannons were developed, driving up the costs of waging war. Crusaders were also sent to recapture holy places occupied by Islamic forces. Their objectives, besides religious, were political and commercial in nature, and successful campaigns helped reopen the Mediterranean Sea for trade and travel.[4]

The development of city states in Europe that became the major centres of trade, together with connections of various trade routes, formed a natural 'world system' of trade. But the fall of Constantinople in 1453 caused by the Ottoman Empire's invasion dealt a heavy blow to Europe as the trade route to the East through the eastern Mediterranean Sea was blocked by the Ottomans, forcing the West to find alternate sea routes to access Asia's riches through the Indian Ocean.[5]

Europe's limited farmland and natural resources, the increasing struggle and competition among factional powers, and greed for wealth and power drove Europeans to venture into aggressive campaigns outside their continent. During this period of excursions, America was discovered and Sub-Saharan Africa was further surveyed. A Portuguese expeditionary force in the early sixteenth century ended the era of peaceful navigation by introducing maritime trade using coercive means. While the West's mission to Asia was mostly to find markets in order to trade commodities, their efforts in Africa were focused on mobilizing slaves for plantation farming in Africa and the New World.[6]

In Latin America, the two powerful Aztec and Inca Empires were known to have flourished by the fifteenth century, but they were conquered by the Spanish expedition and subjected to harsh domination. Also in Africa, before it was colonized by the West, there existed many empires in Sub-Saharan Africa, besides those in Maghreb or the North Africa region. They were mostly concentrated in West Africa, but other empires or kingdoms were identified in central, eastern, western and southern Africa as well.[7] The most prominent ones were the Ghana Empire, the Mali Empire, the Benin Empire, the Mossi Kingdoms, the Aksum Empire and the Ethiopian Empire.[8]

While the features of European incursions into Asia, Africa and America varied, they all had one thing in common, in that they were carried out coercively, by 'gunboat trade', conquest, imposition of terms, etc., based on the Europeans' superior arms and fighting capability. As time passed, the exploitive nature of the West's adventurism intensified and degenerated to the point of doing anything possible, like conducting forced opium sales and the gunboat diplomacy in Asia in the nineteenth century.[9]

The continents that Europeans targeted to advance their wealth and power—Asia, Africa and Latin America, including the Caribbean—were themselves more or less inter-connected in the dynamics of growing international trading system. But the trade in the Indian Ocean, even before Portugal, the Netherlands, Britain and France embarked on the 'armed trade', was robustly carried out by regional players, including Islamic powers, India and China. Natural resources such as gold and silver were introduced to China and India, and from these countries fabrics and other commodities were exported to neighbouring regions. Some items like cotton fabrics were distributed beyond East Africa to reach West Africa.[10]

In the process, the Western imperial powers erected what can be called a world trading system. An example of its sub-system is the one which was based on plantation systems in Africa and South America and Caribbean. The Atlantic world was connected to two triangular trade systems which emerged in the seventeenth century and were completed in the eighteenth century. The most widely known one is that linking the Britain, Africa and America: sugar cane, timber and fisheries from America were exported to Britain, and manufactured goods from Britain were sold to Africa in exchange for slaves, who were exported to America. The other system involved the export of rum to Africa from the North American British colony, the sale of African slaves exchanged for rum to the Caribbean, and the export of molasses from the Caribbean to New England. Through such trade systems, the colonial rulers amassed huge wealth.[11]

How such a large-scale slave trade could have been brazenly and persistently carried out for many centuries is unimaginable today, but at that time human expropriation and exploitation were not uncommon. Muslims are said to have engaged in trans-Saharan slave trade well before this transatlantic slave trade took place, while various kingdoms and states in Africa were operating slavery in one form or another. Of course, slavery itself was prevalent in many regions and throughout our history, and skin colour was of no relevance in terms of becoming a slave. When you look up the word 'slave' in the dictionary, you will find that it is derived from the 'Slavs', who were sold off in great numbers into servitude by conquering forces in the early Middle Ages.[12]

Wars, conquests and subjugation of the weak by the powerful—in other words, the rule of the survival of the fittest—were commonplace among Europeans. The development of modern nation states in Europe in some ways exacerbated the rivalry and divisions in the region, culminating in the two World Wars in the twentieth century. When we reflect on the history of imperialism and colonialism of the West, people may see these as 'sins' committed by the West on others, but back then there were no such thing as universal values like human rights, let alone the kind of international norms or regulations that we take for granted today.[13]

However, the word 'imperialism' in today's context only has negative connotations. It implies greed, exploitation, control and subjugation of the weak. In ancient or medieval times, empires might have been helpful in reducing wars or bringing about stability. However, with growing populations and political entities or states having limited land and natural resources, Europe was increasing engaged in internal rivalries and conflicts, not to mention clashes with foreign (namely Islamic) forces.

Europe's internal tensions could have been relieved as European states focused on expanding into other continents: Portugal and Spain led expeditions to find new sea routes and riches, and embarked on the colonization of foreign lands during the fifteenth and sixteenth centuries, while the Netherlands, Britain, France, Belgium and Germany followed suit. After Asia and America, it was Africa's turn to be subjected to renewed exploitation, culminating in the Scramble for Africa by the European powers in the late nineteenth century. The Berlin Conference of 1894 and subsequent arrangements among the colonial powers largely defined the territorial boundaries of African countries that we see today. The colonial expansion in the late nineteenth and early twentieth centuries is referred to as the New Imperialism.

However, as it turned out, the West's power game did not end with such partitioning of sphere of influence. Meanwhile, the Industrial Revolution that started in Britain and spread to other European countries as well as to the US and Japan, also upgraded the technology and output of weaponry, making wars all the more devastating. The tensions were brought right back to the continent of Europe, where the First

World War was triggered. This was followed by the Great Depression and the Second World War, which was unprecedented in the history of humankind in terms of the scale of its casualties. The surfacing of a whole different form of nationalism in Europe—Nazism and fascism—showed the dangers inherent in Western democracies degenerating into something far worse.

Imperialism and colonialism withered following the World Wars, and as the principle of self-determination of nations was declared. On 14 December 1960, the United Nations (UN) General Assembly adopted a resolution called the 'Declaration on the Granting of Independence to Colonial Countries and Peoples'. Most Asian and Middle Eastern countries were decolonized by the 1950s, while almost all African and Caribbean countries achieved independence by the 1960s. For African countries, decolonization was not the end of the story of international intrusions. They were still being drawn deep into the forces of the international political economy, and faced challenging tasks of nation-building and development both during and after the Cold War and into the era of globalization.

No doubt, for Sub-Saharan African nations, extensive colonization, subsequent decolonization and continued close ties with their former colonial powers have helped them to become open and engaged with the West and the world as a whole. In the process, Western ideas, education, cultures, political, economic and social systems and know-how continued to flow in, having a truly profound influence on the region.

African colonization was a conquest launched by the West equipped with superior armoury and professional expeditionary forces. Before the twentieth century, there were no widely established norms like human equality and non-aggression in the world as we know it today, and many in Europe viewed the white race as being superior.[14] Europeans went about taking the lands and assets of others by forceful means in the context of building empires or enriching themselves and their motherland. The politics of sheer realism prevailed. There were not many objections to those actions taking place outside of Europe and even when Europeans clashed with each other, it was not considered to be extraordinary. With the passage of time, however, the exploitive apparatus of the colonial settlers turned into a more stable and routine governing mechanism that later provided a groundwork for state-building by Africans.[15]

Although Sub-Saharan African countries adopted Western-style modern state institutions and governing systems, and pursued market economics early on, common syndromes such as the weakness of state institutions and the weakness of national identity or a sense of nation persist. Modern states or nation states that we see today began in Europe, although in other continents, such as Asia, there were highly centralized and developed kingdoms or dynasties. As mentioned earlier, there were already empires and kingdoms in Africa before colonization and to this day, some of those sub-national kingdoms persist. Uganda is an example of a country having officially five kingdoms or monarchies: Buganda, Bunyoro, Busoga, Toro and Rwenzururu.

In medieval Europe, there existed a variety of forms of authority or rule over people like feudal lords, empires, religious authorities, free cities and other authorities.[16] Students of international politics have learned that the 1648 Peace of Westphalia, which was the outcome of the Thirty Years' War, gave rise to the development of modern states having a sweeping capability for taxation, a sophisticated bureaucratic system and coercive control over their populations. The form of statehood that became prominent in Europe later spread to the rest of the world through the process of colonization and decolonization. Modern colonialism has deep roots in the Western history of the formation of nation states and we are reminded of its influence on the rest of the world. It is argued that among the countries that were colonized, some types of modern states were developed in Asia and elsewhere prior to colonialism, but they were largely displaced by colonial rule.[17] The West's military capability, technology and expansionist posture made the difference.

Jürgen Osterhammel points out that colonialism contributed to making the European concept of the modern state universal and that this is one of the greatest impacts colonialism had on the world.[18] Before Western colonization, it is said that only centralized despotic powers like the Mughul Empire had the semblance of a modern state. Other than this, political powers in Asia and Africa had the appearance of being rather informal, personal and ritual-religious. These entities were not based on sound institutional structures, but were founded on loose networks of loyalty. On the other hand, colonial states of the nineteenth and twentieth centuries were secularized and administrative states were backed up by a military apparatus.[19]

A problem here was that while the colonial states and subsequent independent states were territorial states, they were hardly nation states. In other words, there was a discrepancy between the concept of territorial state and nation state due to arbitrary territorial boundaries set by the colonial powers. It was an outcome of social Darwinism thinking and the 'divide and rule' policy of European colonialists, which may explain why to this day so many ethnic, religious conflicts occur in Africa.[20] However, a mismatch between territorial boundaries and the peoples does not necessarily correlate to conflicts, and it would be virtually impossible to divide up territories in order to suit every ethnicity or tribe. Correcting the 'territorial mismatch' can still bring about conflict, as can be seen in the case of South Sudan, which became independent from Sudan.

The prime objective of the colonial state was to maintain control over the people conquered and establish conditions or mechanism through which the colony could be exploited economically to serve the interests of the colonial power. In addition, colonial states were equipped with a highly developed bureaucracy. In the case of Sub-Saharan Africa, the current modern state structure that was 'transplanted' by the West and also many of its institutional components emulated by African countries are in most cases functionally weak, inefficient and unreliable, and are frequently riddled with corruption and bad governance.

Unlike in other regions, where the state acquires its sovereignty in the political process of building capacity for the statehood and is eventually recognized by other states, African states gained their sovereign status instantly by collective recognition by the international community, such as the UN. Despite the fact that more than half a century has passed since most African countries gained independence, they are still struggling with the fundamentals of statehood and governance.

Continuing Woes and Dilemmas in Africa's Development

Many decades have passed since the independence of Sub-Saharan African countries, but to this day not much has occurred in terms of fundamental progress in their development. When Ghana, then the wealthiest nation in Sub-Saharan Africa, became independent in 1957, it was more prosperous than South Korea, but by the early 2000s, Korea's gross national product (GNP) per capita was over 20 times that of Ghana. Nigeria collected over $600 billion in oil revenues since the early 1960s when it started oil production, but a study conducted in 2004 revealed that as much as $400 billion has disappeared, while the majority of its population suffers from acute poverty.[21]

How the predicaments have persisted expansively and commonly over many decades throughout the region is quite astonishing, as Martin Meredith observes: 'Although Africa is a continent of great diversity, African states have much in common, not only their origins as colonial territories, but the similar hazards and difficulties they have faced. Indeed, what is so striking about the fifty-year period since independence is the extent to which African states have suffered so many of the same misfortunes.'[22]

Crawford Young also notes African countries' similarities on many fronts, such as in cultural patterns 'that underpin the regular invocation of an "African Society" as a generic entity by leaders and analyst'.[23] Other similarities include the 'defining impact of the colonial occupation', the fact that most of the countries decolonized at the same time, the similarity of regime structures at the outset, the 'high degree of political diffusion in the political arena' and Africa's poor developmental performance.[24]

From the perspective of development, Africa's history since colonization can be broken down into five periods: (1) the period of exploitation by the colonizers; (2) the period of early nation-building (the mid-twentieth century, roughly the 1950s–60s); (3) the period of 'deepening' of international aid (the 1970s–80s); (4) the period of post-Cold War globalization (the 1990s–2015); and (5) period of the Post-2015 Development Agenda (2015 onwards).

Colonial legacies still matter today. It is evident that African countries became independent under the most adverse circumstances. They inherited very meagre agricultural or industrial foundations and lacked human capital and other assets required for rapid growth. The transatlantic African slave trade over some 400 years also had a profound impact on Africa. There were also slave trades within the region and across other regions, but these were smaller in scale. The early phase of colonization was marked by extensive human exploitation and plundering of natural resources. African economies became extractive to serve the colonizers and most infrastructures served the needs of the export market rather than internal development. The coercive force used to manipulate labour turned the economies into monocultures, and Gareth Austin notes that under colonialism 'African societies ceased being self-sufficient as they began to import manufactured goods and basic foodstuffs, while exporting raw materials. To this day, the perceived comparative advantages of many African economies are little more than their colonially derived specializations, even though export agriculture had begun to develop in late pre-colonial times'.[25]

Ever since African countries were decolonized, up until now, they have continuously missed opportunities and faced dilemmas regardless of how international dynamics and environment have evolved, to come to a state of 'African paradox'. During the early nation-building period, the goal of African states was to build autonomous states, but they faced strong counterforces holding them back or even driving them backwards towards structural and psychological dependency.

In the era of 'deepening of aid' in the 1970s and 1980s when emphasis was placed on targeting the poorest and correcting the 'dual economy', Africa again missed the opportunity due to its political unrest, tribal conflicts and wars, continued mismanagement, corruption, etc. Then, entering the 1990s, the demise of the Cold War ushered in the era of political transition, economic liberalization and globalization. Again, what could have been an opportunity disguised as a challenge presented itself to Africa, but the countries were virtually irresponsive. The adaption to the changing world was limited maybe due to failure to fully grasp the weight of dilemma they were in with respect to industrialization under globalization.

The globalization, and especially the financial liberalization, of the 1990s was a force to be reckoned with and not many saw it as such. Even South Korea, which in 1994 espoused *segyewha* (globalization) as a national policy was hit hard by it in the 1997 Asian financial crisis. Given the global economic environment and trends, in retrospect, the 1990s may have been the last real opportunity for Sub-Saharan African economies to solidify their industrialization capacity. The emergence of 'Africa's new tycoons' or 'business giants', while meaningful, cannot be a credible indicator of the countries' transformative economic development.

The global development regime entered a new chapter with the launch of the Post-2015 Development Agenda, and the Sustainable Development Goals (SDGs) in 2015 after the completion of Millennium Development Goals (MDGs). The lesson learned from the MDGs may be that such global efforts may have been good in terms of tackling Africa's humanitarian needs and crisis, but were hardly effective in pushing African countries to have greater ownership and be developmental in substantive terms. The dilemma continues because when the dust settles, everyone is back to their routine business.

The irony is that Sub-Saharan African nations that should be most distressed about their state of development and therefore should be the most eager to undertake the necessary actions to lift themselves out of present situation in fact appear to be the least bothered in this regard. While serious deliberations and debates have taken place in and around the UN and other development forums like the Organisation for Economic Co-operation and Development's Development Assistance Committee (OECD DAC), equally serious soul searching by Africans within the African continent has been lacking.

The syndromes of dependency and 'backtracking' that will be dealt with later on seem to be quite widespread in the region. There is every reason to believe in the positivity of Africa rising in the long term, but for now, the great potential of Africa has not materialized and largely remains as potential. Yet in order to be able to move forward with confidence, countries would need to learn the lessons of their past trials and errors, and come to a clear understanding of where they stand. The dilemma for African countries was that as they were embarking on the path to national autonomy, they soon found themselves held back by the structure of dependency that has re-emerged in the aftermath of decolonization. In the absence of conscientious and sustained efforts to be autonomous, it would have been difficult for the newly independent states to delink themselves from the strong influence of their former colonizers.

A governance crisis was seen as a main culprit for Africa's poor performance in development. But in Sub-Saharan African states, the capacity and institutions of governance have never really been strong since the colonial period, nor was the sense of nation or national identity. Even after gaining independence, many of these states were not effectively prepared for self-government and had to deal with various social and political tensions that were created or neglected by the colonial regimes.

During this time of 'paradox of nation-building and dependency', the most important means sought was foreign aid. Aid was a prime objective for African nations and the main policy tools for developed countries. This was particularly so during the Cold War era, when the developing countries joined the political-ideological blocs. Although some small amounts of aid were given by some European countries for their colonies in the early twentieth century, it was after the Second World War that international aid as we know it began to be institutionalized and expanded to become an international norm.[26]

Initially, aid was primarily targeted at emergency relief, rehabilitation or national reconstruction and was directed at Western countries. After the war, much of Europe was left in ruins and it was the Marshall Plan, or the European Recovery Program, pushed forward by the US, that first set up the international aid regime. The rise of the Soviet Bloc and the beginning of the Cold War increased such efforts. So the purpose of aid during this period was to serve the donor's diplomatic, political and strategic objectives.[27]

Later, mostly in the 1960s, the majority of Sub-Saharan African countries gained independence. Since African countries became independent at the height of the Cold War, from a strategic point of view, they could have used the international political dynamics to advance their own economic development. By all accounts, this should have been a golden opportunity for Africa to grasp because the external conditions were benign. In the 1950s and 1960s, the dominant aid strategy was to focus on developing countries' need for investment capital and modern technology so that they could boost their economies.[28] Emphasis was placed on offering financial assistance and expertise to help plan and manage infrastructure and other economic development projects. The expectation was that modern technology and know-how in institutional building and organization would have trickle-down and spreading effects. But not much consideration was given to promoting links between urban and rural areas, and agriculture and industry.

High expectations and optimism can quickly turn into disappointment. In the 1960s, there was growing dissatisfaction with this approach, as the majority of the populace did not benefit from both the aid and economic growth that followed decolonization. Foreign aid was not having the desired effect on all parts of the targeted areas. It was during this time that much self-criticism in the donor community was voiced towards the tendencies of 'dual economy (a division between a modern, urban-based economy and traditional peasant economy)' in the developing countries, and the term 'white elephants' became popular. In sum, the main point of criticism was that the poor got very little out of such assistance and that the technology used was not adaptable to local conditions.[29]

As early as the beginning of the 1970s, when developed countries already have well-established aid programmes, there were talks about 'donor fatigue' and 'crisis of development' within the donor community. What finally came out of all these debates and criticisms regarding the way forward for aid were 'basic human needs' rather than stimulating long-term growth. Immediate and direct benefit for the poor was the focused goal of donors in this period.[30] The fall in primary commodity prices, the mood of détente, the lessening of rivalry between the West and the East, the international oil shock and the responses of the Organization of the Petroleum Exporting Countries (OPEC) and oil-rich Arab countries may have also contributed to this. In the 1970s and 1980s, the general tendency of donors' approaches was placing greater emphasis on, and distributing more aid towards, the poorest countries, with an increased portion of aid going to Sub-Saharan Africa.

The dominant aid strategy during this time took the form of 'integrated rural development (IRD)' projects, which were aimed at large parts of the local economy, especially small farmers, and engaged much of the central and local government bodies with the goal to reaching out to large parts of the targeted group. Planning units were set up within the central ministries to coordinate multi-sector projects,and international and local non-governmental organizations (NGOs) started to take part in international assistance programmes.[31]

However, the aid strategy of the 1970s encountered various problems, such as the extreme complexity of the integrated development projects demanding a level of coordination that was beyond the administrative capability of most countries and too much faith placed on central planning. Also, the success of the welfare state system that many industrialized countries experienced in the 1960s and the aid strategy that was more or less influenced by such economic development optimism were out of touch with reality, given developing countries' resources and capacity.[32] I think that the international development community was right to bring comprehensive rural development to the forefront of its strategy, but unfortunately this approach lost steam and withered because of the very problem that still haunts Africa today—the lack of initiation for change and corresponding actions on the part of Africans themselves.

While rural development is a fundamental task for any developing country, it is unclear what really ignited the 'integrated rural development approach' to take centre stage in the international development arena in the early 1970s. Interestingly enough, it was in 1970 that Korea's New Village Movement, the *Saemaul Undong*, was launched. But the reason why Korea's movement was successful while IRD projects failed is probably because unlike the former, the latter was driven and assisted by donors and did not induce locals to work voluntarily in a self-help fashion to generate resources and income on their own.

In the 1980s, amid a lack of progress in aid programmes and the looming dangers of further debt crises in developing countries, as the Mexican debt crisis of 1982, soon spread to other parts of the Third World. The International Monetary Fund (IMF) and the World Bank led the structural adjustment programmes that demanded liberalization and the removal of state control for macro-economic stability. The debt crisis turned the 1980s into the 'lost development decade': before the path of development and poverty alleviation could be resumed, they had to implement painful polices of stabilization and structural adjustment.[33]

However, because of the inherent limitations of applying such formulae in rigorous fashion to developing countries and also of the apparent need to continue assistance for building infrastructure and directly targeting those most in need, the structural adjustment programmes were only partially executed, accounting for only a fraction of the total loans. And many bilateral donors and UN organizations continued to work in the same way as they had in the 1970s.[34] From the 1970s to the late 1980s, we can see the aid focus on poverty reduction shifting to structural adjustment and back again to poverty reduction. In the late 1980s, there were growing criticisms in the international development community that adjustment policies neglected the poor.

The end of the Cold War was accompanied by a number of significant changes in foreign aid. Most of all, the disappearance of the East European Communist Bloc and dissolution of the former Soviet Union changed the attitudes of major donor countries' aid policies vis-à-vis their allies and the former Communist Bloc countries. The US and other Western countries were increasingly linking aid to the state of governance of developing countries rather than supporting any friendly countries from a foreign policy standpoint.

As a result of the end of the Cold War, some countries lost the strategic value that the US and others have placed on them, and the amount of aid flowing to them dropped sharply. Also, great attention was given to assisting the political transition processes in former Communist Bloc countries. Therefore, much rhetoric and many efforts were directed towards the governance, democracy and political transition of the developing or newly independent countries in this decade. Amid growing donor fatigue, the total amount of aid funding fell quite markedly, while demands for political reforms became stronger.[35]

The instruments donors used with the focus of aid were sector programme support, capacity-building, policy dialogue, 'selective assistance', etc. All these methods were geared towards responding to the widening scope of aid targets in a more focused manner, with lower amounts of aid available in a bid to achieve greater aid-efficiency. But the development community continued to be dismayed by the lack of progress shown, especially in the poorest nations of Sub-Saharan Africa. Africa's crisis of governance and moral hazard problem were very frequently discussed during this period.[36]

In 2000, the UN adopted the MDGs, which targeted eight areas: (1) eradicating extreme poverty and hunger; (2) achieving universal primary education; (3) promoting gender equality and empowering women; (4) reducing child mortality; (5) improving maternal health; (6) combating HIV/AIDS, malaria and other diseases; (7) ensuring environmental sustainability; and (8) developing a global partnership for development. Each of these goals has specific targets and set dates for achieving those targets.[37]

In 1999, the IMF and the World Bank initiated the Poverty Reduction Strategy Paper (PRSP) approach, a comprehensive country-based strategy for poverty reduction. This approach was the IMF's and the World Bank's recognition of the importance of ownership and the need for a greater focus on poverty reduction, and it has become integral to the negotiation of development assistance for African countries. Its aim was to support heavily indebted poor countries (HIPCs) and provide the crucial link for aid flows with poverty reduction strategies developed by the aid recipient countries. It was to help the countries meet the MDGs, which aimed to halve poverty between 1990 and 2015. The PRSP has become a key benchmark for most countries in Africa for accessing external finance through bilateral and multilateral sources.[38]

In addition to MDGs and the PRSP, at the turn of the new century, there appeared more new initiatives, including Africa's first self-developed initiative. In 2001, the Organisation of African Unity (OAU) (now the African Union (AU)) endorsed the New Partnership for Africa's Development (NEPAD) for economic regeneration of Africa, with the goal of eradicating poverty, promoting sustainable growth and development, integrating Africa into the global economy, and accelerating the empowerment of women. NEPAD, which is a merger of the

Millennium Partnership for the African Recovery Programme (MAP) and the OMEGA Plan for Africa, was hailed as 'Africa's own initiative, Africa's plan, African crafted and therefore, African-owned'.[39]

It was argued that NEPAD 'constitutes the most important advance in African development policy during the last four decades. Undoubtedly it is an ambitious programme and represents perhaps one last hope for Africa to reverse its slide into irrelevance.'[40] But seven years after its launch, President Abdoulaye Wade of Senegal, who was one of its initial backers, accused NEPAD of wasting hundreds of millions of dollars and achieving nothing.[41]

Following the end of the Cold War, special emphasis was placed on aid effectiveness. Besides donor fatigue, recipient fatigue was also acknowledged. The donor community began to realize that its many different approaches and conditions were imposing a huge burden and costs on developing countries, making aid less effective. It began to consult and coordinate closely among its member states and with developing countries to enhance the impact of the aid given. The aid effectiveness movement, led by the OECD DAC, picked up momentum in 2002 with the Monterrey Consensus reached during the International Conference on Financing for Development held in Monterrey, Mexico. The participants of the meeting agreed to increase its funding for development, but acknowledged that more money alone was not enough. A new paradigm of aid as a partnership, rather than a one-way relationship between donor and recipient, was evolving.[42]

As follow-up measures, a series of High Level Forums on Aid Effectiveness was held in Rome, Accra, Paris and Busan (Korea). The fourth meeting in Busan (2011) is considered to have marked a turning point in international discussions on aid and development. It brought together over 3000 delegates to take stock of the progress made in aid delivery and to come up with collective aid plans for the future. The forum culminated in the signing of the Busan Partnership for Effective Development Co-operation by ministers of developed and developing nations, emerging economies, entities of South-South and triangular cooperation and civil society. This declaration established for the first time an agreed framework for development cooperation that embraces traditional donors, South-South cooperators, the BRICS nations (Brazil, Russia, India, China and South Africa), civil society organizations and private funders.[43]

The UN was involved intensively in drawing up the Post-2015 Development Agenda, playing a facilitating role in the global conversation on this subject and supported broad consultations, leading to its launch during the UN Development Summit in September 2015. The process of formulating the Post-2015 Development Agenda was led by member states, with broad participation from major groups of nations, international bodies and other civil society stakeholders. Numerous inputs have been made to the agenda, producing a set of SDGs. This was an outcome of an open working group of the General Assembly, the report of an inter-governmental committee of experts on sustainable development financing, General Assembly dialogues, etc.

These efforts notwithstanding, the era of full-fledged globalization that began in the early 1990s has not been benign in relation to Africa. Thus, it is caught in a very long stretch of a third dilemma that we can call the 'globalization-industrialization dilemma'. In order to realize economic transformation, countries need to first build and strengthen the basis on which economic growth can take place, and then work on building the manufacturing industry sector along with or based on agricultural sector development.

But ironically, globalization which entails trade-investment liberalization, free market access, global competition, etc. perhaps poses a serious obstacle to this African dream. As such, the task of achieving transformation in the era of hyper-globalization from the perspective of African states is quite a big challenge. Certainly, there is an increasing awareness within Africa of this issue, but there do not seem to be clear ideas and answers in terms of what concrete measures should be taken. Figure 1.1 illustrates Africa's continuing predicament. It shows the increasing gap in the average per-capita income level between Africa and rest of the world.

Figure 1.2 illustrates the points made here with respect to Sub-Saharan Africa's paradox viewed from a historical perspective.[44] It also shows Africa's continuing tribulations and challenges. In the colonial era, Africa was subjected to all-out exploitation. Upon independence,

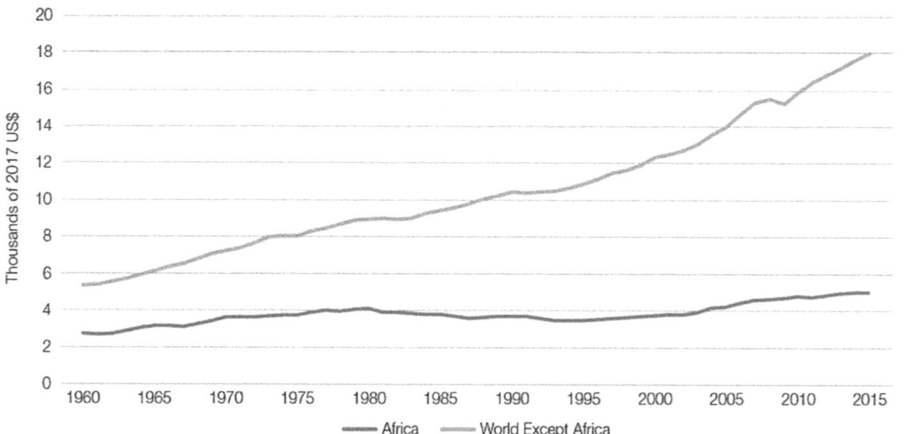

Fig. 1.1 The growing income gap: Africa versus the rest of the world (1960–2015) (*Source* International Futures (Ifs) v. 7.33, data from World Development Indicators (US$ in constant 2017 values). ISS South Africa 'Made in Africa' report 8, p. 4, April 2018)

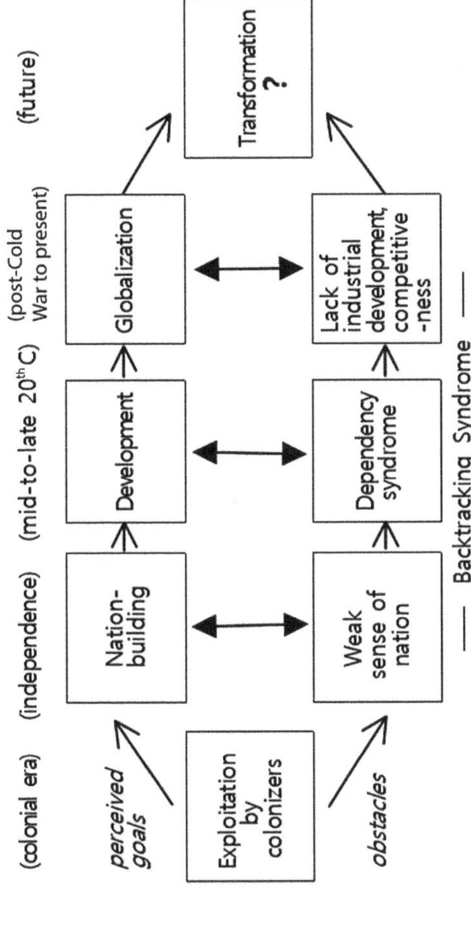

Fig. 1.2 The paradox of Sub-Saharan Africa

Table 1.1 Sub-Saharan Africa at a glance

Country	Area (km^2) (thousand)	Population (millions)	GDP per capita	Country	Area (km^2) (thousand)	Population (millions)	GDP per capita
Angola	1247	22.14	6665	Madagascar	592	23.57	464
Benin	112	10.6	825	Malawi	120	16.83	354
Botswana	581	2.04	6575	Mali	1240	15.77	750
Burkina Faso	274	17.42	725	Mauritania	1030	3.98	1370
Burundi	28	10.48	270	Mauritius	2.04	1.25	11,368
Cameroon	47.5	22.82	1398	Mozambique	800	26.47	624
Cape Verde	4	0.5	4010	Namibia	824	2.35	4997
Central African Republic	623	4.71	363	Niger	1267	18.54	421
Chad	1284	13.21	1040	Nigeria	923	178.52	3080
Comoros	1.86	0.75	942	Rwanda	26	12.1	591
Congo	342	4.56	3226	São Tomé and Príncipe	1	0.2	1746
Congo, DR	2345	69.36	474	Senegal	197	14.55	998
Cote d'Ivoire	322	20.81	497	The Seychelles	0.455	0.093	15,540
Djibouti	23	0.89	1833	Sierra Leone	72	6.21	918
Equatorial Guinea	28	0.78	21,629	Somalia	637	10.81	112
Eritrea	118	6.54	592	South Africa	1,220	53.14	6267
Ethiopia	1104	96.51	559	South Sudan	640	11.74	1269
Gabon	267	1.71	11,805	Sudan	1890	38.76	2221
Gambia	11	1.91	586	Swaziland	17	1.27	2988
Ghana	239	26.44	1265	Tanzania	943	50.76	966
Guinea	246	12.04	606	Togo	57	6.99	598
Guinea-Bissau	36	1.75	655	Uganda	241	38.85	673
Kenya	570	45.55	1593	Zambia	753	15.02	2031
Lesotho	30	2.1	920	Zimbabwe	390	14.6	725
Liberia	113	4.4	467				

Source African Statistical Book (AfDB, UNECA, AUC) (2015)

Table 1.2 Country classification by income in Sub-Saharan Africa

Low income		Lower to middle income	High-middle income
Benin	Malawi	Angola	Botswana
Burkina Faso	Mali	Cape Verde	Equatorial Guinea
Burundi	Mozambique	Cameroon	Gabon
Central African Republic.	Niger	Congo	Mauritius
Chad	Rwanda	Cote d'Ivoire	Namibia
Comoros	Senegal	Djibouti	The Seychelles
Congo, DR	Sierra Leone	Kenya	South Africa
Eritrea	Somalia	Ghana	
Ethiopia	South Sudan	Lesotho	
Gambia	Tanzania	Mauritania	
Guinea	Togo	Nigeria	
Guinea-Bissau	Uganda	São Tomé and Príncipe	
Liberia	Zimbabwe	Sudan	
Madagascar		Swaziland	
		Zambia	

Source World Bank list of economies, June 2017

African states had the opportunity to newly shape their destiny, but failed to move on and were held back by inherent 'limitations', such as a lack of true sense of nation. Then, with favourable international settings, Africans aspired to achieve economic development, but the negativities like dependency syndrome and 'backtracking syndrome' deepened so as to offset what was gained.

Africa continued to miss out on the opportunities in the changing international political-economic environment. The end of the Cold War ushered in an era of full-fledged globalization, but the 'readiness' of African nations in terms of nation-building and development mindedness, let alone industrialization and economic competitiveness, is a far cry from what was expected. To this day, many political leaders, policy-makers and economic experts in African do not seem to fully grasp the nature of the problem. As for the income gap shown in Fig. 1.1, the extended projection shows the gap growing into 2030. The question is: when will African countries break out of this dilemma? The basic country profile information of 49 Sub-Saharan African countries is shown in the Tables 1.1, 1.2, 1.3 and in Chapters 2 and 3.

Table 1.3 Country classification by resource abundance in Sub-Saharan Africa

Resource-rich countries		Non-resource-rich countries		
Oil	Metals/ minerals			
Angola	Botswana	Benin	Gambia	São Tomé and Príncipe
Chad	Congo, DR	Burkina Faso	Ghana	Senegal
Congo	Guinea	Burundi	Guinea-Bissau	The Seychelles
Equatorial Guinea	Liberia	Cape Verde	Kenya	South Africa
Gabon	Mauritania	Cameroon	Lesotho	Somalia
Nigeria	Namibia	Central African Republic	Madagascar	Sudan
South Sudan	Niger	Comoros	Malawi	Swaziland
	Sierra Leone	Cote d'Ivoire	Mali	Tanzania
	Zambia	Djibouti	Mauritius	Togo
		Eritrea	Mozambique	Uganda
		Ethiopia	Rwanda	Zimbabwe

Source World Bank, *Africa's Pulse*, October 2017, vol. 16

Notes

1. 1970 World Bank data (data.worldbank.org).
2. Angus Maddison, *The World Economy: A Millennial Perspective* (Paris: OECD, 2001), pp. 98, 242; Bruce R. Gordon, 'To Rule the Earth', www.hostkingdom.net/earthrul.html.
3. European countries' colonization of Africa can be seen in the context of the 'predatory nature' of state-building and its extension—struggle for survival, their rivalry and competition during and after state-building—as viewed by Charles Tilly in *War Making and State Making as an Organized Crime* (1985) and *Coercion, Capital and European States* (1990). According to Tilly, war-making, state-making, protection and extraction were the four activities in which European countries engaged for survival and development.
4. Robert B. Marks, *The Origins of the Modern World*, 2nd ed. (Lanham: Rowman & Littlefield, 2006). Korean translation by Sa-I Publishing (2014), pp. 91–92.
5. Ibid., pp. 84–86.

6. As for the effects of the African slave trade by Europeans, Warren C. Whatley says that it had a profound effect on Africa's political authority (promoting 'absolutism'), while Nathan Nunn in his 'Long-Term Effects of Africa's Slave Trade', *Quarterly Journal of Economics* 123, no. 1 (2008), pp. 139–176 argues that slaving and slave trade depressed long-term economic growth. See Warren C. Whatley, 'The Transatlantic Slave Trade and the Evolution of Political Authority in West Africa', in Emmanuel Akyeampong, Robert H. Bates, Nathan Nunn, and James A. Robinson (eds), *Africa's Development in Historical Perspective* (New York: Cambridge University Press, 2014), pp. 463–465. Daron Acemoglu and James A. Robinson in *Why Nations Fail* (2012), pp. 252–253 elaborates on the trade of guns for slaves, which, through increased warfare and conflicts, caused major loss of life and human suffering, besides bringing about changes in political authority.
7. In terms of historical development, it is argued that there was significant heterogeneity in Africa, with the most developed parts being North Africa, West Africa and Ethiopia. There are suggestions that these parts of Africa attained levels of development that were close to those of Eurasia. See Emmanuel Akyeampong et al., *Africa's Development in Historical Perspective* (2014), p. 7.
8. See Robert O. Collins and James M. Burns, *A History of Sub-Saharan Africa*, 2nd ed. (New York: Cambridge University Press, 2014).
9. The maritime trade using coercive means at this time could be called a 'gunboat trade', similar to the term 'gunboat diplomacy', which referred to the coercive diplomacy employed by the Western powers against weaker countries.
10. See William G. Clarence-Smith, 'The Textile Industry of Eastern Africa in the Long Duree', in *Africa's Development in Historical Perspective* (2014), pp. 264–266.
11. Robert B. Marks (2006) (Korean translation), p. 138.
12. Robert O. Collins and James M. Burns (2014), p. 201.
13. By all accounts, looking at the history, the universal 'political' values that we take for granted today must have emerged no earlier than the twentieth century. I believe it was in the process of the making of the League of Nations and later the United Nations that the universal values became widely accepted by the global community.
14. See David Olusoga's article 'The roots of European racism lie in the slave trade, colonialism-and Edward Long' in *The Guardian*, 8

September 2015. Olusoga observes that since the fifteenth century, European have viewed Africans as inferior, backwards and barbaric, and this still casts a shadow over the continent.

15. See Jürgen Osterhammel, *Kolonialismus: Geschichte, Formen, Folgne* (Munich: Verlag C.H. Beck oHG, 2003), Korean translation by Yuksa Bipyongsa (2006), pp. 92–97.
16. Karen Barkey and Sunita Karen, 'Comparative Perspectives on the State', *Annual Review of Sociology* 17 (1991), p. 527.
17. Countries in Asia like China, Korea and Japan that were not colonized by the West had achieved a high level of development along with Western Europe prior to the 'Great Divergence' as elaborated by Kenneth Pomeranz in his book *The Great Divergence: China, Europe, and the Making of the Modern World Economy* (Princeton: Princeton University Press, 2000).
18. Jürgen Osterhammel, *Kolonialismus* (Korean translation), p. 112.
19. Ibid., p. 112.
20. Ibid., p. 113.
21. John Campbell, *Nigeria: Dancing on the Brink* (Lanham, MD: Rowman and Littlefield, 2011), p. 12, cited in Crawford Young (2012, p. 8).
22. Martin Meredith, *The State of Africa: A History of the Continent Since Independence* (London: Simon & Schuster, 2011), p. 14.
23. Crawford Young, *The Postcolonial State in Africa* (Madison: University of Wisconsin Press, 2012), p. 5.
24. Ibid., pp. 6–8.
25. Gareth Austin, 'African Economic Development and Colonial Legacies', International Development Policy Series, Geneva: Graduate Institute in Pierre Englebert and Kevin C. Dunn, *Inside African Politics* (Boulder: Lynne Rienner, 2013), p. 215.
26. In the aftermath of the Second World War, various factors like the need to reconstruct Europe, the creation of the United Nations, the emergence of many new independent states and the new international political dynamics (namely the Cold War) are seen as major factors that gave rise to the institutionalization of international aid.
27. Carol Lancaster, *Foreign Aid: Diplomacy, Development, Domestic Politics* (London: University of Chicago Press, 2007), pp. 25–29.
28. John Degnbol-Martinussen and Poul Engberg-Pedersen, *Aid: Understanding International Development Cooperation*, translated by

Marie Bille (London: Zed Books, 2005), p. 44. It was originally published in Danish in 1999.

29. Ibid., p. 45.
30. Carol Lancaster, *Foreign Aid*, pp. 39–40.
31. According to USAID, the Integrated Rural Development (IRD) approach was popular in the 1970s, with the number of and donor allocations to IRD projects increasing rapidly in the mid-1970s and reaching their peak at the beginning of the 1980s. However, follow-up evaluations highlighted the mostly unsatisfactory performance of these projects, resulting in a shift towards broader systemic poverty alleviation initiatives (such as the World Bank's Poverty Reduction Strategies). See 'Integrated Rural Development: Lessons learned', http://pdf.usaid.gov/pdf_docs/PNADF432.pdf. See also John Degnbol-Martinussen and Poul Engberg-Pedersen, *AID* (2005), pp. 45–47; Susan Chase and Elisa Wilkinson, 'What Happened to Integrated Rural Development?', *The Hunger Project*, 10 August 2015.
32. *Aid* (2005), p. 46.
33. Erik Thorbecke, 'The Evolution of the Development Doctrine and the Role of Foreign Aid', in Finn Tarp (ed.), *Foreign Aid and Development: Lessons Learnt and Directions for the Future* (London: Routledge, 2000), p. 33.
34. *Aid* (2005), p. 48.
35. According to Thorbecke (2000), the development strategy in the 1990s retained most of the strategy that was built in the previous decade, at least in the first half of the decade. But as the decade went on, the adjustment-based strategy of the 1980s came under critical review, leading to major changes. Two contending approaches were put forward: the 'orthodox' view and the 'heterodox' view. The East Asian miracle also provided a convincing case for sound institutions, but the Asian financial crisis of 1997 forced a critical examination of excessive trade and capital liberalization policies (pp. 42–43). See also Carol Lancaster, *Foreign Aid* (2007), pp. 45–46. Lancaster explains that the withdrawal of aid and engagement by the West following the end of the Cold War contributed to the rise in conflicts and violence in Africa in the 1990s.
36. Carol Lancaster points out that by the end of the 1990s, four 'new' aid purposes emerged: promoting economic and political transitions; addressing global problems; furthering democracy; and managing

conflict. Concerns for aid effectiveness were not new, but these gained prominence in the 1990s, due, among other things, to the dismal economic performance of Sub-Saharan African countries. See *Foreign Aid* (2007), pp. 48–50.

37. United Nations, 'We Can End Poverty', http://www.un.org/millenniumgoals.
38. Jim Levinsohn, 'The World Bank's Poverty Reduction Strategy Paper Approach: Good Marketing or Good Policy?', G-24 Discussion Paper Series, UNCTAD, 21 April 2003, pp. 1–3.
39. Jeffrey Sachs and George B.N. Ayittey, 'Can Foreign Aid Reduce Poverty?', *CQ Press* (2009), http://www.earth.columbia.edu: 05-09-2013.
40. Hope, K.R. 'From Crisis to Renewal: Towards a Successful Implementation of the New Partnership for Africa's Development', *African Affairs* 101 (2002), pp. 387–402.
41. Reuters, 'Senegal's Wade Slams Africa Development Body', 13 June 2007.
42. OECD, 'Aid Effectiveness', http://www.oecd.org/dac/effectiveness.
43. Ibid.
44. Fig. 1.1 shows the dilemmas that Sub-Saharan African nations have faced. In the early years of independence, their overarching national goal was nation-building, but the irony is that what should be the driving force behind nation-building, a 'sense of nation', 'national identity' or patriotism, was essentially lacking. Hence, the nation-building process is still largely incomplete in most of these countries. The second phase in the dilemma was when the international development community institutionalized various policies and systems of aid, and was actively engaged in assisting African countries. But what should have been the golden opportunity for Africa was missed because Africans could not take advantage of what was provided, and instead fell back on their dependency syndrome and other regressive traits. Since the 1990s, the third dilemma of globalization vs. industrialization persists for Africa, which raises questions as to whether Sub-Saharan Africa can genuinely transform.

2

Assessing the Role of Foreign Aid, Donors and Recipients

Criticisms of Foreign Aid

Since the early 1980s, there have been exhaustive debates on foreign aid focusing on its failures in Sub-Saharan Africa. The literature on foreign aid to Africa, especially among intellectuals, is most often critical of its disappointing performance in terms of poverty reduction and economic development. Critics argue that the aid architecture in Africa presents a sad story of hundreds of billion dollars of aid poured into the continent to virtually no avail. A large number of Africans are today even poorer and many African states are less developed than they were before. Despite continuous massive inflows of foreign aid far exceeding debt servicing outflows, Africa has failed to use aid to make significant improvements in its development. It is the last region in the world where official aid inflows outstrip private capital inflows by a very large margin. And Africa is so dependent on aid not only in terms of quantity but also in terms of the institutional mechanisms.[1]

Among many people from various backgrounds, including government officials, diplomats, development experts, scholars, businessmen, NGO workers and journalists, with whom I have had discussions with

J.-D. Park, *Re-Inventing Africa's Development*,
https://doi.org/10.1007/978-3-030-03946-2_2

over the years in Africa, no one seems to refute the fact that aid in itself cannot lead to development. Aid, in the form of financial assistance or material supply, can be easily diverted to be 'consumed' for various purposes. Facilities and equipment that are donated usually become useless or 'white elephants' as soon as they are handed over. The irony is that the more aid that is provided, the more it will be seen as given and its value will decline in the eyes of its recipients. It is as if aid is 'public goods' provided free and without limits. Hence, conditionality is being applied, but the reality of Africa is such that applying conditionality in itself poses challenges. Some critics go as far as claiming that the provision of foreign aid itself contributes to Africa's troubles and underdevelopment by fuelling dependency syndrome and weakening African states' governance or administrative capacity, or even legitimacy.

Peter Bauer, who was considered a pioneering critic of foreign aid, believed that government-to-government aid was neither necessary nor sufficient for development, as it only entailed the danger of increasing the government's power, promoting corruption and the misallocation of resources, destroying economic incentives, eroding civil initiatives and dynamism. Bauer persistently criticized the big push model (Rosenstein-Rodan 1943), which provided the intellectual support for allocation of aid to stimulate economic growth. He argued that donors do not know which investments are appropriate for developing countries and that aid not only fails to jump-start growth, but actually hinders it.[2]

In his book *Emerging Africa*, Kingsley Chiedu Moghalu suggests that perhaps the main element that has caused the underdevelopment of the African continent is foreign aid. He asks whether several decades of huge amounts of development assistance have failed to produce any significant development, and if this is self-evident, why African leaders have not reacted to this in kind. He stresses that development, by definition, is a process that should be driven internally by organizing the production economy in an efficient manner.[3]

Researchers have found out that the per capita gross domestic product (GDP) of Africans living south of the Sahara declined by an average annual rate of 0.59% between 1975 and 2000. Over that period, per capita GDP adjusted for purchasing power parity declined from $1770 in constant 1995 international dollars to $1479.[4] An observation is made that over the past 60 years, at least $1 trillion of foreign aid is said to have been transferred to Africa, but real per capita income today is lower than it was in the 1970s.[5] For critics, aid has not only impeded economic growth in Africa, but has also led to the huge debt burden that many African countries are saddled with today.[6]

Many point out that aid flows into Africa have left the continent worse off: 'Aid cannot be blamed for all the mistakes made in the projects it bankrolls. However, by providing a seemingly endless credit line to governments regardless of their policies, aid effectively discourages governments from learning from and correcting their mistakes. Giving some Third World governments perpetual assistance is about as humanitarian as giving an alcoholic the key to a brewery'.[7] In their paper 'The Curse of Aid', Simeon Djankev and others liken aid to natural resources, in that it provides a windfall of resources to recipients, which may result in the same rent-seeking behaviour as is the case with the 'curse of natural resources'.[8] Abdoulaye Wade, the former President of Senegal, said: 'I've never seen a country develop itself through aid or credit. Countries that have developed ... There is no mystery there. Africa took the wrong road after independence'.[9]

Bill Easterly has been perhaps the most pronounced critic of aid since the turn of the twenty-first century and his ideas are expressed in a series of books. The central theme of Easterly's book *The Elusive Quest for Growth* is that 'incentives matter': despite all the efforts and money spent trying to remedy extreme poverty in the developing world, the donor countries have repeatedly failed because they have neglected the fundamental rule that individuals, businesses, governments and donors respond to incentives.[10] In *The White Man's Burden*, he contends that existing aid strategies provide neither accountability nor feedback, but without accountability, the problems are never fixed, and without feedback from the poor, no one will understand what exactly needs to be fixed.[11] In *The Tyranny of Experts*, he claims that development experts consider poverty in technical terms and focus on fixing immediate problems without dealing with the political oppression that caused the problems in the first place.[12]

According to Acemoglu and Robinson, the failure of aid for Africa is not due to a vicious circle of poverty per se. Poverty is instead an outcome of 'economic institutions that systematically block the incentives and opportunities of poor people to make things better for themselves'. In sum, the problematic economic institutions that are extractive in nature are blocking their aspirations today in a similar manner to what South Africa's apartheid regime did to black people.[13]

The basic criticism of aid is that it neither goes where it was intended nor helps those anticipated. Paul Collier, in *The Bottom Billion*, highlights the 'four traps' that contribute to this problem—the conflict trap, the natural resource trap, being landlocked with bad neighbours and having bad governance—but aid can potentially help turn things by incentives, skills and reinforcement.[14] And on the question 'is aid part of the problem or part of the solution?', he points out aid is part of the solution, although it has serious problems and is not in itself sufficient.[15] Of course, there are self-criticisms within donor community that they have taken too much responsibility for solving Africa's problems and that aid-dependency syndrome has become deeply rooted in Africa'.[16]

On the other hand, there are strong advocates of aid like Jeffrey Sachs who think that donor countries should increase the amount of aid to poor countries. In *The Age of Sustainable Development*, Sachs again stresses the need to push for global sustainable development, which 'is a way to understand the world, yet is also a normative or ethical view of the world: a way to define the objectives of a well-functioning society, one that delivers wellbeing for its citizens today and in future generations'.[17]

Foreign aid has had a positive impact on health and humanitarian needs. The issue is what impact it has on economic development. According to Sebastian Edwards, the overall findings of a large body of research have been 'fragile and inconclusive', with some experts concluding that 'in the best of cases, it was possible to say that there was a small positive, and yet statistically insignificant, relationship between official aid and growth'.[18] Meanwhile, Steve Radelet observes that 'the pendulum has swung, with more evidence that aid has a modest positive impact on growth' (Table 2.1).[19]

Table 2.1 Official aid received by Sub-Saharan Africa (US$, million, 2015)

Country	1960	2015	Country	1960	2015
1. Ethiopia	15.35	3233.99	26. Chad	0.03	606.67
2. Congo, DR	82.09	2599.24	27. Guinea	0.16	538.45
3. Tanzania	10.36	2580.47	28. Central African Republic	0.03	486.94
4. Kenya	21.11	2473.78	29. Benin	0.02	430.22
5. Nigeria	32.64	2431.60	30. Angola	−0.05	380.09
6. Mozambique	0.02	1815.03	31. Burundi	7.53	366.54
7. Ghana	2.94	1768.29	32. Mauritania	0.04	318.11
8. South Sudan	-	1674.83	33. Togo	0.11	199.62
9. Uganda	20.6	1628.25	34. Djibouti	-	169.56
10. South Africa	-	1420.64	35. Cape Verde	-	152.57
11. Somalia	2.47	1253.55	36. Namibia	-	142.4
12. Mali	0.08	1200.45	37. Gambia	0.54	107.85
13. Liberia	9.92	1094.46	38. Gabon	0.02	98.77
14. Rwanda	7.53	1081.72	39. Guinea-Bissau	-	95.08
15. Malawi	4.16	1049.39	40. Swaziland	8.49	92.63
16. Burkina Faso	0.2	977.05	41. Eritrea	-	92.11
17. Sierra Leone	6.72	946.39	42. Congo	0.02	88.92
18. Sudan	27.59	899.9	43. Lesotho	1.56	83.14
19. Senegal	0.13	897.2	44. Mauritius	0.53	76.55
20. Niger	0.04	865.87	45. Comoros	-	65.78
21. Zambia	0.92	797.14	46. Botswana	3.43	65.58
22. Zimbabwe	-	788.09	47. São Tomé and Príncipe	0.11	48.95
23. Madagascar	2.65	677.01	48. Equatorial Guinea	-	7.51
24. Cameroon	0.38	663.62	49. The Seychelles	1.1	6.78
25. Cote d'Ivoire	0.13	653.4			

Source World Bank, Data—Net Official Development Assistance and Official Aid Received (2015), https://data.worldbank.org/indicator/DT.ODA.ALLD.KD?locations=ZG

Who Is to Be Blamed? Donors or Recipients?

If aid has indeed failed, then who should be blamed for this? Looking at the dismal state of development of Africa, many intellectuals and experts in this field have fallen into a habit of doing two things: accusing foreign aid of being a failure or even evil, and blaming it all on the donor community, sometimes insinuating that they are evil-doers. But the way I see this issue is that aid is only as good as the recipients' ability to make use of it. Foreign aid itself is just a means, with some good intentions behind it at least. Aid can be made very good use of or can bring about unintended outcomes. Sub-Saharan Africa's continuing woes are caused not by foreign aid, but by all the negative elements and inherent problems that have come into play.

The correct assessment would be that Sub-Saharan African countries are experiencing problems *in spite* of aid, not *because* of it. With all the issues that African countries have had to deal with after their independence, they might have done actually worse without aid. In the absence of aid, there could have been more conflicts and political instability, and this could have fuelled more uncertainty and desperation. Remember, in the 1990s, when aid was significantly curtailed, conflicts were on the rise. There could have been more irregularities, corruption, illegal trading, environment destruction, etc. So, if foreign aid was withdrawn and only 'unfettered free market-ism' prevailed, would Sub-Saharan Africa have fared much better?

It is not that the international aid community did not consider various aspects and approaches to development. As already mentioned, the international development community's track record shows that it worked hard to find the right approaches to make aid more effective and relevant, and there was much trial and error. It should be noted that the donor community actually espoused and quite vigorously pursued an industrial policy approach for Africa in the 1960s, although it had to be shifted towards a poverty reduction approach in 1970s, following great disappointment with the former's performance.[20]

Also, there is another important factor worth mentioning. Various entities give various types of aid to Africa. Some are less liable to diversions, and donors have increasingly sought ways to check against the possibilities of misappropriation of funds or materials provided. On the one hand, we have the 'budget support', which is transferring money directly to recipient governments; on the other hand, there are also wide-ranging programmes like capacity-building that are either fully under the control of donors or under strict supervision regarding use of funds.[21] Soft loans, compared to grants which constitute the majority of the type of aid offered by developed countries, are much more susceptible to irregularities, given the state of governance of the recipient countries.[22]

Most of the reports, studies or commentaries that have been made on African development tend to find fault with either the poor performance of foreign aid or the lack of competence and responsibility of donors and development experts. The perception that what donors do only matters is not only wrong but is also detrimental, because this is in effect giving up on the ability of African countries to play their part in the process.

We can easily be hypocritical and out of touch with reality, and what people seem to be oblivious of is the fact that donors do not bear prime responsibility for the development of poor countries. It is not the donors who hold the key to Africa's development. There are plenty of resources to tap into and enormous opportunities for African countries if earnest efforts are made to utilize them. Adversities that African countries face, like the four traps outlined by Paul Collier (see above) and other elements that have been cited as a hindrance to Africa's development (unfavourable climate, epidemic diseases and lack of basic health care, tribalism, neopatrimonialism, etc.) are actually mostly man-made and thus can be overcome.

The reason to be optimistic about Sub-Saharan Africa's future is that there is open-mindedness and receptiveness to the ideas and policies of the outside world. While the word 'dependency' has negative connotations, in certain circumstances, dependency may not the worst thing; rather, exclusivism, isolationism, dogmatism and radicalism are much more dangerous and self-destructive. In fact, inter-dependence has become the general feature of today's world, and maybe African leaders are seeking regional unity and integration to enhance their collective bargaining power vis-à-vis the world in order to develop more interdependent relationships.

Dependence may not be too big a problem in itself if it is short-lived or transitional; rather, fundamentally the bigger problem may be the lack of ambition. If people have true ambitions in life, they will not be satisfied by being dependants of aids. The reason why many people are not as energetic as they should be is not because they are getting enough from donors, but because they have very limited ambitions in life.

Even when people are talking about their aspirations, the first thing that they are looking for could be the funding source. But without breaking the vicious cycle in which poverty, a weak social fabric and 'bad governance', among other factors, are inter-connected, simply pouring in resources for the sake of assistance will not produce positive outcomes. So, the question reverts back to: 'What are the conditions that justify foreign assistance?'

There is no such thing as all-out altruism in the modern world. Everything good and useful entails human endeavour and hence brings with it costs. Sooner or later, it comes with a price tag. Charity in times of calamities and humanitarian crisis comes naturally. But when altruism is expected to be delivered in everyday life for an indefinite period of time by outsiders, this is a sign of trouble and abnormality. So, an appeal by African leaders, like Paul Kagame of Rwanda, that African countries steer clear of foreign aid and dependence on outsiders only makes sense.

One day, when I was giving a lecture to Ugandan local counsellors in a training institute, I challenged them by asking: 'What is development?' I told them that it is essentially about two things: change and speed. How much positive change you can make in a given period; in other words, how fast you can make changes for the better. I asked them again: 'Who should change?' They were all silent, but seemed to understand what I was trying to convey: *it is you, not the donors.*

Those who are quick to criticize donors for not doing enough had better think first whether they are not being overly harsh or unrealistic in light of what donors can actually do. Yes, donors have their professional commitments, but also their national interests, organizational interests and personal interests, and they tend to become bureaucratized over time, and we have to accept this as a reality.

Critics of foreign aid also point out that a significant proportion of aid money is drained before it reaches its intended beneficiaries, the local populace. Basically, two factors contribute to this. First, projects inevitably entail considerable administrative costs. High costs are incurred because from the standpoint of donors, the costs of bringing projects to Africa are high. Many aid projects involve experts and other human resources, materials and equipment from developed countries, and of course these need to be covered by the budget. Allotting sufficient funds to ensure the proper functioning of aid staff on the ground is also important. The level of dedication and service of aid project managers and workers who face very adverse conditions is perhaps the most important determinant of the success of their projects. This is because in a demanding environment like Sub-Saharan Africa, extra devotion and perseverance are required to get things done.

Second, the relevant government departments of the host country usually try to secure some funds of their own from the donors in the name of necessary administrative funds for collaborative activities. Risks lie not only in the planning phase of projects, but also during their actual operation. Hence, persistence in such efforts as fighting graft and reporting irregularities in the work of officials to their higher authorities is important.

Inherent Limitations of Foreign Aid

Debating whether foreign aid is good or bad in a dichotomic fashion misses the point in terms of what the real issues of development are. The usefulness of aid will depend, first, on what types of aid are used in the given circumstances and, second, on how they are planned and implemented. There should be no ambiguity in the fact that foreign aid has inherent limitations and one should not expect this aid to automatically deliver the desired results. This is because most likely, donors have to undertake their aid programmes in the least favourable or most difficult conditions and circumstances in which they can find themselves to begin with.

The usefulness of aid should be judged in terms of what objective it wants to achieve. In the case of a natural or man-made disaster or crisis calling for humanitarian support or emergency relief, the usefulness of aid is obvious. The more acute the needs, the more appealing they will be. Any forms of support—money, food, materials or various human services (by rescue crew, doctors, aid workers, etc.)—will be appreciated. Then there are casual acts of charity like donating basic goods and materials or providing voluntary services to the poor and needy. Here, the goal is achieved through the delivery of the items or services. But things become more complicated as we move into larger-scale and more sophisticated aid programmes. For such types of projects, the work of planning, constructing, operating and post managing are all difficult tasks. When working with locals, which donors cannot avoid, unforeseen events like the local subcontractor suddenly becoming bankrupt and suspending their work may occur, prolonging the duration and hence raising the overall cost of the project.

Development-oriented aid includes construction projects (building factories, hospitals, vocational schools, etc.), consulting projects, facility or systems upgrading projects, training programmes, physical infrastructure projects, technical cooperation, funding programmes (including budget support) and much more. Because the execution of foreign aid involves two collaborators—donor and recipient—with very different standards, practices and levels of skills and technology, expecting positive outcomes to come from aid is always going to be a tough proposition.

We can compare aid with domestic projects that developed countries carry out in their own countries, like social welfare programmes or public facilities construction projects. The governments have to deal with their regulations, public opinions and various stakeholders, but at least things are predictable and manageable from their standpoint. Yet, for foreign aid or development cooperation, donor governments bear the extra burden of having to conduct activities where they not only do not have administrative or legal authority, but where their working conditions are adverse as well. In addition, lack of personnel and staff on the ground, lack of local expertise, etc. compound the problem.

The biggest hurdle is perhaps the issue of ownership, which is also linked to sustainability. Aid projects are implemented over a given period, ending when the contracted term expires, followed by handovers or completion of programmes. Officially, donors' obligations end there and they no longer have the contractual basis to be responsible. Yet, in order for the projects to produce the desired outcomes and be sustainable, the recipients really need to assume ownership of the project in terms of operation and management, otherwise the projects (as they often do) will end up as 'white elephants'. Herein lies a dilemma. The poorest countries need assistance because they lack the necessary resources and skills, but once they are provided with these facilities by donors, their lack of managerial capacity, discipline, commitment to ownership and accountability makes the project untenable and in many cases useless.

There are expectations both in Sub-Saharan Africa and developed countries that aid will contribute substantively to the former's economic and social development. That is the rationale of aid. The most desired outcome would be that aid helps Africans to reduce poverty and generate income. However, there seems to be a basic misunderstanding that wealth can be obtained by transfers. Yet, the fact remains that the wealth of a nation cannot be amassed by transfers, but rather by *creation*. In order to become wealthy in an economic sense, one has to be productive. Wealth is created by producing additional value, goods and services, but there seems to be a tendency in the region where people want to become better off not by being productive, but by benefiting from the work of others, e.g., through simple redistributions.

Donors, on their part, must also find ways to better carry out their assignments. While gearing towards more pragmatic and result-oriented approaches, they need to think more from the viewpoint of recipients' interests in order to have a greater impact. Thus, many aid experts and workers are dispatched to Africa, and their expertise and know-how accumulated over many years no doubt become precious assets in this field. However, as the work of these specialists becomes more regular, their perspective can also become routinized, leading to a 'fixing' of their views on Africa.

Aid specialists who think they have a good understanding of how locals think and behave could subconsciously consider such elements to be a 'given', and hence have low expectations of what can be achieved. When they take action accordingly with such a mindset in place, this can encourage the continuation of the status quo rather than promoting change. Unless they exhibit strong passion to bring about change despite the difficult conditions, their expertise and professionalism may in fact contribute to the 'perpetuation' of Africa's underdevelopment.

Unlike natural science, in the realm of social science, over-reliance on compartmental expertise has its dangers. It is just like the problem of deepening bureaucratization. If you are the head of an organization, having many experts at your service can be convenient and encouraging. They can produce various reports or studies that you can circulate or report to your bosses for recognition. But when it comes to producing 'physical' results in terms of implementing what is in the paper, it can be a very different story; that is, you might have as many experts as you want, but still cannot get the job done.

Deepening of expertise alone may not be the solution to problems. Experts are by definition specialists, as opposed to generalists, and their field of speciality is specified. As such, they are inherently limited in terms of their scope of vision and ability to make decisions on multi-dimensional and deep-rooted issues. Then there is always the danger of being immersed in too many technicalities and details. The need to follow so many reviews, procedures and regulations, and to collaborate with so many players also poses great burden on donors, making the delivery of aid projects that much more challenging.

The moral hazard of aid recipients and development partners alike can be understood in the context of 'bureaucracy' that has been formed in this field. Indeed, there are many competent and dedicated people working in this profession, but there are some from developing and developed countries alike who seem to spend more time enjoying their 'privileged' status than working to make a difference with a true sense of mission.

Aid workers and volunteers on the ground commonly admit that the most difficult challenge they face in Africa is the human factor. When things do not go right, time after time, and frustration mounts, one can feel inclined to give in and 'adapt' to the reality. But it is not easy for people on a mission to give up fighting either. As such, the struggle goes on, but in the end the lessons are learned, usually with mixed feelings.

Another challenge arising from the evolution of donors and their policies that affects both aid recipients and donors is 'aid fragmentation'. This refers to the problem of too many donors providing too little aid (or giving aid in so many small pieces) as to undercut the efficiency of aid.[23] According to International Development Association report, over 50 donor countries, including emerging donors, over 230 international organizations, regional development banks, funds, etc., are involved in development activities, with the result that the average number of donors per recipient increased from three in 1960 to 30 in 2006.[24] This problem was acknowledged in the Paris Declaration on Aid Effectiveness (2005), which called for a pragmatic approach to the division of labour to increase complementarity and decrease transaction costs.[25]

The complex and uncoordinated nature of aid allocation patterns can create gaps and duplications of aid for the aid recipient group. Fragmentation of aid entails transaction costs both for donors and partner countries. The principal drawbacks for donors would be the lack of specialization and scale inefficiency. If donors are active in so many places and sectors, then naturally their staff will need to be spread over a wide area. As a result, they will face an inability, in terms of having enough knowledge or expertise and manpower, to carry out all the projects in a successful manner. At the same time, high fixed costs will be incurred for a limited number of projects. As for recipients, bureaucratic costs to meet the administrative requirements imposed by a multitude of donors will be substantial.[26]

However, in recent years, several donors have also taken the decision to concentrate their aid on fewer partner countries. One reason behind this decision is to rationalize aid in order to achieve better results. However, some of these decisions may also have been brought forward by increased fiscal austerity as a result of the economic and financial crisis. It all comes back to the question of national interests versus multilateral governance.

Since aid fragmentation is a reflection of bilateral donors' tendencies and their competitive nature, it will not be easy to rectify it soon, although some measure of improvement may be found.[27] There may be 'recipient fatigue' for the elites or officials in charge of developing countries, but for the people in general, it is a very different story, which justifies the need for the robust involvement of donors in Africa. A study on aid recipients' attitudes conducted in Uganda several years ago showed that elites and the masses have different perceptions towards foreign aid—the masses strongly preferred aid over government programmes, while the elites preferred government programmes.[28] This attests to the widespread corruption, patronizing and clientelism on the part of the privileged class in the region. The local people know that they will get the benefits from foreign aid agencies, but distrust their elites strongly.

If aid has failed, it is not because aid itself is the problem or that donors had other intentions. At best, donors' responsibility for this failure is no more than being ineffective or being not aggressive enough to 'induce' change on the part of recipients. Reckoning must come from within, from the developing countries. It is not a question of a lack of materials, but is essentially about the mindset and the willingness to act.

The Issue of Reciprocal Compliance

Even scholars and practitioners involved in the development of Africa seem to be still baffled by the 'African paradox' after many decades since the world began trying to address Africa's plight. In the history of humankind, no continent has drawn such worldwide, collective attention and support on a sustained basis as Sub-Saharan Africa. This may seem obvious because the majority of the poorest countries on earth, the least developed countries or 'the bottom billion' are to be found in Sub-Saharan Africa.

But let us not forget that the African continent itself is blessed with natural endowments and has huge potential for growth. In terms of geographical size, Africa is colossal, the second-largest continent after Asia, and is the same size as the US, China, India and Europe combined. It has the greatest number of countries with varying conditions as well as commonalities. In Sub-Saharan Africa, the climate and weather are mostly favourable and there are many large areas of land with fertile soil and plentiful water. The negative description of Africa's geographical and climatic conditions by development experts is quite overblown and misleading.[29]

Meanwhile, the amount of aid provided to developing countries reached an all-time high in 2013, rebounding from two years of falling volumes despite continued pressure on budgets in OECD countries since the global financial crisis. Donor provided a total of US$134.8 billion in net official development assistance (ODA), of which US$55.7 billion went to the African continent in 2013.[30]

At the global level, we have turned a new page with the completion of the UN MDGs and the adoption of the SDGs in 2015. The MDGs focused on the alleviation of absolute poverty, as well as social sector/humanitarian assistance, but even by the UN's standards, only three out of the eight goals were on track in the case of Africa.[31] As the title suggests, the post-2015 goals rightly highlight sustainable development with an emphasis on economic development. But the outcome of MDGs and the lessons learned from them were nothing to be very excited about in terms of having more confidence and clarity in the way forward for Africa's development. Rather, the track record of Sub-Saharan Africa over the past 50 years only seems to add to the lingering sense of disillusionment, doubt, scepticism and uncertainty.

The year 2016 was marked by a series of terrorist attacks in Europe, the refugee crisis and the rise of anti-immigration, nationalistic sentiments in the Western world, while the political developments that unfolded in the US and elsewhere in 2017 only added to the uncertainty of the international order, as if we were entering uncharted territory. In 2018, the world continues to be unsettled by various developments in the international arena, but there are also some encouraging signs like a trend for global economic recovery, so the overall picture is mixed. In any case, it is unlikely that the international dynamics will have a major impact on Sub-Saharan Africa and the global donor community.

The international development architecture of Sub-Saharan Africa will likely prevail, despite the shortcomings and criticisms it has entailed. African countries' strong desire for the continuation of aid, coupled with the 'readiness' of donors and the 'short cycle' of response—decision making, formulation and implementation of projects—characteristic of developed countries in order to meet time constraints, perpetuates the existing framework of aid policies. And it would be naïve to discount the national interests—whether perceived or real—that all donor nations pursue, as well as natural competition among donors. Add to this the pressures coming from various opinion leaders, groups and organizations, and the tendency to stay the course becomes quite clear.

If the existing aid architecture cannot be overhauled in the foreseeable future, what are the practical and realistic ways in which the effectiveness of aid to Africa can be improved? The international community and African countries alike should not stomach continued lacklustre performance in Africa's development. There should be a clear awareness on the part of African nations and the donor community that improved measurements must be applied.

However, it is unrealistic to expect 'sweeping' reform to take place across the continent, irrespective of how good the idea might be, as could be seen in the case of NEPAD. Regional initiatives requiring various coordination efforts among member states present themselves as another challenge rather than as readily applicable solutions. This also holds true for trade and investment initiatives like the African Continent FTA (AfCFTA) and the BRICS-Africa collaboration that are now taking shape. Certainly, there is a sound logic behind the consolidation of regional markets in Africa. But the ultimate bulwark of Africa's development is of course its states. Without enhancing the level of governance and capacity of African states, their sustainable development will not be properly achieved. Regional integration initiatives will not succeed if the member states do not have sufficient capability to govern and manage their own affairs.

The best-case scenario for Sub-Saharan Africa would be that success stories of national development emerge one after another, setting examples for others to emulate. Development cannot be bestowed by others. No matter how much aid a country receives, development cannot be attained by external assistance alone. It is essentially an internally driven process of a nation and is not one which can be injected exogenously by outsiders. Thus, it does not really matter what the international development community discusses or plans if the subject or owners of development—the African nations—are not taking the lead in the process.

Like all other forms of partnerships, the donor-recipient partnership must be based on mutual trust in order to be fruitful and lasting. Let us consider this relationship from the standpoint of 'reciprocity'. For instance, a business partnership can be robust when the participating parties are mutually committed to meeting each other's needs.[32] Logically, a low level of or unequal reciprocity will in all likelihood not yield the desired results compared to a high level or equal reciprocity.

The problem with current state of the aid structure for Africa is not only that the level of reciprocity is low, but, more importantly, that the reciprocity is very much asymmetrical. It takes two to tango, and the parties involved—namely the African countries and the donor community—must find ways to significantly upgrade their partnership in terms of strengthening the reciprocity.

Africa's Compliance to Donors' Needs

Figure 2.1 provides an illustration of the matrix of reciprocity in partnership between Sub-Saharan Africa and the donor community. It depicts the level of 'compliance' of donors and Sub-Saharan African countries towards each other. Donors' compliance can be measured in quantitative and qualitative terms. The amount of aid provided would be a basic indicator of the quantitative response. The qualitative response is about how much attention and effort donors put in their aid programmes to meet the needs of recipient countries. Factors such as areas of assistance, content of aid programmes, level of study, preparation, involvement and coordination with host government agencies, input of experts, 'harmonization efforts', etc. should be taken into account. For aid recipients, their compliance can be gauged by the level of various administrative support and facilitation provided to donors and donor programmes, the degree of ownership and accountability demonstrated with respect to the management of aid projects after their handover, etc. But the irresponsibility and lack of sense of duty of government officials, widespread corruption, poor work ethics, the lack of development mindedness of the people, etc. are impeding efforts for development.

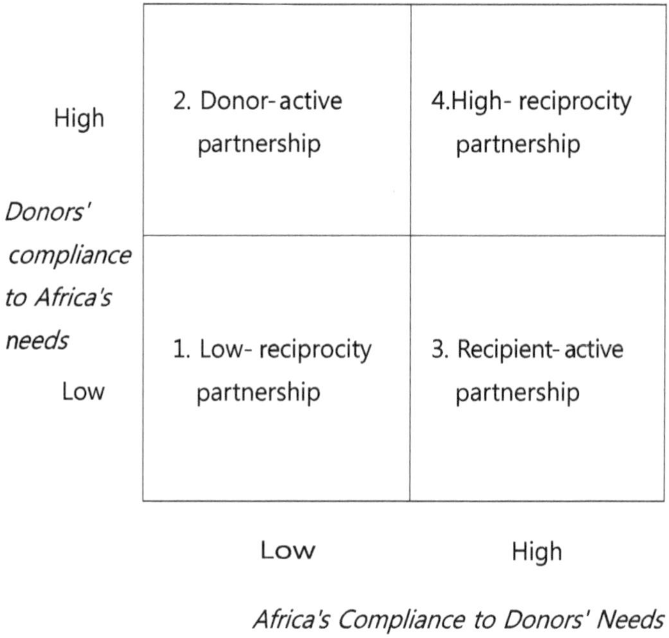

Donors' compliance to Africa's needs	Low	High
High	2. Donor-active partnership	4.High- reciprocity partnership
Low	1. Low- reciprocity partnership	3. Recipient- active partnership

Africa's Compliance to Donors' Needs

Fig. 2.1 Reciprocity in the partnership for African development

Figure 2.1 shows four different combinations of partnerships. The purpose is to gain a general idea of the dynamics in the whole region. The actual situation will, of course, vary depending on each country and project. The present state of partnership between African countries and donor community, in most cases, would correspond to either a no. 1 'low reciprocity' or a no. 2 'donor-active' partnership. Regarding donors' responsiveness towards Africa's needs, they can be seen either as actively engaging or falling short of expectations, depending on how the recipients and others view it.[33]

But the fundamental problem lies in the recipients' attitude. The prevalent low compliance by African countries is what undermines the effectiveness of aid and frustrates the morale of aid officials on the ground, and sows the seeds of doubt. Both donors and African countries seem to have forgotten that the justification of development aid lies in it being temporary in nature. However, things are not as simple as it might appear, and there are clearly limits in terms of how far the donors and African countries can be compliant with each other.

It is true that international organizations and bilateral donors have been struggling with the task of aid effectiveness from their end, while the innate weakness in governance on the part of African countries is cited as a reason for the poor performance of aid. There is a saying that where there is bad governance, aid is ineffective, and where there is good governance, aid is unnecessary. But the governance issue is a matter to be sorted out by African countries.

The 'low reciprocity' partnership represents an untoward state of reality. Aid is provided mostly for the sake of consumption and serves vested interests. A typical feature of this is recipient governments taking aid for granted and making little effort to be forthcoming in relation to the donor's requirements, other than when they see their own interests (such as budget allocation). Donors, for their part, go about 'routinely' with their work, adhering to formalities without worrying much about the outcome (conveniently putting the blame on the environment and recipients) and struggling to make a real impact. However, it is true that the major aid organizations maintain strict guidelines and discipline in their operations in order to try to make them as efficient as possible in the given circumstances.

A 'recipient-active' partnership would be rare in Africa, where countries are highly receptive to donors aid programmes, actively and voluntarily undertaking the necessary measures to make them work (with sound governance), while donors, in comparison, are not as proactive.[34] South Korea in the 1960s may fall into this category. Lastly, a 'high-reciprocity' partnership is an ideal situation where both donors and recipients will get satisfaction and credit for a strong and successful partnership. An example of such a case could be Rwanda.

The most common form of Africa's partnership with mainstream donors is seen to match the 'donor-active' type. In this case, the principal donors, whether multilateral and bilateral, have been making continuous efforts to make their programme more relevant to African countries, while the responsiveness of African countries towards them has more or less remained the same. The compliance gap between donors and African countries must be narrowed so that the partnership status can shift to 'high reciprocity' or 'recipient-active'.

Notes

1. Ravi Kanbur, 'Aid, Conditionality and Debt in Africa', in Finn Tarp (ed.), *Foreign Aid and Development-Lessons Learnt and Directions for the Future* (London: Routledge, 2000), pp. 409–410.
2. Andrei Schleifer, 'Peter Bauer and the Failure of Foreign Aid', *Cato Journal* 29, no. 3 (Fall 2009), pp. 379–382.
3. Kingsley Chiedu Moghalu, *Emerging Africa: How the Global Economy's 'Last Frontier' Can Prosper and Matter* (London: Penguin Books, 2014), pp. 25–28.
4. Thompson Ayodele, Franklin Cudjoe, Temba Nolutshungu, and Charle Sunawabe, 'African Perspective on Aid: Foreign Assistance Will Not Pull Africa Out of Poverty', Cato Institute Economic Development Bulletin No. 2, p. 1, 14 September 2005, https://object.cato.org/sites/cato.org/files/pubs/pdf/edb2.pdf.
5. Dambisa Moyo, 'Why Aid Is Hurting Africa', *Wall Street Journal*, 21 March 2009.
6. 'Honest Accounts? The True Story of Africa's Billion Dollars Loses', Health Poverty Action and 12 Other NGOs, July 2014, https://health-povertyaction.org/wp-content/uploads/downloads/2014/07/Honest-Accounts-report-v4web.pdf.
7. James Bovard, 'The Continuing Failure of Foreign Aid', CATO Institute Policy Analysis No. 65, 31 January 1986.
8. Simeon Djankov, José García Montalvo, and Marta Reynal-Querol, 'The Aid Curse', December 2007, http://documents.worldbank.org/curated/en/206371468155962442/pdf/452540WP0Box331ur-se1of1aid01PUBLIC1.pdf.
9. Norimitsu Onishi, 'Senegalese Loner Works to Build Africa, His Way', *New York Times*, 10 April 2002.
10. William Easterly, *The Elusive Quest for Growth: Economists' Adventures and Misadventures in the Tropics* (Cambridge, MA: MIT Press, 2001).
11. William Easterly, *The White Man's Burden: Why the West's Efforts to Aid the Rest Have Done So Much Ill and So Little Good* (New York: Oxford University Press, 2006). Easterly points out that the true victories against poverty are most often won not by over-ambitious, top-down enactment of big projects, but through indigenous, ground-level planning and incremental measures.

12. William Easterly, *The Tyranny of Experts: Economists, Dictators, and the Forgotten Rights of the Poor* (New York: Basic Books, 2013). Easterly notes that: 'Despite the trampling of rights by Western governments and development agencies, there are plenty of grounds for hope when we see how much global change in freedom is positive anyway … This book does not say that nothing good will happen until some utopian ideals on rights are attained. No, this book argues the opposite: an incremental positive change in freedom will yield a positive change in well-being for the world's poor' (p. 344).
13. Daron Acemoglu and James A. Robinson, 'Why Foreign Aid Fails—And How to Really Help Africa', *The Spectator*, 25 January 2014, http://www.spectator.co.uk/2014/01/why-aid-fails.
14. Paul Collier, *The Bottom Billion: Why the Poorest Countries Are Failing and What Can Be Done About It* (New York: Oxford University Press, 2007), pp. 104–108.
15. Ibid., p. 123.
16. Kurt Gerhardt, 'Time for a Rethink: Why Development Aid for Africa Has Failed', *Speigel*, 15 August 2010.
17. Sebastian Edwards, 'Economic Development and the Effectiveness of Foreign Aid: A Historical Perspective', *VOX, CEPR's Policy Portal*, 28 November 2014.
18. Jeffrey Sacks, *The Age of Sustainable Development* (New York: Columbia University Press, 2015), p. 11.
19. Steve Radelet, 'Angus Deaton, His Nobel Prize and Foreign Aid', *Future Development* (Blog), 20 October 2015.
20. Industrial policy occupies a very low profile in the current aid architecture of the mainstream donor community. Major bilateral donors do not seem to have any interest in industrial policy and it is only in UN agencies like UNIDO that the topic is taken seriously. Industrial policy for development was a part of mainstream development economics in 1960s, but later it came under sustained attack by liberal economists who argued that industrial policy had not worked and could not work because government failures were always worse than market failures. See James A. Robinson, 'Industrial Policy and Development: A Political Economy Perspective', May 2009, paper presented at the 2009 World Bank ABCDE Conference, Seoul, 22–24 June 2009.
21. Budgetary support is a way of giving development assistance: the donor country provides money directly to the developing country through a

financial transfer to the national treasury of the latter. Currently, budgetary support is undertaken by EU countries and is conditional on policy dialogue, performance assessment and capacity-building. 'This is a way of fostering partner countries' ownership of development policies and reforms and addressing the source, not the symptoms, of underdevelopment', according to EU Budget support accounts for around a quarter of all EU development aid. In 2011, the percentages were 26% in Sub-Saharan Africa, 16% in Asia, 23% in Latin America and the Caribbean and 30% in Neighbourhood countries. See European Commission International Cooperation and Development section on its webpage (https://ec.europa.eu/europeaid/policies/budget-support-and-dialogue-partner-countries_en).

22. There is a dilemma in budgetary support, in that this type of aid to enhance the ownership of African countries is in fact becoming an easy target for abuse. Hence, some countries are trying to impose a strict conditionality for this when irregularities are reported, but there are inherent limits in terms of what donors can do about it.
23. See Eckhard Deutscher and Sara Fyson, 'Improving the Effectiveness of Aid', *Finance & Development*, a quarterly magazine of the IMF, September 2008, Volume 45, No. 3. Some experts point out that the problem of aid fragmentation is not the fragmentation itself, but the lack of competition among aid suppliers (Javier Santiso and Emmanuel Frot, 'Crushed Aid: Why Is Fragmentation a Problem for International Aid?', *VOX, CEPR's Policy Portal*, 18 January 2010). Others argue that excessive and uncoordinated aid has helped create governance weaknesses in Africa and that donor-driven governance and corruption control initiatives have failed to deliver results (Brian Cooksey, 'Aid, Governance and Corruption Control: A Critical Assessment', *Crime, Law and Social Change* 58, no. 5 (December 2012), pp. 521–531).
24. Eun Mee Kim and Pil Ho Kim (eds), *The South Korean Development Experience: Beyond Aid* (New York: Palgrave Macmillan, 2014), p. 67.
25. It called for the commitment of partners: ownership, alignment, harmonization, mutual accountability and managing results.
26. '2011 OECD Report on Division of Labour: Addressing Cross-Country Fragmentation of Aid', submitted to Busan, the 4th High-Level Forum on Aid Effectiveness (November 2011).
27. Some experts point out that under the current circumstances, efforts to coordinate aid by donors, however well-intentioned, can backfire and

cause more aid fragmentation and less efficiency. See Kurt Annen and Luc Moers, 'Donor Competition for Aid Impact, and Aid Fragmentation', *IMF Working Paper* (WP/12/204), August 2012, pp. 3, 29.

28. Adam Harris (NYU), Helen Milner (Princeton), Michael Findley (UT-Austin) and Daniel Nielson (BYU), 'Elite and Mass Perceptions of Foreign Aid in Recipient Countries: A Field Experiment in Uganda', 4 April 2013, paper prepared for the annual meeting of the Midwest Political Science Association Meeting, Chicago, 11–14 April 2013.
29. It is largely outsiders who depict Africa's geographical, climatic conditions as unfavourable. The origin of the negative stereotype of Africa's natural environment may date back to the early period of Europeans' travels to and settlement in Africa. But today, the situation is quite different. By all accounts, one could even argue that Sub-Saharan Africa's weather is more modest and favourable than that in most other regions in the world. The vast majority of foreigners who visit Sub-Saharan Africa share such a view. Many Africans boast that their land is blessed with fertile soils and rich endowments.
30. This figure includes aid provided by traditional/mainstream donors, the OECD members. See http://www.oecd.org/newsroom/aid-to-developing-countries-rebounds-in-2013-to-reach-an-all-time-high.htm.
31. *MDG Report 2015—Lessons Learned in Implementing MDGs: Assessing Progress in Africa Toward Millennium Development Goals*, written by the United Nations Economic Commission for Africa, the African Union, the African Development Bank Group and the United Nations Development Program, September 2015, https://www.afdb.org/fileadmin/uploads/afdb/Documents/Publications/MDG_Report_2015.pdf. According to the report, goal 1 (eradicate extreme poverty and hunger) was off track; goal 2 (achieve universal primary education) was on track; goal 3 (promote gender equality and empower women) was on track; goal 4 (reduce child mortality) was off track; goal 5 (improve maternal health) was off track; goal 6 (combat HIV/AIDS, malaria and other diseases) was on track; goal 7 (ensure environmental sustainability) was off track; and goal 8 (develop a global partnership for development) was not assessed.
32. As for addressing the 'needs' of recipients or donors, the question can be raised as to what are the *real intentions* of donors; do they want to genuinely help Africa to develop (for instance, to industrialize) or are they more bent on providing assistance in a way that promotes their

own interests (like opening up markets and making African economies dependent on them)?

33. Even in no. 1, 'low reciprocity partnership', the perceived low responsiveness on the part of donors was either brought about by recipients' persistent failure to even meet the minimum level of irresponsiveness or the drastic deterioration of their condition to receive aid. In other words, increasingly bad governance and the dysfunctionality of the state could cause a drop in the level of donors' responsiveness.
34. From the point of view of the 'development attitude' of a nation, no. 3 combination may be more meaningful and desirable than no. 4 combination because it implies that a country is more proactive than donors when it comes to its own development, which is only logical. This means that a country is less dependent on donors to make use of aid resources without the need for donors' strong intervention.

Part II

Rethinking the Root Causes of Africa's Under-Development

3
Review of Conventional Explanations

Overview

Dismayed by Africa's seemingly never-ending troubles amid concerns that the region may be entrenched in an ever-deepening fix, people from both the region and the development community may be inclined to either find scapegoats to take the blame or to come up with excuses. When things go right, everybody wants some credit for it, but when things go badly, the blame game is on. Passing the buck is particularly serious in Africa, and this is also a problem in itself. In intellectual circles, many observers, experts and academics are seen to come up with standardized, textbook-style explanations in keeping with the line of their thinking rather than searching for fundamental reasons and exploring new ideas or solutions.

What seems to be an insurmountable state that African countries find themselves in may give cover for foreign countries and international organizations, as well as African leaders and the privileged class, to follow the status quo as if nothing can be done to change Africa's fortunes. Unfortunately, in many instances, Africa's political leaders in effect take advantage of the entangled situation to

J.-D. Park, *Re-Inventing Africa's Development*,
https://doi.org/10.1007/978-3-030-03946-2_3

hold on to power. And in some cases, an unexpected and ironic political situation emerges. I was quite appalled to watch *BBC News Africa* (8 October 2017) reporting on Liberia, which aired on the eve of the nation's presidential elections, showing Liberian citizens expressing how much they missed their imprisoned former leader Charles Taylor and that they would vote for him should he run again.

Despite how much conundrum the African issues may pose, the goodwill and enthusiasm on Africa's development on the part of the global community has not been lost, and numerous internationally based private entities are robustly engaged in activities to help tackle Africa's fundamental problems with their professional expertise and international network.[1]

This chapter is a prelude to the next chapter, which will unearth the root cause of Africa's underdevelopment. But identifying or agreeing on the root cause(s) has been very elusive as there have been so many different views and interpretations on this subject. Nonetheless, the objective of this book is to make the case that there is indeed such a thing as a principal root cause for Africa's underdevelopment and to provide ideas on how it can be redressed.

In this chapter, I will very briefly discuss conventional explanations or arguments that are frequently made as to what constitutes a fundamental cause or a set of fundamental causes for Africa's continuing poverty and other troubles. These include: colonial legacies; ethnicism and neo-patrimonialism; institutions, governance and democracy; the role of government; natural conditions like climate and geography; and other factors (geography, corruption, globalization and China).

Colonial Legacies

Can historical experiences have a profound impact on the nations to the extent that they leave a permanent imprint in their lives and determine their fate? Certainly, our civilization, cultures and traditions, social behaviour patterns and even the way in which we view the world can be affected by the events of the past. How much impact they will have will depend on many things, including the scale, intensity, duration and nature of historical events, and how they have been perceived.

But what is also true is that people and nations have the ability and resilience not only to react to various phenomena or forces, but also to 'interpret' them in a context that is variable. The negativities of history can also bring about the opposite in later generations, like renewed positive resolve. And we can see many such examples in our history, both recent and old. It may be more accurate to say that this is not the exception but the rule in our lives.

The history of humanity bears two facets: being subjected to difficulties (adversity, survival, tribulations, struggles and conflicts) on the one hand, while also overcoming hardships (adopting, persevering, creating new things and making progress) on the other. Individuals, people, societies and nations have the ability not only to tame natural conditions but also to respond and overcome various obstacles. Action leads to reaction, and that is how life has evolved. Nothing is static about human beings and their lives. It is one thing to say that European colonizers were utterly exploitive towards Africa, which they were, but quite another to say that Africans are 'bound' by the colonialism of the past and its legacies, even to this day.

The slave trade and the inflow of weapons in exchange of slaves on a grand scale for many centuries must have had a devastating effect on Africa, both economically and socially. And then, during the later stages of colonization, European powers arbitrarily imposed their artificial criteria of creating states in Africa. This, along with the manner in which they managed their colonies, is deemed to have inhibited national identity or nation states from properly emerging and developing in Africa.

In his book *Citizen and Subject: Contemporary Africa and the Legacy of Colonialism,* Mahmood Mamdani argues that colonialism led to systems that impeded the development of democracy in African states. The colonialists' indirect rule in Africa produced 'decentralized despotism', giving rise of new chiefs who become more despotic as they were empowered by colonial authority that was not embedded in local societies, which undermined the existing mode of accountability.[2] Mamdani explains that this led to a 'bifurcated' system: direct rule was exercised in the urban centres where civil powers (mostly the expatriate colonial community) prevailed, while indirect rule was maintained by the rural tribal powers (native authority).[3] Mamdani argues that politicized ethnicity is the source of much of the political-social problem in Africa today and that the colonial politicization of indigeneity was the greatest crime of colonialism.[4]

The colonialists arranged their rule in Africa so as to keep indigenous people separate and under political control. Due to European colonizers' policy of dividing the indigenous population along perceived ethnic lines, the latter's sense of citizenship or individual national identity was never fostered during the colonial era. And when independence was finally achieved, their tendency was towards expanded politicization of the 'ethnic community' rather than pushing for politics at the national level.[5]

Meanwhile, Englebert and Dunn note that the European colonial conquest of Africa was remarkably brief. It took just a few years to bring down the African political systems, some of which had endured for centuries. But the European institutions they introduced were surprisingly shallow and 'the colonial reengineering of African politics was haphazard and superficial'.[6] Interesting but all important point they are making is that while European colonization of Africa is often criticized for 'dividing' the continent and hampering African unity, in reality 'there never was any political African unity, and colonisation actually consolidated a myriad of diverse political systems into some fifty territorial states, dramatically reducing the already Balkanized nature of the continent'.[7]

All in all, it would be fair to say that while Western colonialism had a profound impact on Sub-Saharan Africa, it is too far-fetched to hold it principally accountable for the region's current state of development. The colonial period, the post-colonial era and the period of more than half a century since independence should not be bunched together as one. Some might like to think in terms of historical determinism, but the reality is that the colonial legacy is only one of many factors that have had consequences. Exaggeration of the influence of past history carries with it the danger of vastly underestimating the voluntarism, spontaneity, subjectivity and will of the population. In this regard, 'constructivism' is deemed an instrumental tool to be used alongside conventional method of study.[8]

Proponents of neo-colonialism argue that Europe's colonization of Africa continues even after independence and, similarly, a group of leftist ideologists and scholars influenced by Marxian class theory have forwarded such theories as dependency theory and world-systems theory explaining the systematic exploitation and manipulation of the Western powers in Africa and other developing countries through international trade and economic systems.[9] But with the end of the Cold War and the disintegration of the Communist Bloc and socialist regimes alongside the rise and success of Asian economies, these theories lost their appeal, persuasiveness and relevance. In the post-Cold War era, the topics that draw international attention are globalization, climate change, terrorism, humanitarian crises and so forth, and these pose important challenges to both the developed world and developing countries alike.

Crawford Young sums it up well: 'the explanatory power of colonial legacy, initially compelling, becomes less central as time goes by. The half century of postcolonial existence now matches the historic duration of effective colonial rule'. In other words, the number of Africans having a personal recollection of 'being colonized' is dwindling.[10]

Ethnicity and Neopatrimonialism

Much has been made of ethnicity and neo-patrimonialism when it comes to the problem of Africa's development, and they are interesting themes. Generally, the discourse on Africa's ethnicity and neo-patrimonialism tends to treat these negatively, suggesting that they are inimical to Africa's development. 'Colonial legacy' is more or less an 'imagined' factor, but ethnicism and neo-patrimonialism certainly can have more relevance to real life, in that they are social elements. Certainly, ethnicism can play out to undermine social cohesiveness. For its part, neo-patrimonialism, which is generally understood as the practice of leaders and state officials parasitically using their state offices and resources for the furtherance of informal patron–client relationships in which they are engaged, can also be problematic.

It is true that the prominence of ethnicity is markedly high in Sub-Saharan African compared to the rest of the world. For the entire

Sub-Saharan African region, the probability that two randomly picked individuals belong to different ethnic groups is 66%, compared to 36% for the whole world.[11] However, it should be noted that there are wide variations in ethnic heterogeneity among the Sub-Saharan African countries.

Another salient feature that is observable in the region is the tendency to espouse what seem to be incompatible or contradictory aspects of their perception, to the point that it is mystifying. For example, people basically identify themselves primarily in terms of their ethnicity, but they also show in no ambiguous terms a sense of national identity. Experts of Africa's ethnicity point out that subnational citizenship and national citizenship coexist in Africa. It is pointed out that: 'The simultaneous display of subnational and national identity is one of the most puzzling dimensions of identity politics in Africa.'[12]

In general, people's attachment to their nation seems to fall short of what we call patriotism; rather, it appears to be more associated with opportunism. Perhaps it can also be understood in terms of 'realism', 'openness', 'flexibility' or 'pragmatism'. In other regions, the term 'sense of nation' may mean being patriotic in terms of sacrificing oneself and serving one's country. But the situation seems quite different in Africa. When I was attending a seminar on history in Kampala, we had a chance to discuss Ugandans' perception of their national identity and sense of nation. A Ugandan participant expressed that 'since we already belong to this country, we might as well get along'. His lukewarm response towards nationhood did not sound out of the ordinary under the circumstances. After more than 50 years since Uganda became independent, I thought that at least the Ugandan intellectuals would have a stronger sense of nation. One panellist, a scholar, even said that life in Uganda was better before independence.

As many have pointed out, the duplicity of people's adherence to different identities is common in Sub-Saharan African nations. Moreover, the characteristic of ethnicity is that it is malleable rather than immutable and exclusionary, as different ethnic groups coexist and live peacefully with one another most of the time. A high degree of ethnicity can even have a mitigating effect on the potential division at the national level. The openness and accommodative attitude of Africans with respect to other ethnic groupings and different identities are evident.[13] Ethnic clashes mostly surface in relation to issues concerning land rights and government policies or interventions (or the lack thereof). Ethnic tensions or conflict are also exacerbated when leaders try to use ethnicity for their own political purposes. In the case of 'kingdoms', the issue can relate to local autonomy and authority vis-à-vis the state.

The pursuit of self-interest and opportunism seems to be the prevalent motivation for society. One might be perplexed to see many Africans 'display both ethnic polarization and nationalistic fervour'.[14] Tim Kellstall points out how the tendency of Africans to have multiple identities has led to a 'fragmentation of the self', and in their quest for survival, people develop links to potential patrons in a bid to garner as many favours as possible: 'The ways in which people make a living in Africa encourages them into plural identities, which prevents them from organizing collectively over time, thereby foreclosing certain types of social movement and power.'[15] It may be even called a 'multiple personality'.

Edmond Keller notes that in Sub-Saharan Africa, 'one's social identity is fluid, intermittent, and experimental' and that two forms of citizenship exist in the minds of people in their daily lives: 'a form of communitarian citizenship and a form based on residence in a national community largely created as a by-product of colonialism'.[16] Keller observes that among the most common causes of inter-group conflict in Africa today are disputes over identity and citizenship, exacerbated or prompted by bad politics. And they are inherently linked to land rights and immigration issues, as was the case in Cote d'Ivoire, Nigeria, Rwanda and Kenya.[17] 'Ethnic groups are not closed corporate communities, bouncing off each other like billiard balls; rather, they are permeable at the margins and are entangled with 'the other' in numerous ways. Crawford Young observes that ethnic consciousness can vary widely in its intensity, depending on the depth of cultural resources on which it draws and its degree of mobilization'.[18]

Is Africa's ethnicity the cause or consequence of what is taking place in Africa? Does it negatively impact nation-building or is it like many other factors, being essentially *neutral*, depending on how it is employed? I think what we need to be careful of in this discourse is the possibility of having a 'Eurocentric bias'. From the perspective of Western countries, a sense of national citizenship, civic society, good institutions and governance, and a free-market economy are considered to be factors that are conducive for development. But from the standpoint of developing countries, many feel that these are the features of the end results, not the causes, of development. How can we reconcile such differences?

The identity and ethnicism of Africans seem to be a reflection of how Africans are adapting to reality. The ethnic community, considered as an expansion of one's family and relatives, constitutes a basic foundation or system of people's life. But confronted with the reality of deepening 'dualism' in every aspect of life—the economic, social and political gap or discrepancy between rural and urban areas—people have come to realize the limits of what their ethnic communities can provide to them, in contrast to the opportunities and benefits that can be sought from the state or foreign partners. For Sub-Saharan Africans, differences in terms of religion and political views do not seem to matter and they are rarely made into an issue, except in some isolated cases. For ordinary people, their fundamental concern has been subsistence or survival, while the privileged class has sought the maintenance of the status quo or the protection of their vested interests.

Ethnicism should not be viewed as the primary motivator for people's actions; there are many other elements that account for social dynamism. When problems seemingly taking on an ethnical dimension arise, it is usually the outcome of a combination of various factors at play and is not solely due to ethnicism.

A landmark paper on ethnicity published by the Harvard Institute of Economic Research in 2002 revealed that the Sub-Saharan African nations were the most ethnically diverse in the world.[19] Since many Sub-Saharan African countries are seen as fragile, conflict-ridden and poor, there may be a natural inclination to presume that ethnic diversity leads to more conflicts and hinders economic development and democracy. There have also been quite a number of studies purporting to back such a view, but it is also true that there are many different ways to conduct research and interpret the data.

On the question of whether there is a correlation between ethnical diversity and development, including stability and governance, the more prudent and objective studies seem to suggest that it is inconclusive or conditional at best. Ethnicity is just one factor among many that have an impact. If we think of ethnicity in terms of the 'fragmentation' of a nation, it is all relative. Ethnicity depends on how we define it conceptually and technically. The 'diversity' and 'fragmentation' of a nation is common all over the world. Even if a nation is racially homogeneous, there are sub-regional or socio-cultural divides in most countries. Even in developed countries, cases of regional animosity, stereotyping or even discrimination are not uncommon.

Korea is acknowledged as probably the most homogeneous nation on earth. But ethnical homogeneity does not make democracy or development any easier to come by. Despite being the same homogeneous nation, the two Koreas could not be more different from each other in so many aspects. As the example of North Korea shows, political ideology and the type of regime in place can eclipse all other factors.

There are many examples all over the world where ethnical homogeneity does not guarantee development. In Africa, Somalia exhibits unusual national homogeneity, with the same languages, religion and race,[20] but unfortunately it suffers from extreme internal conflict, destabilization and divisions due to clan warfare and rivalry. On the other hand, Uganda, which is considered one of the most ethnically diverse countries in the world, has enjoyed relatively positive political stability, security, economic growth and business prospects for a Sub-Saharan country. And political and social tensions within homogeneous societies cannot be always less than those of heterogeneous societies.

Rather, I think that conflicts and other problems in Sub-Saharan Africa are not caused by ethnic diversity or 'fractionalization' per se, but fundamentally by the 'concentration' of power that inordinately favours one particular group over others. Paul Collier also notes that except for a few specific cases, ethnic diversity neither increases the likelihood of civil war nor obstructs economic growth: 'multi-ethnic societies can usually be socially and economically fully viable'.[21]

Surprisingly, many African intellectuals that I have met have stressed that in Africa, ethnicism is not the fundamental cause of troubles; instead, it is being used as a rationalization or means to enhance one's leverage whenever political leaders are faced with problems. The conflict in South Sudan that started in December 2013 is a telling example of this. What started as a power struggle between President Salva Kiir and the former Vice President Riek Machar developed into a broader conflict of seemingly 'ethnic' proportions. But as the conflict continued, it became increasingly evident that its nature was more of a personal power struggle rather than a civil war between different ethical groups.

Along with ethnicism, neo-patrimonialism is another distinctive feature of Sub-Saharan Africa. Neo-patrimonialism is a term that is mostly used to characterize the state of Africa and can be defined as 'a system whereby rulers use state resources for personal benefit and to secure the loyalty of clients in the general population'.[22] A more elaborate definition of this term is given by Michael Bratton and Nicolas van de Walle: in a neo-patrimonial state, 'relationships of loyalty and dependence pervade a formal political and administrative system, and officials occupy their positions less to perform public service, their ostensible purpose, than to acquire personal wealth and status'.[23]

There are scholars of primordialism who believe that ethnicity is a deep-rooted, non-negotiable element defining one's identity in Africa. According to primordialism, Africa's ethnic diversity is seen to be a cause of conflict and the reason for the poor functioning of its states.[24] Because there is widespread corruption and continual economic-business failures and poverty in black Africa, it is easy for Afropessimists to blame the region's 'cronyist-neopatrimonial' tendencies for such problems. As a result, 'stressing the cultural or neopatrimonial dimension of African business (and states) promotes a determinism about African business whereby it is ineluctably corrupt: the very nature of patron-client ties in Sub-Saharan Africa would appear to render the expansion of legitimate commerce extraordinarily difficult, if not impossible'.[25]

A typical social culture in many countries in the region is that ordinary people do not distinguish their immediate family members from their relatives (even distant relatives) when it comes to referring them as 'brothers', 'sisters', 'mothers' and 'fathers'. The tradition of 'extended family' persists, and those individuals who have acquired the means or power are expected to help out the other members of the extended family who are in need. Critics would see such cultural elements as making Africa's neo-patrimonial practices even more detrimental to development.

But just like ethnicism, being fixated on neo-patrimonialism without taking into account the wider picture of interacting elements poses the danger of exaggerating or misrepresenting its significance. Based on his case studies on Kenya, Côte d'Ivoire, Malawi, and Rwanda, Tim Kelsall argues that neo-patrimonialism can be harnessed for developmental ends, provided that mechanisms can be found to centralize economic rents and manage them in the long term.[26] Neo-patrimonialism embodies aspects that breed corruption and are not consistent with the practices of developed nations, but it cannot be singled out as a determinant for underdevelopment. Similar traits existed in Asia, Latin America and even Europe. Botswana is a model country for democracy and governance in Africa, despite its patrimonial politics.[27] Rather, it should be viewed more as a sign or outcome of a failure on the part of African countries to meet the challenges and properly adapt to the new environment brought about by their independence.

Theoretically, we can trace the concept of patrimonialism back to Max Weber's famous three types of legitimate authority or rule: traditional, charismatic and rational-legalistic authority. Weber defined patrimonialism as a component of traditional authority, a system in which personal relations dominate in the political and administrative power relations between the ruler and the ruled. Many Africanists observed that traditional patrimonialism has endured into contemporary African regimes in the post-colonial era. Alongside African leaders' essentially patrimonial behaviour coexist formal institutions, laws and bureaucracies, making the task of comprehending Africa ever more complicated. Hence, the notion of neo-patrimonialism was developed to cope with the two dimensions of African states: essentially patrimonial rule coexisting with legal-rational authority.[28]

Neo-patrimonialism is a testament to the lack of or weakness of an authoritative mechanism for the impersonal and rational allocation of state resources, and hence to the disappointing state of nation-building. The crux of the matter is that leaders in general have used the modern state apparatus to serve their personal and immediate interests instead of being 'bound' by it to advance the public interest. Hence, the opposite of modernization or nation-building has been taking place: the state institutions have been adapted to the existing socio-cultural practices instead of institutions bringing about changes and progress in society by making the people conform and adapt to them.

Goran Hyden, Julius Court and Kenneth Mease identified three dimensions of governance from the development context: economic, political and administrative.[29] In order for a nation to properly follow the path of development, a clear separation between the public domain and the private domain must be observed. Equally, economic, political and administrative governance should be pursued 'independently', without their boundaries becoming blurred by personal interests and short-term political considerations. This would require a strong commitment and moral authority from the top. But what is probably more important is the 'empowerment of people' not only as an effective check against the abuse of power and mismanagement by the authorities and the privileged, but also to *make things work* in terms of the everyday business of the nation.

There may be various reasons why neo-patrimonialism is so prevalent in Sub-Saharan Africa, but I think the big issue here is the absence of a critical turning point or occasion to 'break away' from the past and 'shift' the mindset of the people so that it fits into the developmental mode. Western countries underwent political struggles and upheavals, and many Asian countries experienced national movements or political uprisings, both during and after colonization. The political consciousness of the people, the sense of socio-political rights expressed in actions, movements and campaigns that constitute the bedrock of nation-building and development were feeble in Sub-Saharan Africa. To this day, African leaders and elites are largely unable (whether willingly or unwillingly) to change the unwholesome syndromes typical of Africa, a subject I will address in more detail later in this book.

Institutions, Governance and Democracy

Debates on Africa's institutional problems can be taxing to both the proponents and critics of Western institutions. It boils down to the question of what makes institutions work and who is responsible for the weakness or failure of Africa's institutions. There is no question that democracy, the rule of law, human rights and good governance are universal values and principles to which virtually every nation would aspire. The challenge for developing countries is how these goals can be realistically and substantively attained. This is a fundamental task that calls for open-mindedness on the part of all stakeholders.

Is adopting Western-style modern state institutions, good governance and democracy the surest way for Africa to realize development? In other words, are weak institutions, bad governance, and undemocratic and authoritarian rule chiefly responsible for Africa's shortcomings? The mainstream donor community would think that it is a matter of course. However, this seems to be misperception or oversimplification of such a premise, which needs to be viewed in a more objective light.

Much has been made about institutions, but 'institution' itself is a vague term. Sub-Saharan Africa has emerged as a prototype case of the mismatch between 'having' and 'doing'. This mismatch shows no sign of dissipating and the institutional problem is a good example of this reality in the region. Having good institutions is one thing and making them serve their purpose is another. What makes institutions work are the actions of people who uphold them.

In essence, good institutions and governance, the rule of law, freedom of speech, human rights and democracy are essentially ultimate goals or the end state of development rather than the means to achieving development. These are the features that emerge from successful development through the process of 'embodiment', which in itself requires arduous endeavours. They are not what can be simply 'introduced' and 'adopted' upon wish. The same applies to economics. Many seem to be unaware or have forgotten that economic growth and income generation cannot come about by transfers of wealth, but by the creation of wealth or the production of goods and services. Their preoccupation is mostly with the distribution of wealth rather than the creation of wealth.

Another important aspect that may be overlooked is that democracy, the rule of law and good governance are in reality 'modes' rather than 'substance'. In Sub-Saharan Africa, democracy is viewed too much in terms of 'freedom', while the sense of 'responsibility' and citizenship, which is just as important as freedom, is woefully neglected. In a mature democracy, freedom does not mean unfettered liberty that does harm to others, but that is responsible. Freedom of speech and individuals' rights alone cannot guarantee progress, and the obsession to 'duplicate' Western-style institutions and norms only superficially could hinder Africa's path to genuine democracy.

Developed nations and the established international community regard politics and development premised on the notion of 'rationality'. Because in the West 'rational' thinking prevails in life, Westerners may take it for granted that others will think in the same terms. This applies in relation to universal values and norms, business and the market economy, development, science and technology, global challenges, etc. However, as people will soon discover, the reality of Africa seems to be quite removed from such expectations.

The Sub-Saharan African countries have maintained the state system that is the continuation of the former colonial establishments. The introduction of the European rational-legal state has led to a Westernization of the political order in Africa and around the world. But Bertrand Badie states that a crucial consequence of this is the failure in terms of 'loss of meaning' in the relationship between rulers and the ruled which 'discourages the individual in his effort to adapt to an institutional life of no concern to him'.[30]

Not only have Western political institutions and values failed to take firm root in most African countries, but the manner in which they have been pursued or applied is also seen to have inhibited the growth of the very fabric that makes them work. After independence, Sub-Saharan African political leaders 'adapted' to the reality in the way they saw convenient, resulting in the formation of 'hybrid (or mixed) regimes' which are neither true liberal democracies nor the kind of outright dictatorial regimes.[31]

Basil Davidson suggested that the Western colonization of Africa actually held Africa back from forming nation states in its own way: it is the imposition of the European nation state rather than an intrinsic African characteristic that is at the root of the most of Africa's political problems, and colonialism promoted the rise of alienated African elites largely trained in Europe and oblivious to their historical foundations of political legitimacy.[32] According to Davidson, what Africa's leaders inherited was 'a crisis of social disintegration' from which sprang the current problems of Africa: while it was commonly assumed that Africa had no indigenous models for ruling nation states, it was in fact well into the process of evolving its own models for the nation state. The Asante kingdom of modern-day Ghana, for example, was 'manifestly a national state on its way to becoming a nation-state with every attribute ascribed to a Western European nation-state' and even after Africa's independence, the adherence to African tradition was still derided as 'tribalism' and viewed as an obstacle to development.[33]

So what we see today in Sub-Saharan Africa is the perennial gap between what is in spirit and what is actually being practised. African countries all have modern executive, legislative and judicial branches modelled after the Western political system and over many decades, their leaders and political elites were orientated in this modern model of statehood. Every nation should follow good governance, the rule of law, accountability and democracy—the standards that are now taken for granted as global norms. But these values or standards have been achieved over centuries of historical progress in the West through many internal and regional conflicts and social, political, economic turmoil and evolutions. And it was only in the twentieth century that these Western ideas and norms gained the status of being 'universal values'.

There is no denying that Africa's fate and development rests squarely with Africans, not the Western world or the international development community. How deep an impact the colonial legacies have had on Africa is matter of debate, but what is not debated is who are the owners and subjects of development. No matter how convenient and tempting it may be to place the blame on 'outsiders', these 'outsiders' only play a secondary role at best, and the unshakable truth is that the protagonists of Africa's development are none other than Africans themselves. And Africa's development is inexorably tied to nation-building, which is a process that is still very much in the making. But nation-building is not about just 'adopting' or 'adapting'—it should be about carrying out the arduous tasks of making and undergoing change. If African countries have not been able to do this up to this point, after half a century of independence, who should they blame for this other than themselves?

In the meantime, the political dynamics in Africa are seen to follow their own unpredictable course. As stated by Dani Rodrik, according to Freedom House's count, more than 60% of all the countries in the world are electoral democracies, meaning that their regimes have emerged through competitive multi-party elections. But the majority of these 'democracies' are in fact 'illiberal democracies' that brought about the rise of popular autocrats with little regard for the rule of law and civil liberties. Rodrik reminds us that liberal democracy rests on distinct sets of rights—property rights, political rights and civil rights—and that democratic bargaining can work only when the masses are able to organize and mobilize around common interests. And, historically, such mobilizations have been the product of industrialization and urbanization, wars or anti-colonial struggles. But in the developing world, these bargains, by their very nature, produce electoral democracies rather than liberal democracies, so that in practice, the emergence of liberal democracy is rarely seen today.[34]

The 'irregularity' of political developments is common in Africa. For example, in Burundi in May 2015, people took to the streets to protest against the removal of term limits for the President, and a military coup was attempted against President Pierre Nkurunziza, who wanted to remain in power. On the other hand, in Rwanda, with two years left before the next elections, people were petitioning Parliament to amend the Constitution, which limits presidents to two terms, in order to allow President Kagame to stand for President again. Even the second-largest political party, the largest opposition party, has backed the removal of term limits for elected political leaders.[35]

David Booth and Diana Gammack's observation is a telling reminder of the reality in Africa: the reason why the 'development business' most often fails in Africa is because much of the effort of the development community is predicated on false assumptions about how progress takes place in human societies. For the last two decades, development efforts have been based on the thinking that good governance provides a universally valid prescription for economic transformation and social advance, but this 'ahistorical view takes insufficient notice of the fact that Western states did not become economic powerhouses (from the 1750s onwards) … by adopting good governance institutions. Full-blown capitalism creates the social structures and organisational capabilities that lead to democratic governance, not the other way around'.[36]

Brian Levy also makes a case that over the long term, good governance may indeed be a final destination where developing countries can see their governance systems converge. However, he argues that 'the ability to describe the characteristics of effective states does not conjure them into existence out of thin air. Best-practices approaches assume that all policies and institutions are potentially movable and can be aligned to fit some pre-specified blueprint. But they cannot. The central question has less to do with the end point than with the journey of getting from here to there'.[37]

Those who have lived in Africa long enough will agree that one of the syndromes plaguing Africa today is that people by and large are good at expressing their views, but there is very little corresponding action or responsibility taken to make good on the words spoken. Liberal democracy, the rule of law and good governance will bear fruit when they become the way of life and are embodied in the leaders and the people alike. We should not forget that liberal democracy was not bestowed by the rulers, but was earned by the people who struggled for it. Democracy is something that cannot be 'provided for', but which has to be 'won'. What seems to have been forgotten during the course of liberalization and globalization is that democracy cannot be realized by 'free expressions' alone, but requires concrete deeds and toil.

The problem in Africa is that the mismatch between 'lofty expectations' and continued 'disingenuousness' on the ground persists in a kind of vicious cycle, only to breed disappointments and ill feeling without actually getting things done. This has produced the problem where African elites, whether in government or the private sector, talk the talk but do not walk the walk. Often, their motive is to present a good face to donors and receive aid or benefits, whilst knowing they will fall short in their obligations. Despite the challenging environment, efforts to attain sound institutions and governance should not be stopped. Recent studies have shown that the vast majority of people surveyed in Sub-Saharan African countries thought that democracy was preferable to any other kind of government. Obviously, it would be in the best interests of the African countries if they can espouse and 'internalize' these values as much and as early as possible.

Critics may find fault with the way in which the Global North is trying to 'impose' its values, but the Global North will be criticized even more if it was not seen to be steadfastly upholding the universal values. Isn't the European Union referred to as the 'normative power'? But an important thing for Western countries to realize is that it is not enough to only 'assert' these values; equal weight should be given to addressing how to reach the goals, while taking into account the local conditions, indigenous elements and socio-cultural characteristics of African nations.

While most African countries inherited democratic constitutions in the decolonization process, few maintained them. Botswana and Mauritius are just about the only countries that were born democratic and have remained so over the years, although in the case of Botswana, the same political party has been in power since independence. The vast majority of other African countries followed a path that consisted of a few years of democratic multi-party systems, followed by the progressive establishment of single-party regimes or a military takeover.

But most often in this process, there have been frequent political deadlocks and crisis. By and large, formal democratic institutions proved incompatible at the time with the rise of personal rule and neo-patrimonialism. Formal institutions lost their importance and power became concentrated in a close circle around the personal ruler. Many of these rulers then organized single parties, mass mobilization movements that were then seen as plausible instruments of nation-building. The rapid failure of democracy in African is a sobering reminder of its inherent drawbacks to democracy, particularly in light of the fact that in the post-Cold War era, donors made extensive efforts to promote democracy in Africa.

What transpired from this for the majority of African states was the rise of authoritarianism and the deterioration of citizens' rights. Many rulers argued that traditional African values such as consensus-seeking and loyalty justified the adoption of regimes that were seen as dictatorial across the continent. Within a few years of independence, most of the region's democratic aspirations had been stifled. Whatever the merits of the cultural arguments of some African elites to justify their domination, the relative ease with which African dictatorships persisted for decades suggested that many countries shared conditions favouring this type of regime. So what caused this? There must have been some commonalities in effect for the countries to produce such similar results across the continent. I believe that the problem is caused not by the failure of institutions themselves, but rather by the inertia and noncommittal attitude when it came to upholding institutions.

Institutions do matter. Daron Acemoglu and James A. Robinson's book *Why Nations Fail* is an inspiring work that tries to explain why some nations become prosperous, but others remain poor. The authors argue that the answer lies in the difference between inclusive institutions and extractive institutions. The former 'are those that allow and encourage participation by the great mass of people in economic activities that make best use of their talents and skills and that enable individuals to make the choices they wish', while the latter have the opposite properties 'designed to extract incomes and wealth from one subset of society to benefit a different subset'.[38] They argue that nations that develop inclusive institutions have far greater potential for growth than those that support extractive institutions that transfer rather than create wealth.

The authors have also pointed out the stark contrast between South and North Korea. They described the former as having inclusive economic institutions, while the latter has extractive economic institutions. Koreans are homogeneous people with a history of many thousands of years of sharing a national identity, language and culture. No doubt, it was the nature of North Korea's institutions—its regime and ideology—that turned North Korea into a failed state.

However, despite their appeal, the terminology of 'inclusive' and 'extractive' institutions comes with some question marks. I cannot help thinking that the term sounds tautological, as if to say 'what is good (inclusive) is good (prosperity) and what is bad (extractive) is bad (poor)'. 'Institution' is instead an abstract term that implies many things like ideologies, policies and actions of the state besides formal governing bodies. The question remains as to why such institutions came about in the first place and what drives them to continue functioning in this way. And the authors seem to have come up short in proposing specific mechanisms for encouraging better institutions.[39]

Institutions, however well thought out and meticulously stipulated into law, are only as good as the intention, persistence and capacity to 'operationalize' them. The success of institutions depends not on the existence of seemingly good institutions, but rather on the commitment and ability to make those institutions work, including continuous efforts to improve or reform public service mechanisms. The majority of Sub-Saharan African countries may have the 'right' institutions, but the pace of moving ahead with governance and development is all but gratifying.

Perhaps from a developmental perspective, what should draw our attention the most is the Human Development Index (HDI): out of 188 nations in the world that were surveyed, the bottom ten countries are all Sub-Saharan countries, and among the 'low human development' group of 41 countries having the lowest scores, 36 nations are from Sub-Saharan Africa. The Fragile State Index (2018) shows the top ten most fragile states and includes seven Sub-Saharan African countries (South Sudan, Somalia, the Central African Republic, Democratic Republic of the Congo, Sudan, Chad, Zimbabwe). In Freedom House's Country Freedom Index (2017), five Sub-Saharan African countries were included in the top ten least-free countries (Eritrea, South Sudan, Somalia, Sudan and Equatorial Guinea). Transparency International's Corruption Perception Index (2016) found that four countries in the region ranked in the top ten most negatively perceived states (Somalia, South Sudan, Sudan and Guinea-Bissau).

As Pierre Englebert and Kevin C. Dunn explain, what is troubling for both the donors and Sub-Saharan African countries alike is that there has been no visible progress in the region's governance during the period from 1985 to 2012 over which the study was conducted, no matter what indicators (Country Policy and Institutional Assessment,

World Governance Indicators, the Ibrahim Index or the Political Risk Service) were used.[40] The World Bank's latest Country Policy and Institutional Assessment (CPIA), which measures four areas (clusters) of governance—economic management, structural policies, policies for social inclusion and equity, and public sector management and institutions—illustrates that there was a slight downward trend in the regions' governance over the period from 2008 to 2016.

However, there are countries in the region that usually rank in the top ten in most of the indicators—the usual suspects like Mauritius, Botswana, Cape Verde, the Seychelles, Namibia, South Africa, Ghana, Senegal, São Tomé and Príncipe, Benin and the new rising star Rwanda—that should also be given due attention. An exception might be Ethiopia, which is the fastest-growing economy in the region, sustaining around 10% growth per annum in recent years.

Lastly, what cannot be stressed enough is the importance of governance in Sub-Saharan Africa. From a worldwide perspective, while debates on the correlation between democracy and economic development remain largely contentious and inconclusive in the light of the Asian experience, and notably China, which is a recent example, in Sub-Saharan Africa things seem to be quite different. In this region, it is clear that the countries exhibiting a high level of democracy and governance also fare well economically. For example, countries that are categorized as 'free' by Freedom House like Mauritius, Namibia, Botswana and South Africa are all ranked as 'high-middle income countries', and other countries scoring high in governance like Cape Verde, the Seychelles, Ghana, Rwanda, Senegal, São Tomé and Príncipe, and Benin are some of the fastest-growing economies in the region.

The reason for this may be found in the difference in the level of the work ethic: in Asia, a strong work ethic and government's role, and discipline in bureaucracy are seen to offset the negativities of weak democracy and corruption, but in the case of Africa, which is seen to lag behind in such traits in comparison to Asia, there is an extra burden posed by rampant corruption, ethnicism, nepotism, neopatrimonialism, rent-seeking, etc., and here, as a result, democracy and governance must make up for such drawbacks in order to catch up with other regions. Yes, institutions, governance and democracies should be fervently upheld, but the path to reaching the point where these become effective would require a massive endeavour by society as a whole, entailing enhancement of performance in virtually every segment and sector of the nation (Tables 3.1, 3.2, 3.3).

The Role of the State

According to Irma Adelman: 'No area of economics has experienced as many abrupt changes in the leading paradigm during the post-WWII era as has economic development. These changes have had profound implications for the way the role of government has been viewed by development practitioners and their advisors in international organizations' (see Note 40). The issue of the role of government regarding development is nothing new, but it continues to plague African countries and must be re-examined.

On the face of it, African governments have a high degree of centralization and strong presidential systems. Apparently, out of 49 states in Sub-Saharan Africa, no less than 40 have presidential executives. The centralization bias is considered both the colonial legacy as well as the reflection of reality: the inclination of the colonial administrations was to retain central authority and personal rule prevailed, while African societies were forcefully integrated into the post-colonial mold.[41] Another distinct feature of African governments is that they have a rather large number of ministerial posts.

However, despite their large 'horizontal' government structure, African executives do not have big 'vertical' bureaucracies in terms of formally employed civil servants. More importantly, African governments suffer from weak capacity to undertake given tasks in terms of implementing policies, solving problems and providing public services. The Fragile States Index (formerly called the failed states index), published annually by the Fund for Peace, assesses states' vulnerability to conflict and collapse, using a total of 12 indicators that fall into one of the following three groups: social (4), economic (2) and political indicators (6). Among the political indicators are state legitimacy, public services, human rights and the rule of law, security apparatus, etc. The

Table 3.1 The Mo Ibrahim Index of African Governance (2016)

Country		2015 score	Trend 2006–2015	Country		2015 score	Trend 2006–2015
1.	Mauritius	79.9	+2.3	28.	Liberia	50.0	+8.7
2.	Botswana	73.7	−0.5	29.	Swaziland	49.7	+1.0
3.	Cape Verde	73.0	+1.9	30.	Sierra Leone	49.4	+3.8
4.	The Seychelles	72.6	+4.0	31.	Ethiopia	49.1	+7.0
5.	Namibia	69.8	+3.6	32.	Gabon	48.8	+1.5
6.	South Africa	69.4	−1.9	33.	Madagascar	48.5	−7.6
7.	Tunisia	65.4	+3.4	33.	Togo	48.5	+9.7
7.	Ghana	65.4	−2.1	35.	Gambia	46.6	−3.9
9.	Rwanda	62.3	+8.4	36.	Djibouti	46.5	+2.3
10.	Senegal	60.8	+3.7	36.	Nigeria	46.5	+2.5
11.	São Tomé and Príncipe	60.5	+2.9	38.	Cameroon	45.7	−2.1
12.	Kenya	58.9	+5.1	39.	Zimbabwe	44.3	+9.7
13.	Zambia	58.8	+4.3	40.	Mauritania	43.5	−2.7
14.	Morocco	58.3	+5.7	41.	Guinea	43.3	+1.9
15.	Lesotho	57.8	+0.3	42.	Congo, Rep.	43.0	+2.6
16.	Benin	57.5	+0.7	43.	Burundi	41.9	−2.1
17.	Malawi	56.6	+1.1	44.	Guinea-Bissau	41.3	+4.0
18.	Tanzania	56.5	−0.6	45.	Angola	39.2	+5.0
19.	Uganda	56.2	+3.4	46.	Congo, DR	35.8	+2.7
20.	Algeria	53.8	−0.6	47.	Equatorial Guinea	35.4	+2.0
21.	Cote d'Ivoire	52.3	+13.1	48.	Chad	34.8	+2.3
21.	Mozambique	52.3	−1.8	49.	Sudan	30.4	−0.6
23.	Burkina Faso	51.8	+1.0	50.	Eritrea	30.0	−5.6
24.	Egypt	51.0	+3.5	51.	Libya	29.0	−18.0
25.	Mali	50.6	−4.7	52.	Central African Republic	25.7	−4.9
26.	Comoros	50.3	+3.7	53.	South Sudan	18.6	
27.	Niger	50.2	+5.9	54.	Somalia	10.6	+0.3

Source Mo Ibrahim Index of African Governance (IIAG) 2016
Governance as the provision of the political, social and economic goods that citizens have the right to expect from their state
The IIAG assesses progress under four main conceptual categories: safety & rule of law, participation & human rights, sustainable economic opportunity, and human development

Table 3.2 Freedom country scores for Sub-Saharan Africa (2017)

Not free			Partially free			Free		
Country	Rating	Score	Country	Rating	Score	Country	Rating	Score
Uganda	5.5	35	The Seychelles	3.0	71	Cape Verde	1.0	90
Gabon	5.5	32	Lesotho	3.0	64	Mauritius	1.5	89
Mauritania	5.5	30	Malawi	3.0	63	Ghana	1.5	83
Congo	6.0	27	Burkina Faso	3.5	63	Benin	2.0	82
Djibouti	5.5	26	Liberia	3.5	62	São Tomé and Príncipe	2.0	81
Rwanda	6.0	24	Sierra Leone	3.0	61	South Africa	2.0	78
Angola	6.0	24	Tanzania	3.5	58	Senegal	2.0	78
Cameroon	6.0	24	Zambia	3.5	56	Namibia	2.0	77
Gambia	6.0	20	Madagascar	3.5	56	Botswana	2.5	72
Congo, DR	6.5	19	Comoros	3.5	55			
Burundi	6.5	19	Mozambique	4.0	53			
Chad	6.5	18	Cote d'Ivoire	4.0	52			
Swaziland	6.5	18	Kenya	4.0	51			
Ethiopia	6.5	12	Nigeria	4.0	50			
Central African Republic	7.0	10	Niger	4.0	49			
Equatorial Guinea	7.0	8	Togo	4.0	48			
Sudan	7.0	6	Mali	4.5	45			
Somalia	7.0	5	Guinea	5.0	41			
South Sudan	7.0	4	Guinea Bissau	5.0	40			
Eritrea	7.0	3	Zimbabwe	5.0	32			

Source Freedom House, Freedom on the World 2017 country scores
Freedom rating is an average of political rights (PR) and civil liberties (CL): 1 = most free and 7 = least free
Above score is aggregate: 0 = least free and 100 = most free

Table 3.3 Other state performance indicators

Country	Human development	Corruption perception	Fragile states	Country	Human development	Corruption perception	Fragile states
Angola	0.533 (150)	18 (164)	91.1 (32)	Madagascar	0.512 (158)	26 (145)	84.0 (55)
Benin	0.485 (167)	36 (95)	77.6 (73)	Malawi	0.476 (170)	31 (120)	88.0 (44)
Botswana	0.698 (108)	60 (35)	63.8 (120)	Mali	0.442 (175)	32 (116)	92.9 (31)
Burkina Faso	0.402 (185)	42 (72)	88.0 (44)	Mauritania	0.513 (157)	27 (142)	93.7 (28)
Burundi	0.404 (184)	20 (159)	98.9 (17)	Mauritius	0.781 (64)	54 (50)	41.7 (148)
Cameroon	0.518 (153)	26 (145)	95.6 (26)	Mozambique	0.418 (181)	27 (142)	89.0 (40)
Cape Verde	0.648 (122)	59 (38)	70.1 (106)	Namibia	0.640 (125)	52 (53)	70.4 (103)
Central African Republic	0.352 (188)	20 (159)	112.6 (3)	Niger	0.353 (187)	35 (101)	97.4 (20)
Chad	0.391 (186)	20 (159)	109.4 (8)	Nigeria	0.527 (152)	28 (136)	101.6 (13)
Comoros	0.497 (160)	24 (153)	84.8 (52)	Rwanda	0.498 (159)	54 (50)	90.8 (34)
Congo, Rep.	0.592 (135)	20 (159)	93.4 (29)	São Tomé and Príncipe	0.574 (142)	46 (62)	72.1 (97)
Congo, DR	0.435 (176)	21 (156)	110 (7)	Senegal	0.494 (162)	45 (64)	82.3 (60)
Cote d'Ivoire	0.474 (171)	34 (108)	96.5 (21)	The Seychelles	0.782 (63)	55 (47)	59.4 (125)
Djibouti	0.473 (172)	30 (123)	88.9 (41)	Sierra Leone	0.420 (179)	30 (123)	89.1 (39)
Equatorial Guinea	0.592 (135)	19 (163)	85.0 (51)	Somalia	NA	10 (175)	113.4 (2)
Eritrea	0.420 (179)	18 (164)	98.1 (19)	South Africa	0.666 (119)	45 (64)	72.3 (96)
Ethiopia	0.448 (174)	34 (108)	101.1 (15)	South Sudan	0.418 (181)	11 (174)	113.9 (1)
Gabon	0.697 (109)	35 (101)	73.8 (91)	Sudan	0.490 (165)	14 (170)	110.6 (5)
Gambia	0.452 (173)	26 (145)	89.4 (37)	Swaziland	0.541 (148)	43 (70)	88.8 (42)
Ghana	0.579 (139)	43 (70)	69.7 (108)	Tanzania	0.531 (151)	32 (116)	80.3 (65)
Guinea	0.414 (183)	27 (142)	102.4 (12)	Togo	0.497 (166)	32 (116)	83.9 (56)
Guinea-Bissau	0.424 (178)	16 (168)	99.5 (16)	Uganda	0.493 (163)	25 (151)	96.0 (24)
Kenya	0.555 (146)	26 (145)	96.4 (22)	Zambia	0.579 (139)	38 (87)	87.8 (46)
Lesotho	0.497 (160)	39 (83)	81.7 (62)	Zimbabwe	0.516 (154)	22 (154)	101.6 (13)
Liberia	0.427 (177)	37 (90)	93.8 (27)				

Source UNDP Human Development Index (2016); Transparency International CPI (2016); Peace Foundation Fragile States Index (2017) Parenthesis: ranking (HDI 188 countries, CPI 176 countries, FSI 178 countries)

2017 Index showed that 32 Sub-Saharan African countries were ranked in the top 50 most fragile.[42]

A conspicuous feature of Sub-Saharan African countries is the weakness of their governing power and hence their weakness in performing the basic functions to serve the public and realize economic development that is worthy of their potential. Many African governments apparently lack the drive and persistence to achieve short and mid to long-term national goals. And as is often the case, well thought-out national policies are rendered nominal when confronted by hard realities.

Unfortunately, corruption, bad governance and inefficiency have become almost synonymous with African governments, so that donors and the African people may be wary of the notion of governments being 'strengthened'. Yet, for developing countries that are still in the midst of nation-building, discrediting the need for strong government and giving up on the state could be extremely detrimental.

European countries built their nation-state system with centralized government and a highly developed bureaucracy over a long period in their tumultuous history. On the other hand, in comparison, Sub-Saharan African countries lacked a strong social fabric, political norms and systems that form the basis of state. And such elements as tribalism and neo-patrimonialism, while they cannot be branded as definitive causes of underdevelopment, are still very much prevalent and pertinent. Under the circumstances, if African leaders, elites and people are serious about developing their country, it is imperative that they find ways to make their government much more functional, and naturally this will take some time to achieve. But what is more disconcerting is that Africans themselves may not be well aware or concerned about this problem. And development partners do not seem to be particularly interested in helping 'empower' African governments either.

However, the donor community tried various approaches in the early stages of development assistance for poor countries, including efforts to empower the state with optimism. As John Harris notes: 'In the 1950s and 1960s, the centrality of the role of the state and the need for regulation of markets was hardly questioned. It was generally understood that economic development must involve industrialization.'[43] In the

1960s, donors indeed espoused such a stance in their aid policy, putting trust in working with African governments so that the latter would follow the course of state-building and economic development, counting on a trickle-down effect for rural development and industrialization. But the approach was short-lived, due to unforeseen disappointing results and also because of the inherent restraints in the political dynamics of the donor community that was impatient with ongoing failures and was under pressure to seek alternative measures.[44] Kingsley Chiedu Moghalu also notes that: 'In the 1960s, the main focus of aid was on large-scale industrial and infrastructure projects. This was the golden age of foreign aid; one which could be justified as a catalyst of growth and development. Dams, roads, bridges and railways were constructed across the continent. But this phase didn't last long.'[45]

The approach that focused on building infrastructures and creating local industries, preferably starting with the agricultural sector, should have been pursued for far longer, instead of quickly shifting to poverty reduction programmes in the 1970s. The policy choice was right and timely. However, what was lacking was commitment as well as fundamentals like 'internalization' efforts and a sense of ownership on the part of developing nations.

The golden opportunity for African countries seems to have been missed in this period encompassing the 1960s and 1970s. If they had indeed capitalized on this opportunity and exerted themselves, many success stories would have emerged in the region, as was the case in Asia. While African countries today have registered high economic growth, this masks many worrying features: overdependence on raw materials; continued underdevelopment and low-value addition of the agricultural sector; the 'curse of resources' and the extractive industry; the dominance of foreign companies; a lack of industrialization; overreliance on foreign, multi-national companies and negligible indigenous manufacturing industries; rapid population growth and youth unemployment, etc.[46]

Turning to the international development architecture, the world has witnessed transitions in mainstream development theories and policy orientations: the structuralist/modernization theory-dominant period (from the end of the Second World War to 1979); the neo-liberalism ascendency period (1979–1996); and the 'revisionist' or 'Post-Washington Consensus' period from 1996 onwards. The 'revisionist' school advocates a dynamically changing mix of state and market interactions. The World Bank published a report, 'The State in a Changing World (1997)', in which it stated that development without an effective state is impossible, stressing the need to find a balance between the market and the state, and recognizing that there are market failures as well as state failures.[47]

The Structural Adjustment Programme (SAP) was introduced into African countries in the mid-1980s to reduce the role of the state in the development process and give market forces a greater role in the allocation of resources, but ended in failure and worsened Africa's economy. As a result, an overall policy shift was made, and the New Orthodoxy Era (1996–2010) unfolded for Africa.[48] But, apparently, African countries have not yet learned to 'right' the role of the government.

The global economic and financial crisis of 2008–2009 was another turning point in the thinking on economic development. Following the crisis, there appears to have been a convergence of ideas, at least within the African Union Commission (AUC) and the United Nations Economic Commission on Africa (UNECA), on the imperatives of economic development. The two reports, the 'UNECA/AUC Economic Report on Africa (2011)' and 'Governing Development in Africa: The Role of the State in Economic Transformation (2011)', suggest that the state has a crucial role to play in meeting the development challenges in Africa. Their recommendation is that the 'developmental state' approach should be used through disciplined planning, while avoiding the pitfalls of state intervention.[49] The notion is quite sound, but putting this into practice this still remains a big challenge in the absence of concrete actions.

African countries missed the golden opportunity discussed above because successful development through industrialization is becoming increasingly difficult for developing countries to achieve. Dani Rodrick reminds us that historically, rapid growth has always been associated with industrialization. But today, even BRICS countries, including China and India, have not realized the full-scale development (in terms of percentage of employment by economic sectors) of the manufacturing industrial sector that characterizes the growth path of Western economies, but instead have prematurely dipped in the industrial structure, that is, deindustrialization. Rodrik mentions that only South Korea succeeded in achieving sufficient industrialization before, making a transition to an advanced industrial structure that we see in Western economies. He points out that 'less room for industrialisation will almost certainly mean fewer growth miracles in the future' and that 'today's developing countries will possibly have bumpier paths to democracy and good governance'.[50]

Capitalism's most important components include private property, production factors, capital accumulation and competition.[51] Private property rights are a central tenet of capitalism, and the land ownership question can be most problematic but crucial for developing countries. In classical economics, labour, land and capital constitute production factors, but today elements such as technology, entrepreneurship and innovations are considered as crucial means for enhancing production. This is all the more so in the increasingly competitive international environment under globalization.

According to Kingsley Chiedu Moghalu, the fundamental requirements for successful capitalism are innovation, property rights, and financial and capital markets, but none of these is present to any significant extent in Africa.[52] This is a fair assessment, but the interesting thing is that these three fundamental factors—innovation, property rights, and financial and capital markets—all invariably demand focused, disciplined and 'intrusive' government intervention. Hence, on the question of whether African countries need strong government, the answer seems to be self-evident. First of all, regarding land reform, only the government can authoritatively certify, allocate and regulate land ownership for the people. Technical innovation requires active, systematic and long-term investment and support of the state. Developing, regulating and reforming financial markets, and operating capital resources to assist the private sector are all rudimentary tasks of the government.

The responsibility for the lacklustre development of African countries rests with Africans themselves, not the donors or the international environment. And 'to imply that entrepreneurs can carry on in environments in which governments are failing in their duty to provide an enabling environment for value-adding business activity is to make a case for failed states dominated by stunted entrepreneurs'.[53] But few people in the region seem to take this seriously enough. The reality is that both market failures and government failures are commonplace. As long as we are talking about the development of 'nation states', mindful that Sub-Saharan African countries are still a long way from completing the task of nation-building, it is imperative that strong, functioning governments must be zealously sought. And the scope of governance that is required is not what the international community can provide on behalf of African states.

The international community must also be reflective and understand that in order for African states to properly tap into and implement policies, and to enhance their output, the latter need to have an effective government. In light of all the problems that African states have experience up to now, it could be argued that it would be better to have as little government as possible. But outsourcing just about everything that the government should be doing while forgoing their task of 'learning by doing', which is the case in most African countries, is tantamount to the state's self-denial of its raison d'être.

Sub-Saharan states are marked by the weak functioning of the government and an inappropriate or 'wrong' policy orientation for economic growth. Many Sub-Saharan African regimes have the facade of authoritarian power, but in reality they lack the focus and determination to get things done and to push the agendas through, as East Asian countries were able to do. The Asian experience provides fertile ground for sober reflections on the part of both African countries and the donor community. In this vein, not enough lessons have been learned, while some experts are dismissive of the East Asian examples, claiming that the 'conditions are different' and they are not applicable. We need not simply stick to the examples of the East Asian Tigers, since there are also good case studies in other Southeast Asian countries.

In his book *Asia-Africa Development Divergence: A Question of Intent*, David Henley explains why Southeast Asian countries have become much more prosperous over the last half-century compared to African countries, which have stumped without visible signs of a major turnaround. Regarding the scope of divergence, he points out that:

> [I]n [the] 1960s, South-East Asians were on the [sic] average much poorer than Africans; by 1980 they caught up, and by 2010 they were two and a half times richer. In South-East Asia the whole of the intervening half-century was a period of almost continuous growth, apart from a brief hiatus at the turn of the century caused by the Asian financial crisis. In Africa, per capita income stagnated in the 1970s, declined in the 1980s, grew weakly in the 1990s, and in 2010 was still barely higher than it had been in 1975.[54]

Henley argues that state-led rural and agricultural development that led to higher incomes for peasant farmers has been central to Southeast Asia's economic success, while its absence in Sub-Saharan Africa was critical for the continent's failure. The policy prescriptions by the world development agencies like the World Bank and IMF demanding liberalization, deregulation, and privatization and austerity measures in Africa were contradictory to the reality of strategic planning of the national economy that underpinned the success in East Asia. For developing countries, the weaker the government, the more it is likely to be dependent on outside forces, jeopardizing their chances of development.

When coming up with initiatives, especially in multilateral forums, African leaders did show a certain level of energy and enthusiasm. For example, in 1980, African governments adopted their own economic blueprint—the Lagos Plan of Action for the Economic Development of Africa 1980–2000 (LPA)—calling for collective self-reliance. But this was scarcely implemented and, moreover, did not sit well with the international development community, as it repudiated the logic of neo-liberal thinking, ending up in failure.[55] After the aborted LPA, African leaders launched a second major attempt to reclaim African development agenda and adopted the New Partnership for Africa's Development (NEPAD) in October 2000. But again, African countries failed in this endeavour, drawing considerable criticism because it was never properly implemented.

The reason why Sub-Saharan African countries continue to struggle with economic transformation and remain poor while being heavily dependent on foreign aid and capital may be attributable to the inability to push for development or a lack of determination and willingness.

Natural Conditions

The geographical and natural conditions of Sub-Saharan Africa, characterized by the existence of many landlocked countries and vast inland territories that are very difficult to access due to very poor and sparse roads, the harsh tropical climate and widespread diseases like malaria, are often cited as obstacles to development for the region. The narrative of the history of colonization of Africa by the Western powers that we are familiar with might have contributed to the stereotypical worldview of the continent.

However, two things must be pointed out: first, foreign explorers and settlers back then must have faced great hardships, but the geographical condition for development should be judged not from the outsider's point of view but from the locals' position; and, second, objective assessment should be made based not on historical documents, but on the present situation.

In *The Age of Sustainable Development* (2015), Jeffrey Sachs, a pioneer in the research on geographical differences between places, reiterates that the geography of Africa and adversity of the African climate matter for development. Paul Collier similarly views that being 'land locked with bad neighbours' makes African countries' development harder. In his book *Prisoners of Geography*, Tim Marshall depicts Africa as a historically remote and isolated continent cut off from the centres of trade and disadvantaged in terms of lack of navigable rivers and having too large a land mass to be effectively connected as a single region or even as sub-regions.[56]

The effects that geographical and climatic factors can have on the development of countries should not be downplayed and it is a fact that landlocked countries face huge challenges in making their economy competitive in terms of exporting commodities and attracting foreign investment. For the majority of foreigners who have never been to Africa, the mere notion of travelling to this region would entail great adventurism and a psychological challenge.

But this is just one aspect of Sub-Saharan Africa in its natural form, and to a certain degree it is deceptive, masking the overall, accurate picture of Africa. When the Ebola epidemic broke out in West Africa in 2014, it alarmed the international community and travel to and from Africa was greatly curtailed. However, I remember an international health expert telling CNN that people should not be panicking because Africa is not a country but a very big continent.

We must bear in mind that Africa is a huge continent with diverse geographical and climatic features. I know all too well that Africa is not only attractive for foreigners to live in, but undeniably also has a huge potential for growth and development due to its rich natural resources and many other things. Thus, we should be careful not to be simplistic and prejudiced when talking about the 'conditions' of Africa. If there are places where the conditions are adverse, there are also places where the conditions are most favourable. And when one visits Sub-Saharan Africa, it doesn't take long for one to realize that here so many places are far more 'favourable' than other parts of the world.

The geographical and natural conditions of Sub-Saharan Africa should not be construed as a root cause of its underdevelopment. Instead, it is the human factor, the failure to deal with these conditions that has led to the perpetuation of the problems. Strictly speaking, even endemic and epidemic diseases are largely man-made. But sadly, we tend to attribute the failures of human beings not to humans, but to what we think is convenient. We do not need to mention Arnold Toynbee's famous axiom 'challenge and response', as it is apparent that human endeavour to overcome adversities makes all the difference. Many rich nations had to tame geographical and natural conditions much harsher than those in Africa in order to arrive at where they are now.

Uganda provides a good example at this point. Its nature—the weather, agricultural conditions and natural resources—provides all that one could ask for. It is no wonder that it is called the 'Pearl of Africa'. Other East African countries like Rwanda, Burundi, Tanzania, Kenya,

Ethiopia and even South Sudan all boast wonderful natural conditions. We need not mention countries in the south like South Africa, Zimbabwe, Mozambique, Botswana, Zambia and Namibia. And there are so many countries in western Africa that are richly endowed. I have not heard of instances where great natural calamities such as earthquakes, volcano eruptions and tsunamis have occurred in Sub-Saharan Africa. Because of global warming and climate change, the whole world is suffering from unexpected or extreme weather conditions. In sum, it is Africa's negative and stereotyped image, along with many other things, rather than the actual workings of the geographical and natural conditions that has far more debilitating effects. Unduly exaggerating the given conditions will only breed despair and dependence.

Other Factors (Population, Corruption, Globalization and China)

We also could conceive of various other factors that may not necessarily be the root cause of Africa's underdevelopment, but can affect the region's development. Corruption readily comes to mind, but there can be other elements like population size and the effects of globalization that also have a bearing.

Regarding population size, conventional wisdom would suggest that it will be easier to foster and run democracy in a smaller nation than a larger one. Direct democracy like the Athenian democracy would only be possible if the size of the community of the people is limited. It could also be argued that the formation of identity and consensus of the people and maintaining of social order will be easier when communities are small. Certainly, in Sub-Saharan Africa, the least-populous nations, such as the Seychelles, São Tomé and Príncipe, Cape Verde, Mauritius, Botswana and Namibia, are among the highest scorers in governance and freedom. But countries like Djibouti, Guinea-Bissau and Equatorial Guinea, which have very small populations, score very low in terms of governance and freedom, so this is not a reliable criterion. Another factor that may need to be considered along with population is the size of the territory or the sparseness of the population.

The correlation between the size of the population and economic development in Sub-Saharan Africa is not easy to gauge either. GDP and per-capita income are generally in a trade-off, hence it is difficult to rank highly in both. GDP represents economic influence or market size, while per-capita GDP represents the level of wealth enjoyed by the people. For developing economies in particular, both of these matter, and the degree of income or social inequality should also be counted in assessing a nation's overall economic performance. In terms of GDP, the top five countries are Nigeria, South Africa, Angola, Sudan and Ethiopia in that order; however, the top five in per-capita GDP are the Seychelles, Equatorial Guinea, Mauritius, Gabon and Botswana.

A major issue for Sub-Saharan Africa is the population explosion that has produced an extraordinarily large youth population, which poses huge social economic challenges, given that most of the countries experiencing such phenomenon are the poorest and most fragile countries. It is pointed out that the SSA's population, which is currently over 1.0 billion (that of the entire African continent is over 1.25 billion) may double by 2050.[57] The population of Nigeria, the biggest in the continent, is expected to grow from 191 million in 2017 to 411 million in 2050 to become the world's third-most populous country, behind India and China. However, it would all come down to how the population is managed. The youth population can turn out to be an asset or a huge liability depending on how the state and society respond to this, which in turn hinges on their ability, commitment and mindset for development.

Compared to the demographic timebomb, corruption is viewed as being outright negative, and many suggest that this is the biggest reason for Africa's problems. But corruption can also be viewed as a reflection or outcome of more fundamental problems, in addition to being a reason for underdevelopment. Corruption exists everywhere, in any society and country, but is more conspicuous and widespread in developing countries and is seen as a general attribute of a weak social fabric. But in Sub-Saharan Africa, corruption is so rampant that it is relentlessly exposed time after time in the news.

As a continent, Africa continues to top the list in the category of having the most highly corrupt countries, with 12 countries ranking in the top 20 and five in the top ten, according to Transparency International's Corruption Perception Index (2016), which surveyed 177 countries worldwide. An African Union study conducted in 2002 estimated that corruption cost the continent roughly $150 billion a year. The foreign aid that Sub-Saharan Africa received from developed countries amounted to $22.5 billion in 2008, according to the OECD.[58] According to the East African Bribery Index of 2009, compiled by Transparency International, over half of East Africans polled paid bribes to access public services that should have been provided for free. Corruption in Africa, which ranges from high-level political graft to low-level bribes given to public officials, has a hugely corrosive effect on basic institutions and unduly increases the cost of doing business. It is argued that academic research shows that curtailing corruption can drastically enhance the economic productivity of a country, and some economists propose that African governments need to fight corruption instead of relying on foreign aid.[59]

There are several reasons why corruption in Sub-Saharan Africa is particularly detrimental to the region's development. Its regularity and rampancy are unmatched. Corruption can be defined simply as 'the abuse of entrusted power for private gain'.[60] Hence, discussions on corruption usually centre on 'public sector corruption', but corruptive behaviours or 'irregularities' are not confined to political leaders and public officials; they extend far beyond to include the private sector and the public in general.

Except for a very small number of countries, Sub-Saharan African nations experience corruption as the 'norm' rather than the 'exception', with people taking advantage of the 'opportunities' whenever they arise, political graft and systematic extortion by the powerful (leaders and their inner circles) being deeply entrenched and persistent without being challenged, politicians and top officials routinely and incessantly engaging in private business, officials at various levels in government departments and public offices frequently being involved in 'organized' irregularities, and police, customs officers and other officials in public service taking bribes. And this is not the end of the story.

Another form of corruption is 'absenteeism', which is also a very serious problem in the region: government organizational (central and local) officials, teachers, doctors, etc. frequently being absent from their offices to the detriment of the public interest. Corruption in Africa is linked to many other facets and problems inherent in African societies and therefore its scope and impact is as much far-reaching. And the negativity of neo-patrimonialism, ethnicism and other issues related to various syndromes, the mindset and ethics, etc. all contribute to corruption.

While 'corruption' is broadly defined to mean all the 'irregularities' taking place in a society, corruption is also widespread in the private sector as well. It is difficult to distinguish between corruption and theft, and maybe it is meaningless to make the distinction. Especially for foreigners, the difficulty in countering corruption in Africa is that one doesn't know who is involved and at what level. The widespread and common practice of seeking 'commission' is another good example of how corruption can take many forms in the region. Not only are the most fundamental public services that are taken for granted in the developed world not properly provided, even those expensive utility installation services, for instance, that users have to pay high cost to access do not come automatically.

Foreign aid projects can also (and often do) become the targets of corruption. They can be subtle in their approach, but it is customary for officials who are involved to explicitly or implicitly ask donors to give them some kind of 'commission' for receiving aid. It is true that donors often feel they have to 'pay' for the good deeds they are trying to do, instead of being fully embraced and appreciated.

What makes Africa's corruption more nuanced compared to that in other regions is that it is combined with many other negative factors. The case in point is that although corruption was widespread in Asian countries, this did not prevent these countries from achieving fast economic growth. Hence, we need to look at the whole picture, taking into account all the relevant factors and the reality on the ground. An interesting observation has been made that 'corruption in African countries tends to be of the decentralised and disorganised type in which paying a bribe to one official does not guarantee that a service will be provided. This type of corruption may be more deleterious to growth and development than the centralised and organised type found in Asia. For all these reasons, it is most likely that corruption could have a different effect on economic development in African countries than elsewhere'.[61]

The state of Africa's corruption is a reflection of the African reality. Fundamentally rectifying this problem will by no means be an easy feat and would require all-out and sustained responses. Nonetheless, various supervisory, sanctioning mechanisms to enforce transparency and discipline in the relevant institutions and offices, along with pressure exerted by the development community, should be stringently applied.

Another subject that deserves our attention, I believe, is the consequences of globalization on Sub-Saharan African countries. While globalization can in general be seen in a positive light in terms of Africa's business and cultural connectivity with the world, its overall impact is anything but simple to assess, and it can entail various risks and side-effects, depending on the capacities of the countries. There is no denying that today African countries find themselves in a quite different international setting compared to when they gained independence. And globalization—inter-dependence and inter-connectivity among economies—may be the most potent force affecting developing and developed countries alike in today's world.

The impact of globalization is clearly felt in Sub-Saharan Africa, as this was reinforced by the acts of both the international community and the African countries. Perhaps the first major shockwave of globalization to hit the continent came in the form of policy measures: the neo-liberalist policies prescribed by international financial and development institutions during the period of structural adjustment and the Washington Consensus. In order to obtain aid and loans from donors, African countries had to show commitment to market-oriented economic reforms and good governance. And while African countries did not have much choice but to conform to donors' terms, they actually opted for a pro-business liberal economy for a number of reasons.

The elites of Sub-Saharan African countries are pragmatists, who are keen to obtain wealth by seeking business opportunities with foreign companies and partners. The limited financial resources and capabilities of African states is understandable, but the major problem is really the lack of entrepreneurship, commitment and perseverance to successfully pursue business demonstrated in African business circles, and their inability or hesitation to make the necessary investments for future returns. This has left a huge vacuum that foreign investors and partners have had to fill. In many instances, even in remote provinces, landlords and local communities are willing to sell off chunks of land they possess at low prices to foreign investors. Since the locals do not have the means to make use of their land in any case, it would make sense to find an option with those who can develop it. For landlocked African countries in particular, the need to remove trade barriers and make their markets more accessible and appealing is deemed to be crucial in order to offset their disadvantages.

Obviously, there are also downsides to globalization, which are the ultimate price developing countries have to pay for being integrated into the global economy. For example, over the years, East African currencies have undergone a continuously sharp drop in their value against the US dollar, but the East African governments have admitted that there is not much that they can do to counter this phenomenon.

The deepening of liberalization over recent decades and the way in which African countries have 'adapted' to it have no doubt undermined their economic 'autonomy'. For them, the window of opportunity to approach the ranks of industrialized economies has been narrowing because of the slow pace of structural changes and the absence of strategic thinking and genuine efforts to 'catch up', amid increasing international competition and faster cycles of technological ratcheting-up. Confronted with the economic tasks at hand, African leaders have opted for convenient solutions like inviting foreign capital and expertise to fill their financial and capacity gaps, without concurrently taking competitiveness-enhancing measures at their end. This is mostly true throughout the region, including South Africa, where there is a juxtaposition of the 'First World' and the 'Third World', making it an interesting testing ground for 'radical economic transformation'.

For developing countries, continuously relying heavily on foreign firms and capital would not be the best solution in relation to economic development. The goal should be for African countries to build an industrial economy that is suited to their own specific situation in which they enjoy ownership, even while they trade freely with the outside. Unfortunately, many Sub-Saharan African countries have opened up and sold off their precious economic rights too soon to foreign companies, without even realizing their long-term value. The prospect of earning immediate profits, perhaps with 'premiums', can override consideration for the long-term national interests. A good example of this is the telecommunications market. African countries easily gave away their frequency usage rights to foreign companies, unaware that this is tantamount to giving up their strategic leverage and valuable economic sovereignty that could be used for many decades to come.

Lastly, as a feature of globalization, China's increasingly proactive economic engagement with Africa deserves our attention. But the impact that China has on the landscape of Africa's development, the ODA policy of traditional donors and the overall economic dynamism of Africa are uncertain. What is clear is that China's method of economic cooperation is quite different from the mainstream donor community, so African countries tend to think of China as an alternative to Western partners.

China's greatest strength lies in its financial capability and readiness to do business with Africa. China, employing generous assistance and sumptuous loans as tools, has made tremendous inroads in infrastructure-building and the energy development market in particular, based on their price competitiveness of labour, which is unmatched. For African countries desperate to find any financial resources for large-scale construction and engineering projects, China's partnership becomes handy. As both China and African countries will point out, these come with 'no strings attached'.

However, while there might not be any strings attached, various socio-economic costs may be incurred. The impact on the already-fragile governance and business practices in Africa comes to mind. Furthermore, it is no secret that Chinese goods and work that are found in Africa often turn out to be substandard, while Chinese merchants' businesses in retail frequently attract complaints from local competitors.

A latest report by the McKinsey Global Institute shows the profile of China's economic footprint in Africa in comparison to other countries, including the US, Germany, France, the UK and India, in terms of trade, FDI, aid and infrastructure financing. We can see that China's lead is absolute in trade and infrastructure financing, and while China's FDI is comparatively low, it is registering fast growth; its ODA level is also considerable, on a par with the UK.[62]

In the past, corruption scandals involving Chinese firms appeared frequently in the African news, and the region's overall perception of China's economic expansion and mode of doing business in Sub-Saharan Africa is mixed, as is captured by surveys. However, we should not be unduly critical. Many Chinese firms enter African markets taking risks in the areas where no one else is likely to venture. Contrary to conventional thinking, aggressive as they may seem, Chinese companies are not necessarily successful in Africa. In fact, they commonly face stiff competition even among themselves and many withdraw from African markets after incurring losses. Maybe the biggest downsides to such a 'no-strings-attached' way of doing business with Africa lies in the possibility that it can make African countries more complacent and exacerbate the already-serious dependency syndrome, moral hazard and poor governance. And it is my impression that there is still a considerable misperception amongst African leaders and elites about the situation of their markets and economies, and how companies do business and operate to make profit.[63]

In this regard, the presence of big multi-national corporations and aggressive Chinese firms may have had an undesirable impact in terms of making people overestimate the capacity of these entities and to have inaccurate views on how business works. For instance, they seem to think that big foreign companies can operate and make a profit for as long as possible and can do anything.

Notes

1. Among many private entities involved in international development, a notable example that I encountered is the Geneva Institute for Leadership & Public Policy based in Switzerland. The Institute organized, jointly with South Korea's Science & Technology Policy Institute and with its partners Kumi University and the Uganda National

Council for Science & Technology, the Conference on National Transformation with special focus on science & technology, business & industry, in Kampala, Uganda, 5–7 October, 2017 (Africana Hotel). The special guest speaker was David Beasley, Executive Director of the World Food Programme.

2. Mahmood Mamdani, *Citizen and Subject: Contemporary Africa and the Legacy of Colonialism* (Princeton: Princeton University Press, 1996).
3. 'Native authority' refers to the indigenous chiefs or black elites who were granted power by the colonialists according to Mamdani. In a way, the vestiges of this remain in many parts of Africa as dual legal systems, in which power is divided at both the national and local levels.
4. Mahmood Mamandi, 'Beyond Settler and Native as Political Identities: Overcoming the Political Legacy of Colonialism', *Comparative Studies in Society and History* 43, no. 4 (2001), pp. 651–664.
5. Edmond Keller, *Identity, Citizenship, and Political Conflict in Africa* (Bloomington: Indiana University Press, 2014), p. 23.
6. Pierre Englebert and Kevin C. Dunn, *Inside African Politics* (Boulder: Lynne Rienner Publishers, 2013), p. 25. The authors point out that new states were created without much attention and resources being devoted to them. It is argued that, fearful of the expense, colonial offices were rather reluctant and lacked a master plan.
7. Ibid., p. 27.
8. Constructivism is a philosophical viewpoint about the nature of knowledge and is widely applied in various social science disciplines like education, sociology and cultural studies, including studies on ethnicity, international relations, etc. According to Englebert and Dunn, constructivism has displaced primordialism as the mainstream approach to ethnicity among Africanists. Constructivists view ethnic identity as something that can be invented or constructed, and they stress perception, an interactive process, mobility or evolution of behaviourism and relationships among individuals and people. See Englebert and Dunn, *Inside African Politics*, pp. 70–71.
9. The idea of neo-colonialism was created by Kwame Nkrumah, Ghana's first post-independence president, in his book *Neo-colonialism, the Last Stage of Imperialism* (1965). Dependency theory makes the point that through economic transactions and international systems, resources flow from the 'periphery' of poor and underdeveloped countries to the 'core' of wealthy countries, enriching the latter at the expense of the

former. Dependency theory originates with Singer-Prebisch thesis on comparative advantage. Dependency theorists include Latin American Marxists like Celso Furtado, Aníbal Pinto, other Americans like Paul Baran, Paul Sweezy and Andre Gunder Frank, and many others. Immanuel Wallerstein refined the Marxist aspect of the theory to form the world-systems theory.

10. Crawford Young, *The Postcolonial State in Africa* (Madison: University of Wisconsin Press, 2012), p. 339.
11. Englebert and Dunn, *Inside African Politics* (2013), p. 65.
12. In East Africa, for instance, even after the nations gained independence, different people of different ethnicities or tribes have been 'migrating' or seeking refuge regularly in one another's territory without any noticeable opposition from the host tribes. The massive inflow of South Sudan refugees into Uganda has not changed such attributes on the part of Ugandans.
13. Englebert and Dunn (2013), p. 75.
14. Ibid., p. 74.
15. Ibid., p. 75.
16. Edmond Keller (2014), p. 27.
17. Ibid., pp. 147–150.
18. Crawford Young (2012), p. 320.
19. Alberto. F. Alesina et al., 'Fractionalization', *Harvard Institute Research Working Paper* No. 1959, June 2002.
20. However, there is an argument that in Somalia, despite such racial and social homogeneity, division of clans or sub-clans was always existent. See Max Fisher, '5 Insights on the Racial Tolerance and Ethnicity Maps, from an Ethnic Conflict Professor', *Washington Post*, 17 May 2013, https://www.washingtonpost.com/news/worldviews/wp/2013/05/17/5-insights-on-the-racial-tolerance-and-ethnicity-maps-from-an-ethnic-conflict-professor/?utm_term=.48cfd79a2c28.
21. Paul Collier, 'Implications of Ethnic Diversity', *World Bank Working Paper* Report No. 28127, vol. 1, World Bank, 17 December 2001, p. 2. See also Paul Collier, 'Ethnicity, Politics and Economic Performance', *Economics and Politics* 12, no. 3 (2000), p. 225. Collier points out that '[ethnic] diversity is highly damaging to growth in the context of limited political rights, but is not damaging in democracies'.
22. Daniel C. Bach and Mamoudou Gazibo (eds), *Neopatrimonialism in Africa and Beyond* (New York: Routledge, 2012).

23. Michael Brandon and Nicolas van de Walle, *Democratic Experiments in Africa: Regime Transitions in Comparative Perspective* (Cambridge: Cambridge University Press, 1997) in Crawford Young, *The Postcolonial State in Africa-Fifty Years of Independence 1960–2010* (Madison: University of Wisconsin Press, 2012), p. 68.
24. Englebert and Dunn (2013), p. 68.
25. Scott D. Taylor, *Globalization and the Cultures of Business in Africa* (Bloomington: Indiana University Press, 2012), pp. 5–6.
26. Tim Kelsall, 'Rethinking the Relationship Between Neo-patrimonialism and Economic Development in Africa', *IDS Bulletin* 42, no. 2 (2011, March 2).
27. Anne Pitcher, Mary Moran, and Michael Johnston, 'Rethinking Patrimonialism and Neopatrimonialism in Africa', *African Studies Review* 51, no. 1 (April 2009), p. 145.
28. Englebert and Dunn (2013), p. 132.
29. Goran Hyden, Julius Court, and Kenneth Mease, *Making Sense of Governance: Empirical Evidence from 16 Developing Countries* (Boulder: Lynne Rienner Publishers, 2004).
30. Bertrand Badie, *L'État importé: l'occidentalisation de l'ordre politique* (Paris: Fayard, 1992), p. 227.
31. Other terms describing typical African politics, I believe, are 'electoral democracies' and 'semi-democracy'.
32. Basil Davidson, *The Black Man's Burden: Africa and the Curse of the Nation-State* (New York: Times Books, 1992), pp. 9–24, 99–161.
33. Ibid.
34. Dani Rodrik and Sharun Mukand, 'The Puzzle of Liberal Democracy', *The Independent*, 22–28 May 2015, p. 40. Rodrik writes that this is because 'the dispossessed minorities who have the strongest stake in civil rights play no role during the democratic transition for the simple reason that they cannot normally bring anything to the bargaining table'.
35. President Kagame commanded the rebel force that ended the 1994 Rwandan genocide and is noted for steering his country towards socio-economic transformation.
36. David Booth and Diana Gammack, *Governance for Development in Africa* (London: Zed Books, 2013), Introduction.
37. Brian Levy, *Working with the Grain: Integrating Governance and Growth in Development Strategies* (Oxford: Oxford University Press, 2014), p. 8.

38. Daron Acemoglu and James A. Robinson, *Why Nations Fail: The Origins of Power, Prosperity, and Poverty* (New York: Crown Business, 2012), pp. 74–76.
39. Homi Kharas, 'Development Assistance', in Bruce Currie-Alder, Ravi Kanbur, David M. Malone, and Rohinton Medhora (eds), *International Development: Ideas, Experience, and Prospects* (Oxford: Oxford University Press, 2014), p. 858.
40. Irma Adelman, 'The Role of Government in Economic Development', in Finn Tarp (ed.), *Foreign Aid and Development: Lessons Learnt and Directions for the Future* (London: Routledge, 2000) p. 48. According to Adelman, there have been three phases in the dominant view concerning the optimal role of government in development: the prime mover phase (1940–1979); the problem phase (1979–1996); and rehabilitating government (1996 onwards, in the making).
41. Englebert and Dunn (2013), p. 156.
42. Failed State Index, http://fundforpeace.org/fsi/data.
43. John Harris, 'Development Theories', *International Development* (2014), p. 39.
44. John Degnbol-Martinussen and Poul Engberg-Pedersen, *Aid: Understanding International Development Cooperation*, translated by Marie Bille (London: Zed Books, 2005). This was originally published in Danish in 1999.
45. Kingsley Chiedu Moghalu, *Emerging Africa: How the Global Economy's 'Last Frontier' Can Prosper and Matter* (London: Penguin Books, 2014), p. 30.
46. Regarding the emergence of indigenous or black-owned firms in Sub-Saharan Africa, Kenya and Nigeria are frequently cited as examples. South Africa, on the other hand, is seen in a negative light, as locals continue to struggle in comparison to white businesses, which are dominant in the country. But even for Kenya and Nigeria, more detailed and accurate data needs to be accumulated and analysed in order to come to a better understanding of their situation.
47. John Harris, 'Development Theories (2014)', p. 45.
48. Olu Ajakaiye and Afeikhena Jerome, 'Economic Development', in Bruce Currie-Alder, Ravi Kanbur, David M. Malone, and Rohinton Medhora (eds), *International Development—Ideas, Experience, and Prospects* (Oxford: Oxford University Press, 2014), pp. 786–787.
49. Ibid., p. 745.

50. Dani Rodrik, 'The Perils of Premature De-industrialisation' in the *Opinion*, *The Independent* (Uganda), 18–24 October 2013, p. 8.
51. Greg DePersio, 'What Are the Most Important Aspects of a Capitalist System?' *Investopedia Academy*, 7 April 2015, http://www.investopedia.com/ask/answers/040715/what-are-most-important-aspects-capitalist-system.asp.
52. Kingsley Chiedu Moghalu (2014), pp. 64–66.
53. Ibid., p. 67.
54. David Henley, *Asia-Pacific Development Divergence—A Question of Intent* (London: Zed Books, 2015), p. 5.
55. Olu Ajakaiye and Afeikhena Jerome, 'Economic Development (2014)', pp. 742–743.
56. Tim Marshall, *Prisoners of Geography: Ten Maps That Tell You Everything You Need to Know About Global Politics* (London: Elliot and Thompson, 2015), pp. 116–139.
57. 'World Population Prospects the 2017 Revision', ESA.UN.org (custom data acquired via website), United Nations Department of Economic and Social Affairs, Population Division. It was retrieved on 10 September 2017.
58. See the article written by Stephanie Hanson, 'Corruption in Sub-Saharan Africa' for the Council on Foreign Relations, 6 August 2009.
59. Ibid.
60. Huguette Labelle, 'Corruption', in *International Development* (2014), p. 240.
61. Kwabena Gyimah-Brempong, 'Corruption, Economic Growth, and Income Inequality in Africa', *Economics of Governance* 3 (2002), pp. 183–209, 185.
62. McKinsey Global Institute, 'The Closest Look Yet at Chinese Economic Engagement in Africa', June 2017 report, https://www.mckinsey.com/featured-insights/middle-east-and-africa/the-closest-look-yet-at-chinese-economic-engagement-in-africa.
63. Some Western experts who have long served in Africa have expressed the view that many African leaders still run their economy following the socialist mindset.

4
Uncovering the Main Root Cause: The Mindset Factor

The Forgotten 'Mind Over Matter'?

As we grapple with the question of what went wrong with Africa's development and what the way forward should be, it is no surprise that so many studies have been done on Africa in wide-ranging fields by various experts and organizations. However, in the eyes of the global community at large, Africa is still very much an unknown, yet-to-be-discovered region and hence much academic, scientific and fact-finding research on Africa will follow suit. In business circles, Sub-Saharan Africa is described as 'the last frontier' but the region is already open for the outsiders to take advantage of its potentials.

Africa's development can be an interesting and fascinating subject to ponder on. What makes the field of development most challenging is that, in sum, it is about carrying out the task of bringing about changes where normally the conditions are the least favourable for doing so. Development bears an aspect of international relations and is an inter-disciplinary field, but it is unlike any other, especially from the practitioners' perspective. For example, development cooperation has a fundamentally different working structure compared to other

J.-D. Park, *Re-Inventing Africa's Development*,
https://doi.org/10.1007/978-3-030-03946-2_4

areas of engagements or dealings, including conventional diplomacy, public diplomacy, trade and investment, security, the environment, etc. In these fields, countries participate as 'equal entities' and each party focuses on advancing its position from its own end. Whether it is about negotiating or carrying out PR activities, the process is simple and predictable. It is not necessary to worry about the situation of one counterpart or its capacity to play its part; the responsibility that one bears is confined to one's own responsibility.

However, in development cooperation, things are very different and practitioners cannot go about conducting their own business in a matter-of-fact fashion, paying no attention to the situation of others. It is not enough to have shared goals and reach an agreement, and doing well on your part: one has to involve one's counterpart or partner in doing the difficult and necessary things. Development projects are conducted and assessed over the long haul, and for donors, their assignment is not substantively fulfilled until the collaborative work bears fruit in the end. People cannot feel lighthearted when things break down or become white elephants immediately after they have handed over the facilities or programmes to African countries.

Hence, 'rationality' and standard procedures that we are used to following in most fields in international relations do not necessarily apply in development cooperation. If aid projects are to be responsibly carried out in order to produce tangible results, then extra 'human toil' is required, such as a greater level of patience, perseverance and devotion. Frustration and stress levels can become very high when officials in charge in the aid recipient country do not properly respond and follow up.

I think development as a specialized field in its own right has, over time, lost the zeal it needs to have and has settled for the pursuit of human needs and stability. This was driven largely by the unmitigated challenges that the development community has faced in its conventional domain, but current events have also played a part. For instance, what could have been a promising second decade for the world in the new millennium began with an uncertain and troubling international landscape: political destabilization, the eruption of new conflicts, a new form of international terrorism, and a refugee crisis impacting Europe and having global ramifications, among others.

We could be overwhelmed by the challenging developments and contingencies around the world, but development initiatives must be focused on the development agenda instead of following the fickle of times. The more the current situation appears to be entangled, the greater need there is to focus on the fundamentals, root causes and 'ultimate solutions'. This is because development is possibly the best answer to most of the ills and problems we face today. As such, it was heartening when, recently, even David Beasley, the Executive Director of the World Food Programme (WFP), said that 'humanitarian dollars should be turned into development dollars'.[1]

We need to have a better misunderstanding of what foreign aid can do. Not all aid is geared towards economic development and, all things considered, the actual portion allotted to economic development is quite small. This is because the spectrum of foreign assistance has expanded over decades to include just about everything, as is reflected by the adoption of universal Sustainable Development Goals (SDGs). The clear phenomenon observable in African development is that the distinction between 'economic development' and 'economic welfare' is increasingly blurred, which I think is a big problem in itself.

To simplify matters, foreign aid can be broken down into four categories: (1) humanitarian assistance; (2) 'social welfare'-type assistance; (3) development assistance; and (4) the promotion of democracy and governance. Humanitarian assistance is for the emergency relief of those suffering as a result of disasters and crises. Social welfare-type programmes target the socially vulnerable or disadvantaged, providing various services to meet their basic needs. While the first two types of assistance are meant to serve the immediate or basic requirements of the recipients, development assistance is for the mid- to long term sustainable development of the recipient nations. These include various types of cooperation like capacity-building, technological cooperation, the construction and handover of facilities and infrastructures, the provision of materials and equipment, the injection of funds, etc. in multiple sectors. Lastly, the promotion of governance, democracy and human rights, and regional security are also important areas in which Western donors provide assistance.

Therefore, foreign aid that directly supports economic development in African countries is not particularly apparent. And this is further 'compromised' by how the recipient countries utilize this aid. The problem is that various economic projects often turn out to be short-lived programmes that mainly benefit the officials of counterpart agencies or a limited number of the people concerned. In sum, even these have turned into 'welfare' programmes instead of acting as sustainable means to assist economic development.

Basically, universal economic activities can be considered as either wealth creation or wealth distribution. Wealth creation is about realizing additional production and value that drives economic growth, leading to overall development. Wealth distribution, in policy terms, is the act of 'correcting' market failures from a socio-political standpoint like addressing income inequality and providing public services. If there is no wealth creation, then there is no wealth to distribute. Thus, for Sub-Saharan African countries, the priority should be 'enlarging the pie' through wealth creation, but their general mindset is fixated on the transfer of wealth. Under such circumstances, various assistance programmes are likely to fail. The 'welfare mentality' is so widespread in the region that everyone is looking for solutions to come from somewhere else, while readily blaming outsiders and external factors for their own poverty and troubles. More troubling is the failure or unwillingness to take action, and the deep-seated practice of 'non-implementation' poses the biggest mystery, obstacle and threat to development in Sub-Saharan Africa.

The 'mindset' of people should be brought to the forefront of our attention and considered as a key term in the discourse on Africa's development. If people were to ask what the single most important root cause is of underdevelopment of Sub-Saharan Africa, the best answer I can think of is the 'mindset'. Among the myriad of things that can be considered, the ultimate solution to break the impasse lies in a change of mindset. It is one thing to find reasons for past failures, which is what everybody has been doing, but quite another to make things right in practice, which seldom takes place in the region.

The 'mindset change approach' beings with it great benefits, in that it is conducive to the 'internalization' of development, enhancing awareness for ownership, and is action-oriented. It brings home what people have forgotten: the plain and simple truth of *mind over matter*. 'Mindset' can be an elusive term, but it would be useful to confine its meaning to what is relevant to development. Bringing the 'mindset' to the fore in discussion propels search for answers 'from within', which is what development ought to be about in the first place. Too much energy has been spent on secondary and peripheral issues without addressing the core issue of *mind over matter*.

To make this kind of attitudinal change will not be an easy task, but it is not impossible. It is certainly achievable and there are precedents to prove it. The most prominent example, I would argue, is South Korea. In Africa, Rwanda is seen as an emerging case, following a similar model. Uganda has already adopted this mindset change programme, although it is still in the initial, exploratory phase of doing so. Sub-Saharan African nations should go beyond acquiring knowledge and capacity to espouse mindset change if they are indeed serious about 'radical transformation', and rightly so.

The good news is that in some places in Sub-Saharan Africa, people are beginning to at least be aware and are talking about the mindset issue in an open manner. Uganda is one of those where Korea's experience and know-how in this field has had an influence. Since 2009, the Canaan Farmers School, an institution in South Korea which specializes in mindset change and agriculture programmes, has worked with Uganda. Born out of the destruction of the Second World War and the subsequent Korean War, the Canaan School is reputed to have played an instrumental role in leadership and agriculture training in the early stages of Korea's economic development. The objective of this institution was to eradicate poverty and attain sustainable development through changing the mindsets of rural leaders, who, in turn, would spearhead the change of mindsets in their communities. The School's methodology was adopted later in the model of the New Village Movement (*Saemaeul Undong*) that became a national campaign in South Korea from 1970. The *Saemaul Undong* became an icon of a successful community-driven, self-help rural development endeavour of Korea that contributed to its overall success in economic development.

The 'Mindset Change' Issue in Sub-Saharan Africa

Few international experts and observers know that South Korea's economic miracle began with the mindset change campaigns conducted at a national level. When you see various books and articles on Korea's rapid economic growth or 'miracle' written by economists, both Korean and foreign, there is hardly any mention of the mindset change campaigns like the *Saemaul Undong*. It is only in recent years that the *Saemaul Undong* was recognized and promoted internationally as a development model, and the *Saemaul Undong* archives were added to UNESCO's Memory of the World Register in 2013.[2] In the international development community, UN bodies like the UN Economic Commission for Africa (UNECA) and the United Nations Development Programme (UNDP) are the pioneers in embracing this approach.[3]

There may be many reasons for this, but two things come to mind. One is the tendency or influence of mainstream economics and the other is the fundamental 'political' propensity or bias. First, mainstream economists do not deal with 'extraneous' factors like the people's 'mindset'. What approximates 'mindset' according to scholars is the 'hard work' or 'work ethic' of Koreans. Even Alice Amsden's *Asia's Next Giant* (1992) does not mention the *Saemaul Undong* at all. Also, it might be that orthodox economists would have shunned such an 'interventionist' movement.

Another reason why the *Saemaul Undong* has not received universal praise inside Korea is because of the 'political divide' in the nation. No sooner had Korea achieved rapid economic development, the process of its socio-political evolution, democratization began to unfold. Despite the fact that the *Saemaul Undong* had a substantial impact on rural development, because it was initiated by the authoritative government, the progressive-minded population half-heartedly admitted, or were even critical of, its outcomes. Also, as times have changed and people have become wealthier and more self-centred, they tend to be dismissive of things done in the past and do not enough thought to the situation back then, regarding these things as 'outdated' or 'irrelevant'.

Korea and Sub-Saharan African countries share many similar historical experiences. No sooner had Korea been liberated from Japanese colonial rule in 1945 than it became divided. The subsequent Korean War that started in 1950 devastated the nation. But the great turnaround started with the public programmes to empower the people in the 1950s, and the story of South Korea that unfolded provides valuable lessons for Africa's development.

No one will disagree that without a fundamental change in the mindset of the leaders and the populace, there cannot be real progress. Setting up goals and expressing aspirations is an easy part, but this would be of no avail if they are not followed up with concrete actions. There have been serious misperceptions, negligence or intentional 'looking the other way' on the subject. Development is not a 'stock' but a 'flow' concept in economics, and it is all about change and dynamism, not the maintenance of the status quo. But many in the region seem to mistakenly believe that national wealth can be transferred and stocked up like material goods. But even materials and equipment need proper usage and maintenance in order to be useful. Many facilities built to serve the public, like medical clinics, factories, schools and welfare centres, become useless shortly after they are opened and handed over due to a lack of care and ownership, accompanied by corruption.

Although many factors come into play, the real issue is not the lack of resources or means, but the mindset of the people who are involved and responsible for undertaking the work. Evidently, poor work ethics—the habit of not thinking ahead and making necessary preparations, not being focused and devoted in relation to one's work, easily quitting one's task, not keeping to deadlines and promise, etc. does so much harm, but this is not mentioned enough. When people imagine poverty in Africa, they tend to think of poverty in terms of lack of means, but one has to think further that poverty can be caused or sustained by the failure to manage oneself, like saving money and having plans for making a living and for spending.

In Sub-Saharan Africa, it is customary to see people attributing their problem to outside elements. One East African journalist writes:

> [W]hat is it that inhibits our ability to produce our own technologies? Note that most sub-Saharan nations possess political institutions and public policies that (we are told) ensure prosperity. Is it, therefore, our education system which is the problem? Is it our social organization? Is it our colonial history that destroyed our self-belief in our ability to produce our own technologies? Is it the hegemonic ideology of global capitalism that keeps us looking outward for the solutions to our problems?[4]

There are different ways to deal with these needs and problems. People can be introspective, inclined to seek answers and solutions from within, or can have the opposite tendency and put blame on others or expect others to solve their problems. If we had two distinctly different societies, one being 'introspective' and the other having 'disowning' tendencies, which one would fare better? The answer is obvious.

The value of being 'introspective' is that over time, individuals are likely to improve and achieve something because of the 'know thyself' kind of effect that it will have. Skills and technologies can be gained when one strives for them. On the other hand, knowledge and institutions are of no consequence when people are idle and irresponsible. Worse, this 'disowning' tendency breeds a 'don't care' mentality. Because people are not the drivers of their own life, they cannot have high expectations of what can be achieved.

It is baffling as to why people should be reluctant to do the things that will only benefit them, particularly in the longer term. This is not limited to the economic field. Institutions, the rule of law, governance and democracy are only worth anything if they are put into practice. We studied at school that the essence of democracy was deeds and practice. It can be a hollow echo of rhetoric which can degenerate into endless political strife if democracy is not properly understood and embodied by the people.

Development is about making difficult changes, and admitting and targeting one's own weakness and problems rather than trying to conceal them, so that they can be overcome. Development is what is earned and not what is bestowed by others, and there is no magical formula for it, except that people and the government all have to work conscientiously with a common purpose. In this regard, much more harm is done by being ambiguous, disingenuous, hypocritical and manneristic than being honest, straightforward and practical. Being politically and diplomatically correct all the time may not be a good thing for the sake of development, and straightforwardness could yield better outcomes.

Fortunately, within Africa, people are showing an increasing awareness that the mindset needs to be changed. The call for mindset change has been aired in various regional bodies including the African Union (AU), and it is not uncommon to see African leaders and intellectuals speaking out on this.[5] Everyone seems to agree that people's mindset should change, but when it comes to how this should be done, people seem to be at a loss and lack clear ideas. This is where we need to break out of the box. Rather than give up or try to avoid the matter, it should be tackled head-on. The ideal scenario would be that the African people themselves take the initiative and make full-fledged efforts in this regard. Development partners can approach this issue with good intentions and without prejudice, being circumspective in relation to the nature of the matter.

Efforts to this end have already been made in Uganda through such projects as the establishment of the National Farmers Leadership Centre (NFLC), which is a training round for mindset change and agricultural development.[6] Perhaps the best way to break the yoke of the inaction or powerlessness of the people is to 'provoke' them to change. This is because as far as human behaviour is concerned, 'voluntarism' is the surest way forward. The 'mindset change' of the people, if effected, can have far-reaching and 'explosive' repercussions on their lives and society.

There are a number of parallels between Korea's experience and the situation in which Sub-Saharan African countries currently find themselves. One of the areas that Korea identified as crucial for national transformation was the mindset of the people, and the campaign for mindset change was essentially about empowering the people. The Korean experience will be examined in Part 4 of this book.

With respect to the substance of the problematic mindset in Sub-Saharan Africa, I believe that the following can be identified as the syndromes or traits that commonly exist in the region: (1) the dependency syndrome; (2) the 'what's-in-it-for-me' syndrome; (3) the 'backtracking syndrome'; (4) expediency or short-sightedness; (5) a lack of action and implementation; (6) a weak sense of responsibility or ownership; (7) a weak sense of nation or patriotism; and (8) a 'commission culture'.[7]

First, we are all so familiar with the talk of a 'dependency syndrome' in Sub-Saharan Africa that it sounds like a cliché. It is so widespread throughout the region, at all levels in society and the state. For instance, at the provincial level, the general tendency is that the locals wait indefinitely, hoping that the government will come to their aid for the most basic things that they can do for themselves. I had the opportunity to participate in a series of 'community clean-up' exercises in and around Kampala, and on one occasion I was appalled to see first-hand the scene of total negligence and irresponsibility. The site was not a slum by any measure, but apparently the residents were waiting for the city authority workers to show up and remove the rubbish. Even on the very day we were conducting clean-up exercise, many locals, particularly young men, were sitting idly and gazing at us, smiling but declining to take part in the exercise. It was an awful state to witness because this had nothing to do with the people lacking knowledge, capacity or financial resources (the reasons frequently cited for people failing to act), but was a simple matter of willingness.[8]

The 'what's-in-it-for-me?' syndrome is also a widespread phenomenon among the population in the region. This is a tendency to consider one's own interests at all times before anything else. In Sub-Saharan Africa, it is a well-known fact the poor delivery of public services wrought by civil servants who are devoid of any sense of duty and responsibility is a major hindrance to development. It is a common practice for government officials to engage in personal businesses, and even in their official duties their priority is often misplaced, putting their personal interests over the public interest. There is a tendency to put the official assignments on the back-burner or neglect them altogether if they fail to see what is in it for them. Such practice not only breeds conflict of interests and corruption, but also, more fundamentally, drastically undercuts the government's performance. Economic loss due to disruptions and delays in public service, not to mention outright acts of corruption, is said to be enormous.

The 'backtracking syndrome' is the tendency to hold back or back pedal instead of moving forward to build on what has already been achieved. I have always thought of this as a great paradox. It is the problem of failing to 'keep pace', stopping short of meeting the target, and not being consistent and living up to expectations. Where dynamic economic growth is enjoyed, people take it for granted that things improve over time. But this is generally not the case in Africa. There are actually many things that get worse over time, the most noticeable being the deterioration of physical infrastructure and facilities, but it goes well beyond that.

The backtracking syndrome is observable on many fronts and it has huge accumulative or multiple effects at the national level. What is so disheartening is that in many cases, local employees, if they are not placed under the 'special attention' of the management, end up causing problems or missing out on the opportunities that will definitely benefit them (like long-time employment). What we can call the 'self-regulating' or 'self-disciplining' ability of workers is visibly poor. Overall, their will to 'appeal' to their bosses in terms of diligence and performance is short-lived and they do not respond well to the continuing pressures of work. Because Africa's organizations and companies have a weaker management or governance structure compared to foreign entities, their overall organizational output or efficiency is also weaker. In contrast, those who do receive greater recognition in foreign organizations enjoy many benefits and opportunities. They can even be headhunted by higher-paying government organizations and companies.[9]

In any organization, local workers can only benefit if they are attuned to maintaining their level of work because normally, over time, they will gain expertise and productivity in relation to their work. Their pay will increase and it should be a win-win situation for the organization and the employees. But, to our dismay, many show 'regression' instead of steady progress, with the result that they are eventually fired from their job. The strange phenomenon is that when rewards and incentives are given to employees, one should expect them to perform more positively, but often the opposite occurs—rather than responding in kind, employees become spoilt, complacent and ask for more. This results in an ironic situation where the good intentions of one party are met by the negative reaction of the other party, which defies logic and rationality.

The next trait is expediency or short-sightedness. This is quite evident in daily work practices. Cutting corners is a tendency of most technicians and workers in the region, meaning that in order to avoid this as much as possible, customers' intervention in terms of continuous on-site 'supervision' is required. This applies to a whole variety of work, ranging from menial chores to construction projects. Sloppy work, the habit of leaving things undone, a failure to keep to deadlines and promises, etc. are the 'norm' rather than the exception.[10] Generally, there is a lack of attention to detail and thinking ahead, so that even the most basic things to expect like the standardization and linear, geometric correctness of products are not met most of the time.

The lack of implementation or action is another distinctive feature of Sub-Saharan Africa. Ian Clarke, an Irish missionary doctor who became the Mayor of Makindye Division in Kampala, gives a vivid account of such a problem:

> Uganda was a great country to live in: the weather was lovely, the vegetation beautiful, and the people friendly and outgoing. Some foreigners came to work in Uganda and were at first enthralled by what they found, particularly by the social life and by how articulate people are, but they often got a rude awakening when it came to the work practices and work ethic. If people could talk their way into making things work, Uganda would have been the best developed country in the world. Donors were impressed with people's grasp of problems and understanding of the steps which should be taken in finding solutions, but then confused as to why so many basic issues on the ground remained unresolved. The problem lay in implementation: many public servants were good at analysing and talking about what should be done, as if the very talking was the same as doing it, but then nothing happened. This lack of implementation of simple things in the public domain was so common that it was accepted as the norm, and one only remarked when anything actually changed.[11]

The disinclination to act is a very serious problem under any circumstances. Everybody seems to agree that there has been too much talking and too little action. There is the saying 'easier said than done', but the wise have admonished us against frivolity and talkativeness: 'silence is golden', 'an empty wagon makes more noise', 'action speaks louder than words', 'the superior man acts before he speaks, and afterwards speaks according to his action', etc.[12]

Lack of responsibility and ownership is also a serious obstacle to development. Institutional mechanisms to enforce accountability are important, but what is much more needed is a greater sense of responsibility of the people. The seriousness of the problem is frequently expressed:

> It's very hard to get things done, even at the smallest level. But it is very easy to sit and complain about things. Reading social media, one gets the sense that we have increasingly become a complaining nation, not a doing nation. Everywhere complaints abound about our failing healthcare and education system, of corruption and abuse of office. But one hardly reads a story of what those complaining are doing to change the situation. Are we waiting for intervention from God?[13]

What I also see as typical of Sub-Saharan Africa is the practice of offering amnesty in the name of national reconciliation. Political leaders are quick to call for amnesty, thereby promoting impunity. Betrayal and treachery are also common. When I was in West Africa, I saw internal conflicts in many countries where the military as well as political leaders conveniently 'switched sides'. Opportunism prevails, and this leads to a protraction of conflicts because there is no clear will for or path towards its closure. In eastern Africa, South Sudan provides the latest worst-case scenario of what personal greed for power and impunity of leaders can do to a nation.

Weakness in the sense of nation and patriotism is another general trait in the region. The weak sense of nation and patriotism correlates with the weak functioning of states and these two feed off each other. From a national standpoint, the spread of patriotism that transcends tribalism and sectarianism will be an ideal goal to achieve. Many

African countries suffering from internal strife and disunity ought to realize the fact that this could easily be exploited, engulfing the whole country and the region into a state of crisis.

So how can a sense of nation, national identity, solidarity or patriotism be fostered? The greatest responsibility rests with the political leaders and elites, who should be leading their nation forward by example. But this need not be top-down only—it can work both ways, from top-down and bottom-up, in an interactive fashion with people's voluntarism. Sometimes tragic events can serve as a critical turning point for nations. A good example is the case of Rwanda. What the country has been able to achieve in the aftermath of the genocide is remarkable and has set a high bar for other African countries to match. For an African country, Rwanda has tackled seemingly improbable tasks: good governance, the civic-mindedness of the people, social order and discipline, national solidarity, etc. Most surprising is the cleanliness and orderliness of the capital city Kigali to the extent that it makes one wonder if it is indeed a city in Sub-Saharan Africa. What developing countries desperately need is the government setting an example to 'empower' the people rather than simply trying to curry favour with the people, but without enacting essential reforms.

Lastly, there is a widespread practice of people at all levels wanting to be given 'commission' as if they are entitled to it. Foreign investors are the easy targets and can be hassled by various people, including high-level government officials, who are hell-bent on rent-seeking. The 'commission culture' is one of the many facets of corruption, but because it stands out so prominently in Sub-Saharan Africa, it can be regarded as a syndrome.

Notes

1. David Beasley, speaking at 'Geneva Conference on National Transformation—With Special Focus on Science & Technology, Business & Industry', 7 October, Africana Hotel, Kampala, Uganda. The conference was jointly organized by the Geneva Institute for

Leadership & Public Policy and the Science & Technology Policy Institute (STEPI) of South Korea.

2. UNESCO, Memory of the World, http://www.unesco.org/new/en/communication-and-information/memory-of-the-world/register/full-list-of-registered-heritage/registered-heritage-page-1/archives-of-saemaul-undong-new-community-movement.
3. Internationally, UN development bodies are believed to be the pioneers of recognizing and accepting the *Saemaul Undong* as a model for rural development. For instance, the United Nations Economic Commission for Africa (ECA) chose the *Saemaul Undong* as a base model for the Sustainable Modernization of Agriculture and Rural Transformation (SMART), programme in 2008, and the *Saemaul Undong* was officially introduced to the UNDP in 2015 at the same time as the adoption of the SDGs. Edward Reed, the former country representative of the Asia Foundation to Korea, is a noted international scholar who had studied and written about the *Saemaul Undong*.
4. Andrew Mwenda, 'Africa Through North Korean Eyes', *The Independent*, 6 April 2017, https://www.independent.co.ug/columnists/andrew-mwenda.
5. For instance, Dr. Nkosazana Diamini-Zuma, the African Union Chairperson, stressed the need for Africans to change their mindsets to achieve development while briefing the Speakers of the African Parliament regarding Agenda 2063 in August 2014. When I came to Uganda in 2011, I noticed that the term 'mindset change' was already a familiar term in government circles perhaps due to Korea's Canaan Farmers School's activities in Uganda.
6. The National Farmers Leadership Centre was formally opened in Uganda in May 2016. This centre, which focuses on mindset change (*Saemaul Undong*) and agricultural training, is the first of its kind to be created by the Korean government in Sub-Saharan Africa. It is dealt with more in detail in other parts of this book.
7. The observations and propositions made in this book, including the description of typical syndromes in Sub-Saharan Africa, are based on my own experiences in Africa. My personal involvement in development cooperation, including the planning and implementation of development projects in Uganda, provided the inspiration and the empirical grounds for my work.

8. However, I was very pleased to learn later on that this community did indeed turn itself around and became one of the recognized examples of community environment improvement.
9. Africa's prominent executive bodies that are highly sought-after by white-collar workers also struggle to keep their employees disciplined and in check. So, those who have had a 'good training' and a track record of working in foreign organizations are often preferred by those offices.
10. African countries approach this issue from the viewpoint of 'skilling', but I think this is a fundamental mindset or work ethics problem. The advocates of skilling have the point of correcting identifying the problem as essentially vocational rather than academic in most African countries. But limitations in 'skilling programmes' is that skilling alone cannot address what skilling is purported to achieve; it has to be complemented with work ethics and social ethics.
11. Ian Clarke, *How Deep Is This Pothole?* (London: Ian Clarke, 2010), p. 195.
12. 'An empty wagon makes more noise' is a Korean proverb and 'the superior man acts before he speaks, and afterwards speaks according to his action' is a saying of Confucius.
13. Andrew Mwenda, *The Independent*, 20–26 February 2015, p. 9.

Part III

Africa's Forgotten Mission of Nation-Building: What are Missing

5

Finding the Missing Links

Internalizing Development: The Question of Intent

One would think that by now, more than 50 years since the majority of Sub-Saharan African countries gained independence, they would have completed the task of nation-building. But the reality is that a big mismatch exists between Africa's legal, political and economic institutions in name and what these actually deliver in practice. This appears to be an outcome of a serious lack of ownership and a failure to 'internalize' development. Such a perception is shared by African scholars.[1]

Before people can 'internalize' development (that is, being oriented towards development as individuals), some kind of visions or schemes for development at the national level to which people can ascribe would be required. Hence, the government's 'moral authority'—which derives from leadership, credibility, performance, etc.—is vital to encouraging people to actively comply with government initiatives. Certainly, the formation of a national consensus and unity will be a huge boost for development. But as many Africans would divulge, their national identity, sense of nation and patriotism are comparatively weak and

J.-D. Park, *Re-Inventing Africa's Development*,
https://doi.org/10.1007/978-3-030-03946-2_5

ambiguous. This, together with the weakness of the role of the states, has impeded the ability of African countries to pursue development. As a result, many African nations have spent decades following independence with the facade of development, like electoral democracy and economic liberalization, without substantively making much progress in the essence of nation-building and modernization.

There is a popular saying that poverty should not be passed on to the next generation. The task of development has to be taken seriously by African countries because they are certain to face mounting social, economic and political pressures that can erupt and unleash untenable consequences.

As far as the political system is concerned, the 'hybrid regime' that is typical of Sub-Saharan Africa has proven to be unsuccessful and should also be redressed. Africa's hybrid regimes which combine the formality of liberal-democratic polity with neo-patrimonial authoritarianism are the outcome of the adaptation of the Western political system to 'local needs'. The problem is that they have the attribute of being neither democratic nor transformative, but in essence are status quo-oriented. Rather than being transitory, this type of polity coupled with problematic electoral democracy appears to be assuming permanence in Africa.

The downsides of this kind of system are that it seemingly satisfies (even if in a minimalist fashion) popular demand, while protecting the vested interests of the privileged class, so that it is ultimately status quo-promoting. But what may be a comfort zone for political leaders can turn out to be exactly the opposite of what 'national development' requires. David Booth and Dianna Cammack rightly point out the clear gap that exists between formal democratic institutions and the reality in Africa: 'The trouble with democracy, as a substantive reality and not just a set of formal arrangements, is that its effectiveness depends on social and economic conditions that are not yet enjoyed in most developing countries'.[2]

African countries should pause and think about how to comprehensively and meaningfully alter their approach of development rather than following the same course that will only yield the same results. This is a critical task of 'internalizing' development, and it comes down to the basic question of intent. There are so many variables that can have an impact on the livelihood of nations, but African countries should be able to discern between 'external variables' and 'internal variables' and understand their implications.

The reason why Sub-Saharan Africa's 'development frame' has been ineffective in comparison to other regions like East Asia is that Africa got the priorities or sequencing wrong: it treats the external variables as the 'principal' variables while relegating the internal variables to a 'secondary' status. Sub-Saharan African countries have always tended to seek explanations and solutions 'outside' of themselves, and they continue to do so, even though they talk about ownership. Many Asian countries, and particularly South Korea, understood that development is what comes from within, like taking action to catch up with rich countries with a strong sense of responsibility and ownership.

South Koreans could have placed the blame for the country's predicaments on a range of external factors like the colonial legacy, the Korean War, geopolitics, geographical and natural conditions, etc. They could have relied on foreign aid without making strenuous efforts for development, leaving the nation's destiny in the hands of outsiders and external dynamics. If this had been the case, Korea would never have even come close to what it achieved.

So the real question lies in the *intent* of Sub-Saharan African nations. How much do African leaders, elites and the general public want to see change? What is the thinking of political leaders and are they really prioritizing national development or are they more interested in amassing wealth for themselves and simply staying in power as long as they can? What is certain is that economic transformation and the overall national development that entails structural changes will not occur as a result of technical prowess and the introduction of systems only.

One of the misguided thoughts that is widely held in the region is that people cannot do things and need assistance from outsiders because they lack the necessary 'capacity'. But capacity is not something that can be injected into someone and then have an immediate effect like vaccination; there is the 'knowledge' part and the 'application' part, and while the former can be gotten from others, the latter is totally up to oneself. In the absence of determination and implementation, knowledge will end up merely as knowledge. When there is a willingness to learn, it will simply be a matter of time before knowledge and skills will be acquired. Nothing can happen all at once and everything is achieved through the 'building-block' approach, as no one has skills and expertise from the beginning.

An overwhelming number of invitation programmes for capacity-building, study tours, conferences, education, cultural exchanges, etc. are offered to Africans of various backgrounds by donor countries and organizations. Many entry points are provided, but apparently many Africans are not fully taking advantage of these programmes to promote their individual and collective capacity.

Edmund Phelps, the recipient of the Nobel Prize in Economics in 2006, rightly points out that 'economic growth is dependent on the character of the nation'.[3] Mindful of this, it will be worthwhile to figure out what would be the 'missing links' to development. In my view, they are the following three elements: (1) a sense of nation or national identity; (2) 'development-mindedness'; and (3) a strong role played by the state—coherent industrial policy, prioritization of agriculture-rural development, etc. For African countries, securing these missing links is certainly achievable if there is the intent to do so.

But we also need to take account of the realities such as the 'odd' electoral democracy, the influence of the internet/social media and globalization, the government's policy of providing handouts, etc. The development of ICT enabling greater access, sharing of information and inter-connectivity, along with economic globalization, are also affecting the lives of African people. These would make people conscious of global trends and raise their expectations of the things to come.

This, coupled with the dependency syndrome which seems to have only been exacerbated over time by the government's policy of providing handouts, has fostered a troubling environment where people's demand keeps growing to the extent that meeting these demands becomes unsustainable. The paradox is that while political leaders and civil servants struggle to respond to people's demands with what available resources they have, the population do not become any more empowered in terms of becoming more responsible and productive. Social pressure mounts when African states continue to fail to deliver public services and mismanage the economy.

African countries and the international community alike should take a long hard look at what takes place underneath the facade of African dynamics. Let us take economic growth, for example. It is true that over the last decade or so, many Sub-Saharan African countries have achieved quite impressive growth and this is to be commended. However, when one looks at the substance, growth was led by extractive industries (and now the downturn because of this), and multi-nationals or foreign companies were the ones that profited the most. Business, investments and economic growth did not translate into meaningful industrial transformation, the creation of a manufacturing sector or the creation of significant job opportunities for the masses.

When African economies are assessed in terms of the key parameters of economic development like industrial structure, infrastructure and agriculture, there is hardly any country that would qualify as a success.[4] A raw materials or commodity-based industrial structure, absolute shortage and poorly maintained physical infrastructure, a rudimentary and non-competitive agricultural sector, etc. are the causes and at the same time the reflections of chronic weaknesses of the Sub-Saharan African economies.

Many countries are belatedly prioritizing the expansion of physical infrastructure and the increase in power-generating capacity. It is surprising to see that the countries are still struggling to achieve the minimum level of the most basic features of infrastructure, like roads, railways and electricity supply. This is often attributed to a lack of funding, but human failure, which manifests itself as mismanagement, diversion of funds, lack of will and follow-up actions, is more responsible for such deficiencies.

In many cases, the conditions and efforts for 'economic take-off' were not put together from the start. Rural-agricultural development, a backbone for economic transformation, has not been given due attention and pursued energetically because of a lack of understanding of the basics of economics and a reluctance to foresee the problems ahead. When it comes to the formulation and, more importantly, the implementation of national policies, the myopic approach has always incurred heavy costs.

Many things that people are hoping for in developing countries may not easily come about when the leaders' and people's way of life and work patterns are steadfastly maintained. The situation is that people are unwilling to change their attitudes and yet they want to become better off. But how you change without changing? This demands a holistic and long-term view of the problems and solutions, and self-reflection.

What African countries can easily do if they have the willingness to do so is to hold national dialogues, leading to action-oriented national campaigns to enhance people's awareness of national tasks and to build a national consensus on the way forward. Nation-building is far from being achieved in the region. The identification and pursuit of societal and national objectives and values are vital for the nation to move forwards, and common goals or interests should be established at the national as well as the community level.

But what will be counterproductive is sectarianism or sectarian interest-seeking at the extreme, especially when the social fabric and social capital are weak, as is the case in Africa. There is no shortage of public gatherings or events, and very long hours are spent conducting protocols and listening to what everyone has to say. These should become venues for leaders and the people to engage in fruitful discussions and debates on public agendas and how to work together to achieve national goals.

A Sense of Nation and National Identity

It is generally recognized that the sense of nation and national identity in Sub-Saharan African nations are not as strong as in many other nations in different regions. A high level of ethnic diversity is what stands out as a distinct characteristic of Sub-Saharan Africa, but ethnic diversity in itself cannot be correlated to instability or considered to be a direct cause of underdevelopment. And ethnicism and loyalty to the state do not necessarily come into direct conflict. This is all the more so when people realize that the state and their ethnic entity are at different levels. What impact ethnical divergence or multi-ethnicism would have on the nations would vary from country to country, and the overall outcome of the studies on ethnicity and development tends to be inconclusive.

Crawford Young talks about Africanism, territorial nationalism and ethnicity as 'the ambiguous triple helix of identity' and concludes that they operate on different tracks: 'Territorial nationalism usually does not compete directly with ethnicity; in contrast to what happens in Europe, in Africa ethnic groups are never referred to as "national minorities" juxtaposed to a titular nationality … the prevalence of multilingualism lowers the temperature of language issues that are so volatile in India, Sri Lanka, Turkey, Belgium or Canada'.[5]

One thing that is quite remarkable and should be taken note of regarding territorial nationalism in Sub-Saharan Africa is that the territorial boundaries of African states that were drawn during the peak of the colonial era remain virtually intact today, long after the independence of nations. While the artificially set linear territorial boundaries did not match the ethnic identity map, Africans have been able to maintain their existing state boundaries. A more accurate way of putting it may be that they have opposed the fragmentation of their territory or, because of the apparently huge task that any effort for re-alignment of territories would entail, they might have accepted living with what has already been given. Pierre Englebert and Kevin C. Dunn point out that 'for all the talk of the emphasis on ethnicity in Africa, one of the most salient and puzzling features of African politics is actually the surprising degree of national identity that African states have managed to produce among their citizens, and the extent to which the latter profess nationalist sentiments despite their subnational divisions'.[6] As mentioned by these authors, this is somewhat paradoxical, given the colonial origins of these states.

Considering the degree of Africa's ethnic diversity, nationalism in this region (or, to be more precise, territorial nationalism) can be viewed as quite remarkable. But in reality, Sub-Saharan Africa's nationalism is neither forceful nor ideological. It is rather weak, as is in the case for the role of the state. Territorial nationalism might have been maintained because it is conveniently in compromise with ethnicity, not superseding it. Another reason could be that from the standpoint of ethnic entities, since the ethnic composition is complex, they would see no point in seceding to form a separate state entity when they lack the capacity and self-sufficiency in terms of resources and infrastructures, as well as being impeded in terms of geographical remoteness, etc.

Nationalism, which originated in Europe centuries ago, evolved in other regions around the world in the twentieth century with the rise of anti-colonialism and doctrine of self-determination during the independence struggles of the colonized. In the process of fighting for independence, the inhabitants of colonial territories became a nation. By the early second half of the twentieth century, 'nationhood' became universal and the international political norm. Sub-Saharan African countries, in the wave of independence, strived for nation-building which was necessary in order to gain not only internal legitimation but also international respectability. Crawford Young points out that 'the nation-building project generally did succeed in representing territorial nationalism as a higher form of identity distinct from ethnicity, existing on a different identity track. Ethnicity was deemed legitimate within a purely cultural and private kinship realm but not as a discourse of statehood'.[7]

In Sub-Saharan Africa, ethnic tensions can be latent, subdued, sporadic or exploited, but they do not often degenerate into all-out violence, although there are some exceptions to this. It would be fair to say that in the case of Sub-Saharan Africa, ethnicity does not directly challenge or pose a danger to territorial nationalism. In some instances, a high degree of ethnicity can have a moderating effect on potential cracks or the break-up of a nation. Uganda provides a good case study in this respect. It is viewed as the most ethnically diverse nation on earth, but its very multi-ethnicity makes the predominance of any single ethnic group virtually impossible as others will be united against it. Ethnic checks and balances, even if they are far from ideal, are having an effect. The people of Uganda have lived through tough times and lengthy civil wars in the past, during the eras of Idi Amin and Milton Obote, the Bush Wars and the fight against Joseph Kony and his Lord's Resistance Army. And over the course of time, they have learned the lessons of the dangers of ethnical sectarianism getting out of hand. Rwanda, by African standards, is one of the least ethnically diverse countries, but it experienced the most horrific genocide in Africa.

The 'backtracking syndrome' is also at work here. At the time when Sub-Saharan African countries gained independence, a major feature of nationhood was about differentiating it from, and transcending, tribalism or ethnicity. At the beginning, many African leaders considered that ethnicity would soon become a relic; the Guinean leader Sekou Toure declared that 'in three or four years, no one will remember the tribal, ethnic or religious rivalries which, in the recent past, caused so much damage to our country and its population'.[8] Like Toure, subsequent nationalist leaders of the new African nations vehemently rejected ethnic nationalism, seeing it as a threat to their states.[9] But, as it turned out, this was all an illusion. Ethnicism never withered, but the existence of states itself was not seriously threatened either. Later on, the leaders themselves would often take advantage of ethnicism for their own political purposes.

Nation-building with the sense of nation or patriotism at its core is not the task of leaders or government only, but should also be supported and driven by the people. If the masses have no part in it, there is no point in pushing for nation-building in the first place. How nation-building was achieved in most other countries was through 'movement' rather than in a customary fashion. The realization of nation-building without the people's support and fervour is hard to imagine.

So why has nation-building still not been accomplished in Sub-Saharan African countries? Why has the weakness of nationhood in Africa continued for so long? Many have attributed this to colonial legacies and the way in which post-colonial transitions took place. Normally, new nations around the world have developed a sense of nation and national identity over the course of their history or through their struggle for independence. But as some have pointed out, Sub-Saharan Africa's independence by and large did not feature 'vehement' struggles in a political sense, as was the case in many other countries outside the region, and the colonialists' state apparatus was virtually handed over to them. Since independence was not earnestly fought for, the result is a weak sense of nation and patriotism.[10] The mismatch between the euphoria of independence and the reality that unfolded thereafter in Sub-Saharan Africa is still repeating itself in the twenty-first century in a rather dramatic fashion in South Sudan: no sooner had South Sudan become independent than it was drawn into a much deeper turmoil of constant internal conflict and chaos.

A sense of nation—the feeling of togetherness as a nation—that has a special meaning and value of its own as an integral part of people's lives and which matters for their livelihood is what constitutes an essential foundation for nation-building and national development. But in Africa, not only is this noticeably weak, but it is also often misinterpreted or purposely distorted.

Many still blame the 'colonial legacy' for this, but what should be considered even more seriously is the 'Africans' legacy of missteps'. It does not make logical sense to blame the former while being silent about the latter, which is much more pertinent to the reality of Africa today. So how can the sense of nation and patriotism, which should have been cemented a long time ago at the outset of independence, be erected at this time of ever-heightening liberalization and inter-dependence on a global scale? I believe this will be a true test of the commitment and readiness of Sub-Saharan African countries to move on to the next stage of development. The answer is simple: make conscientious effort now before it become even more difficult.

Development-Mindedness

Now, we are coming down to the crucial part in the discourse on development: development-mindedness. It seems that everyone in Africa wants to see their country develop, but not many seem to genuinely understand, let alone do, what it takes to being about that development. This could be due to many things, but in my view, what is most fundamentally missing is 'development-mindedness'.

So what is development-mindedness? It is a matter of definition and I have purposely simplified it to mean what is 'functional'; it falls within the realm of 'work ethics'. Development-mindedness is a mindset that is conducive to the development or *fulfilment of one's work*. This book takes a logical viewpoint (of 'structural functionalism' in sociology) that a nation ('the whole') is made up of its members, the individuals ('parts' or 'entities'), and that national development is the aggregate sum of their actions. I base my proposition on the premise that human factors or actions are the single most important component of national development, because the essence of development lies in 'doing' or 'taking action', and not on 'possessing' materials or resources.

So, what constitutes development-mindedness? In an effort to search for the answer to this question, I had to think about what cycle people generally go through or what the things are that people have to do in order to successfully achieve their aims. What I have deduced is the following, 'KPOP': (1) knowledge; (2) practising (embodying); (3) owning; and (4) passion (devotion). The sequencing may not necessarily occur in this order and could vary, and these elements tend to be interactive. I may refer these elements, which are pertinent to national development, as 'steps' or 'phases' for the sake of convenience.

The first thing anyone must do is to *know* what and how to do things. But know-how itself will be of no help if it is not put into practice. As the saying goes, knowing and doing are two very different things. It should also be plain that practising involves 'embodying' process, and these two tend to go together. 'Practising' means going beyond just knowing—to really digest and put into action what needs to be done. The next phase is taking 'ownership', which means that the individuals themselves are 'taking charge' of their work in an active, responsible manner. This would entail broadening of thinking on the planning and execution of tasks. The last phase is 'passion', where people show genuine devotion and motivation for their work. This is what really pushes people to excel and reach the culmination of their work.

This rule applies to everybody from all walks of life and at every level: national leaders, politicians, bureaucrats and public service workers, CEOs and businessmen, labourers, farmers, students, specialists, technicians, academicians, etc. 'Knowing'—that is, acquiring knowledge or expertise—is an initial but important step. One learns through natural process, studying and training in various forms. Many upper and middle-class people are well versed in the category of 'know-how' and have a grasp of the issues and the way forward, thanks to their enthusiasm for, and early exposure to, higher education and frequent contacts with the outside world. In fact, their ability to express themselves in an organized manner impresses many visiting foreigners. In elite circles and the well-to-do class, their level of knowledge and expression is up to the 'world-class'. But the domain of 'knowing', while essential, is only an introductory part, and it has to followed by the 'main body' of embodiment, application, ownership and passion.

But 'knowledge' is by no means a given. This is especially true for ordinary people like the youth and the rural populace. What is encouraging to see is that at least the students are enthusiastic and have a yearning for education in many parts of Africa. Of course, a great disparity in terms of the quality of education exists between urban centres and rural areas, where teachers' absenteeism is very high and the contents of education or knowledge imparted often have little relevance to reality.

Practising or applying knowledge is a much more challenging part. The main issue here is twofold: either very little work has been done or things are done improperly. No doubt, a widespread propensity of inaction and non-implementation is evident in Africa. Even worse, people frequently apply their know-how not to where it is due, but to do things that are detrimental to society and the public interest. This is common among civil servants throughout Sub-Saharan Africa. Government departments, law enforcement authorities and local governance bodies are deeply entrenched in irregularities, corruption and abuse of power, so that the problems have become institutional and undermine what little progress is made.

The picture outside the public sector is no less bleak. Sometimes workers have little regard for the most basic things. We can see many instances where knowledge, practice, ownership and devotion are all missing. Many things break down easily, but people tend not to mind and take it for granted. What is clearly visible and can be very easily fixed is often ignored. For example, I heard a story of local employees at a training institute in Uganda who did not bother to do anything about newly purchased classroom chairs. They were new and in good condition, except for a few loose joints that could be easily fixed manually. The employees were blaming the product and saying it was now useless. The principal of the institute, a foreigner, was at a loss in relation to their utter irresponsibility, and he fixed the chairs himself by simply tightening up the screws.

Unnecessary wastage and loss due to such indifference and carelessness is beyond our imagination. In general, some point out that it is not only the 'commoners' but also the 'capitalists' of Africa who are known to be wasteful.[11] In Sub-Saharan Africa, the 'mismanagement' is so prevalent, ranging from something small to something on a national scale, that 'good management' is considered rather rare. Probably the more profound harm done is that people become numb to the seriousness of the problem. A question that comes to mind is: 'If expectations and standards for work are set at such a low level, will development ever be possible?' A testimony by an Asian national who runs a mechanic shop in Kampala is reflective of this; he half-jokingly said 'a good thing about working in Uganda is that customers don't complain about my work, even when my equipment they purchased is not working properly. Better still, they never call me up late in the night to ask me to come and fix it'.

In our world, this KPOP combination can sound like an ideal type. But logically speaking, if the mindset or work ethics cannot keep pace with basic standards, what are the chances of progress? As such, strenuous efforts should be made to bring about the enhancement of quality and productivity of work to meet the acceptable 'standards'. Let us take an imaginary salesman, for example. In the phase of 'knowing', the salesman has to learn the basics—the nuts and bolts of sales and marketing, and company rules and policies. The next 'practising' step would require him to *act* as a salesman, 'embodying' the routines, being customer-friendly, service-oriented, keeping up with his work schedule and so on. Then in the 'ownership' stage, he would be going beyond routine work to have a sense of responsibility and attachment towards his organization. And finally, he would become fully devoted to his work, exhibiting the level of passion to make him a competent and professional businessman.

It is generally recognized that many African nations suffer from mismanagement or a lack of management capabilities. The reason for the scarcity of successful and sustainable businesses run by those native to the region is due to this. And the reason why government projects and services fail time after time, businesses go bankrupt, factories, hotels and restaurants need foreign managers to keep their business and reputation alive, etc. is because of this shortcoming in development-mindedness.

The human factor of ownership, responsibility and implementation is particularly important. But so much time has been wasted looking elsewhere for answers without addressing the real root causes of the problems of the region. Everybody involved, including the development partners, will have a share of responsibility for this, but no one could deny that the primary responsibility rests squarely with the African people.

This is where mindset change approach can come in. Instead of waiting for the lengthy process to be completed in a sequence, if the mindset change campaign can cause the people to be self-driven and passionate, that is, to go directly to the fourth stage, then stages one, two and three will be taken care of easily and almost automatically. This is the reverse engineering of development-mindedness. Those who feel passionate about doing something will be driven to learn, execute and own the things they want to do *of their own accord*. The reason why 'knowing' is not often followed by 'practising' and 'devoting' is that people are, for some reason, 'involuntary' or 'half-hearted'. In such a situation, coercing people would be counterproductive.

This 'reverse engineering' method can succeed where conventional approach fails. There are examples of such a model of development being tested and applied in Africa. The National Farmers Leadership Centre (NFLC) situated in Kampiringisa in the Mpigi District of Uganda is a prominent case in point. This institution, constructed by the Korea International Cooperation Agency (KOICA) in Uganda, was formally opened in May 2016, following the completion of all the facilities, but it had actually been operational for about a year and a half by this point.

During its trial operating period, in January 2015, about 50 Ugandan farmers from the Millennium Village Project in the Isingiro District were selected for a two-week mindset change and agriculture-livestock development courses. What I witnessed was striking. I have not seen such remote villagers attending a training course this elated, energetic and determined. They were said how much gratified

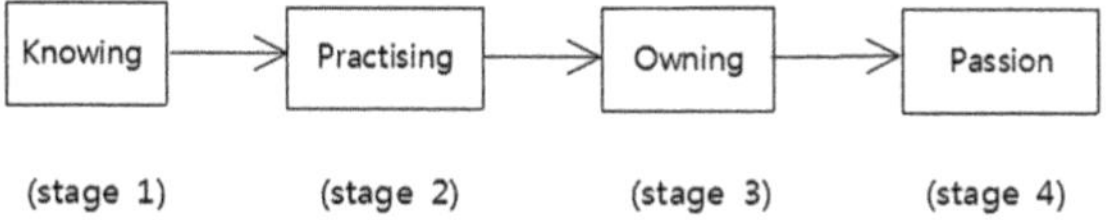

Fig. 5.1 Basic stages of development-mindedness (KPOP)

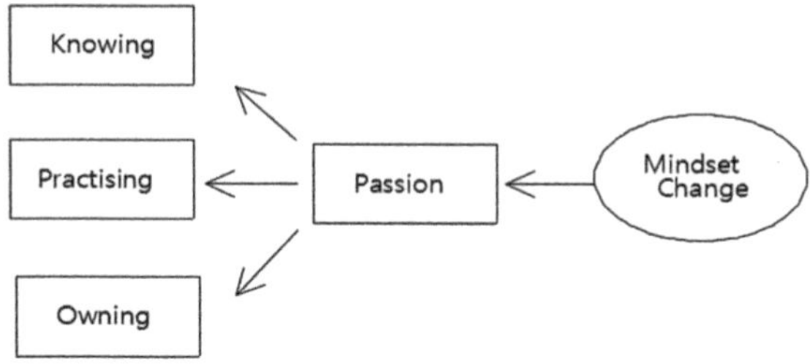

Fig. 5.2 Reverse engineering of development-mindedness

they were, and impressed by, the mindset change training which was something they had never experienced before. What was surprising is that this Canaan Farmers School style mental-disciplinary programme had such a strong appeal to the locals. The aim of this course was to 'reform' the trainees' mind to become self-confident and disciplined.

The benefits of this programme are having a sense of self-esteem, confidence, responsibility and being motivated to work. Those on the programme have to wake up at 5 a.m. every morning to participate in jogging and cleaning-up exercises before having breakfast and starting their classes. To my amazement, I later learned that these farmers, long after having returned to their villages, had stuck to this daily routine, chanting 'I can do it' slogans well before dawn. And this sounds almost like magic because it is all done *voluntarily*. The reason why it appeals to them in such a way may be because it felt innately 'natural' for them.

Figures 5.1 and 5.2 illustrate the basic stages of evolution of development-mindedness and the reverse engineering scheme respectively. The sequencing shown in Fig. 5.1 need not be taken literally; it is simply to illustrate a general idea and the order may vary depending on the individuals involved and the relevant circumstances.

Figure 5.2 shows the logic of the mindset change programme that was successful in South Korea. A successful drive for mindset change has the advantage of instantly impacting human attitudes and behaviour. Instilling people's mind with a can-do spirit, positive motivation and encouraging them to work cooperatively so that they become the spontaneous agents of rural transformation is the logic behind the *Saemaul Undong*, the New Village Movement. When people are motivated and passionate, their intensity of learning and practising will naturally become greater, if not automatic.

Figure 5.3 illustrates a repetitive pattern in Sub-Saharan Africa: the 'backtracking syndrome'. The biggest problem here is not so much the scope or level of knowledge, but the low level of intensity of actions like, in many cases, a surprising lack of attention to basics and details. It cannot be emphasized enough that what is steady, consistent and predictable is much better than what is irregular, arbitrary and unpredictable. The advantage of the former is that over time, it will have positive accumulative effects, while the latter will entail so many impediments like slow and meagre performance, frustration, uncertainty, rise in costs and loss of confidence.

As shown in the figure, backtracking syndrome is represented by 'regressions', the act of falling back and failing to stay on track towards progress. People may give up very early in their work or may not quite make it to or keep up with the 'practising' or the 'owning' phase. 'Tentative actions' is when the 'embodiment' of knowledge has not properly taken root in the individuals. While the term 'backtracking

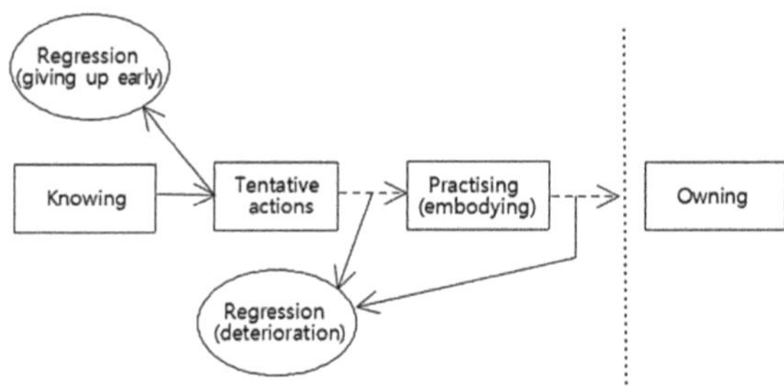

Fig. 5.3 'Backtracking syndrome'

syndrome' is used here for the first time, this is a common and recognizable phenomenon typical of Sub-Saharan Africa that many locals frankly acknowledge. Moreover, it occurs both in individuals and in organizations, including the government.

The Strong Role of the State

The weak role played by states poses another major vulnerability for Sub-Saharan African countries. From a broader context, the perceived lack of capacity and credibility of African governments seems to be due, in no small part, to the issue of the mindset or development-mindedness. The inefficiency or poor output of governments is deemed to be more attributable to lack of commitment and the problem of 'not doing' the basics than to the matter of policy choices because there are always many ways to make policies work.

As for the role of government in economic development, different theoretical perceptions have been put forward: the neoclassical view, the revisionist view, 'market-friendly view', the 'functional approach' and so on.[12] But today, the prevalent view in the development community is that the government's role matters and is important for economic development. No doubt, the successes of 'developmental states' in Asia is a powerful testament that developing nations can indeed achieve fast and successful economic transformation based on the positive role of state.

I believe that the developmental states model still is very relevant and deserves to be examined because its lessons and applicability can certainly benefit African countries. Jordan Kyle points out that 'between 1960 and 1995, the economies of 10 East Asian countries – Taiwan, South Korea, Singapore, China, Thailand, Hong Kong, Indonesia, Vietnam, Malaysia, and Japan – grew faster than those of nearly any other country in the world … In each of these economies, the government played a significant role in development process'.[13]

Nations should not treat the maxim 'actions speak louder than words' as a cliché. Countries in the region had ample time for nation-building and economic transformation, but the desperation was lacking. Thandika Mkwandawire is absolutely right that 'neither Africa's post-colonial history nor the actual practice engaged in by successful "developmental states" rules out the possibility of African "developmental states" capable of playing a more dynamic role than hitherto', but equating a scholarly 'misreading (in this case Myrdal's concept of "soft state" that he coined in 1968)' to 'denying Africa of the opportunity to think creatively' is far-fetched.[14] As long as the leaders and society as a whole fail to take measures to rectify the situation and scholars continue to justify the reality on their behalf, little progress can take place; taking responsibility and ownership is key.

The tasks requiring direct action to be taken by a nation, like nation-building and economic development, should not left to be initiated, planned and shaped by theorists and directed by international organizations that do not and cannot bear responsibility on behalf of developing countries. South Korea and other Asian countries did not develop because they were guided by theories and the donor community. Explanations or model-building comes after, not before, the accumulation of results and samples. If Sub-Saharan African countries find themselves at odds with the international development community, the chances are that this is due mostly to donor fatigue exacerbated by the slow-paced, non-committal response of the former. Everyone involved in the partnership suffers from consequences like delays, breakdowns and rising costs when parties repeatedly renege on their obligations. International recognition and favourable terms are won on the basis of merit, not on insistence.

The role of the state is deemed to have become more important in light of growing global challenges and inter-dependence. It is true that globalization in the form of greater economic and social inter-dependence calls for complex decision-making processes, which take place at various levels (namely sub-national, national and global), paving the way for a growing multi-layered system of governance.[15] The need for enhanced cooperation and regulation on a wider scale in the international arena justifies the more robust and effective role of states in the process. Imagine the uncertainty and chaos that would ensue should states start reducing and abandoning their role. The emergence of global civil society or world government that was once imagined by transnationalists seems less likely than ever.

African countries have every reason to push for a strong state in which the government plays an active role in relation to economic and social development. Developed countries and international organizations, on their part, should be supportive of Africa's endeavour in this regard. Economic stability and predictability that countries around the world need would come from credibility in actions. The question is how African countries can move in this direction. With respect to the success of East Asian economies, debates have taken place as to whether this was due to policy choice, i.e., selecting the right polices, or to initial conditions like better state capacity and autonomy, higher human capital formation, etc. While both policy choices and initial conditions were proper, the more fundamental and decisive factor was the latter, as stressed by Keun Lee.[16] But 'initial conditions' should not be taken literally as something already given that cannot be replicated. The lesson for African countries is that there is no shortcut to development, but that it is achievable when the necessary effort is indeed made.

Western nations undertook a variety of mercantilist policies to increase national wealth and pursued aggressive industrial policies to develop and transform their industries; the latecomers to industrialization followed this course in order to catch up with the forerunners. Ha-Choon Chang observes that the role of the state was central in the initial stages of the evolution of economics and in Western Europe the role of states increased with the emergence of nation states and the development of capitalism. During the golden era of capitalism, the rise of the state both in terms of economic theory and practice was dramatic.[17]

The states were not only preoccupied with exercising sovereignty for the defence and maintenance of order, but also actively promoted economic transformation. European countries have incessantly pushed forth, tested and refined the state's functions or roles in order to meet domestic and international needs or challenges. The welfare state, which is seen as a distinctive combination of democracy, welfare and capitalism, is another example of the state playing an active role in the social and economic wellbeing of its citizens.[18] Originating in Europe, the welfare state has spread to different regions, taking different forms as it has done so. Others have retained significant government roles, as can be seen in the strong regulatory role played by the US government. Western nations, which started economic development in the primary industry, are still materially involved in protecting and promoting the agricultural and other sectors.

Today, developing and developed nations alike need to have a strong and well-functioning government to handle various economic and social tasks, in addition to security challenges that take many different forms. The role or intervention of active government to promote economic growth in itself should not be regarded as simply being protectionist or anti-free market. Despite all the clamour of neo-classical liberalism and neo-liberalism in the theoretical or academic realm, in practice, how many countries would indeed fit the description of 'laissez-faire capitalism' or a 'night-watchman state?' In reality, there is no such thing as a free market without the government's involvement. Even in the most neo-liberal economies such as the US, the 'invisible hand' is a myth. Today, the role of government in developed countries remains robust and is even upscaled to meet the challenges of economic globalism.

So what are the lessons to be drawn for Sub-Saharan Africa? One of them could be that the so-called adverse international development regime that many hold accountable for Africa's continued economic plight, such as structural adjustment policies, the Washington Consensus and neoliberalist policies, cannot be an excuse of giving up the strong role of government. Since independence, Sub-Saharan African countries have had every opportunity to build a consolidated and effective state to push for economic development with the backing of the international community.

Back in the 1950s and 1960s, the centrality of the role of the state and the need for market regulation was widely accepted, and there was a general perception that economic development called for industrialization, following the path of many Western economies.[19] At the time, Gerschenkron, who analysed the cases of France, Germany and Russia, which wanted to emulate Great Britain, suggested that a backward economy might take a considerably different form of development from the advanced economies and that 'there could even be advantages for late industrializers because they might be able to leapfrog into more technologically advanced sectors, by learning from and imitating the pioneers'.[20] He later argued that 'the greater the degree of backwardness, the more intervention is required in the market economy to channel capital and entrepreneurship to nascent industries'.[21] Hence, in this period, the goal of development was growth and the agent of development was the state.

Despite an optimistic worldview on the part of 'modernization' and 'big push' theorists, and the developmentalist zeal of first-generation African leaders, the disappointing performance of African countries in this regard brought about a great shift in development thinking around the late 1970s and early 1980s influenced by neo-liberal thought, which was well reflected in the World Bank's report *Accelerated Development in Sub-Saharan Africa*, commonly known as the Berg Report.[22] The report attributed the failures of Africa's development to all the negativities of African governments' problematic intervention, missteps and mismanagement.[23]

The essence of the problem was not the strength of government or governmental intervention per se, but rather the failure of states to assume their roles as developmental states. In the meantime, countries in East Asia, namely the NICs, were making strides in terms of economic growth and development. Without addressing the fundamental problem of underperforming or dysfunctional government, the pendulum shifts in policy adoptions are not likely to bring about the desired outcomes.

Liberalization and privatization have become popular catchwords and norms for Sub-Saharan Africa's leaders, policy-makers and business sectors. But many have also cast doubts, in hindsight, on the appropriateness of this policy orientation, especially with regard to the manner in which they were implemented, in the absence of sound governance and oversight of the state. The United Arab Emirates case of Dubai provides a good example of a successful marriage of proactive economic liberalization and highly disciplined and effective government oversight.

Fortunately for the United Arab Emirates, it has the riches, the oil, but many other resource-rich countries have not capitalized on their resources. Generally, the hallmark of the strong role of the state in developing countries should be industrial policy. Developing countries, as latecomers to industrialization, should be able to drive economic development forward with a sufficient level of ability and authority. The more a country lags behind others, the more it will need to exert itself through an industrial push to catch up with the others, instead of leaving everything up to the markets. The word 'transformation', which has become fashionable in the region, implies making real change and breaking the status quo, which is contrary to the general inclination of African states. It is an irony that people want change and yet they themselves are not willing to change.

Regarding the Korean model of latecomer development, Keun Lee argues that Korea's sustained economic growth is due to the capacity of the people and enterprises rather than the role of government, departing from the conventional debates on the state-market dichotomy. According to Lee, the real lesson to be learned from Korea is not the role of government, but the fact that it was able to build up the capabilities of people and companies, thus inducing sustained growth for decades.[24] He makes a powerful statement that neo-classical economics focuses on macroeconomic stability and trade liberalization, but these are hardly connected to capacity-building, and such 'bias in economics dates back to the intrinsic limitations of neoclassical economics when the word "capabilities" (and by implication, "learning") did not exist'.[25] The classical theory advocates effective allocation or 'optimization' of resources, with an implicit assumption that the necessary resources are already available. But for developing countries, optimization of resources cannot be their preoccupation because they lack such resources as capacity to begin with, and so the more pressing and critical task for them is how to build such capabilities.[26]

Sung-Hee Jwa proposes that economics must take governments and business firms into account alongside market mechanism because governments and corporations also drive the economy. Hence, he calls markets, governments and corporations the 'holy trinity' or the three key entities of economic development. He claims that markets are old as human civilization and are not a new feature of the capitalist world. As the case of South Korea shows, what also matters is the role of the government and firms in addition to market mechanism. Korea in the 1960s and 1970s, during the tenure of President PARK Chung-Hee, successfully combined these three components to achieve the 'miracle on the Han River', according to Jwa (2015, 2017). Its secret was *sin-sangpilbhur*, a Korean axiom meaning 'reward good deeds and punish wrongdoings', which he termed 'economic discrimination (ED)'. He argues that the sustained economic growth of Korea during the tenure of President Park was possible because economic policy-making and implementation was insulated from political influence; the strict application of 'economic logic'—efficiency, incentives and competitiveness—while disallowing political influences and considerations for welfare was the key to success.[27]

The examples of South Korea and other East Asian countries demonstrate that governments and firms can be formidable 'pro-capitalist', 'pro-market' agents or forces complementing and reinforcing market mechanism. In this respect, Jwa's theorizing work on the 'extended market mechanism' that brings government and firms into the equation is a valuable contribution to economics. In developing countries in particular, market distortions and failures often occur not necessarily due to too much government intervention, but more often due to weak institutions and a weak role played by the government; this is all the more true in view of their imperfect economic environment.

When the functioning of government is meagre, not only will government projects fail, but the general public will suffer the most. Since poor public service delivery reflects a lack of discipline amongst and responsibility of civil servants, this will have a negative effect on the society as a whole. In many countries in the region, the spirit of 'serving the people', whether it concerns public service by government workers or customer service by the private sector, is markedly weak. The perennial poor delivery of service lowers people's expectation of service and they take this to be the norm. This translates into less pressure on those on the government payroll to do their job. Hence, the vicious cycle of poor service and performance, wastage of public resources, marginalization or disempowerment of the public, and weak accountability in the public sector continues. Furthermore, officials are engaged in widespread corruption, aggravating the problem in the public sector. According to the Mo Ibrahim Foundation's Index on Governance released in October 2016, the level of red tape and corruption in governments in Africa has increased over the last ten years.

Agricultural-rural development in the wider context of industrial policy deserves the special attention of African leaders because this should be the bedrock of industrialization and economic transformation for any developing country. There is clearly a renewed advocacy for agricultural development in the community of African elites, Africanists and international development organizations.

David Henley sheds light on Asian states' pro-poor agriculture-rural development policies, which African countries have not been able to successfully adopt and implement. He views that the divergence in performance between Africa and Asia boils down to the ways of combining rapid economic growth with mass poverty reduction, and the fact that African leaders have never shown a serious intention to pursue such pro-poor development: 'Their development models, implicitly or explicitly, have focused not pragmatically on mass outreach and rapid impact in the battle against poverty, but on ideas of technological and cultural modernity based on conditions in already rich countries'.[28]

Joe Studwell outlines the crucial roles that governments of Asia played in economic development: (1) the restructuring of agriculture as a highly labour-intensive household farming to maximize output alongside land ownership reform that provided land for small farmers; (2) using the proceeds from surpluses in agriculture to build an export-oriented manufacturing sector; and (3) intervening in the financial sector to direct capital towards the small farming and export-oriented manufacturing sector.[29]

Let us revisit the classical economic growth theory of Walt Rostow. This is a theory of modernization development postulating that developing countries go through the following five stages: (1) traditional society; (2) establishing conditions for take-off (underdeveloped economy); (3) economic take-off (developing economy); (4) drive to maturity (developed economy); and (5) high mass consumption (post-industrial economy). The first stage, traditional society, is associated with the country having the majority of its people engaged in subsistence agriculture. The second stage is entails change in order to build up the conditions for growth and take-off. It is characterized by the massive development of raw materials, increase in capital use in agriculture, and the mobilization of funding and investments. There is also a shift from an agrarian to an industrial or manufacturing society, and trade and other commercial activities are broadened. In the third, take-off stage, urbanization increases, new industries expand rapidly and a technological breakthrough occurs. This is characterized by dynamic economic growth and the reinvestment of increasing profits in new industrial plants. The fourth, drive to maturity stage features the diversification of the industrial base, the expansion of multiple industries, the shifting of manufacturing from investment-driven capital goods to consumer durables and domestic consumption, and the rapid and large-scale development of social infrastructure. The fifth stage is about high mass consumption, with the industrial base dominating the economy and with widespread consumption of high-value consumer goods.[30]

An important point to make here is that economic development started from the agricultural-rural sector. For non-Western countries, the development path need not follow such an order, but this is not the central issue. What should be recalled is that not only the East Asian economies but also the Western economies that have industrialized much earlier have taken the course of achieving economic transformation on the basis of successful agriculture-rural development.

In *Common Wealth*, Jeffrey Sachs lays out his version of the economic development stages of poor countries rising to the status of wealthy economies in which agricultural development plays a key role: (1) subsistence economy; (2) commercial economy (large boost in agricultural productivity); (3) emerging market economy (expansion of infrastructure); and (4) technology-based economy. And he observes that 'once the economy gets an initial surge in food productivity (stage 2), it begins to grow and prosper on its own. This is because the initial surge in wealth allows private citizens and the government to make investments in health, education and infrastructure'.[31]

All in all, we can argue that what is fundamentally lacking in Africa that East Asian countries and much earlier Western economies were able do during the early phase of their development are: (1) the construction and operation of strong government functioning mechanisms; and (2) an effective policy drive for rural-agricultural development.

So why haven't most of the countries in the Sub-Saharan African region been able to take advantage of these historical facts and lessons? The models of development did not emerge out of a vacuum; they are the outcome of decades or even centuries of efforts. It is up to developing nations to figure out what best suits their situation, given all the facts and experiences. What is obvious is that true economic transformation takes objective, consistent and broad-scoped thinking, planning and, most of all, action.

After popular optimism of the 'Africa rising', indications of the flaws in the economic state of Sub-Saharan Africa continue to show themselves. For example, the deterioration of the economic situation in Zambia has threatened to send the copper-rich country that was hailed as a middle-income nation to a point of near-collapse. For decades, Zambia reaping heavily from its sole mineral export, copper, which accounted for nearly 70% of the country's export earnings, and was the second-biggest copper producer in Africa behind the Democratic Republic of Congo. But today, Zambia provides a lesson on the perils of overdependence on a single commodity and a handful of multinational mining companies. Declining copper prices and a severe electricity shortage were the biggest reasons for its fall from grace. Zambia's economic growth rate, which had averaged seven per cent annually for the previous five years, fell to an estimated 3.4% in 2015, leading to speculation that it might have to turn to the IMF for assistance.[32] Fortunately, however, for Zambia and other resource-rich African countries, commodity prices are on the road to recovery in 2018.

Nigeria is just one of many countries that have suffered in recent years from over-reliance on oil production without having proper governance in place. As of early 2017, as the largest oil-producing nation in Sub-Saharan Africa, where oil income accounted for 35% of its GDP and 75% of government revenue, Nigeria was facing a serious shortage of electricity even in Lagos, following a 35% fall in the value of its currency over the previous year amid rampant corruption, which saw billions of dollars of oil revenue disappearing into thin air. Nigeria has been the biggest tomato-producing country in Africa, but was importing tomato pastes from abroad because it did not have sufficient manufacturing facilities to make the product domestically.[33]

Rick Rowden noted that: 'Africans were told to simply privatize, liberalize, deregulate, and get the so-called economic fundamentals right. The free market would take care of the rest. But this advice neglects the actual history of how rich countries themselves have effectively used industrial policies for 400 years, beginning with the U.K. and Europe and ending with the 'four tigers' … This inconvenient history contradicted free market maxims and so has been largely stripped from the economics curriculum in most universities'.[34] It is up to African countries to decide how they want to develop but they should be at least cognizant of historical facts and lessons to be able to make the right decisions.

Notes

1. See George J. Sefa Dei and Paul Banahene Adjei (eds), *Emerging Perspectives on African Development* (New York: Peter Lang Publishing, 2014), p. 5.
2. David Booth and Diana Gammack, *Governance for Development in Africa* (London: Zed Books, 2013), p. 87. Booth and Gammack argue that evidence tends to support E. A. Brett's thesis ('Problematising the Democratic Imperative: The Challenge of Transition and Consolidation in Weak States', draft paper, London School of Economics, 2012) that open democratic processes have only ever been established in countries that have strong states, cohesive societies and liberal capitalist economies'. And they make an important case that 'careless promotion of elections and economic liberalisation – the trappings of democracy and capitalism – in countries where inter-communal relations and political settlement are fragile can be very costly in terms of violence and human life'.
3. 'Secrets Behind Korea's Economic Success', Korea Foundation DVD (October 2014).
4. In this respect, South Africa can be categorized as a different class. But when we discount the 'white minority run-economy' if we can describe it as such, then the situation is comparable to other countries in the region. There are 'pockets' of developed or industrialized areas in countries like Kenya and Nigeria, but when we see them from the holistic perspective of the 'national economy', they lag considerably behind other regional economies.

5. Crawford Young, *The Postcolonial State in Africa* (Madison: University of Wisconsin Press, 2012), p. 332.
6. Pierre Englebert and Kevin C. Dunn (2013), pp. 89–90.
7. Crawford Young (2012), p. 312.
8. Ibid.
9. Asongazoh Alemazung, 'Leadership Flaws and Fallibilities Impacting Democratization Processes, Governance and Functional Statehood in Africa', *African Journal of Political Science and International Relations* 5, no. 1 (January 2011), p. 32.
10. Edward Kirumira, Principal of the College of Humanities and Social Sciences, University of Makerere, speaking at the workshop 'Colonial Legacy and National Development: Comparative Post-colonial Impact Assessment and Lessons Learned between South Korea and Uganda', 15 August 2015, Sheraton Hotel, Kampala, Uganda.
11. See Thandika Mkandawire, 'Thinking About Developmental States in Africa', http://archive.unu.edu/hq/academic/Pg_area4/Mkandawire.html. See also Thandika Mkandawire, 'Thinking About Developmental States in Africa', *Cambridge Journal of Economics* 25 (May 2001), pp. 289–313.
12. Oh-Seok Hyun (President, Trade Research Institute, Korea International Trade Association), 'The Role of Government and Economic Development', November 2006 (PPT presentation), http://siteresources.worldbank.org/PSGLP/Resources/Session2Oh.pdf. The government's role involves the mobilization and allocation of resources, the stabilization of the national economy and the promotion of technological development. The neo-classical view emphasizes a stable macroeconomic environment, the absence of price controls and other distorted policies, a reliable legal framework, free trade, investments, etc. The revisionist view is that industrial policy and interventions in financial markets are not easily reconciled within the neo-classical framework, and some policies in some economies are much more in accordance with models of state-led development. The market-friendly view prescribes the appropriate role of the government in the market-friendly strategy (the World Bank's *World Development Report*, 1991). The functional approach identifies successful cases like South Korea, considering that South Korea achieved rapid growth based on the 'three functions of growth': accumulation, efficient allocation and rapid technological catch-up.

13. See Jordan Kyle, 'Perspectives on the Role of the State in Economic Development—Taking Stock of the "Developmental State" After 35 Years', *IFPRI Discussion Paper* 01597, January 2017.
14. Thandika Mkandawire, 'Thinking About Developmental States in Africa' (2001).
15. Guido Bertucci and Adriana Alberti, 'Globalization and the Role of the State: Challenges and Perspective', paper drawn from *United Nations World Public Sector Report*, 'Globalization and Public the State' (2001).
16. Keun Lee, *Economic Catch-Up and Technological Leapfrogging: The Path to Development and Macroeconomic Stability in Korea* (Cheltenham: Edward Elgar, 2016), p. 15.
17. Ha-Joon Chang, *Globalization, Economic Development and the Role of the State* (London: Zed Books, 2003), Korean translation (2006) by Bookie Publishing House, pp. 37–39.
18. T.H. Marshall, *Citizenship and Social Class and Other Essays* (Cambridge: Cambridge University Press, 1950).
19. John Harriss, 'Development Theories', in Bruce Currie-Alder, Ravi Kanbur, David M. Malone, and Rohinton Medhora (eds), *International Development: Ideas, Experience, and Prospects* (Oxford: Oxford University Press, 2014), p. 39.
20. Ibid. See Alexander Gerschenkron, *Economic Backwardness in Historical Perspective: A Book of Essays* (Cambridge, MA: Belknap Press, 1962). Gerschenkron stresses the importance of capital for overcoming technological gap confronting 'backward' nations. He argued that state intervention compensated for inadequate supplies of capital, skilled labour or entrepreneurship in late-developing economics.
21. Ibid. See Albert Fishlow, 'Review Essay on Gerschenkron's *Economic Backwardness in Historical Perspective*', for the Economic History Network (www.eh.net/node/276).
22. Ibid., p. 42. The Berg Report faults Africa's 'inappropriate state dominated policies' for leading governments to take on more than they could handle, distorting economic incentives and creating all the opportunities for unproductive rent-seeking.
23. Thandika Mkandawire (2001), p. 289.
24. Keun Lee, 'Korean Model of Latecomer Development: Capability-Building and Smart Specialization Leading to Structural Transformation', a policy report, Center for Economic Catch-up, Seoul National University, December 2016, pp. 2–3.

25. Ibid., p. 3.
26. Ibid.
27. Sung-Hee Jwa's PPT presentation 'Korean Economic Development and Saemaul Undong: Experience and Lessons' (8 September 2015, Kampala, Uganda) and the presentation paper at the Korea Forum for Progress (1 September 2015, Seoul, Korea), 'Success Factors of Saemaul Undong' (Korean). Dr. Jwa, Sung-Hee is the Chair Professor of the Park Chung-Hee School of Policy and Saemaul, Yeungnam University, Korea.
28. David Henley, *Asia-Pacific Development Divergence: A Question of Intent* (London: Zed Books, 2015), pp. 209–210.
29. Joe Studwell, *How Asia Works: Success and Failure in the World's Most Dynamic Region* (London: Profile Books, 2013).
30. W.W. Rostow, *The Stages of Economic Growth: A Non-communist Manifesto* (Cambridge: Cambridge University Press, 1960), pp. 4–16.
31. Jeffrey Sachs, *Common Wealth*, 2008, http://www.povertyeducation.org/stages-of-economic-development.html.
32. 'Declining Copper Prices a Large Factor in Zambia's Economic Tumble', *Globe and Mail*, 26 October 2015.
33. *Nigeria Crossroads*, CNN International, broadcast on 3 May 2017.
34. Rick Rowden, 'Here Is Why "Africa Rising" Is Just a Myth', *The Observer* (Uganda), 6 January 2016, p. 24.

6
Reasons for Optimism and the Tasks at Hand

Positive Signs and Reasons for Hope

The challenges and tasks facing African countries may seem daunting, but this does not warrant an overtly pessimistic judgement, as there are in fact positive aspects in the countries that when properly recognized and utilized can be instrumental in the development of the region. Africa's problems, which have been cited by so many, are exhaustive, but I have reason to be optimistic and believe that Africa can indeed succeed in transforming itself. Here I would like to explain why.

I can think of at least seven reasons to be positive. First of all, the root cause of underdevelopment of Sub-Saharan Africa is essentially a matter of 'intent' rather than being structural or environmental in nature. Second, there is a prevalence of openness and pragmatism in the region. Third, Africa's political, economic and social structures are not 'fixed', but dynamic. Fourth, there is great potential for development because of the 'cushions' they have: an abundance of land, including vast fertile soils, untapped natural resources and a growing young population that can be turned into 'assets'. Fifth, there have been so much disappointments and shortcomings that now the time is ripe

J.-D. Park, *Re-Inventing Africa's Development*,
https://doi.org/10.1007/978-3-030-03946-2_6

for accepting the inevitability of 'change' and doing things differently on the part of Africans and the international development community alike. Sixth, an increasing number of Africans are beginning to understand that not only the world but also their sub-regions are becoming ever more competitive and that they need to develop competitiveness in order to survive and prosper. Seventh, there are a number of very positive traditions or customs conducive to development in Africa that have been overlooked, forgotten or underestimated, but which should be duly recognized or brought back into play.

Regarding the first question of intent, changing the mindset of the people is by no means easy and some say that it can be the most difficult thing to do. But when mindset change actually does occur, even partially and incrementally, it can unleash a powerful force that brings about changes beyond people's imagination. Mindset change is important not only for development but also for dealing with social problems like violence, killings and abuses that plague the people, because such problems cannot be resolved through law enforcement alone. If the mindset change of the individuals takes place *collectively*, its impact will be huge and can bring about a sea change. As much as there are aspirations for growth and prosperity in the region, there has to be an equal level of seriousness for mindset change.

I do not see Africa's development problem as a fundamentally structural one that cannot be overcome despite human efforts to do so. Africans are not subjected to perennial wars, natural disasters and diseases on a grand scale, although it tends to be big news when these do occur. Africa is a huge continent and except for some limited trouble-spots and isolated cases, the vast region is mostly calm, peaceful and stable. There is nothing that coercively suppresses the people from developing. Wars are man-made and epidemics are, strictly speaking, also man-made. To treat Africa differently from the rest of the world by depicting it as always being in a more adverse state than other regions is simply wrong. I have met so many locals who were very proud of their heritage, and some even suggested that Africa lags behind other regions because it is blessed with an overabundance of so many things.

What is also striking is that there is a genuine passion for education and learning among the populace. In every circumstance, education is the key and it will make all the difference. But apart from regular academic teaching, subjects on socialization or 'national ethics' should be newly introduced and pragmatic, vocational skills training must be expanded. In the end, Africans have to, and eventually will, come to terms with this critical matter of 'intent' because this is unavoidable, if not quintessential.

The second reason is closely related to the first one. I personally think that the most attractive and promising feature of the people in Sub-Saharan Africa is that they are predominantly open-minded and pragmatic, and not ideological, self-closing or dogmatic. In fact, I find virtually everyone—elites, intellectuals and the general populace—in the Sub-Saharan African region to be very receptive and friendly. Nearly all African countries are seen to pursue pro-development, pro-liberal market economy policies and want to very much enhance business in collaboration with foreign firms and partners. Religious extremists and terrorist organizations are mainly confined to Somalia and northern Nigeria. What is interesting, however, is that South Africa, which is economically the most advanced country in Sub-Saharan Africa, is perhaps the most ideologically charged nation in the region, mostly due to the legacy of apartheid.

Third, Africa's political, economic and social structures are not 'fixed', but are dynamic and still in the making. I think that many will agree that this is true, which is why I am rather optimistic about the future of Africa. I have a sense that in due course, Sub-Saharan African countries—and if not all of them, then at least an increasing number of them—will experience an 'awakening' with respect to their reality and will take charge of their destiny.

Fourth, Sub-Saharan Africa is promising in terms of its sheer size of the 'untouched' fertile land mass. It is also abundant in untapped natural resources and boasts a growing young population, which should be regarded as a potential asset rather than an economic and social burden. Some point out that the demographic dividend could be a huge advantage for Africa: 'You don't need to stay long in any African city to feel the entrepreneurial energy on the streets. For those of us who grew up on the continent, it is very much a fact of life. But for those visiting, perhaps for the first time, it can seem overwhelming. There is no single reason, of course, for this bustle and energy. But a big part of it comes from the fact that Africa has the youngest population of any continent.'[1] It is a matter of how people perceive things and what choice of actions they take.

These are all valuable 'cushions' that Africa can take advantage of in the future exigencies of this world. Ironically, the uncertainties of the world like global climate change, shortage of foodstuffs, the impact of ageing society in industrialized countries, etc. may make Sub-Saharan Africa increasingly attractive. There is also a special 'affection' and eagerness on the part of international community to recognize its positive developments.

The fifth point I want to make is that now many people appear to be craving something new and different that can work. People are literally fed up with the rampancy of corruption, mismanagement, breach of laws, and irresponsible and immoral acts that mar the basic functioning of society and the state. In this respect, we should acknowledge that there is an apparent variance on this point across the African continent: at one end of spectrum, some countries are viewed in a positive light, giving rise to optimism, while at the other end, certain countries are suffering from prolonged crises involving unending internal conflict, destabilization and human suffering. Even within a country, the situation may vary depending on the region, but hopefully good practices will prevail and spread.

The sixth argument is that even in Sub-Saharan Africa, 'competition' has set in as a stark reality. By now, state leaders, elites and businessmen should know that economic performance or capacity is what matters. They are not only competing among themselves for foreign development assistance, but also—and more importantly—for trade, investment and tourism. Competitiveness is becoming a key word in Sub-Saharan Africa and there will be countries 'running away' and receiving increased recognition and opportunities, while others lag further behind. The pursuit of equality and welfare is like a double-edged sword for development: it can hurt if it is too little or too much. But the principal driver of economic growth is competition and comparative advantage.

Lastly, Africans nations and donors alike should 'rediscover' the valuable 'gems' of Africa that have been underestimated. African people greatly value recognition, like earning academic certificates and degrees, and winning citations and awards. The sense of pride that I see in ordinary African people for being honoured for their achievements is immense. Another positive element is the tradition of community-based self-help work. In Uganda, this is called *Bulungi Bwansi* (for the good of the nation) and in Rwanda *Umuganda* (coming together for a common purpose), while in Burundi it is called *Ibikorwa Rusangi*. Many other countries, including Ethiopia, have similar traditions. In Uganda, the *Bulungi Bwansi* movement has weakened following the influx of foreign aid and the popularization of the 'welfare' policy of the government that exacerbated the dependency syndrome of the local populace. The situation is more or less the same in most other African countries.

It will not be difficult for devoted Africanists to soon recognize that 'Africa has rich, ancient traditions of what we call public work—self organized communal labours. These are crucial foundations for a democratic way of life that existed long before Europeans brought the term to the continent'.[2] But many such traditional virtues have been neglected, discouraged or sabotaged with political intent by African rulers after independence. The unwholesome electoral democracy prevalent in the region is seen to have smothered the voluntarism that would have really empowered the people.

In any case, we should neither be naive and optimistic nor overly pessimistic and cynical. Only being truthful and candid about the problems will be of help. As the saying goes, 'truth will set you free'.

The Task of the Donor Community

What are the things that donors should do to improve the situation and the efficiency of aid? Compared to what African countries need to do, which are basically fundamental things, the tasks facing donors are more technical in nature, including features like coordination, know-how transfer, supervision, etc. But the reality obliges donors to not only carry out such technical tasks but also to constantly 'press' others, the aid-recipients, to do their necessary part as well. From the donor community's perspective, aids provided to African countries since their independence were not having desired outcomes and African countries needed to assume greater responsibility as aid recipients. The end of the Cold War brought about fundamental changes in international political dynamics and this lead to a basic change in donors' stance as well:

The 1990s was an era of the re-examination of aid's effectiveness and imposition of 'conditionality' with increased donor fatigue and call for good governance to root out corruption. Emphasis was also placed on reducing aid dependence as well as liberalization and privatization, while there was a resurgence of the poverty alleviation objective.[3]

As for the development doctrine in the 2000s, the development community ran out of 'big ideas'. Following the turn of the century, it seems that no one was confident to lay out a clear prescription in terms of theory and policy. Instead, the international community came up with action-oriented plans like the Millenium Development Goals (MDG), and the problem of aid fragmentation was seriously considered. Since the new millennium, while the Washington Consensus has been 'muted', there have been bits of everything without a clear aid policy-orientation.

Development paradigms before the MDGs lacked formal international agreement, but the MDGs emerged as the first ever of their kind in terms of their formality (although the agreement was incomplete) and specific action goals. The MDGs were mainly the outcome of the work by a small group within the OECD Development Assistance Committee (DAC) and UN Secretary General Kofi Annan's Millennium Declaration, which lacked the formal approval of the UN General Assembly. Hence, developing countries tended to view MDGs as part of the developed countries' agenda, but the SDGs were an outcome of much more broader deliberations and were formally adopted at the UN summit. Therefore, it can boast greater legitimacy in that both developed and developing countries can claim its ownership.[4]

Good governance is also rightfully stressed, as political stability and sound institutions are vital to sustainable growth. The need for industrialization and building infrastructure, and private sector participation in the funding for development, among other factors, are also underscored. On the other hand, the fact that SDGs have a very broad scope in terms of issue areas and items, and that these goals are designed to be taken up on a voluntary basis by the states will likely prompt both developing countries and developed countries to act in a discretionary and selective manner suited to their national interests.[5]

So, what should the task be for the donor community? First, the international community should take a long hard look at the reality and limitations of existing approaches, and realize the need to be more open-minded and creative about making improvements. Second, the donor community as a whole must forge closer collaboration, and where it is appropriate and possible to do so, should try to be less competitive and be more complementary.

We have seen the evolution of the aid doctrine since the 1950s. At the multilateral level, the aid doctrine and policies have been driven by developed countries through their organizations, namely the OECD DAC, along with the World Bank and IMF. While international organizations ensure the consistency, predictability and stability of international aid policies, as well as providing specialized or tailored assistance for a whole range of needs, bilateral donors are the major funders of international organizations and at the same time are their collaborative clients or partners on the ground.

Looking back, the MDGs were touted by the UN as 'the most successful anti-poverty movement in history'.[6] But it would be fair to say that the MDGs had limited success in terms of the overall development of Africa, as the goals were focused on poverty reduction and assistance for 'basic needs'. The lessons learnt are already incorporated to a certain extent in the action plans of the SDGs, and as this is the general framework of development at the global level, the UN is doing its fair share to spearhead this. But the UN cannot be guarantors of Africa's transformation, and it is only at the national level of African countries that the successful implementation of the SDGs can be achieved.

While the donor community has inherent limitations, it also provides a meaningful support that we can call 'limited external governance'. To understand the value of this 'limited external governance', one only needs to think what would have happened if foreign aid personnel—officials, experts, workers and volunteers—were suddenly withdrawn or aid programmes were stopped. Hence, the basic challenge regarding aid is twofold: how to overcome dependency syndrome and how to improve the overall governance. And I think the theme of enhancing aid effectiveness captures both. But things have to change and can change for the better. One way to do this is by avoiding the 'Samaritan's dilemma'.[7]

Aid can end up just as one-time transfers of wealth or can be 'wealth creating' if used properly. Therefore, the principle of 'rewards and punishments' should be applied and the tools of incentives and competition should be employed, along with consideration of the needs of African countries. Foreign aid should be value-adding and 'giving credit where it is due', 'reward based on merit' or 'effective resource reallocation' ought to be the catchphrases that donors should be honouring.

I have already mentioned that democracy and governance are basically an outcome of development rather than its precondition. Western countries were not democratized when they were industrializing, and the East Asian economies achieved rapid growth under authoritarian political regimes and imperfect governance. Of course, the better the governance, the better it will be for development. This is all the more true for Sub-Saharan African countries. Corruption, irregularities and political repression were also common in East Asian countries, nut Asian nations were much more development-oriented in terms of state leadership, policy focus and work ethics compared to African nations.

Countries that ranks high in terms of development in the region, such as Mauritius, Botswana, Namibia, Cape Verde, the Seychelles and South Africa, all boast high marks in governance and democracy. But needless to say, the ideal condition for developing countries will be to have both strong a work ethic and good governance. While it will be no easy feat to achieve both at the same time, if at least steady improvements can be made in these, the countries will no doubt make great progress.

The vast majority of official development assistance (ODA) is provided by the OECD Development Assistance Committee (DAC) members. The DAC is comprised of 29 countries, plus the EU, of which all except for two (Japan and South Korea) are Western countries. In 2016, the OECD DAC's net ODA totalled USD 142.62 billion, which represents an 8.9% increase compared to 2015; the top five donors were the US (USD 335.9 billion), Germany (USD 246.7 billion), the UK (USD 180.1 billion), Japan (USD 103.7 billion) and France (USD 95.0 billion); the DAC has provided USD 267.4 billion to Africa, of which 88.9% has been directed at Sub-Saharan Africa.[8]

The official donors, which comprised 20 countries in 1960, has now become 48, including non-OECD DAC members that report to the OECD DAC. This excludes some countries like China, India, and Brazil that do not report to the DAC.[9] In Africa, the non-OECD DAC, emerging donors such as China, India, Brazil, Kuwait, Saudi Arabia, Turkey and the United Arab Emirates—the so-called seven emerging donors—have been active to varying degrees for many decades.[10] China, the outright biggest donor in this group, is estimated to have dispensed USD 7.1 billion in 2013, making it the sixth-largest donor in the world.[11]

So what does diversification of donors mean for Africa? We may start by comparing traditional donors with emerging donors. The OECD DAC is the mechanism that spearheads established donors' development agenda; it is the body of policy consultations and coordination and lays out principles and guidelines for its member states. Among them is the criterion for evaluating development assistance: relevance, effectiveness, efficiency, impact and sustainability.[12] And the emphasis it places on aid recipients' governance is clearly enunciated.[13] The basic difference between the established donor community and the emerging donors can be summed up by the words 'governance' and 'concessionality'. According to Courtney Meyer, 'the emerging donors have begun to establish a new status quo, one without policy strings attached and one which focuses on infrastructure, innovation, exports and health, rather than governance'.[14]

Among the emerging donors, China is the most important provider of aid to Africa that resembles ODA provided by the OECD DAC, and according to one study, China's share represented about 76% of the total commitments from the seven emerging donors for Africa over the period from 2003 to 2012.[15] Hence, the role of China's aid to Africa and its implications on the current aid architecture in Africa will be an interesting and noteworthy theme of Africa's development. There is a need to view the relationship between traditional donors and emerging donors in terms of possible partnership, but basically the relationship is seen as being competitive. Yet, in reality, they can be complementary in nature, even enabling some kind of division of labour. But forging a meaningful and systemic collaboration between the two donor groups, while ideal, would be not so likely, at least in the near future, for the following reasons: (1) political and strategic calculations; (2) a technical logjam; and (3) inherent limitations in the capacity of recipient countries. However, some degree of de facto division of labour can emerge, given the basic differences in their fields of assistance.

From the traditional donors' perspective, their aid 'leverage' towards African countries could be curtailed if countries like China, which pursues a fundamentally different aid approach compared to the OECD DAC, provides African countries with an alternative to traditional donors' aid. Some leaders even express publicly that the West's support mostly goes into 'consumptive' areas that do not yield sustainable economic benefits and want Western countries to invest more in infrastructure building like China. Many Sub-Saharan Africans admit that their leaders have been trying to play the West off against other non-Western players to elicit as much benefit from all these countries as possible.

How much commonality in substance will the BRICS countries find with one another and whether BRICS will prevail as a coherent and forceful body wielding influence on the global stage is still uncertain. This is true because China, India, Russia, Brazil and South Africa all derive their economic power and status from their links with the global economic system in which the Western world is dominant; furthermore, these countries' interests and positions could diverge more than converge when it comes to regional and international politics.

The 10th BRICS summit that was held in July 2018 in South Africa gathered many African heads of state as the host, South Africa, was promoting BRICS-Africa business and investment. The summit was held under the theme: 'BRICS in Africa: Collaboration for Inclusive Growth and Shared Prosperity in the Fourth Industrial Revolution'. As expected, China's investment charm offensive highlighted the event, along with the call for free trade and multilateralism by the participants. Many African leaders voiced their wish to collaborate with BRICS for employment opportunities for the youth, industrialization and infrastructure development.

The traditional donors, in principle, may want to espouse China and draw it closer to the OECD DAC framework. However, considering China's strategic stance in Africa as well as its foreign policy orientations, I see little reason why China would want to adapt itself to the OECD DAC regime, which essentially reflects Western values. In this sense, everyone—traditional donors, China and other emerging donors, and Sub-Saharan African countries—would all want to maintain the status quo because the current dynamics in regional aid architecture serve their interests under the given circumstances.

The 'technical logjam' that I mentioned above relate to the difficulty of coordinating aid policy among donors. Given that aid coordination is difficult enough among the OECD DAC members, we can only imagine how challenging will it be to coordinate both the OECD DAC members and emerging donors. The third element, 'inherent limitations in the capacity of recipient countries', is another reason why concerted action or coordination between traditional donors and emerging donors will not easily occur. Donors do not simply give away aid and African countries do not simply take aid as it comes. Both sides have to work out arrangements and plans, and follow procedures. If the two groups were to engage in some sort of consultation or coordination mechanism with regard to aid plans for Africa, naturally, aid recipient African countries would have to be brought on board as well.

ODA is here to stay, despite all the criticisms it has attracted. Considering the trend and the demand of African countries, in all likelihood, the amount of global ODA will continue to increase for the foreseeable future, barring extraordinary circumstances like a drastic downturn in the global economy. The proliferation of donors means that while it would be difficult to establish formal coordination mechanisms among donors, nonetheless, some kind of donor 'inter-connectivity' could emerge across the board, leading to a de facto 'division of labour' among donors.

The growth of donors and inter-connectivity or inter-dependence among various donors or donor groups also needs to be considered. There is no denying that today's engine for economic growth is global free trade and investment, and that the rise of emerging economies is attributable to them being closely integrated into the global economy. Different countries with different political regimes may have different ways of running their economies, but the universal ticket to national pre-eminence depends on wealth creation and this can only come by actively engaging in global economic transactions.

In this regard, China draws our attention in light of its perceived growing influence and assertiveness on the global stage and especially its aggressiveness in advancing into African markets. Is China a rival, a potential threat to the existing development norm and order or can it be a benign force, a constructive partner of traditional donors? Economically, China's growth has been possible by taking advantage of the global market economy, and many countries have also benefited from China's economic power. The trend seems to be that China is economically increasingly linked to the world. When I visited the Brookings Institute in July 2009, I found an interesting book entitled *Power and Responsibility* in its bookstore. This book advocated resurrecting US global leadership by building partnerships and institutions for cooperation with traditional and emerging powers, mindful, as the authors pointed out, that rising powers such as China 'recognize that their economic growth relies on a strong and resilient international and finance system'.[16]

With respect to China's economic rise, the principal architects of US foreign policy at that time seemed to have concluded that there was no cause for concern as long as China was integrated into the prevailing international regimes. Their logic was that the US might no longer be the hegemonic superpower it once was, but that it has sufficient power to lead the world through smart multilateralism. This seems to be the correct perspective. Joseph Nye asserts in his book *Is the American Century Over?* that the US will remain the strongest power in the world, with no visible sign that its status will be altered in the foreseeable future. He recognizes that China poses the biggest challenge to the US, but China still lags considerably behind it in the three aspects of power: military, economic and soft power.[17]

On the third point that there should be a division of labour among donors, we should see this from the standpoint of international collaboration and coordination, being mindful of the difference in the 'lifetime experiences' of donors. To a certain extent, this is already happening in a natural way, as donors would have certain areas of expertise that they would wish to impart to developing countries.

Notes

1. Yemi Lalude, 'There Is Huge Entrepreneurial Energy in Africa; How Do We Harness It?', in 'Opinion', *The East African* (weekly newspaper), 6–12 May 2017, p. 15.
2. Harry Boyte, 'Conversations on Democracy—The John Dewey Society and Civic Studies', *Huffpost* (blog), 27 April 2016, https://www.huffingtonpost.com/harry-boyte/conversations-on-democrac_b_9776550.html?guccounter=1.
3. Erik Thorbecke, 'The Evolution of the Development Doctrine and the Role of Foreign Aid, 1950–2000,' in Fin Tarp (ed.), *Foreign Aid and Development: Lessons Learnt and Directions for the Future* (London: Routledge, 2000), pp. 17–45.
4. The 17 SDGs are: (Goal 1) end poverty in all its forms everywhere; (Goal 2) end hunger, achieve food security and improved nutrition and promote sustainable agriculture; (Goal 3) ensure healthy lives and promote wellbeing for all at all ages; (Goal 4) ensure inclusive and equitable quality education and promote lifelong learning opportunities for all; (Goal 5) achieve gender equality and empower all women and girls; (Goal 6) ensure availability and sustainable management of water and sanitation for all; (Goal 7) ensure access to affordable, reliable, sustainable and modern energy for all; (Goal 8) promote sustained, inclusive and sustainable economic growth, full and productive employment and decent work for all; (Goal 9) build resilient infrastructure, promote inclusive and sustainable industrialization and foster innovation; (Goal 10) reduce inequality within and among countries; (Goal 11) make cities and human settlements inclusive, safe, resilient and sustainable;

(Goal 12) ensure sustainable consumption and production patterns; (Goal 13) take urgent action to combat climate change and its impacts; (Goal 14) conserve and sustainably use the oceans, seas and marine resources for sustainable development; (Goal 15) protect, restore and promote sustainable use of terrestrial ecosystems, sustainably manage forests, combat desertification, and halt and reverse land degradation and halt biodiversity loss; (Goal 16) promote peaceful and inclusive societies for sustainable development, provide access to justice for all and build effective, accountable and inclusive institutions at all levels; (Goal 17) strengthen the means of implementation and revitalize the global partnership for sustainable development.

5. Kang Seonjou, 'Adoption of Post-2015 Sustainable Development Goals (SDGs) and its Implications for Development Cooperation Diplomacy', *International Analysis*, No. 2015–29 (23 October 2015), Institute of Foreign Affairs and National Security, Republic of Korea (Korean).
6. 'What have the millennium development goals achieved?', *The Guardian*, 6 July 2015. The UN released the final assessment of MDGs on 6 July 2015 (http://www.un.org/millenniumgoals/2015_MDG_Report/pdf/MDG%20report%202015%20presentation_final.pdf).
7. The term 'Samaritan's dilemma' was coined by the economist James M. Buchanan. See James M. Buchanan, 'The Samaritan's dilemma', in E.S. Phelps (ed.), *Altruism, Morality and Economic Theory* (New York: Russell Sage Foundation, 1975), pp. 71–85.
8. 'Aid spending by Development Assistance Committee (DAC) donors in 2016', *Development Initiatives*, 12 April 2017, http://devinit.org/post/aid-spending–by-development-assistance-committee-dac-donors-in-2016.
9. 'The rise of new foreign aid donors: why does it matter?', *Devpolicyblog*, 4 August 2017, http://devpolicy.org/rise-new-foreign-aid-donors-matter-20170804.
10. Of seven emerging donors, China's ODA-like aid represented about 76% of the total of this group over the period from 2003 to 2012, according to the EU Commission's paper 'The European Union, Africa and New Donors: Moving Towards New Partnership', Highlights (2015). Monday, 11 May. https://ec.europa.eu/europaaid/sites/devco/files/com-411-africa-final_highlights_11052015_en.pdf.

11. 'Estimating China's Foreign Aid 2001–2013', *Working Paper*, JICA-RI, JICA USA May/June 2014, https://www.jica.go.jp/usa/english/office/others/newsletter/2014/1405_06_02.html.
12. The DAC Principles for the Evaluation of Development Assistance, OECD (1991).
13. http://www.oecd.org/dac/accountable-effective-institutions.
14. Courtney Meyer, 'Emerging Donors: Ushering in a New Aid Era?', *Think Africa Press*, 25 July 2012.
15. EU, 'The European Union, Africa and New Donors: Moving Towards New Partnership', 2015.
16. Bruce D. Jones, Carlos Pascual, and Stephen John Stedman, *Power and Responsibility: Building International Order in an Era of Transnational Threats* (Washington, DC: Brookings Institution Press, 2009), p. 23.
17. Joseph S. Nye, Jr., *Is The American Century Over?* (Malden: Polity Press, 2015).

Part IV

Understanding Korean Development Model

7

Korea's Path of Development in Retrospect

Historical Background, Liberation and State Building

There is an advantage in studying the Korean case of development because it provides a clear-cut picture of economic transition due to its 'compressed' story or timeframe of dynamic economic development spanning only 50 years. There are different ways to describe and analyse its phases of development. First, it can be divided into decades: (1) the 1950s: post-war reconstruction; (2) the 1960s: laying the groundwork for a self-supporting economy; (3) the 1970s: upgrading industrial structure and rural development; (4) the 1980s: transition to an open and liberal economy; (5) the 1990s: globalization and structural adjustment.[1] Or we can divide the period into: (1) liberation and state-building (1948–1959); (2) export promotion and industrialization (1960–1979); (3) stabilization and liberalization (1980–1997); and (4) economic crisis to the present day (1997–).[2] Another way of defining the phases can be as follows: (1) state-building; (2) economic take-off; (3) policy adjustments and liberalization; and (4) new challenges and policy responses.[3]

J.-D. Park, *Re-Inventing Africa's Development*,
https://doi.org/10.1007/978-3-030-03946-2_7

At this juncture, it would be useful to briefly sketch Korea's historical heritage. One thing that stands out on the global map is that Korea is a nation in the Far East surrounded by neighbours much bigger than itself. Moreover, it is the divided nation and there is a psyche among Koreans and outsiders that Korea is a small country. But when the area of the Korean Peninsula, South and North Korea combined, which is about 220,000 square kilometres, into account, it is not actually undersized as it approximates the size of the UK or Italy. In terms of population, South Korea's population is over 50 million and North Korea has over 24 million, making a total of 74 million, which is larger than that of UK, France or Italy and a little less than Germany, which stands at 81 million.

Historically, Korean society is a composition of varied peoples who gradually forged together culturally and ethnically as a homogeneous nation. Scholars point out that the core cultural traditions of Korea are shamanism and Confucianism: its shamanism was able to survive into modern times and has influenced the Korean way of life in general and its 'sub-consciousness', while Confucianism (or Neo-Confucianism to be more precise) has heavily influenced the social consciousness and cultural orientations of the majority of Koreans for many centuries.[4] Kyong Ju Kim points out that: 'In Korean Shamanism, the notion of absolute truth and goodness is denied. Everything is placed on a continuum … and everything can change depending on the vicissitudes of society and nature.'[5]

Korea has only been divided since 1945, when it was effectively partitioned by the US and the Soviet Union following the end of Japanese colonial rule. Before this division, Korea was one of the oldest continuously unified states in the world. The Korean Peninsula became unified in 676 and remained so until the mid-20th century. And today, it is considered as one of the most homogeneous nation on earth. Korean people merged into a single ethnicity sharing one language. It was their language in particular that bound them together and distinguished them from their neighbours.

There were times when China seemed to wield considerable influence over Korea, and Korea imported China's ideas about government and politics, as well as its culture, but Korea maintained its independence, cultural distinctiveness and national identity:

> Koreans were fiercely independent. Much of their history has been the story of resistance to outside intruders. Korea's position as a tributary state was usually ceremonial, and for Koreans it did not imply a loss of autonomy. Chinese attempts to interfere in domestic affairs were met with opposition. Indeed, some today view the Korean past as a saga of the struggles of a smaller society to resist control or assimilation by larger, more aggressive neighbours.[6]

Another notable feature of Korea is the remarkable continuity of its history:

> From seventh to the twentieth century only three dynasties ruled Korea. The second ruled for almost five centuries and the third for more than five centuries; both were among the longest-ruling dynasties in history. The two dynastic changes that did take place did not bring about a vast upheaval. Elite families as well as institutions were carried over from one dynasty to another. This, along with a Confucian concern for examining the past, contributed to a strong sense of historical consciousness among Koreans.[7]

In the nineteenth century, Korea remained a 'Hermit Kingdom' adamantly opposed to Western demands for diplomatic and trade relations. Over time, a few Asian and European countries with imperialistic ambitions competed with each other for influence over the Korean Peninsula. Japan, after winning wars against China and Russia, forcibly annexed Korea and instituted colonial rule in 1910. The colonization process stimulated the patriotism of Koreans. Korean intellectuals were infuriated by Japan's cultural assimilation policy, which even banned Korean-language education in schools. On 1 March 1919, a peaceful demonstration demanding independence spread nationwide. Although it failed, the 1 March independence movement created a strong bond of national identity and patriotism among Koreans, and led to the establishment of a provisional government in Shanghai, China, as well as an organized armed struggle against the Japanese colonialists in Manchuria.

Koreans rejoiced at Japan's defeat in the Second World War in 1945. However, their joy was short-lived as the liberation did not instantly bring about the independence for which the Koreans had fought so fiercely. Rather, it resulted in a country divided by ideological differences wrought by the emergence of the Cold War. Korean efforts to establish an independent government were delayed as the US forces occupied the southern half of the peninsula and Soviet troops took control of the northern half.

In November 1947, the UN General Assembly adopted a resolution calling for general elections in Korea under the supervision of a UN commission. But the Soviet Union refused to comply with the resolution and denied the UN commission's access to the northern half of Korea. The UN General Assembly then adopted another resolution calling for elections in areas accessible to its commission. The first elections in Korea was carried out on 10 May 1948 south of the 38th parallel, and accordingly the new government was inaugurated on 15 August. Meanwhile, the communist regime was set up on 9 September with the support of the Soviet Union.

The American military government, which was in charge of South Korea between 1945 and 1948, tried to introduce a modern market economy system there. The sale of confiscated Japanese-owned properties during the US military rule was an important first step towards establishing a market economy based on private property ownership. Divesture continued under the newly established Korean government and sales reached the peak during the Korean War in the early 1950s. By 1958, as a result, most Japanese-owned properties were converted into privately owned assets. Such an achievement is deemed significant in light of the tendency towards socialism, even on the part of right-wing politicians, at the time.[8]

It is said that the colonial government's land surveys and registration conducted in the 1910s established the first modern system of property rights in Korea, which significantly reduced land transaction costs. But measures to protect small farmers were not followed, leading to a wide disparity in land holdings. After independence, the Korean government tackled the increasing demand for agricultural land reform by enacting the Farmland Reform Act in 1949 and revising it in 1950. The land reform was based on the principle of 'compensated forfeiture and non-free distribution', whereby the government bought farmland from landlords at predetermined prices and sold it to farmers at below-market prices.

Agricultural land reform contributed not only to state-building, but also to redistributing wealth and reducing income inequalities. Everyone was now placed on a more or less equal footing, and individual effort and ability rather than family wealth became the most important determinant for people's success. Many believe that the Koreans' typical diligence and their emphasis on education were motivated by this perception of equal opportunity. However, on the negative side, restrictions on farmland holdings hampered the growth of large-scale farming and contributed to the low productivity growth of the agricultural sector in later years.[9]

Syngman Rhee, an intellectual educated in the US and former independence fighter, was elected as the first President of the Republic of Korea in 1948. His foresight was instrumental in establishing a separate government in South Korea, laying the groundwork for a democracy and a market economy. He strived to rebuild the economy with a series of reconstruction plans aimed at expanding economic infrastructure, building key industries like cement and steel, and increasing the production capability of manufacturing.

Rhee's desire to construct a self-sufficient Korean economy with such plans was in direct conflict with the US government's intention to rebuild an East Asian economic bloc with industrialized Japan at its centre. The US urged Korea to liberalize its market, stabilize the value of the Korean currency and expand cooperation with Japan. To Rhee, this implied nothing but the revival of the Greater East Asian Co-Prosperity Sphere and the re-colonization of the Korean economy. Rhee made full use of Korea's geopolitical value to frustrate America's efforts, while promoting import-substitution industries through reconstruction plans.[10]

The Korean government also differed with the Americans on the issue of what kind of foreign aid it would receive. The Korean government preferred project assistance, while the US government wanted to provide non-project assistance to private enterprises for civilian use. In the end, the preference of the US prevailed, with non-project assistance making up 73% of the total, while project assistance made up only 27%. In any event, various reconstruction plans envisioned by Rhee's administration failed to spark economic growth in Korea, as they were not substantively executed.[11]

On 25 June 1950, North Korea launched an unprovoked invasion into the South, triggering a three-year war that devastated the nation, with millions losing their lives. In the South, 42–44% of manufacturing facilities and 40–60% of power-generating capacity were destroyed. Basic infrastructure like housing, schools, health centres, water and sewage, roads and communication facilities were utterly razed. The scale of total civilian damage reported was bigger (1.05 times) than Korea's GNP of 1953.[12]

Hence, the economic policy objective was then to bring the nation back to life from the ashes of war, restoring and rebuilding basic infrastructures, and stabilizing people's livelihoods. In order to do this, massive funding was necessary, but the only thing Korea could do was to turn to foreign assistance. From 1945 to 1960, South Korea received a total of $2.94 billion in aid, of which the amount provided by the US accounted for over 80%.[13] Although the government tried hard to build the necessary structures for industrialization, there was an inherent limitation in that Korea's economic performance in the 1950s was wholly dependent on foreign assistance, the vast majority of which came from the US

The US aid comprised projects, non-projects and technical assistance: projects were mainly for the restoration or expansion of social infrastructure like power, communications, transportation, education and health facilities; non-projects mainly included the supply of necessities such as wheat, oil, fertilizer, raw rubber, spun rayon, medicine, etc.; technical assistance was minimal in terms of scale and involved training and consulting. The ratio of projects to non-projects was around 4 to 1 on average.[14]

In the post-war reconstruction period, the government's economic policy focused on rehabilitation following destruction, and its efforts to curb inflation was largely successful. The assistance provided by the US was crucial, but there were also friction between Korea and the US over the usage of aid funds. While the Korean government wanted to use the resources to purchase more equipment and build factories, the US insisted on allocating them primarily for commodities and raw materials to increase the counterpart fund. Non-project aid (the commodities), were sold to civilians and the profits were turned into a counterpart fund that was in turn used for reconstruction projects.

Rhee was finally ousted from power in 1960 by student demonstrations protesting against his protracted rule and election frauds as he was strengthening his authoritarian rule. The situation deteriorated when many demonstrators were shot by the police. Rhee announced he was stepping down and took refuge in Hawaii. Shortly afterwards, the Constitution was amended and the cabinet system and bicameral national assembly were adopted.

Under the new Constitution, the regime led by Prime Minister Jang Myeon was launched, but the political situation became extremely fragile with political struggles and protests by students continuing unabated. In May 1961, a group of young army officers led by General Park Chung-Hee seized power in a military coup. In the presidential election that was held in October 1963, after two years of military rule, Park Chung-Hee, having retired from the military, was elected President and was inaugurated in December.

The Economic Take-off Period

The government led by President Park set up a five-year economic development plan under the slogan of 'modernization of the fatherland' and achieved rapid economic growth by implementing an export-oriented policy. Subsequently, a heavy and chemical industries (HCI) plan was boldly but successfully launched.

In the following decades, Korea achieved unparalleled economic growth. It was one of the poorest countries in the world in 1948 when the government was formed following independence from Japan. Korea is considered a unique case of an aid recipient having successfully turned into an advanced country in terms of full-scale economic transformation and democratization in the latter half of the 20th century. Korea's rapid development has been dubbed 'the Miracle on the Han River'. This began with the all-out efforts launched in the 1960s. The country vigorously pushed ahead with the development of national land, the construction of the Gyeongbu Expressway and subway lines, the Pohang Iron and Steel Company (POSCO), and the creation of heavy and chemical industry.

After having become President, Park proclaimed that economic development would be the central feature of his administration. He and his policy team were well aware of the importance to reaping economic success in order to legitimize their seizure of power by force. The new government set out to depart from the foreign aid-dependent economy and lay the groundwork for a self-sustaining economy so as to terminate the vicious cycle of poverty and to realize high economic growth. Although Korea at that time was a predominantly agricultural nation and food shortages were serious, the government focused on industrialization. In the early 1960s, over 40% of the Korean population was suffering from absolute poverty and the government believed that the only way to offset this was by achieving high growth through industrialization.[15]

It seemed that the regime did not have a clear ideology or scheme on free market economy from the very outset, but somehow it managed to adopt active export promotion, which in effect turned out to be a critical factor for its resounding performance. Initially, export promotion was pursued in response to the rapid depletion of foreign exchange reserves.[16] Exports began to quickly increase following the devaluation of the currency in 1960 and, encouraged by the success, the government undertook more serious efforts to promote exports in 1964–1965. First, a new exchange rate regime was put in place in 1964, and various ad hoc export subsidies and the export-import link system were phased out, while a comprehensive and consistent export incentive mechanism was introduced. Key measures were export credits that were extended to exporters who turned in letters of credit, and tariff exemptions on imports of intermediate inputs. And these incentives were reinforced by administrative measures like 'export targeting', the holding of monthly export promotion meetings, the establishment of the Korea Trade Association and the Korea Trade Promotion Agency, etc.[17]

Industrialization was the focus of the five-year economic plans that began in 1962. With the first five-year plan (1962–1967), the government laid out its ambition to modernize the industrial sector and enhance its international competitiveness by rapidly expanding the key areas (cement, fertilizer, industrial machinery, oil refineries, etc.).[18] The government promoted exports, but maintained restrictions on imports to contain current account deficits and protect domestic industries. Tariff rates began to decline slowly in the early 1970s, but their levels remained high until the early 1980s.

In the early 1960s, the government increased its intervention in domestic financial markets to support the economic growth strategy. It took full command of commercial and special banks, while strengthening its grip on the central bank. The primary role of the monetary authorities during the government-led growth period was to supply 'growth money' and price stabilization was treated as being a far lower priority. One of the key measures was the credit programme: by controlling the financial sector, the authorities were able to provide vast amount of directed credit with low interest rates and share the investment risk with private enterprises.

In pursuing the five-year development plans, the most fundamental problem the Korean government confronted was the question of how to come up with the funding. To encourage domestic savings from which capital can be funnelled to development projects, interest rates were raised substantially in 1965 to match the demand and supply of capital. Accordingly, savings grew rapidly. In addition, the taxation system was reformed and strengthened in 1966, greatly increasing revenues. These encouraged an active pursuit of development projects and government expenditure was greatly enhanced.

But the major injection of the necessary funds had to come from abroad and there was a large increase in foreign borrowing during this period. While foreign capital inflow was encouraged to fill the gap in domestic savings, capital liberalization remained selective and partial. What was of significance in terms of the accumulation of capital funds was the agreement reached between Korea and Japan in 1966 to normalize their diplomatic ties in return for Japan's reparation payments of $500 million and commercial loans of $300 million. The payments were used to build the POSCO and make investments in various sectors.

The success of the first five-year plan encouraged the government to continue pushing ahead with its ambitious plans. The emphasis of the second five-year plan (1967–1971) was placed on HCIs, including the steel, machinery and petrochemical industries. The Steel Industry Promotion Act was enacted in 1969 to support the construction of a large-scale integrated iron and steel mill and other kinds of mills by granting them tax exemptions. For other industries, similar laws were introduced to provide financial and tax incentives: the Machinery Industry Promotion Act (1967), the Shipbuilding Industry Promotion Act (1967), the Textile Industry Modernization Act (1967), the Petrochemical Industry Promotion Act (1970) and the Nonferrous Metal Producing Business Act (1971).

What the government considered as particularly important then and which later proved to be a strategic move was the construction of an integrated iron and steel mill and a petrochemical complex. The Pohang Iron and Steel Company (currently POSCO) and Ulsan petrochemical complex, which were built in the early 1970s, had to rely almost entirely on foreign technology and capital, and they faced a multitude of difficulties at the outset.[19] Meanwhile, a Korean oil refinery had already been built as early as 1964.

In hindsight, Korea undertook a very bold and seemingly inconceivable number of projects of such magnitude despite of its 'capacity', but it successfully undertook what other developing nations were not able to do, which is the 'synchronization' of all fronts of industrialization. And this was done despite doubt, disapproval and reluctance on the part of donors. But scepticism turned into praise as Korea continued to deliver results that far exceeded the international community's as well as its own expectations.

Projects were also vigorously pursued to ease the shortage in the economic infrastructure, like power and roads. What is remarkable is the fact that soon after electric power development projects were launched from 1962, the supply of electric power came to exceed demand by the mid-1960s. Another major accomplishment to facilitate economic activity was the construction of roads, the most noticeable being the completion of major expressways: the Seoul-Incheon, Seoul-Busan and Honam Expressways were opened in 1968, 1970 and 1973, respectively.

The economic achievement in the 1960s was a resounding success in view of the situation in which Korea found itself. Despite various challenges, Korea was able to fulfil the first and second five-year development plans with a level of performance exceeding targets and expectations. The GDP growth registered 8.5% and manufacturing sector growth 17.0% on average during the 1960s; per-capita income jumped from USD 82 in 1961 to USD 253 in 1970, a threefold increase. Unemployment rate fell from 8.1% in 1963 to 4.4% in 1970. The driving force behind rapid industrialization was strong exports. During 1962–1971, exports increased annually by 38.6% on average. And the timing was just right, with the favourable international trade environment in the 1960s.[20]

Korea made good use of labour, which it had in abundance, and also financial capital, which was scarce and had to be borrowed from overseas. The light industries of labour-intensive manufacturing such as wig-making, clothing and footwear absorbed the surplus labour force discharged from rural areas. As these industries launched their production in industrial complexes near urban areas, they also contributed to the growth of large cities and the urbanization of the population.

The success in building up a manufacturing industry in Korea was due to a number of factors, including the entrepreneurial skills of early generations of pioneering businessmen who started as small traders, and the unlimited supply of labour from the agricultural sector that generated explosive growth in the light industry sector. Wage levels in Korea were one of the lowest in the world, and the workers were relatively well-educated and diligent, making labour-intensive industries of Korea competitive.[21]

Rather than restraining its ambitions, the government launched a full-scale drive towards HCIs in 1973. Six strategic industries—steel, nonferrous metal, machinery, shipbuilding, electronics, and chemical engineering—were selected under the HCI initiative.[22] The committee to drive forward HCIs was created and the targets were set to achieve per-capita income of USD 1000 and annual exports of USD 10 billion. The reasons for adopting HCI drive were twofold: national security and the need to upgrade industrialization to ensure exportation. First, concerns about national security grew with North Korea's increased military provocations and US government's announcement in 1968 that its ground troops would be gradually pulled out of Korea. Second, the government felt it was necessary to upgrade the industrial structure to compete with newly industrializing countries over export markets.[23]

In the 1970s, compared to the 1960s, the level of wages, savings and exports all increased, along with the heightening of industrialization. As wage levels rose and competition from low-wage economies intensified, capital-intensive, high-productivity manufacturing assumed importance over labour-intensive, low-productivity manufacturing. The share of services increased continuously in terms of both value-addition and employment, while that of agriculture declined. Within manufacturing, HCIs increased their share at the expense of light industries. Meanwhile, the domestic saving ratio increased from an average of 15 in 1961–1970 to 23% in 1971–1980, while the investment ratio increased from 19 to 29% respectively in these periods.

The focus of industrial policy shifted from the export drive in the 1960s to the building of HCIs in the 1970s. To successfully undertake an ambitious task of upscaling industrialization, the government intervened more forcefully in the economy in the 1970s. The HCIs required not only enormous capital but also significant technological expertise. Very few, if any, Korean firms were able to take up such a task without the proactive support of the government. The Vietnam War became another source of foreign currency income to support industrialization as Korea received US economic aid for its military participation in this war. The government's bold intervention and active support led to the inflow of investment in HCIs. The growth of HCIs registered an average of 20.0% over the period from 1971 to 1979, driving the growth of the overall manufacturing sector, which stood at 18.2% over the same period.

In summary, what Korea was able to achieve in the 1960s and 1970s is unique and unmatched in the history of industrialization and development. The growth was led by the manufacturing sector, the output of which grew annually by 17% in the 1960s and 16% in the 1970s. Korea was considered to be a high-risk country in the international capital market, so it experienced difficulties in terms of finding lenders. Furthermore, because its natural resources were not abundant, Korea only had human resources to rely on to build the economy: an abundant labour force and the hard work of the people.

The role of the government was critical in accelerating the growth of manufacturing. During the first and the second five-year economic development plans that were undertaken in the 1960s, the government invested heavily in physical infrastructure to lay the foundations for export-driven industrialization. It established state-owned enterprises in key industries and mobilized other policy measures, involving foreign exchange, taxation, finance and customs regulations to promote exports.

The export structure underwent dramatic changes. In 1970, the primary industries amounted to 17%, the light industries 70% and the HCIs 13% of total exports. By 2008, these shares changed to 2, 6 and 92% respectively. The share in the gross value addition of sectors also underwent huge changes (comparison between 1953–1960 and 2001–2009): agriculture 41.9 → 3.4%; manufacturing and mining 13.4 → 27.3% (it reached 30.0% in 1987); public utilities construction 3.7 → 9.6%; and services 41.1 → 59.6%.[24]

This pattern of structural change is similar to that experienced in other developed countries. It has been pointed out that the industrial structure of Korea in the early 1960s was comparable to that of the UK in 1700, the US before 1880 and Japan in the early decades of the twentieth century. In all these countries, during the process of industrialization, the manufacturing and service industries replaced the agricultural sector in terms of their importance to the national economy. What sets Korea apart from these developed countries is the speed with which it achieved structural changes. Korea's industrial structure in 1990 came close to that of the UK in 1890, the US in 1950 and Japan in 1970.[25]

Korea's phenomenal economic growth in the 1960s and 1970s, accompanied by economic and industrial structural changes, placed it on the path of transformation that other advanced countries had taken. Exports and industrialization are not the only things that were pursued actively by the government; vigorous campaigns were waged for rural development (*Saemaul Undong*) and the promotion and application of agricultural technology (the Green Revolution and the White Revolution) that benefited and enhanced the productivity of this sector. All these measures contributed to the economic growth and modernity of the nation.

The pace and energy with which the massive mobilization of labour and capital, heavy investment in technology and the effective reallocation of resources from less to more productive sectors were carried out made the difference. But what Korea was always conscious of and targeting was foreign trade and markets. For Korea, foreign trade played a pivotal role by encouraging innovation and accelerating resource reallocation, learning from advanced countries and taking advantage of the rapidly expanding global market.

The Period of Policy Adjustments and Liberalization

The 1980s marked an important turning point in the economic development strategy of Korea. The government's deep intervention in allocating resources in the 1960s and 1970s was the crystallization of a state-led economic development strategy. The impetus behind the five-year economic development plans was the role played by the government, with markets playing 'supplementary' roles. This was deemed inevitable in the early stages of development where the market mechanism was imperfect.

However, as Korea's economic scale grew and the role of the private sector increased, it became harder for the decision-making of bureaucrats alone to manage the allocation of resources. Thus, entering into the 1980s, the thinking in the government was that the greater involvement of the private sector and markets was necessary. Among other things, this was especially so in light of the side-effects of the HCI drive in the 1970s: misallocation of resources (excess and duplicate investments), inflation and income inequality.

Tackling inflation had been a concern of the government as early as 1978, but the new government formed in 1980 took up the task of stabilizing the economy much more prominently.[26] A radical departure from the past was made in the early 1980s, as the government emphasized price stability over economic growth. The 'growth-first' strategy gave way to 'consolidating growth on the basis of stability'. Private initiatives were encouraged and liberalization of the market began. Greater attention was paid to social policies, and public spending on health, welfare and education was increased.

Of course, there were downsides to such an aggressive growth strategy. Reconciling rapid growth, concentration of resources and efficiency on one the hand, and equality, stability and fairness on the other would not be an easy task in any case, and all the more so for a newly developing country with scant resources. Still, a factor that was in Korea's favour was that the transitions were swift and progressive, in effect considerably mitigating the overall 'costs' of fast-paced development.

The commonly cited problems faced by Korea during this period are as follows: financial repression since the 1960s that held back the financial sector from developing into a fully competitive service industry; large business conglomerates, namely the *chaebols*, increasing their influence on the back of government support; increasing economic disparity amid the phenomenon of concentration of economic wealth and power; and a failure to establish sound worker–management relations (until labour movements arose in the mid-1980s).

Corporations also wanted greater autonomy from economic institutions. The financial market became increasingly liberalized in the 1980s and early 1990s, particularly as many *chaebols* that were the proprietors of non-bank financial institutions demanded deregulation. Deregulation began to emerge as an important priority in the late 1980s and continued to be addressed seriously in the 1990s.[27]

Meanwhile, import liberalization measures were announced in 1978, but progress proved sluggish owing to the second oil shock that picked up speed in 1984. In 1986, Korea registered a current account surplus for the first time and the surplus increased in the following years. In 1989, the government began to reduce quantitative restrictions amid intensifying trade conflict with the US. As Korea's trade performance and economic status improved, in January 1990, it moved into a different category of the General Agreement on Tariffs and Trade (GATT) provision and was no longer allowed to impose trade restrictions for balance-of-payment purposes. The average tariff rate dropped from 34.4 to 9.8%, while import liberalization from quantitative restrictions increased from 60.7 to 92.0% between 1981 and 1995.[28]

Compared to trade liberalization, the opening of the capital market was markedly slow, as there was a major concern over the control of the domestic money supply and the real exchange rate movement. When the current account showed large deficits in the late 1970s and early 1980s, restrictions were strengthened on capital outflows. But when the current account moved into a considerable surplus in the latter half of the 1980s, the government relaxed restrictions on outward FDI while tightening other regulations. The public sector halted borrowing from abroad and started to repay foreign debts. Then in 1990–1993, the government began liberalizing long-term capital inflows.

In November 1997, a foreign exchange crisis hit the country, forcing it to turn to the IMF for a bailout. This was the first ordeal Korea had to face after decades of rapid economic growth. The crisis was such a great shock as it was totally unforeseen. Even immediately before the outbreak of the crisis, there were no warning signs or abnormalities that could be detected. Foreign exchange reserves were quickly depleted and a drastic devaluation of the currency ensued as international creditors rushed to withdraw their loans to Korean banks. Many explanations have been put forward for this, ranging from the weak fundamentals of the Korean economy, including 'crony capitalism', to the intrinsic instability of international financial markets.[29]

At the time, Korea's macroeconomic indicators were sound, but there was an external shock coming from a worsened terms-of-trade shock wrought by plummeting semi-conductor prices and a substantial increase in external liabilities (especially short-term ones). The increase in non-performing loans and the low profitability of businesses led to the bankruptcy of *chaebols* and the general shortage in liquidity afflicted businesses. The Asian regional financial crisis exacerbated the situation for

Korea, so that the international credit rating agencies began to downgrade Korea, causing the financial crisis fallout at the end of November 1997.

The crisis inflicted extreme hardship on the Korean people, but worked as a catalyst for improving the fundamentals of the economy. The IMF bailout required Korea to undertake austere economic measures and wide-ranging structural reforms. The sudden depreciation of the Korean currency wreaked havoc on businesses and the austerity policies were difficult to bear and unpopular. But the nation, led by the new administration of Kim Dae-Jung, faced the challenge head-on. Poorly performing businesses were driven out of the market and industrial restructuring was pushed ahead. In just two years, the country recovered its previous growth rate, levels and current account surplus. In the process, some 3.5 million people joined in the campaign to collect gold to help the government repay the fund borrowed from the IMF, something unheard of in global history.

The Korean economy came out of the crisis in an entirely different shape: it became much more open to international capital flows; transparency of corporate management was substantially enhanced; and the functioning of financial market improved substantially.[30]

New Challenges and Policy Responses

Despite Korea's remarkable economic success in the past, concerns have been raised on the growth potential of the Korean economy. Economic growth began to slow down in the 1990s with the decelerating growth of the working-age population. Income distribution also started to deteriorate in the early 1990s, with the expansion of the knowledge-based economy and globalization leaving low-skilled workers at a disadvantage. At the same time, productivity gaps between manufacturing and services, between HCIs and light industries, and between large and small companies widened, and access to quality jobs has become more difficult.

In 2008, Korea was hit by another financial crisis, this time a global one, coming from the heart of Wall Street, the global financial centre. Korean financial markets were thrown into disarray. The sudden capital outflow led to a plunge in the stock market and domestic banks faced serious difficulties in foreign debt servicing. A precipitous fall in exports and investment also battered the industrial sector. But the repercussions were considerably less painful than had been the case in 1997, as Korea's economic output went back into positive growth in the first quarter of 2009. This time Korea was able to recover from the crisis even more rapidly because, among other reasons, the vulnerability of the financial and corporate sectors had been reduced as a result of the reforms and restructuring that had been undertaken following the 1997 crisis.

From the standpoint of maintaining economic competitiveness, Korea has confronted two basic challenges since the 1990s: technology development and market opening. Korea had to tackle the reality of developed countries not wanting to transfer advanced technology to newly industrialized nations like itself, while also having to worry about new competitors. It decided that the best way to respond was to develop new industries based on new technologies, while improving the technology for existing industries so that their productivity could be boosted.

In the early phases of development, Korea was able to benefit from learning technology from developed countries, but as this became increasingly difficult, the government and industry had to gear up technology development of their own. Since the mid-1990s, Korea has relied more on technologies that it developed on its own than on foreign-adopted technology. In the 1960s and 1970s, state-financed research institutes had already been established to foster development in key industrial sectors, and full-scale efforts were launched in this field in the 1980s. And since the 1990s, Korean enterprises were able to expand their own research and development (R&D) activities and set up private-sector research institutions.[31] Not only the Ministry of Commerce and Industry but also the Ministry of Science and Technology actively supported technological development. During the period from 1982 to 1991, the Ministry of Science and Technology invested a total of 964.2 billion won, of which 65% was allotted to core industrial technology (semi-conductors, computers, etc.), 18% to public technology and 17% to basic technology.[32]

The major investment in corporate R&D was vital for the Korean firms to develop core technologies in order to attain self-reliance in such new areas as semi-conductors and telecommunications in addition to existing industries. The rise of the ICT industry in the 1990s, which was possible due to developments in technology, marked a key turning point in the industrial development of Korea.[33]

A series of developments like the launch of the World Trade Organization (WTO) in 1995, Korea's entry to the OECD in 1996 and the 1997 Asian financial crisis pushed Korea towards the full opening of its market. Korea has constantly adapted to international markets and globalization trends: at an early stage, Korean manufacturers were encouraged to focus on export markets rather than depend on a limited domestic market; and later, in the era of full-fledged globalization, Korean manufacturers took the next step of 'industrial globalization' by diversifying partnerships, establishing production facilities overseas, etc., which has contributed to the increased competitiveness of Korean industry in its respective sectors. This brought Korea into the top five rankings of countries in the fields of automobiles, shipbuilding, electronics and steel.

The IMF financial crisis in the late 1990s forced the Korean industrial sector to restructure, and some industries, like ICT, came out stronger and more competitive following the crisis. However, the primary industries faced great difficulties. By the 2000s, the challenge was how to go about restructuring industries, yet being mindful that while some were able to handle changes in terms of market opening and technological advancement, others were having trouble meeting these challenges. Also, there was the question of how to effectively select and promote future engines of growth.

After the era of rapid economic growth followed by the liberalization and stabilization period, since the turn of the century, Korea has been pursuing 'new growth engines' that will sustain economic dynamism and growth in order for it to secure the status of an advanced economy. Up to the 1980s, Korea successfully implemented an 'industrial targeting' policy for economic transformation. But with the advent of the WTO regime in the mid-1990s, the government's direct fiscal and monetary support for businesses was no longer possible and only its indirect support in R&D was allowed. Hence, Korea's industrial policy turned into technical development policy, and from the 2000s, the government started to nurture new growth industries by focusing on technological development.

In 2001, Kim Dae-Jung's government promoted the so-called 'five technological industries': IT, biotechnology (BT), nanotechnology (NT), environmental technology (ET) and cultural technology (CT). In 2003, the Noh Mu-Hyun administration announced ten industries that would spearhead growth: robots, future cars, next-generation semi-conductors, digital TV and broadcasting, new-generation mobile communication, display, intelligent home networks, digital contents/SW solutions, next-generation batteries, new biomedicine and organs. In 2009, the Lee Myung-Bak administration presented a vision for a new growth engine and strategy, with emphasis on green growth, high-tech fusion and a high value-addition service industry. The overall performance of these initiatives was mixed, showing partial success.[34]

Then, the Park Geun-Hye government laid out the vision of achieving a 'creative economy' and planned to develop future engines of growth in 2013. In 2014, the government announced economic goals of a 4% economic growth rate, USD 40,000 GDP per capita and a 70% employment rate.[35] This was to be realized through a three-year plan for economic innovation built on the three pillars of 'strong fundamentals', a 'dynamic and innovative economy' and 'balancing domestic demand and exports'.[36]

However, this administration came to a halt with the impeachment of President Park in March 2017, before these goals could be attained. What should be noted is that since Korea recovered from the Asian financial crisis in the late 1990s, it has experienced a steady slip in its economic growth rate, which reflects the typical trend in developed economies. During the four years of Park's administration (2013–2016), GDP growth averaged 2.9%, the lowest ever. Since the late 1990s, when Korea suffered the IMF crisis, the administrations had achieved an average growth rate of 5.1% (Kim Dae-Jung 1998–2002), 4.5% (Roh Mu-Hyun 2003–2007) and 3.2% (Lee Myung-Bak 2008–2012).[37]

The new President Moon Jae-in, who was inaugurated on 10 May 2017, pledged to enhance the livelihood of ordinary people, taking care of employment, reforming business conglomerates, reining in collusion between political and business circles, and promoting equal opportunities.[38] Evidently, Korea has already entered the phase of slow growth, given its industrial structure and income level and the size of its economy. But managing the economy and meeting people's demands is likely to be increasingly difficult with heightening global and domestic competition, and an increase in people's demands and expectations amid the enhancement of their living standards, socio-political awareness and rights.

Besides upgrading technology and focusing on developing new growth engines, Korea's task is to nurture development and enhance the competitiveness of existing industries which are vital for the overall socio-economic stability of the nation. The issue becomes tricky in the case of the primary industries, especially the agriculture sector.

What characterized Korea's economic development for some 50 years was its exceptionally high economic growth: for the period from 1961 to 2004, the average GDP growth rate for Korea was 7.1%, compared to a global average of 4.0% (83), 3.3% for developed nations (22), 5.7% for East Asia (5), 3.7% for Latin America (22) and 4.9% for South Asia (4).[39] What was the key to Korea's high growth was the accumulation of capital, and until the IMF financial crisis, the accumulation of capital led the economic growth; however, since the IMF crisis, the per-capita accumulation of capital rate dropped sharply and increases in productivity led the growth.

Manufacturing drove Korea's rapid economic growth. Over the period from 1953 to 2000, Korea's manufacturing averaged a high growth rate of 13.1% annually. Although Korea maintained one of the highest industrialization ratios in the world of close to 30% even after it dipped slightly in the 1990s, it is deemed to have reached its limits.[40]

But as Korea achieved high growth, the problem of 'bipolarization', the widening of the disparity between large corporations and small and medium-sized enterprises (SMEs), and between exporting and domestic-oriented industries, has surfaced. Too much concentration of economic power in the *Chaebols* and their overexpansion alongside such problems as moral hazard, loose management and bad debt have rekindled debates and deliberations over how to appropriately regulate and control their activities. How to deal with low growth and worsening wealth distribution, balancing or simultaneously pursuing economic growth and strengthening welfare remain fundamental tasks for the nation. In addition, matters such as revamping the ever-growing service sector and fostering innovative SMEs to attain a position of global competitiveness are drawing increased attention.

Recapping the Overall Achievements

In 1962, when Korea launched its first five-year development plan, its per-capita income was only USD 87, lower than most African countries at that time. Korea's drastic economic transformation is summed up in its attainment of '20-50 club' status in recent years. This is a measurement of economic development that combines population size and the level of per-capita income. Literally, it means having a per-capita income of over USD 20,000 at the same as having the population of over 50 million. When Korea entered this club in 2012, it was only the seventh country in the world to achieve this feat. The other countries are Japan (1987), the US (1988), France (1990), Italy (1990), Germany (1991) and the UK (1996). Furthermore, Korea has reached another milestone of the '30-50 club' in 2018. As of 2017, Korea is the eleventh-largest economy.

In terms of trade volume, Korea was the fifth-largest exporter and the seventh-largest importer as of 2014. In 2012, Korea has achieved, for the first time, a landmark total trade volume of over 1 trillion dollars, making it the eighth major trading nation. In terms of foreign reserves, Korea ranks sixth in terms of foreign exchange reserves with 369.6 billion dollars (2015), while it ranked thirteenth in the Human Development Index (2013). In addition, it topped the rankings in the Bloomberg Innovative Country Index for five consecutive years (2014–2018).[41]

By every account, Korea has already entered the threshold of advanced economies, which is also symbolized by its joining of the OECD DAC in 2009. This has all taken place without Koreans themselves being well aware of their achievements. The work to be done is how to explain the reasons for success and draw lessons from it.

Coming up with a credible 'Korean model of development' that can be benchmarked in practice by the African countries will be an even more significant task, but the purpose of this book is to try to invite and provoke greater deliberations in this field in the years to come. In this vein, making sense of what has transpired and what indeed were the key factors that drove Korea to success is deemed to be important.

In my view, the essence of the Korean model of economic development in its simplest terms can be broken down into two main elements: (1) compressed economic growth; and (2) effective social mobilization for change. Korea's development is considered so impressive and unique because it has somehow found a way to 'accelerate through' industrial transformation and also has been able to instil the 'can-do spirit' into its people and has induced them to be active agents of development.

This has taken place against the backdrop of positive role of the government. And there were four fundamental cornerstones upon which compressed economic growth and effective social mobilization were realised: land reform; empowerment of the people; revolution in education; and governmental reform. These seemingly basic but 'profound' reform measures were taken at appropriate moments, in some ways helped by 'pressures'—constraints, limitations and adversities Korea faced as a nation. Of these, I think land reform and empowerment of the people were most crucial.

Based on such measures, Korea's economy evolved, but the whole picture of Korea's development will not be complete without adding to it the important aspect of social dynamics, that is, the formation and evolution of social or popular mindset change and action-oriented campaigns. Addressing Korea's development from a purely economic dimension misses the point entirely. With regard to East Asian developmental states, so many academics and experts have already mentioned the key role of the state. But in the case of Korea, besides the government's critical intervention, the people's mindset and action-oriented movements played an equally important part in Korea's overall development.

Korea in the 1950s, after having gone through the Korean War, focused on reconstructing the war-torn nation, relying heavily on foreign aid, mostly from the US, and employing import-substitution as

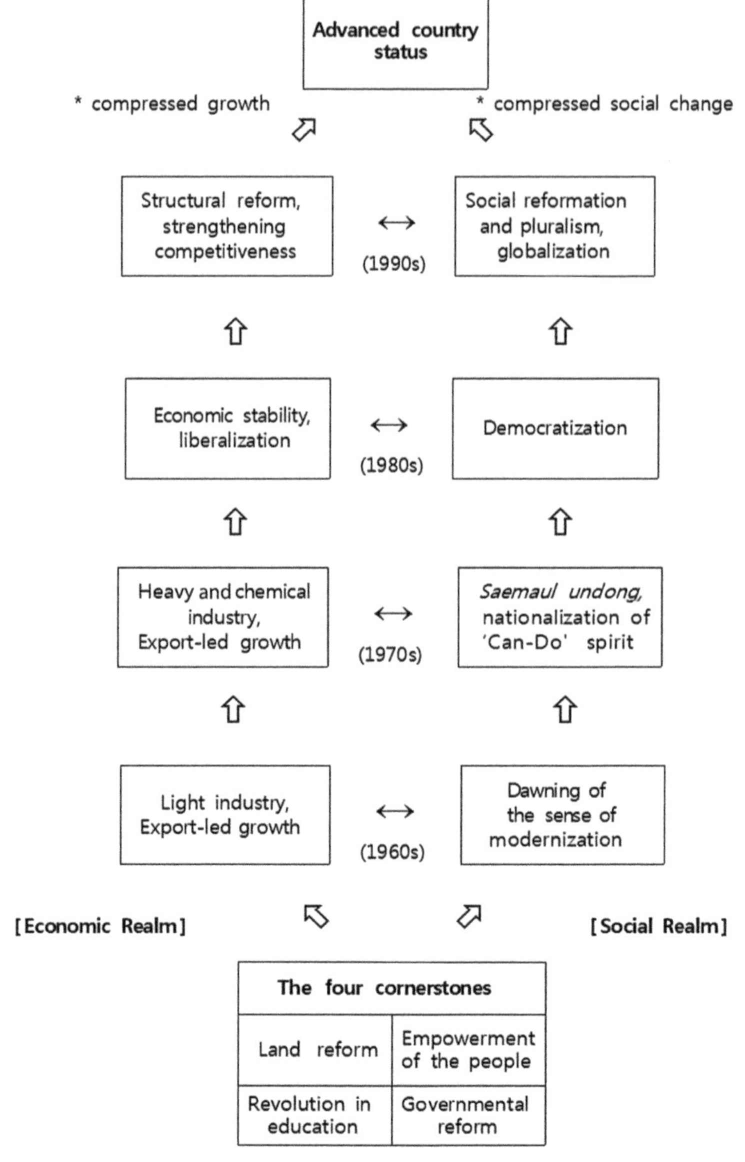

Fig. 7.1 Schematic itinerary of Korea's development

a mainstream economic policy. It was in the early 1960s that Korea embarked on a full-scale and systematic effort to develop its economy. But earlier, in the 1950s, a number of crucial measures such as land reform and government-driven campaigns to empower the people were enacted. Broadly speaking, we can say that the compressed economic growth of Korea lasted until the end of the 1990s, with Korea achieving the status of an advanced economy at the turn of the new millennium. Figure 7.1 above provides an illustration of a summary of Korea's path of development that I have mentioned. This cannot be considered as a road map because Korea did not pre-plan the scheme of development over a period of decades to achieve compressed growth.

Notes

1. Chuk Kyo Kim, *Korean Economic Development*, 2nd ed. (Seoul: Parkyoungsa, 2016) (Korean Edition), p. 11.
2. Il Sakong and Youngsun Koh (ed.), *The Korean Economy: Six Decades of Growth and Development* (Seoul: Korea Development Institute, 2010).
3. In this book, I will freely use different categorizations where it is deemed suitable for the sake of convenience and ease of explanation.
4. Kyong Ju Kim, *The Development of Modern South Korea: State Formation, Capitalist Development and National Identity* (London: Routledge, 2006), pp. 44–47.
5. Ibid., p. 45.
6. Michael J. Seth, *A Concise History of Korea* (Lanham, MD: Rowman & Littlefield, 2006), p. 2.
7. Ibid., p. 4.
8. Sakong and Koh (2010), p. 11.
9. Ibid., p. 12.
10. Jung-en Woo, *Race to the Swift: State and Finance in Korean Industrialization* (New York: Columbia University Press, 1991), p. 52. It is argued that Taiwanese government was much more cooperative than Korea with the US.
11. Sakong and Koh (2010), p. 13.
12. LEE Dae Geun, *Korean Economy in the Post War 1950s* (Seoul: Samsung Economic Institute, 2002) (Korean), p. 253.

13. Edward S. Mason, et al., *The Economic and Social Modernization of the Republic of Korea* (Cambridge, MA: Harvard University Press, 1980), p. xxx.
14. Chuk Kyo Kim (2016), p. 17.
15. Ibid., p. 25.
16. Sang-cheol Lee, 'Switching to an Export-led Industrialization Strategy and Its Outcome', in Dae-geun Lee (ed.), *New Korean Economic History: From the Late Joseon Period to the High-Growth Period of the 20th Century* (Seoul: Na-nam, 2005) (Korean), p. 394. The decrease in US aid to Korea from 1958 is said to have contributed to Korea's foreign reserve crisis, prompting the government to shift from a fixed exchange rate system to a unitary fluctuation exchange rate system in 1964.
17. Sakong and Koh (2010), pp. 17–19. 'Export targeting' refers to a practice of setting a target for each year's total exports by adding up the export forecasts of individual firms. In the Monthly Export Promotion Meetings, government officials and business representatives gathered to monitor export performance, compared it to export targets, identified problems and sought solutions. The President himself chaired these monthly meetings. The Korea Trade Promotion Agency (KOTRA) took charge of building overseas networks, helped the marketing activities of domestic firms and collected market information.
18. The new government set an ambitious task of achieving 7.1% growth, but was confronted with various obstacles from the start, so that the target economic growth rate was later lowered to 5% for 1964–1966. The government tried to mobilize domestic capital through monetary reform in 1962, but failed, and in 1963 faced a foreign exchange crisis amid lukewarm support from the US for the Korean regime. However, at the end of the first five-year plan, Korea actually exceeded the goal of 7.1%.
19. Sakong and Koh (2010), pp. 20–21.
20. Chuk Kyo Kim (2016), p. 33.
21. Sakong and Koh (2010), p. 21. By deepening the industrial structure and upgrading the export mix, the share of HCIs in total industrial production was to be increased from 35 to 51% between 1972 and 1981, and their share in total exports from 27 to 65%.
22. Chuk Kyo Kim (2006), pp. 32–34. Governmental support to HCIs took various forms: providing long-term credit and tax incentives

to selected industries, establishing and expanding vocational schools and training centres to supply skilled manpower, creating government-funded research institutions to carry our R&D activities as a public good.

23. Sakong and Koh (2010), p. 104.
24. Bank of Korea, http://ecos.bok.or.kr.
25. Sakong and Koh (2010), pp. 87–90.
26. The need for change was initially brought up within the government, resulting in the announcement of the Comprehensive Economic Stabilization Program in April 1979.
27. The Fair Trade Commission, which was set up in 1981, formulated deregulation plans in consultation with the private sector and related ministries. In 1990, the Administrative Deregulation Committee was set up in the Prime Minister's Office to direct deregulation efforts across government in compliance with the Comprehensive Economic Vitalization Program. These efforts were carried on by the Kim Youngsam government from 1993.
28. Kwang Suk Kim, *Korea's Industrial and Trade Policies* (Seoul: Institute for Global Economics, 2001) (Korean), p. 82.
29. Some of the factors cited were that Korea failed to take appropriate measures to counter the reckless management of banks; moral hazard arising from business–politics ties; a failure to put in place a fair and transparent process; excessive dependence on foreign loans (short-term debts), etc.
30. With the lifting of restrictions on inward FDI at the end of the 1997, FDI flowed in and the accumulated amount of FDI inflows reached USD 100 billion in October 2004, making Korea the fifth largest foreign reserves-possessing country in the world. Corporate governance was strengthened by such measures as requiring *chaebols* to prepare consolidated financial statements and applying stiffer penalties. And, most importantly, interest rates were fully liberalized.
31. DoHoon Kim and Youngsun Koh, 'Korea's Industrial Development', in Il Sakong and Youngsun Koh (eds), *The Korean Economy: Six Decades of Growth and Development* (Seoul: Korea Development Institute, 2010), pp. 111–112.
32. Chuk Kyo Kim (2006), p. 165.
33. Kim and Koh (2010), p. 112. The success of the ICT sector also helped create a new development vision for Korean HCIs just as they were

emerging from the period of industrial rationalization and were searching for ways to achieve future-oriented growth.

34. DoHoon Kim, 'In Search of Future Growth Engine: Tasks and Solutions', *Korea Economic Forum* 8, no. 2 (Seoul: Korea Economics Association, 2015) (Korean), p. 54.
35. According to OECD Data, https://data.oecd.org/emp/employment-rate.htm, employment rates are calculated as the ratio of the employed to the working-age population. The employment rate is different from the 'unemployment rate', which refers to the percentage of the total labour force that is unemployed but actively seeking employment and willing to work. Thus, these two concepts are not the two sides of the same coin.
36. These three pillars or strategic goals are in turn each composed of three sub-tasks. 'Strong fundamentals' consists of public sector reform, developing a principled market economy and building a strong social safety net. As for 'dynamic and innovative economy', the sub-tasks are developing creative industries, investing for the future and making inroads into overseas markets. 'Balancing domestic demand and exports' is composed of expanding domestic demand, de-regulating to improve investment, and job creation to stimulate domestic demand.
37. *Yonhap News* (Korean), 10 March 2017, http://www.yonhapnews.co.kr/dev/9601000000.html. See also Evan Ramsdat, 'South Korea's Economic Challenges After the Park Geun-hye Era', *CSIS Newsletter*, 17 March 2017. In 2016, exports dropped by 5.9% to USD 495.5 billion, registering a decrease for two consecutive years. This marked the first time that Korea had experienced a two year-consecutive drop in exports since 1957–1958. Although exportation is showing signs of recovery, there is weariness that it is largely being driven by a limited number of products like semi-conductors. However, the employment figure improved with an annual increase of 388,600 thousand jobs compared to around 250,000 in the previous two administrations. But the employment rate (for 15–64 year olds) registered an average of 65.4%, falling short of the 70% target. On the other hand, the unemployment rate did not improve, being recorded at 3.5%, about the same level as Roh's (3.5%) and Lee's (3.4%) government. The 'youth unemployment rate (for 15–29 year olds)' was at a record high of 9.0%.
38. 'Inaugural Address to the Nation by President Moon Jae-in', unofficial translation by the Ministry of Foreign Affairs, Republic of Korea,

10 May 2017. See also Maeil Business News (Business Department), *Moon Jae-in nomics* (Seoul: Maeil Business News Korea, 2017) (Korean).

39. Chin Hee Hahn and Shin Sukha, 'Understanding the Post-crisis Growth of the Korean Economy: Growth Accounting and Cross-Country Regressions', in Takatoshi Ito and Chin Hee Hahn (eds), *The Rise of Asia and Structural Changes in Korea and Asia* (Cheltenham, UK: Edward Elgar, 2010), pp. 97–110.
40. The heavy industry ratio (the portion of heavy industry in the total manufacturing sector) continued to increase from 58% in 1980s to 88.5% in 2007, and Korea tops the world in this category.
41. 'The U.S. Drops Out of the Top 10 in Innovation Ranking', *Bloomberg Technology*, 23 January 2018, https://www.bloomberg.com/news/articles/2018-01-22/south-korea-tops-global-innovation-ranking-again-as-u-s-falls.

8
The Essence of the Korean Model of Development

Conceptualizing the Korean Development Model

Below, in Fig. 8.1, I have attempted to construction, with a schematic map, what can represent a model of Korea's development. While Fig. 7.1 depicts how the course of Korea's development unfolded, Fig. 8.1 expresses *what* actually made the transformation possible, that is, the central elements of development.

In sum, the Korean development model starts with the four cornerstones. Based on these cornerstones, the economic realm and the socio-political realm of Korea each realized a 'compressed' developmental process with more or less common characteristics in each stage of development. The top row representing economic domain and the bottom row representing socio-political domain show a full range of Korea's development.

Choi, Joong-Kyung observes:

> among the countries that were disconnected from Western industrialization up until the beginning of the 20th century, Korea is the only country

J.-D. Park, *Re-Inventing Africa's Development*,
https://doi.org/10.1007/978-3-030-03946-2_8

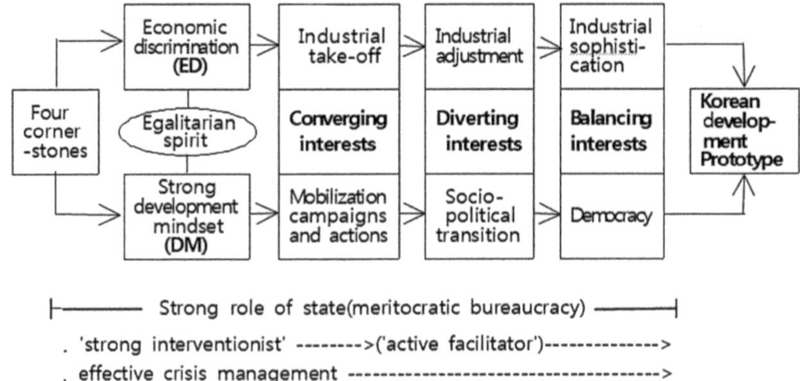

Fig. 8.1 Korea's development model

> that achieved both Western industrialization and Western democracy. Both Israel and Singapore are also regarded as having achieved industrialization and democratization, but there were historical reasons … Israel was formed by a Jewish population that came from Western industrial countries. Singapore was a small city economy and had been a base for the UK's East India Company for a long time, and this was exposed to Western-style industrialization from early on.[1]

In the economic domain, the rule of 'economic discrimination' (ED) was the principal driving force for growth during the rapid industrialization period. The rough timeline for 'industrial take-off' was the 1960s and 1970s, while 'industrial adjustment' occurred in the 1980s and 1990s, and 'industrial maturity' took place the period from 2000 up to the present day. As mentioned earlier, 'economic discrimination' is the concept coined by Professor Jwa, Sung-Hee. This concept is instrumental in understanding the success of Korea, particularly in the economic take-off period.

Meanwhile, in the socio-political realm, the emergence and expansion of a 'strong development mindset (DM)' in the nation was critical in terms of motivating individuals and mobilizing the general public to work harder in order to attain a better life and the modernization of the nation. There is no denying that the economic domain and the socio-political domain must have had a substantial correlation or interactions. In my mind, what reinforced the rationale and effectiveness of both the DM and ED was the 'egalitarian spirit' typical of Koreans up to now. If we recognize that ED and the strong DM were crucial factors for development, 'egalitarian spirit' is more of a psychological element deeply ingrained in people's minds that expeditiously matched well with those two factors to produce maximal outcomes.

I have already pointed out that Korea boasts notable historical continuity and homogeneity as a nation. In the twentieth century, Korea's liberation from colonial rule and the Korean War largely demolished the existing socio-economic hierarchy and the vested interests structure. After being devastated by the Korean War, the nation had to start again from scratch and everybody was literally on an equal footing. The Korean people were all very poor, so there were basically two tendencies: either people could resign themselves to their lot or they could try to do something special to get out of the misery in which they found themselves. Fortunately, the nation did not opt for the former because unlike many Sub-Saharan countries blessed with abundant natural resources and a favourable climate, making year-round farming possible, Korea's land was resource-poor, rugged and mountainous, making an easy lifestyle simply unsustainable. And a strong sense of egalitarian-mindedness in the people prompted them to jump on the bandwagon of social mobilization.

An egalitarian mindset was important because this encouraged competition and emulation among the people to 'keep up with the Jones', as if they were saying: 'If others can do it, why can't I?' People were envious of their neighbours' or acquaintances' wealth or success, and this made them exert greater effort to try to catch up with them. I think the can-do spirit of Koreans is rooted in this egalitarian thinking. It has also been observed that: 'Korea's development is also remarkable because it constituted development with equity, with rapid poverty reduction and no increase in inequality throughout the development process.'[2]

In addition, socio-cultural norm that emphasizes 'saving one's face' and maintaining one's dignity, along with the typical 'shame culture', has contributed greatly to the emergence and expansion of a hard-working, self-sacrificing populace. As illustrated in Fig. 8.1, the period of ‘industrial take-off’ can be characterized as an era of ‘convergence of interests’. The interests of the country’s leader, the government, the people and companies converged, leading to phenomenal and unparalleled economic growth. In the early 1960s, Korea had just experienced the troubled government of Rhee, Syng-Man, who was ousted following popular opposition. The cabinet system administration that was newly formed also found itself unpopular and in turmoil, and as a result, the military, led by a group of young officers, staged a coup with the rationale of saving the nation.

The strong role of government based on meritocratic bureaucracy is the hallmark of Korea’s success, particularly in the rapid industrialization period, but is also the overarching feature in the overall development of Korea that continues to this day. What started as the government’s strong interventionist stance in the early 1960s over time underwent adjustments and changes so as to become that of an ‘active facilitator’. But this does not mean that the government’s function has basically ‘weakened’; instead, it reflects changes in government policy.

What is not marked in the Korean development model diagram, but is deemed as another important feature for the success of the nation is the timely and effective management of crisis or, even better, *taking advantage of a crisis*. This notable feature has crystallized on many occasions throughout Korea’s development path. Not only was Korea able to successfully cope with crisis time after time, but it also came out stronger than before. The responses to crises or challenges were bold and immediate. And Korea made many correct policy choices when confronted with big challenges or tasks. Even when some of these turned out to be failures, the government was on track to fix them.

The collapse of Rhee’s government and the ensuing new government at the turn of the 1960s was in itself a crisis for Korea. But as it turned out, the 1960s marked an important turning point in relation to Korea’s development. So, what enabled Park Chung-Hee’s government to be successful in driving forward its policies? A combination of factors must have been in been in effect, but the ‘right timing’ of the advent of a new state leadership and the ‘synchronization’ of policies, national demands and aspirations, etc. should also be recognized. The test for the new democratic politics in Korea failed due to various reasons. The people were wary of politics, and uncertainty and instability prevailed. Park came from a poor peasant family and his style of leadership was perceived to be down to earth and in touch with the grassroots. Korea was at a low point in every aspect and people were willing to support and take part in new initiatives.

Meanwhile, because of North Korea's propaganda and the perception held by some South Koreans that North Koreans might be better off living under a communist state, there was a constant pressure on the government to outperform North Korea in terms of economic development. This was all the more reason for Park to vigorously launch the national modernization campaign in order to consolidate the legitimacy of his rule.

This was a time when the Cold War was at its peak, with the threat of North Korean communist military adventurism being very real. The ongoing Vietnam War was a stern reminder of what might happen in the Korean Peninsula. South Korea was in competition with North Korea on multiple fronts: economic, military, political and ideological. It was also in a fierce contest with the North to win the 'approval' of the international community. Korea depended heavily on the US for its military capability and national security, but this also represented a vulnerability for Park's regime.

There were also disagreements with the US in certain areas, such as Korea's pursuit of its export-drive policy instead of import-substitution. President Park was at times wary of a possible US military pull-out from the South, knowing all too well that the US security commitment to Korea hinged on the decisions taken in Washington, DC and that it should not be taken as a given. This led Park to hasten economic development in order to try to acquire industrial capability including defence.

'Modernization of fatherland', the motto of Park Chung-Hee's government, was timely and appropriate for the nation, and it would have been hard to argue against its logic, given the circumstances in Korea at the time. Rather than being populist and trying to cater to the short-term needs of the masses, Park emphasized the great challenges that lay ahead and the magnitude of the work that needed to be done to pull the nation out of poverty. The term 'modernization' implies moving from 'backwardness' to modernity, realizing economic development and adopting advanced modes, systems and institutions necessary to upgrade the nation so as to join the ranks of the rich nations. Hence, the government asked people not only to support the vision and policies but also to actually participate vigorously and physically in the 'mobilization' campaigns.

But the effectiveness of winning popular support and generating social mobilization hinged on the government's leadership and performance, and the development momentum of the nation was sustained because the government was able to deliver concrete results promptly. During the take-off period, Korea's policies and industrial structure underwent big and continuous changes. Korea's conversion from protectionism and import-substitution in the 1950s to export-oriented policies in the 1960s is hailed by many experts as the most dynamic transition since the Second World War. It was in 1962 that the first five-year economic development plan was launched. The targeted goal of economic growth was set at a very high level of 7.1% average annual growth, but the actual growth rate attained exceeded this, reaching 8.5%. The second five-year economic development plan (1967–1971) yielded an even more remarkable result of 9.7% average annual growth against the original goal of 7.0%.

What was also remarkable about President Park was that he took very bold economic measures against the advice of international organizations and principal donors by pursuing an export-drive policy, establishing Pohang Iron and Steel Company (POSCO) and building the eight-lane Gyeongbu Expressway. Choi, Joong-Kyung, who served in Korea's Ministry of Finance and the World Bank, observed that:

> at the time, the projects seemed like nonsense and the tasks appeared impossible. President Park Chung-Hee was not an economist. He witnessed the success of other countries that faced similar situations as Korea and he believed in his intuitions. The case of West Germany (which had success with an export-drive policy and hardly had any natural resources) caught his attention. The unified Germany still continues to adopt [an] export-drive policy. As a small country with a small domestic market and with scarce natural resources, such a policy is almost inevitable.[3]

According to Choi, for an economy to achieve successful development, four basic elements are required: a strong and stable leadership with a clear vision; well-organized economic development plans; a competent bureaucracy to carry out these plans; and the financial resources necessary to execute meet them. In the case of Korea, these conditions were met and 'without any doubt, the late President Park Chung-Hee was the architect who exerted leadership and created the strong foundation of the modern Korean economy. The zeal for education and a competitive and objective civil service exam made it possible to recruit and maintain a competent bureaucracy. Through visionary leadership and the efforts of an efficient bureaucracy, it was possible to establish highly effective five-year economic development plans'.[4]

In the 1950s, Korea was seen as a 'hopeless' and high-risk country, with the possibility of war breaking out again in the eyes of foreign agencies, including the United States Agency for International Development (USAID) and the World Bank. Korea was unable to obtain the necessary loans to push forward with its economic development scheme in such circumstances where Samuel D. Berger, the US ambassador to Korea, made a negative report to his headquarters regarding Korea's development plans and the World Bank was equally reluctant to extend financial assistance to Korea. Despite the unreceptive mood of the international community towards Korea's needs, in 1962 Korea was finally able to sign a commercial loan agreement with West Germany. By the terms of agreement for a loan of USD 150 million, Korea had to send nurses and miners that West Germany needed and the salaries of the workers were set as collateral.[5]

The first job assigned to the Korean nurses who were sent to an alien country was cleaning stiffened dead bodies. The miners worked so painstakingly hard, risking their lives in caves over 1000 metres deep underground fighting geothermal heat. The Korean workers' zealous work deeply impressed the people of West Germany and so President Park was invited by President Heinrich Lübke to visit West Germany in December 1964. Anxious to greet their President, who has come all the way to West Germany to meet them, Korean miners and nurses gathered in an auditorium all dressed up: the miners in suits and the nurses in traditional Korean dress. Prior to the Korean President's speech, they all began singing the Korean national anthem but none of them could finish the song because they were all sobbing. President Park put his prepared speech into his pocket and said repeatedly 'let's work hard'. He went on 'let's work hard until our bodies turn into shatters so that our sons and daughters would not be sold to a foreign country'. The Korean workers cried out 'we will do anything. Please help our country, please help our President', as they knelt down and bowed low to the ground for the President of West Germany. Leaving behind sobbing Korean workers, on his way back to the hotel, President Park could not hold back the tears. President Lübke give him a handkerchief and comforted him by saying 'we will help you; the people of West Germany will help your country'.[6]

Through such hardships and the sacrifice of the people, Korea was able to build the stepping stones towards modernization. In addition, sending troops to Vietnam helped accelerate the economic growth of Korea as the soldiers' combat allowance money was used to fund the Gyeongbu Expressway. The Korean government also obtained a reparation payment of USD 500 million and commercial loan of USD 300 million from Japan following the normalization of diplomatic ties with Japan in 1965. The payments were used to build the Pohang Iron and Steel Company and other investments. Money earned by Korean construction workers from construction sites in the scorching desert heat of Middle East in the 1970s was another valuable foreign currency inflow for Korea. Fabric, shoe and wig factories were packed with teenage boys and girls who were saving money to pay for their younger siblings' education.

And yet another drama unfolded when Koreans achieved democratization. There are two common misperceptions held by many foreigners when it comes to the state of Korea's democracy. One is that Korea is still run by an authoritarian or non-democratic regime and the other is that Korea was democratized long ago and it achieved development under democracy. But neither is the case. First of all, the Korean democratic movement ran its full course and could possibly be the most successful case of a Third World nation-turned full democracy since the second half of the twentieth century. Korea's compressed development featured 'compressed democratization' in addition to compressed economic growth and transformation. It would be no exaggeration to say that the level and dynamism of democracy exhibited by South Korea is highly exceptional in the non-Western world.

Korea's compressed democratization was fuelled by democratic uprisings or movements, although even during the absence of such events, there were ongoing awareness and a drive for democracy in society, albeit in a subdued fashion. In the post-war era, the first democratic movement erupted in 1960 against the Rhee Syng-man regime, culminating in the 19 April Revolution that finally toppled the government. But the new democratic government that was formed was seen to be incompetent and powerless, and was overthrown by a military coup just after a year.

If President Park lacked full legitimacy because he had taken power through a coup, his delivery on impressive economic development more than offset this, as shown by his landslide win in the 1967 presidential election. But he faced increasing opposition to his prolonged rule in the 1970s, as he announced a plan to amend the Constitution to allow him to run for a third term in October 1972. The new *Yushin* Constitution was legislated in December of that year. Park was assassinated in October 1980 by his aide, the chief of the intelligence service. The assassination is largely considered to be an outcome of a collision between the repression of Park's regime and the resistance of the democratization movement, which was preceded by years of confrontations and escalating tensions in political parties under the *Yushin* system. After Park's assassination, the prospect of democratization appeared to be evident in South Korea.

During the early years and up until the mid-term of Park's rule, successful economic development enhanced the legitimacy of the regime. However, by the time of Park's death, the regime had lost much of its popular support due to changes in people's attitudes and values brought about by economic growth and the enhancement in people's standard of living, and also because Park reinforced coercion to prolong his rule. There were high expectations that the end of Park's dictatorial rule would open a new era of democracy, giving rise to the 'Seoul Spring', which was the period from 26 October 1979 to 17 May 1980.

But the 'neo-military forces' snatched power from the transitional government with a military coup and imposed martial law on 17 May 1980. General Chun Doo-Hwan soon became President and after his term finished, Chun's chosen successor, Roh Tae-Woo, a retired general and an army academy classmate, took over. In the meantime, a massive anti-government uprising occurred in the city of Gwangju on 18 May 1980, which is referred to as the Gwangju Democratization Movement. During this period, citizens rose up against Chun's dictatorship. During the course of the uprising, citizens took up arms by raiding police stations and military depots to oppose the government and the imposition of martial law, but were ultimately crushed by the army. Hundreds of people died in the process. There was another major democratic uprising in June 1987, which pressurized the regime to accommodate some institutional and policy changes demanded by the people and the opposition.

The democratization movement in the 1980s was no longer limited to the student and the dissident movement. Instead, it was aligned with social movements and particularly with the labour movement. Moreover, the opposition party which had been excluded from the political scene re-entered the political arena following the general election in 1985 and expressed opposition to dictatorship and support for democratization more clearly. Accordingly, the democratization movement was able to muster the largest coalition of social and political forces comprising workers, opposition party and dissidents, and students.

Although the democratic transition ended up in the emergence of the Roh Tae-woo regime, which succeeded the Chun Doo-Hwan regime, the political environment of Korea did change after the transition. Above all, the constitutional system began to operate normally under the amended Constitution in 1987 and subsequently, the arbitrary exercise of the state's power was considerably reduced. In addition, political and civil society, which had been repressed by authoritarian rule under the dictatorial regime, also became normalized due to democratization.

A normal political party system based on popular support was created, although it was under the influence of 'regionalism', and civil society also regained autonomy and developed rapidly afterwards.

The election of Kim Young-Sam, the leader of the democratic movement, as Korea's President in 1993 ushered in a new era of civilian rule. Then, after ten years of democratic transition since 1987, Kim Dae-Jung was elected President in the fifteenth presidential election held in December 1997. The emergence of the Kim Dae-Jung government was a historic feat because it marked the first 'parallel' regime change by election and also because the regime change was made by a democratic opposition party. The Kim Dae-Jung government was followed by a successive liberal government led by President Roh Moo-Hyun, who came to power in 2003.

After ten years or two terms of rule by liberal-progressive party leaders, the political landscape of Korea shifted back to conservative party rule as a businessman-turned politician Lee Myung-Bak from the conservative party became President in 2008. Then, the conservative party's candidate Park Geun-Hye, the daughter of the late President Park Chung-Hee, won the subsequent presidential election to become the first female Korean President in 2013. However, Park was implicated in a corruption scandal and faced massive public demonstrations demanding that she step down. She was removed from power after being impeached in March 2017.

The liberal party opposition leader Moon Jae-In became the new President in May 2017. Likewise, the political pendulum continues to swing back and forth between the conservative and liberal political parties since the peaceful transition of power was first realized in Korea in 1998.

Going back to Fig. 8.1, I have pointed out that in the 1960s and 1970s, the interests of the government and that of the people and businesses largely converged, producing positive synergy effects that led to high economic growth. But afterwards, the bond or unity between the government, corporations and the populace loosened, although it did not diverge strongly to cause instability of the country.

What characterized this era of the 1980s and1990s is, I think, 'diverting interests'. I chose the word 'diverting' for a lack of better word, to avoid the word 'divergent'. This is to suggest that the interests of the government, the people and businesses started to 'differentiate' somewhat, but were not really in conflict with one another.

By this time, South Korea has extricated itself from poverty, so economic stability, distributional justice, workers' rights and democracy were higher priorities. One of the signs of change was that the Korean private business sector, especially the large business conglomerates, the *chaebols*, now wanted to be more autonomous vis-à-vis the government. Labour unions, opposition political parties, intellectuals and social activists wanted their voices to be heard and increasingly confronted the government and the establishment.

During the Park Chung-Hee era, modernization was the single most important goal of the nation and most of its energy and resources were devoted to achieving economic development. But afterwards, many things were set to change. The early success in economic growth is deemed to have set off a chain reaction of: economic development; social, political demands and changes; economic policy adjustments; evolution of democratization and social dynamism; deepening of economic reforms and sophistication of industrial structure, and so on.

But Korea might have started celebrating too early and was complacent without ever suspecting what was to come. To the shock of the whole nation, Korea was on the verge of bankruptcy and had to receive a financial bailout from the IMF in December 2007. Moral hazard and problems in corporate governance on the part of big business, the weakness of the government and its failure to monitor and regulate the problems, as well as excessive borrowing and spending by the people gave rise to a major crisis. This led to a change in the tide, the reassessment of unfettered free market economy and the re-alignment or rebalancing of interests. The 1997 Asian financial crisis and the 2008 global financial crisis were stern reminders to Korea that a sound regulatory role of government is very much in order and that economic globalization poses such a grave, immediate and extensive risks to economies if they lack the necessary discipline and governance.

For Korea, this was an occasion to become 'united' once again. To help the government pay back the IMF debt, the Korean people voluntarily launched a movement to donate gold. This was in effect a revival of the *Saemaul Undong*. Such an act of the people giving up their personal possessions for the public cause is unheard of in the world history. The business conglomerates had to undergo serious restructuring, and they became more conservative in their investment activities. The last phase of 'industrial sophistication' is still an ongoing process.

Politically, Korea has become a full democracy, while economically it is faced with increasing global competition. The interests of various players or entities in Korea can be said to be in the 'balancing' stage. They do not converge to the extent that they did in the 1960s or 1970s, but nor are they as divergent as was sometimes the case in the 1980s or 1990s. We can say they are somewhere in the middle.

Koreans have responded and adapted appropriately to challenges and crises. The '*Palli Palli* (hurry hurry)' culture, which is typical of the Korean people, is deemed to have been instrumental in bringing about the rapid development. There is a tendency that people cannot stand staying idle or doing nothing, because this will make them uneasy as if some kind of penalty will be incurred for doing so. They feel more comfortable keeping themselves busy.

Without question, the strong role of government was essential in propelling the nation forward. The government was effectually 'interventionist' during the high growth period, but even during later phases, its active role persisted in the form of engagement in regulating and 'facilitating' the national economy, which has become increasingly complex to manage.

Jongryn Mo and Barry R. Weingast explain Korea's development using an analytical method devised by North, Wallis and Weingast (2009) referred as the 'NWW approach'. They attempt to explain how the transition of Korea's political economy from an underdeveloped to a developed country took place, that is, from a 'natural state' or 'limited-access order' to an 'open-access order'.[7] Countries have different levels of openness or accessibility in their political order and economic order, and when the disparity between these two becomes large, it causes social tensions that require 'rebalancing' measures.[8]

According to the authors, Korea's successful development came about because an increase in economic access was followed by a corresponding increase in political access (democratization).[9]

The Four Cornerstones of Development

Land Reform

The first major impetus for change in Korea came from the land reform, that was a powerful and innovative policy based on the land-to-tiller's and market-oriented principles. Korea's land reform is internationally known as one of the most successful cases of its kind. The Korean case of land reform stands out as it was rapidly implemented, resulting in the collapse of landlords who dominated rural communities at the time. This is in stark contrast to the disappointing results seen by many other developing countries in their land reforms.

Park, Hyung-Ho observes that:

> Korea's land reform was implemented based on a compound combination of political, social and economic factors. In the way that Korea abolished a semi-feudal tenancy system as well as landlordism in a relatively short period of time, Korea's land reform is acclaimed as the most successful case of land reform all over the world. Therefore, a redistributive land reform at an early stage of development can be a crucial means to lay the basis for agricultural productivity gains while enhancing growth and poverty reduction prospects. Such government interventions can lead to both equity and efficiency gains.[10]

When Korea was liberated in 1945, it was an agrarian economy in which most of the population were tenant farmers without ownership of farmland. In view of the slave-like status of the tenant farmers who were subordinate to landlords, the 1948 Constitution that established South Korea guaranteed private land ownership and proclaimed the adoption of a capitalist economic system. While the land reform's social objective was to free the populace from the shackles of servitude, its 'economic objectives were to improve agricultural productivity and the income of farmers by dismantling the oppressive tenant farming system, to encourage reinvestment, and to provide incentives through ownership of land and production'.[11]

Korea's land reform and the Korean War in effect brought about equality in income and property in Korea. The vested interest class of landlords was disbanded and educational opportunities were extended to the people, thereby promoting greater social migration and an egalitarian society. The land reform had a huge impact on Korean society. The proprietary class, the landowners, inherited lands handed down to them generation after generation from their ancestors, while tenant farmers remained where they were, leading to 'the rich get richer, the poor get poorer' phenomenon. But with the sudden collapse of the proprietary class, the conflict between these two classes also came to an end.

The land reform that was undertaken during the time of war was considered the most important measure during this phase of development. The government purchased the land and redistributed it to farmers in consideration of its market value. The government bought land by issuing land securities to the owners, and the farmers paid for the land in kind by instalments. In South Korea, landlords were compensated, unlike in North Korea, where land was confiscated and redistributed forcefully.

The land reform offered the chance for farmers, who made up about 75% of the Korean population, to farm on their own land. Being given the right of ownership was another big change for the vast majority of the populace. In itself, the reform did not have an immediate impact in terms of increases in agricultural production and income, due to the fact that war broke out and the new independent farmers, unlike the past landlords, lacked the necessary funds to invest in agriculture. However, it had a considerable impact in promoting the capitalist system and economic development in South Korea in the 1960s and afterwards. It helped South Korea nurture a capitalist society by giving property rights to farmers, unlike in North Korea, where collective farms were the norm. The guaranteeing of private farmland ownership in effect also created the necessary conditions for the guaranteeing of private property rights in other economic activities.

An important point to note was that the Rhee government promoted both land reform and education reform at the same time, so that human capital could be successfully accumulated in Korean society, and this led to successful industrialization after the 1960s. The land reform and education reform produced synergistic effects.

It has been pointed out that thanks to the land reform, farmers were able to increase production and own what they farmed. They could think of climbing the social ladder and becoming rich. That's how they worked harder and created more wealth. Thus, it laid the groundwork for economic development and overall social development.[12] Scholars have recognized that among the fast growing economies in the world, the case of South Korea, which has exhibited a remarkable degree of overall fairness in terms of income distribution, is exceptional. Many Korean experts argue that the roots of such success should be traced back to President Rhee Syng-Man's land reform, as there is a recognition that Korea was able to embark on a modernization path as an egalitarian society without this tension between the classes. Under such conditions, the possibility of acute conflict between the classes that has commonly occurred during the course of the progression of capitalism was shielded. It is said that this is the biggest benefit that Korea derived from the land reform.[13]

In the case of East Asian countries like Korea, Japan and Taiwan, the successful land reform helped bring about a large middle class, which acted as a cornerstone for economic growth and a social 'buffer' or balancer. This is in a stark contrast to many Latin American countries, where such a wide gap between the rich and poor exists due to their failure to properly enact land reform. The effective abolition of the social class system in Korea led to the realization of equal opportunities for all, and this in turn later gave rise to the spread of a 'can-do spirit' typical of Koreans.

Hyung-Ho Park states the lessons learned from Korea's experience of land reform: (1) the resistance of the privileged class on behalf of landlords should be overcome; (2) land reform should be accompanied by follow-up measures to ensure an increase in agricultural production and farmer households' income; (3) educational reform should be promoted concurrently to maximize the social benefits of land reform; and (4) the government's ability to implement reforms is important.[14]

Empowering the People

As I have pointed out earlier and illustrated in the Korean development model in Fig. 8.1, strong development-mindedness (DM) and ED were the two key drivers of Korea's sustained development. What propelled and reinforced these two elements further was the egalitarian spirit of Korea that was fostered during this time. In turn, the government's policy of 'empowering' people, along with the land reform, significantly contributed to the burgeoning of this national ethos.

The Korean government, in the circumstances in which it found itself and with the means at its disposal in the 1950s, was naturally inclined to pursue 'miserly' policies that sometimes called on the populace to do its part or help out the country. This is in stark contrast to many Sub-Saharan African countries that in effect use the plague of their people and poor state of their economy as leverage to get more offerings or concessions from donors. Korea tried to turn things around by itself through self-reflection instead of 'outsourcing' the burden of finding solutions to its problems to the international community. This 'outsourcing' trend, rather than diminishing, is seen to be becoming more pronounced in Africa.

Because Korea was not only devastated by the war but was also poor in terms of its natural resources, it had to rely heavily on foreign aid. With the massive flow of aid, the society developed a dependency syndrome that was seen by the government and intellectuals to have reached an alarming level and was having a very negative impact on the country. In such an environment of poverty and despair, men became idle, drinking and gambling their life away, while women did most of the household chores and laborious work.

The campaigns to empower the people led by the government had two purposes: other than the need to motivate and instil a work ethos in the people, there was a requirement for large-scale labour mobilization for pressing public works like land reclamation and reforestation.

Because of Korea's lack of fuel due to its dearth in natural resources, the practice of timbering was widespread, meaning that many hills and mountains in populated areas were barren. This caused perennial flooding following heavy rainfall, accompanying mudslides, and sanitary and environmental problems.

Something had to be done to rectify this state of affairs, as well as to address people's problematic behavioural and 'mentality' issues, and the response came in the form of 'empowering the people'. This campaign started as early as the late 1940s under the Rhee government. The government wanted to change people's mindsets and values, and infuse a new work ethos: nothing would be free and everyone had to work hard; people were asked to work for food under the government-led projects and they were paid in wheat flour given by the US as aid. The materialization of such a policy showed the willingness of the people to change and empower themselves.

This kind of environmental protection public works initiative turned out to be a resounding success. The government was not only able to get people to participate in it actively, but also managed to sustain it in the long term. Preservation of the country's greenery through the planting of trees became a 'norm' for the people, and this public campaign has survived to this day. Nearly 21 million people participated in the land reclamation and reforestation programme led by the government. Over ten billion trees were planted over 30 years, bringing Korea's once-desolate landscape back to life. South Korea had been barren of trees after years of excessive deforestation and war, but trees once again covered 65% of the country. It was a remarkable achievement and the opportunities to make a living and to be rewarded for hard work helped establish a new set of values that would serve Korea well during its rapid development.[15]

I believe that the success of programmes to empower the people provided a useful basis for the *Saemaul Undong* that was launched in the 1970s. The former were the government-driven projects to conduct specific tasks, while the latter was essentially a bottom-up-style people's voluntary movement with the government's guidance and backing. The benefit of this was that it made people realize the value and necessity of collective work, and become used to the new culture of the mobilization of the workforce that was absolutely necessary at the time to initiate effective development.

It was not only the government that tried to empower the people. The need to 'enlighten' the people was perhaps felt widely across the nation and certain entities were engaged in this effort. One institution that is renowned in this field is the Canaan Farmers School, which specializes in mindset change training. It is founded on the Christian faith, with the goal of creating a humanistic society and prosperous future through moral value education, community education and leadership education.

While the school was formally established in 1962, its origins can be traced back to a model village that was created in 1931 by the founder of the School Kim, Yong-Ki. At the time, Koreans were suffering from Japan's severe colonial oppression and he led a farming movement, which was in a way a nationalistic movement to bolster people's self-esteem, determination and hope. The vast majority of the people were farmers and the leader of Canaan farmers' movement saw a fundamental national challenge in the form of the mindset of the people, and waged a fight against the shortcomings of the populace, like powerlessness, idleness, over-indulgence in drinking and dissipation. He embarked on the farmers' enlightenment movement in a bid to change the culture of dishonesty and vanity. He claimed that independence would come about faster when there were a growing number of people with the right attitude. The motto was 'pioneering spirit'.

The Canaan Farmers School is said to have been an inspiration for President Park Chung-Hee to launch the *Saemaul Undong*. As Korea had attained high economic growth and the agriculture sector continued to shrink, the focus of this school also underwent some changes. I remember in the 1980s, when I was in my twenties, Canaan Farmers School was considered as a sort of mental-reform institution teaching the values of self-discipline, thrift and diligence, social responsibility and ethics, etc. Many groups of people from various backgrounds, including public officials, businessmen, students, leadership course trainees and farmers, entered the school to be trained. Individuals also enrolled on a voluntary basis. Decades later, the school extended its scope of activities to international programmes or development projects both domestically and in foreign countries.

There were other similar mindset reform campaigns led by various religious entities and social groups, like the Catholic Church's revival of the moral rearmament movement with the motto 'it's my responsibility'. In Korean society, you can very often see civil society groups expressing slogans for the reforming of citizens' mindsets. This means that Korean society is basically a self-reflecting society and that the empowerment of the people is self-generated by the people. This is the opposite of how the 'empowerment' of the people is understood and pursued in some African countries, where grants to a large segment of poor people are provided in a way that makes them more dependent on the state.

Revolution in Education

It would not be an overstatement to say that Koreans understand the value of hard work and education probably more than anyone else. In the 1950s, illiteracy among adults was a staggering 77%, and an all-out war was waged to fix this. In 1954, the first campaign of the war was launched by making primary education compulsory. Primary education was deemed most important because in this period in one's life, people learn the basic knowledge and social skills that serve as the foundations for human development. What is even more important is that it made primary education accessible to girls. So, lack of money was no longer an obstacle to receiving primary education.

After 1945, enrolment in primary schools grew rapidly. In less than a decade, Korea reached an enrolment rate of 83% in primary education, up from only 54% in 1945. By 1959, primary education was within reach of everyone. The war on illiteracy was waged in community centres scattered across the country. Millions of adults learned to read and write in schools with US assistance. It was made compulsory that illiterate adults took up more than 200 hours and over 70 days of education. In five short years, illiteracy rate among adults fell to just 22%, which was a remarkable achievement. Within a decade of the launch of this mandatory education, the number of primary schools grew from 2800 to 4600, and students from 1.36 million to 3.6 million. Universities also grew rapidly, from 19 to 68, with university students increasing from 8000 to 100,000. Numbers of middle-school students grew by 10 times, high-school students by 3.1 times and university students by 12 times.

When we look at the government budget in the 1950s, the portion spent on education accounted for about 20% of the total, which is seen as an impressive statement of the government's commitment to education, even in a time of war when defence spending took up about 50% of the entire budget. This laid the groundwork for what turned out to be an icon of Korea: a nation enthusiastic about education. It is often said that the ingredients for Korea's success lie in its human resources. About 17 years ago, when a Korean law-maker who was visiting Cote d'Ivoire was asked by his counterpart what brought about Korea's economic development, he replied without hesitation that 'it is the education and the will of the people'. I would add to this that what really made the difference was the education that went beyond regular academic studies, like inculcation and regeneration of social values, and pragmatic and action-oriented courses like technical training.

Governmental Reform

While three of the 'four cornerstones of development'—the land reform, empowerment of the people, and a revolution in education—were launched during the Rhee Syng-man government, governmental reform, namely the creation of Korea's National Tax Service, was undertaken during the Park Chung-Hee government.

In 1966, the National Tax Service, the first of its kind, was established. If educational reform was the war against illiteracy, establishing the National Tax Service was waging a war against deep-seated corruption in government and business. This was symbolic of the government's efforts to undertake self-reform to tackle corruption and improve services. The effect of the reform was almost immediate, as tax revenues grew by 51% on average from 1966 to 1969. The increase in tax revenue provided critical fiscal resources and helped Korea to become self-sustainable.

During the time of President Park's tenure in office, various efforts were made for nation-building and accordingly, many government agencies, mechanisms and policies were created or launched. To name just a few, within the five years since Park Chung-Hee assumed power, the Economic Planning Board, the Rural Development Administration, the Ministry of Construction, the Board of Audit and Inspection, and the Ministry of Science and Technology were established. These were all very important and foundational organizations, but President Park is said to have particularly favoured the National Tax Service, and this organization soon became an all-powerful and authoritative government watchdog and enforcer of national revenue collection.

It is widely accepted that a meritocratic bureaucracy was critical for Korea's fast development and this is one of the things that set Korea apart from most other developing countries. The advent of disciplined, capable and patriotic bureaucrats may have been bred by the Korean culture, but this would not have been possible in Korea without strong leadership and the commitment of the ruling elites to motivate government officials in such a way. Recognition and promotion were effective tools that were used to maintain the meritocratic bureaucracy.

The 'governmental reform'—in a wider context of rejuvenating and empowering the entire bureaucratic circle to become substantially more goal-oriented and 'functional'—took place during the time of Park's government. As we have seen, the principle of 'incentives and punishment' that the government applied to businesses was also in fact applied to civil servants and, in this regard, to the general public as well.

On Koreans' Temperament and Egalitarianism

As Korea went through a half-century of upheaval to enter the mature stage of development, it seemed timely that Koreans looked back and assess what their ingredients of success were with greater depth of perception. Over the years, a number of interesting works by Korean experts shedding light on the 'secrets' of the Korean people's temperament have emerged. Among them are Baek, Suk-Ki's

Koreans' Success DNA (2007) and Shin, Gwang-Chul's *Extremist Koreans, Extreme Creativity* (2013).

What is interesting to note in this regard is that recent efforts to find explanations for Korea's economic or developmental success from a Korean perspective are being increasingly drawn to the domain of national traits. Early observations both within and outside of Korea cited the general traits of Korean people as 'hard-working' or 'diligence'.

But recent studies on the temperament of Koreans have become more sophisticated. Baek observes that this temperament has evolved over the course of Korea's history. Traditionally, Koreans were known for their paternalism, veneration of literature, respect of traditional and moral values, respect for the elderly, originality and optimism, emotional sensitivity, etc. But on the other hand, they also showed vanity, disunity, disregard for economy and pragmatism, laxity in terms of morality, obsessions with the past, lack of ambitions, lack of rationality and courage, irresponsibility, self-righteousness, exclusivity and ignorance of the rule of law.[16] However, as the people entered into a dramatic phase of transformation in the 1970s, they showed active and aggressive traits, blending Western rationality with their traditional values. Veneration of literature, social orderliness, courage, a challenging spirit, love of peace, ethics, paternalism, a taste for distraction and amusement, an egalitarian spirit, democratic values, creativity and humour were stressed. At the same time, emphasis on face-saving, emulation and accommodation of others, intervention in the affairs of others, superstitions, lack of cohesiveness, collective egotism, dichotomic thinking of what is just and unjust, and hastiness were pointed out as shortcomings.[17]

Baek lays out six uniquely Korean facets that drive Koreans to try to become 'number one' in the world: (1) emulating and meddling in others' affairs in order to surpass them; (2) employing full creativity and dynamism to create new values; (3) a *bibimbap* (mixed rice) culture of fusion and harmony (the icon of today's network society); (4) a *palli palli* (quick, quick or hurry, hurry) temperament, which is 'an advantage in the digital age'; (5) a *shinbalam* (love of merriment) spirit serving as an impetus for the creation of new cultures; and (6) a zealous passion for education.[18]

Shin, Gwang-Chul's work is much more historical, detailed and analytical in terms of identifying and tracing the many originalities and facets of the Korean national ethos. He traces back as far as the ancient Korean kingdoms and highlights Korean cultural heritage as evidence. Here, the word 'extremist' or 'extremism' is used as a term to depict not religious or ideological radicalism, but how Korea has accommodated and embodied different things that are so different or in contrast to each other. Reading his book, I came to realize that the Korean national flag is a good reflection of this: the circle in the middle of the flag is derived from the philosophy of yin and yang, the balance and harmony of opposing forces.

According to Shin, Koreans have traditionally accepted 'extremities' or 'opposites', and this would be quite unique in this world. The characteristics of Koreans are elaborated and summarized as the following four points: first, Koreans accommodate totally different and opposite elements, internalizing and socializing them; second, Koreans have the dynamism to 'traverse' between the two extremes to create new things; third, Koreans provide 'middle grounds' to avoid collisions between the extremes; and, fourth, Koreans have the ability to 'integrate' differing factors to bring about a greater whole.[19]

For example, when foreigners are asked to name one single trait that best describes Koreans, many would say it is the *palli palli* temperament. There are both positive and negative connotations to this, such as diligence, motivation and a positive work ethic, but also hastiness, quick-temperedness, social stress, etc. But interestingly enough, on the opposite side of *palli palli*, there is this trait of 'composure and perseverance' that is typical of Koreans. Patience, endurance and a 'never give up' spirit have been the hallmark of the Korean people. On the surface, these two may seem to have no links whatsoever, but what drove Koreans to achieve success was not only the *palli palli* spirit, but, perhaps more importantly, this contrasting 'composure and perseverance'.[20]

In fact, South Koreans do have many inconsistent and conflicting attributes. For instance, when there is a 'get-together night' for office workers, everyone is expected to take part in the fun and revelry until very late into the night. They are allowed or encouraged to go to the 'limits'. Often they are told they should not worry about work the next day. But it turns out that no one is excused for tardiness and laxity, and they are expected to show up on time to work the next day as if nothing had happened.

In Korea, different thoughts and ideologies, religion and culture are all merged to be re-created. During the last 2000 years, Koreans were subjected to Confucianism in every aspect, spiritually as well as in daily life. While China and Japan came into direct contact with Western powers and half-coercively opened their doors to let in capitalism, Korea was more receptive to Western civilization and influence because the US liberated Korea from Japanese colonial rule. Koreans were so envious of Western ideas, science and technology to the point that Koreans' own traditions and values were being discounted, and hence the sense of Korean national identity was seriously curtailed. Korea's traditional values were considered obsolete and the strong sense of urgency to 'change' led to Korea's compressed economic development.

Having achieved modernization in an unprecedented manner and also having experienced the positives and negatives of rapid economic development in a competitive environment, Koreans have started to look back on their history and national identity. As Shin observes, now in Korea, traditional Confucianism and Western capitalism might be heading towards a collision. The ongoing talk of 'economic democracy' in Korea is consistent with the Confucian task of taking care of 'people's economic plight'. Confucianism values equality and humanism, while capitalism is based on competition and materialism. For a long time, Confucian values were seemingly put on the back-burner, but they have been flowing in the veins of Koreans and, according to Shin, are now on the rise.

Koreans may well be at a crossroads in terms of their value system and attitudinal orientations. They have achieved both unprecedented compressed economic development and democratization. Western ideas and system have fuelled the former, while the latter might be attributable to the 're-emergence' of the Confucian values of egalitarianism and humanism. Western countries experienced industrialization and rapid economic growth before realizing democracy, and the Korean model of development is consistent with this modernization. But there is no denying that the innate Korean national ethos made this transition possible in such a compressed manner.

Na, Jong-Seok has written a very insightful book on Korea's Confucianism and democracy, in which he claims that Korea was able to achieve democracy based on its traditional Confucian values rather than through its adoption of the Western ideals of democracy. Na asserts that Korea's democracy has flourished because it is rooted in its Confucianism and, unlike conventional thinking, Confucianism and democracy are not conflicting values.[21] This may be true, and it provides food for thought for other developing countries struggling with political challenges and social cohesion.

The rise in people's expectations, a rapidly ageing society, the increasing influence of globalization, along with other factors pose new challenges to Korea. As competition and the income gap increase, so does social tension. Furthermore, there are increasing concerns that the youth today are mentally vulnerable and weak. Thus, Korea finds itself in need of once again reflecting on its national values and the way forward. The new developments in the Korean Peninsula surrounding the issue of North Korea's denuclearization, if it continues to make progress, can have no small impact on the national visions.

As Korea fully embarked on the modernization drive, the egalitarianism spirit of Koreans re-emerged, albeit in a different form. The traditional egalitarianism was more of a 'passive' right or idealism bestowed or upheld by the kings and the leaders. The new modern egalitarianism in Korea was born in the very trying conditions, like the struggle against Japanese colonialism, the Korean War and the devastation of the land. As mentioned earlier, the 1950s set the stage for a series of bold reforms like the land reform that revamped the vested interests, leading the way towards a greater egalitarian mindset of the people.

The 1960s can be seen as a turning point in the history of Korean egalitarianism: 'passive egalitarianism' turned into 'proactive egalitarianism'. This proactive egalitarianism was built on the traditional egalitarianism and humanism with the new 'empowerment of the people' policy pursued by the government. The government's all-out modernization drive propelled the people to be more motivated and 'egalitarian minded', and this proactive egalitarianism in turn helped the government's agenda of economic growth and rural development such as the *Saemaul Undong*. When Korea was well on its way to rapid industrialization, this egalitarian spirit was turning into a formidable force for political change. Korean democracy finally came of age in 1998 with the first-ever peaceful transfer of political power from the ruling party to the opposition party. What seemed impossible happened 'overnight' when votes were tallied for the presidential election, and the perennial opposition leader Kim Dae-Jung was declared the winner.

This showed that Korea is a land of surprises and dynamism that constantly reinvents itself. The year 2002 was marked by the 'eruption' of the Korean people's passion when Korea co-hosted the FIFA World Cup with Japan. It was an important occasion for the Korean people, especially the younger generation, to uplift their pride and confidence, and rediscover themselves. It was also the year when a tragic accident took place, in which two Korean junior high-school girls were hit by a US army armoured vehicle. The US military court's acquittal of the two servicemen in the vehicle sparked unprecedented anti-American sentiments and protests in Korea. In that year, the presidential election was won by Roh Moo-Hyun, the most progressive President the nation had ever seen. Roh's election ushered in a new generation of Korean politicians to power.

The *Saemaul Undong* (The New Village Movement)

In the 1960s, Korea posted record growth under the five-year economic development plans, but this policy drive, centred on industrialization, deepened the gap between urban and rural areas. Many people left rural areas to start new lives in the cities, and the growing discontent of the farmers became a political problem. Unemployment and poverty emerged as social issues, and the agricultural sector was faced with labour shortages, causing a rise in agricultural production costs and threatening the viability of the sector.

President Park Chung-Hee realized that economic development could not be fulfilled without rural development. It was necessary to improve the income of rural households and encourage people to remain in rural areas by providing more income-earning opportunities and employment. This called for drastic measures to reverse the problems caused by the unbalanced growth that was fuelled by rapid industrialization. The *Saemaul Undong*, which in the beginning had the appearance of a campaign for improving rural living conditions such as roads, housing, water supply, sewage and irrigation, soon turned out to be an all-out movement for transforming the rural sector and the nation as a whole.

The *Saemaul Undong* is a Korean community development model which contains the spirit of diligence, self-help and cooperation that is also shared in the urban areas as well. It is said that during those times, most rural areas in developing countries, including those in Asia, were trapped in a vicious cycle of poverty, despite the flow of international aid and the government's efforts. In this regard, the World Bank pointed out that it would be difficult to resolve the poverty situation without a special reform programme being in place.[22]

Korea was no exception, and before the *Saemaul Undong* started in the 1970s, in rural areas, about 80% of households were thatched roof houses and only 20% had an electricity supply. As there were no village entry roads for vehicles, even cultivators could not enter the villages. The situation in Korea back then is comparable to or even worse than what most Sub-Saharan African countries are facing today. But Korea was able to overcome this common and perennial dilemma, the underdevelopment of the rural-agricultural sector of developing countries, and enter the next threshold of development because of the drastic or 'revolutionary' measures initiated by the Korean government in 1970.

Complementing this community movement was the government's efforts to develop new varieties of rice as part of the Green Revolution and conducting large-scale land reclamation projects to create farmland. In the early stages, the Ministry of Internal Affairs played a leading role in this campaign by providing cement and other materials through the local administrative network. Later on, more ministries took part in conducting the movement-related programmes, such as assisting rural households to find alternative sources of work out of season, forming cooperatives for the production of rice and barley, supplying electricity to rural areas and building factories.

The *Saemaul Undong* was launched as a mentally reformative movement to make villagers aware of the spirit of diligence, self-help and cooperation, and a mental reform was achieved through practice and action instead of words and theory. The secret of the *Saemaul Undong* lies in its practicality, and it was a success because people themselves practised it. As was suggested earlier, the *Saemaul Undong* could not have been launched at a more opportune time. There was a sense of urgency in the population to get out of the misery in which they found themselves, and with the limited resources they could rely on, it was like they had no other choice but to work hard in order to earn a better living. If Koreans did not embark on such a movement at that time, they could have missed the critical opportunity to do so. It would have become increasingly difficult for the Korean people to take on hardships or make 'sacrifices' for tomorrow as they might have already lost hope or motivation, or have fallen into the sinister trap of the vicious cycle of dependence that we witness today in many Sub-Saharan Africa countries.

The positive thing about the *Saemaul Undong* was that it bred a virtuous cycle of voluntary collective work producing concrete results, and this reinforced the 'can-do spirit' of the people, which, in turn, brought about competition among villages and widening participation in the movement. The spreading of the *Saemaul Undong* not only in rural areas but also in urban areas and factories was like a 'wild-fire'. What appears to have helped the farmers to be enthusiastic and confident was that Korea was already witnessing changes in the form of high growth in exports and industrialization in the 1960s.

At the beginning of the movement in 1971, the government is said to have provided 335 sacks (40 kg per sack) of cement to 33,267 villages, leaving it up to the villages to decide for themselves which projects they would use the cement for. As a result, villagers held community meetings in which they elected *Saemaul Undong* leaders and agreed on which projects they would undertake and how they would undertake them following long discussions. For instance, if the villagers decided to construct a village entry road, they would work out specific plans on how to secure the necessary workers and land, and how to acquire and transport gravel and sand, the raw materials needed to make concrete.

The Korean government evaluated the projects of all villages in 1972, one year after enacting the movement, and named 16,600 villages (approximately half of all villages in Korea) as 'outstanding villages'. These outstanding villages were those that had successfully implemented *Saemaul Undong* projects and were provided with an additional supply of 500 sacks of cement and one ton of steel by the government. The villages that were not given additional government support were stimulated by the government's differentiated support system and, as a result, when all the villages were evaluated again a year later in 1973, some 6000 villages were found to have implemented *Saemaul Undong* projects with their own resources and without government support.

Against this backdrop, the government classified villages into three categories: basic villages, self-help villages and self-reliant villages. Different projects were implemented in accordance with the level of performance and the level of government support was varied as a result. The principle of prioritized support to successful villages was applied. The strategy of *Saemaul Undong* can be summed up as being three-pronged. First, the government played the role of jump-starting or igniting the villagers' participation by giving limited support to spur the spirit of diligence, self-help and cooperation. Second, villagers started with practical projects in which they can participate and benefit from, and implemented the projects in a democratic process. Third, villagers fully embraced the principle of prioritized support to outstanding villages designed to induce the spirit of self-help and cooperation.

Jai-Chang Lee elaborates and sheds insights on the spirit of the *Saemaul Undong*: as the *Saemaul Undong* is a mental reform movement, its underlying spirit is emphasized all the more; however, in the past, many developing countries around the world attempted to develop the rural sector through so-called community development movements without success; the most important reason for their failure was that they were devoid of the component of mindset reform given that such type of rural transformation initiatives, in essense, requires mindset reform based on its own social-moral fabric like cultures, traditions and national spirit; this was in contrast to Korea's *Saemaul Undong*, which was implemented based on the home-grown spirit of diligence, self-help and cooperation.[23]

There are many proverbs that underscore the virtue of the *Saemaul Undong* spirits: 'the early bird gets the worm (diligence)', 'heaven helps those who help themselves (self-help)' and 'two heads are better than one (cooperation)', to name but a few. In Korea, there was a traditional cooperative agricultural group called *durae* and a traditional culture called *hyangyak*, a village code of conduct followed within agricultural communities. These traditional Korean heritages became the basis of the *Saemaul Undong* spirit, and the people's strong yearning to escape poverty ignited the *Saemaul Undong* spirit of diligence, self-help and cooperation.[24]

In the initial stage of the *Saemaul Undong*, the government supplied villagers with basic raw materials such as cement and steel, while providing them with some technical guidelines. The villagers were able to execute by themselves the projects to improve their basic living environment with the backing of the government. For example, kitchens, fences and sewages were modernized in households, and village entry roads were widened and paved, and public laundry facilities as well as public wells were constructed through the *Saemaul Undong* living environment projects. In addition, training was conducted in order to enlighten villagers with the *Saemaul Undong* spirit and to nurture their leadership.

The second stage involved building communal infrastructure and implementing production and income-generating projects with the SMU spirit and project experience that had been acquired. The main projects for improving infrastructure included the construction of bridges, clearing of village streams, paving farming roads and building irrigation facilities. Meanwhile, livestock breeding, horticulture, non-agricultural income-generating business, cooperative productions, greenhouse farming and speciality crop farming, such as of herbs, can be cited as examples of the income-generating projects implemented at the time. During this stage, professional education on construction and farming as well as mental training was conducted.

In the third stage, various projects for common profit were implemented based on the SMU spirit accumulated through previous projects. Public funds were raised through the *Saemaul Undong* credit union, cooperative project committees, village stores and the selling of food during special events. In addition, public village facilities such as village libraries, barber shops, baby care centres, public storages, rice mills, workshops and public farming machines were provided.

The fourth stage saw the expansion of the *Saemaul Undong* to urban areas. SMU, which started as a rural development movement, further developed nationwide during this stage. Urban *Saemaul Undong* was implemented in the cities by promoting public order, kindness and cleanliness. Energy saving, the promotion of frugal lifestyles and the improvement of product quality as well as productivity were promoted through quality control campaigns in companies and factories.

In more recent times, efforts have been made to promote the *Saemaul Undong* as a new national movement that can adjust to changes in Korean society under such slogans as 'Green Korea, Smart Korea, Happy Korea, and Global Korea movement'. Good examples of the new *Saemaul Undong* are the national campaign to gather gold in order to recover from economic crisis, a win-win movement to promote cooperation between employers and employees in businesses, and various social service movements.

Even though great progress was made through the *Saemaul Undong*, trial and error could not be avoided. But the important thing was that improvements were made as villagers searched for ways to rectify shortcomings in themselves, while the government provided timely and adequate guidelines.[25]

Lastly, according to the Korea *Saemaul Undong* Centre, the success factors of the *Saemaul Undong* can be identified as follows: (1) voluntary participation of villagers; (2) democratic decision-making; (3) dedicated leaders; (4) differentiated support by the government; and (5) grassroots-level (village unit) execution.[26]

Notes

1. Joon-Kyung Choi, *Upside-Down Success Story of Korea's Economic Development* (Seoul: Daewon Publishing, 2013), translated by Christy Hyun-Joo Lee, pp. 6–7.
2. Irma Adelman, 'From Aid Dependence to Aid Independence: South Korea', http://www.un.org/esa/ffd/wp-content/uploads/2007/11/20071116_IrmaAdelman.pdf.
3. Joong-Kyung Choi (2013), Prologue XX.
4. Dr. Choi, Joong-Kyung, a former chief economic advisor to the President and Minister of Industry, Trade and Energy, also served in the World Bank as Executive Director and was appointed Ambassador to Philippines.
5. Chosun.com (Korean daily news), 1 September 2014, http://pub.chosun.com/client/news/viw.asp?cate=C03&mcate=M1002&nNewsNumb=20140915514&nidx=15515.
6. 'Miracle of South Korea' (2011) (video), http://cafe.daum.net/yogicflying/Cia1/145214?q(2012.3.1).
7. M.O. Jongryn and Barry R. Weingast, *Korean Political and Economic Development—Crisis, Security and Institutional Rebalancing* (Cambridge, MA: Harvard University Press, 2013).
8. Ibid., pp. 3–4.
9. Ibid., p. 9.
10. Hyung Ho Park, *2012 Modulation of Korea's Development Experience: Land Reform in Korea* (Seoul: Ministry of Strategy and Finance, 2013), p. 121.
11. Jung Jay Joh and Young-Pyo Kim, 'Territorial Development Policy', in Sakong and Koh (2010), p. 183.
12. 'Miracle on the Hand River', DVD made by KDI (2012).
13. Kim Young-Sam, 'Korea Owes RHEE Syngman for the Nation's Egalitarianism', *New Daily Korea*, 9 April 2014, http://web2.newdaily.co.kr/news/article.html?no=199491.
14. Hyung Ho Park (2013), p. 122.
15. 'Miracle on the Hand River' (2012).
16. Suk-ki Baek, *Koreans' Success DNA* (Seoul: Maekyung Publications, 2007) (Korean), pp. 122–124.
17. Ibid.
18. Ibid.

19. Shin Gwang-chul, *Extremist Koreans, Extreme Creativity* (Seoul: Sam & Parkers, 2013).
20. Ibid., pp. 30–32.
21. Jong-seok Na, *Daedong Democratic Confucianism and 21st Shilhak* (Seoul: Dosochulpanb, 2017) (Korean).
22. 'Saemaul Undong in Korea', lecture given by Jai Chang Lee, President of the *Korea Saemaul* Undong Centre at Makerere University, Kampala, Uganda, 19 October 2012.
23. Ibid. Joong-Kyung Choi, in *Upside-Down Success Story of Korea's Economic Development* (2013), points out that many countries including China have tried to emulate the *Saemaul Undong*, and the *Saemaul Undong* in development economics is understood as a concept of Community-Driven Development (CDD) and is promoted as one of the main policy items by international organizations like the World Bank; however, the CDD is more of a NGO-led social development programme and thus differs from the prototype of the *Saemaul Undong*, which is self-help.
24. Ibid.
25. Typical mistakes or shortcomings include villagers being faced with technical gaps in the process of autonomous implementation. For example, there were cases of large bridges constructed by villagers breaking down after a while due to villagers' lack of technical skills; in some instances, villagers were burdened by some projects that were beyond their capacity of implementing. This is the consequence of too much emphasis on competition; also, some village projects aimed at only 'visible' results.
26. To elaborate, villagers' voluntary participation was induced through efficient and timely support from the government. Villagers became participative as their confidence was raised through the possibility of economic development and rural improvements as part of the government's efforts to make Korea industrialized. Second, *Saemaul* projects were implemented in a democratic way in which villagers made their own decisions. The government only provided technical guidelines, while villagers elected *Saemaul* leaders and selected the projects to conduct in their villages. This autonomous policy induced the spontaneous participation of villagers. Third, there were dedicated *Saemaul* leaders and their strong leadership was nurtured by the *Saemaul Undong*. The *Saemaul* leaders were unpaid voluntary workers who were elected

by villagers and played the role of a leader based on the *Saemaul* training they received at the *Saemaul Undong* Central Training Institute. *Saemaul* awards were given to leaders in accordance with their accomplishments to raise their morale. Fourth, the government prioritized support to well-performing villages to induce competition based on self-help spirit. The government also differentiated its level of support to villages categorized into three levels: basic villages, self-help villages and self-reliant villages. As a result, villagers worked harder on their projects to upgrade their village level and receive more support from the government. Fifth, *Saemaul* projects were executed in village units. Traditional villages in Korea were able to bring about cooperative spirit and common profit that worked for the *Saemaul Undong* (Jai Chang Lee, 2012).

Part V

Application of the Korean Model for Africa

9

Applicability of the Korean Development Model for Africa

Lessons of Fundamentals of Economics and Industrialization

Sub-Saharan African countries are still grappling with the issue of how to tackle poverty and move up the economic ladder. For any poor country wanting to break out of its lot and join the ranks of rich nations, realizing structural, wide-ranging and continuous changes in all sectors is a necessity. Those economies that have successfully emerged in a transformative fashion were able to do so because they were progressing on multiple fronts, as was the case in many East Asian and Southeast Asian nations. South Korea pushed forward many social, educational, economic and governmental 'reforms' and launched industrialization and rural development in a 'concurrent' manner.

The worst-case scenario would be where a poor country with no resources remains idle and fails to undertake any significant economic initiatives. Resource-rich countries are better off as they can rely on these resources, but the danger of the Dutch Disease (the problem of production of natural resources causing a decline in other sectors like manufacturing) wrought by a commodity-based monocultural economy

J.-D. Park, *Re-Inventing Africa's Development*,
https://doi.org/10.1007/978-3-030-03946-2_9

looms in these countries. Hence, an unsavoury recipe for the countries would be a combination of a resource-rich, commodity-dependent structure with bad management, and a lack of sense of ownership or a workable strategy. Evidently, hardly any countries have successfully developed simply by relying on their natural resources.

An IMF report released in April, 2017 confirmed that oil-exporting countries and other resource-intensive countries in Sub-Saharan Africa were showing the worst economic performance in the region.[1] Even countries like Botswana and Zambia that enjoyed a reputation for good governance and were regarded as models in Sub-Saharan Africa experienced problems related to a commodity-dependent economy. Traditionally, African economies which are primarily reliant on agricultural produce like cacao, coffee and tea have experienced vulnerability with the fluctuation of international market prices. While commodity prices have been recovering in 2018, various economic forecasts point to rather sluggish growth for the resource-rich African countries.

And then, of course, we see a preponderance of economic liberalization, free trade and investment in Africa. Somehow, the myth that privatization, liberalization and the influx of foreign companies will, *in themselves*, unleash the full economic potential of their country has settled in Africa. In appearance, this has all the bearings of a positive trend and can certainly help, but it masks the untoward side of the reality. In order or any policy to be successful, the government must assume responsibility and a hands-on posture. All policies have drawbacks as well as advantages, and this should not be forgotten. Furthermore, different policies require different conditions and although trial and error is inevitable, appropriate rectifying measures must follow. However, the tendency seems to be that the authorities opt for convenience and the easy way out.

Basically, in order for any organization to function properly, it would require positive leadership from the top and adherence to its rules or policies by the members. The stronger such traits are, the more efficient the organization will be. And in the case of governmental bureaucracy, this should be all the more evident. The bigger the hierarchical structure of an organization, the greater the 'trickle-down effect' the quality of leadership will have on the organization. There is an old Korean saying that 'upper stream water must be clean for downstream water to be clean'.

There is also a cliché that says 'action speaks louder than words'. Public services are delivered by actions, and the timely provision of services is of the utmost importance. The credibility, authority and efficiency of the state stem from the everyday performance of the governmental bureaucracy, which is determined by the devotion and actions of civil servants. When we are talking about producing real outcomes, that is, being productive, we mean making an improvement over time. The variables are intrinsically 'change' and 'speed', or how fast this change can be made. Change or improvement can be either quantitative or qualitative, or both. The measure of progress is how much and how fast things can be done.

Myopic vision, which is not looking ahead, and expediency, which is choosing what is convenient now rather than what will yield better results tomorrow, both come with costs. A typical example is when requests are made to build factories, training institutes, etc., but after they have gotten them from development partners, the familiar pattern of mismanagement ensues. Often the training and consulting provided to local officials and operators are rendered futile as soon as they are handed over. Of course, some projects manage to survive and last as intended, proving to be useful, but these are the exceptions to the rule.

Also, in many countries, there seems to be a tendency for people wanting things for the sake of 'possession', as an end in themselves, rather than to utilize them as a means to extract additional or greater benefits. I have met many African officials, businessmen and rural leaders who would say that once they receive investments and factories, everything else will take care of itself. But in order to run a factory, people need utilities, management, maintenance, skills and capacities, funding, etc. Securing a facility in its physical form is one thing, but operating it successfully is another thing entirely.

In the context of addressing poverty, African leaders are urging their rural populace to get out of the subsistence way of life and engage in more productive activities to generate income. For peasants, subsistence means getting by with what they can find around them without being far-sighted and having a long-term plan in place. However, the problem of 'subsistence' is also inherent in other sectors, including the public sector.

As laid out in the African Union (AU)'s Agenda 2063, all African countries aspire to growth and sustainable development, and aim for a 'structurally transformed' economy. And every leader seems to have industrialization in mind. It will be difficult to imagine having structural transformation of economy without industrialization or a manufacturing sector. Figure 9.1 represents manufacturing as a percentage of GDP, comparing Sub-Saharan Africa with East Asia, Southeast Asia, and Latin America and the Caribbean. It shows the persistently low level of Africa's manufacturing sector in its post-independence era. Interestingly, in the early 1960s, Sub-Saharan Africa started with a higher percentage compared to East Asia, but now there is about a 15% difference between them: the figure for East Asia is about 25%, while Sub-Saharan Africa is hovering around 10%, and this is even lower than Southeast Asia, and Latin America and the Caribbean.

The challenge, as well as the opportunity, facing Africa's manufacturing is shown in the composition of import and exports in Fig. 9.2. Manufactured goods make up almost 60% of its imports, while energy (mostly oil) constitutes the dominant export. Agriculture makes up

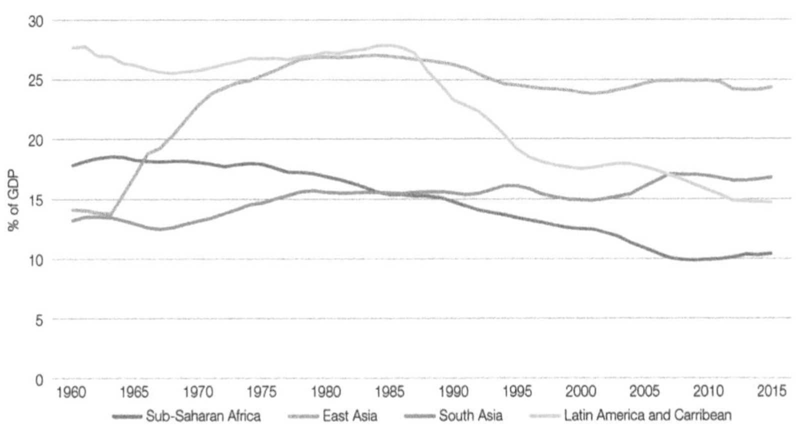

Fig. 9.1 Manufacturing as a percentage of GDP by selected global regions (*Source* calculation in Ifs v. 7.33 (five-year average); ISS South Africa, 'Made in Africa' (April 2018))

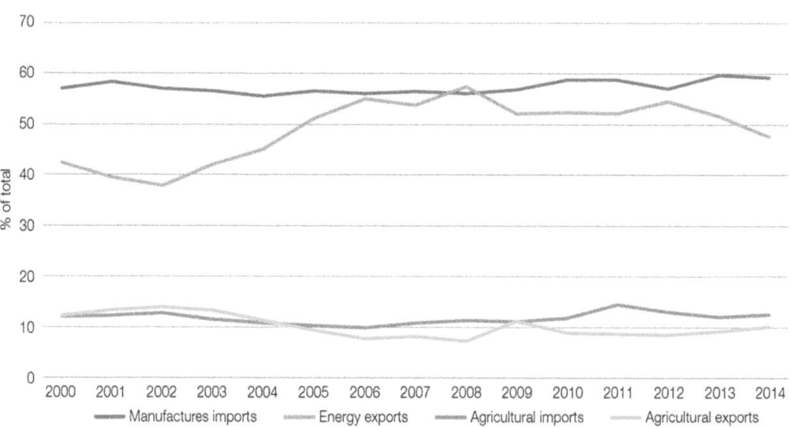

Fig. 9.2 Most important import and export sectors: Africa's trade with world (rest) (*Source* calculation in IFS? v. 7.33; ISS South Africa, 'Made in Africa' (April 2018))

around 12% of imports and around 10% of exports. Sub-Saharan Africa has a huge agricultural potential, but its dependence on food imports is growing, with nine countries depending on imports for more than 40% of their demand.[2] The weakness in African countries' manufacturing is closely related to the uncompetitiveness or high cost of its labour force relative to their average income levels, which is the combination of many things: workers' skill levels, poor infrastructure, institutions, health conditions, etc. Hence, it is generally considered that 'African labour cost needs to be cheap enough to compensate for other benefits. South Africa stands out as a middle-income country with particularly high labour costs and a very capital-intensive industrial sector'.[3]

Exports are what African countries have counted on, but their share of global exports has declined over the past 35 years from 4.5% in 1980 to 3.0% in 2015, and the exported items are mainly commodities, with the share of manufacturing exports declining from 0.4 to 0.3% over the same period.[4] Even maintaining their level of exports, let alone expanding and upgrading industrial capacity, is not a simple task. In 2016, Africa's GDP growth fell to 1.4%, its slowest rate for more than two decades.[5]

There is a choice that Sub-Saharan African countries have to make: first, they can either accept the hard reality and make the most of (or do what best they could with) the given economic conditions; or, alternatively, they can make extraordinary efforts to transform and upgrade their industrial and economic structure adopting a set of different and bold measures. But neither of these two options would be comfortable ones for African countries to espouse. The first choice would be difficult for countries to bear because what it really means is resigning to the reality and the status quo, while the second choice entails significant burdens, commitment, endurance, focus and effective mobilization of work.

The choice is up to each Sub-Saharan African nation to make, but most African countries can end up stuck in the middle between these two options. What Africa leaders and elites really have in mind, and what they intend to do, matters. But in any case, what they seem to prioritize is to lure as much foreign investment and companies as possible to stimulate businesses and the economy. However, the possibility of a quick fix in the economy is virtually non-existent if it is to be transformational. Such approach will have inherent limitations without the expected increase in income and employment, and capital accumulation or reinvestment, if many other conditions that Africans themselves need to satisfy are not met. And these are essentially all human factors: strong oversight for business support, a business-facilitating environment, sound corporate governance, a high level of economic-mindedness and rational thinking, a sense of public duty and ownership, discipline amongst officials, etc.

Should African economies undergo structural transformation, the conventional path would be to move from a traditional economy to an industrial economy, and then to a tertiary industry economy. The world is buzzing about 'industry 4.0' or the fourth industrial revolution, which is the new generation industrial revolution that combines manufacturing technologies and ICT.[6] Such a development path is that which developed countries have undergone. The UK was the leader in industrialization, and other European countries and the US followed suit. In Asia, Japan was the first to successfully transform and later South Korea realized unprecedented compressed economic growth.

There is no economically developed country that remains a primarily agricultural economy without a manufacturing industrial capability. Even an agriculture-based economy will need a certain level of manufacturing capability in order to reap meaningful benefits from its agricultural sector. And it requires much greater industrialization to move to the second phase of development, and then to the third phase of tertiary industry or the service sector, which includes commerce, finance, insurance, tourism, public health, mass media, consulting, education, entertainment and logistics.

Unfortunately for developing countries, we are now living in the era of globalization that is so much more competitive. Such an environment inhibits the growth of domestic industries in the 'fragile' economies of Sub-Saharan Africa. Rather than moving along each stage in a linear trajectory, developing countries may have to pursue all these three phases concurrently, given the circumstances of today's globalized world.[7]

However, African countries should not give up industrialization because they need to, and actually can, achieve industrialization, even while the age of 'new globalization' of industrial robots and 3D printers is dawning before us: their best chance of industrializing in the coming decades will be to focus on intra-regional trade and targeting agriculture-based industrialization, because these are less affected by global competition and trends. The developing agricultural sector is also crucial in that it can absorb the fast-growing youth population into rural areas.[8]

On the other hand, while Africa's industrialization lags behind, the new global developments may now work to Africa's advantage: the impact of digitization of production and the trend towards locating manufacturing closer to markets—what Baldwin termed the new globalization and the phenomenon of the 'great convergence'.[9] Such characteristics of the 'new globalization' like greater participation by emerging economies and the growing role of small enterprises is I think worth noting from Africa's perspective.

According to the McKinsey Global Institute, the 'new globalization' that has emerged in the twenty-first century is different from the 'old globalization' of the twentieth century, and these two forms of globalization have contrasting features: tangible flows of physical goods vs. intangible flow of data and information; flows mainly between advanced economies vs. greater participation by emerging economies; capital and labour-intensive flows vs. more knowledge-intensive flows; transportation infrastructure being critical for flows vs. digital infrastructure becoming equally important; multi-national companies drive flows vs. the growing role of small enterprises and individuals; the flow mainly of monetized transactions vs. more exchanges of free contents and services; ideas diffusing slowly across boarders vs. instant global access to information; and innovation flows from advanced to emerging economies vs. innovation flows in both directions.[10]

Some argue that leapfrogging in terms of technology is both possible and desirable for many Sub-Saharan African nations. To a certain extent, this is already happening in the region, like the widespread usage of wireless internet and mobile phones forgoing communication requiring wire connection, and economic transactions using ICT like mobile money services. Others point out the global trend of the expanding service sector and the dwindling manufacturing sector, but this does not negate the need for Africa to continuously pursue industrialization.

Reflecting on the Korean Experience and Africa's Reality

Korea's economic dynamism is a testament to the veracity of the principles of the market economy. As we have seen, Korea did not rely solely on market mechanisms, but it certainly used markets to its full advantage. There are differing views on whether Korea's economic success is due to the adoption of orthodox capitalism and free market-oriented policies, but it is fair to say that Korea utilized other measures to *supplement* and *reinforce* capitalism and markets, and not to substitute them. In hindsight, this was perhaps inevitable and necessary. Otherwise, Korea would not have achieved such a feat if it were not for the extraordinary measures it took, considering the disadvantageous conditions and state of underdevelopment in which it found itself.

All things considered, the Korean model of development does provide good lessons and reference points for emulation for Sub-Saharan African countries. Although the Korean case can be considered an exceptional and dramatic example, and hence difficult for others to replicate with success, this does not diminish its value and relevance—it serves as a forceful reminder of what is possible for developing nations.

One of the lessons to draw from Korea's experience is that development efforts can only work if they are supported by the essential 'foundations' that must be put in place at the early stages of development. This is to say that a sort of 'multi-tasking' is required. The reason why economic and development policies do not work well in Sub-Saharan African countries is that the basic foundations that are necessary to support them are very weak or almost non-existent.

There cannot be a quick fix to economic challenges and the fundamentals must always be observed. If development is to take place nationally and sustainably, then industrialization should go hand in hand with rural-agricultural development and empowerment of the people. The industrial sector cannot be built out of thin air. Even if the physical conditions are favourable for industrialization, there is still a need for human resources to make it work. In order for factories to properly operate, what is required are capital, a skilled labour force, good management, a steady supply of utilities, satisfactory infrastructures, etc. In the region, things tend to degenerate into vicious circles because one thing after another is lacking, and there is little effort made to fix the situation.

Returning to the fundamentals of economics, the basic production factors—land, labour and capital—are all necessary means for industrialization, and technology, which is treated as an exogenous variable in economics, is a key element for enhancing production. In order for any underdeveloped country to modernize, it would need capital in the form of both physical and human capital. So, how can countries amass the necessary capital for development in the first place? The answer is that they should start with utilizing what is already available to them. In the early stages of economic development or industrialization, except for city states or commercial hub cities, the majority of the populace would be living in rural areas, working in the primary sectors that include agriculture, livestock, forestry, fisheries, etc. Without the development of these sectors, there cannot be wealth creation enabling a transition to the secondary industry of reprocessing and manufacturing, ranging from light industries to heavy industries.

As we have already seen, the Korean government laid the groundwork for industrial transformation with rural reform, namely land reform and pro-poor empowerment of people policies, before embarking on an export drive in the early 1960s. The *Saemaul Undong* was launched in 1970, and following this, urban and rural development was concurrently pursued, while export promotion and the *Saemaul Undong* produced synergistic effects.

The ideal for developing countries would be to push for agricultural-rural sector development and industrialization at the same time in a way that results in these two producing mutually reinforcing effects. But in Africa, the primary industry largely remains 'traditional agriculture'. A sensible path for economic development would be prioritizing industrialization in the agricultural sector, where their comparative advantage lies. This makes sense not only economically but also politically, because the vast majority of people are villagers and farmers. Today, as the marginalization of the rural populace continues amid a population explosion and worsening income disparities, the countries should have no choice but to deal with this challenge more proactively.

The example of Korea is not the only case of vindication of the pro-poor rural-agricultural policy for developing countries. Unlike many African countries, Korea is resource-poor and has unfavourable natural conditions. Africa, with its vast arable land, fertile soil and abundance of natural resources, has all the more reason to be enthusiastic and focused on rural-agricultural development. Scholars who have studied the divergence in development between Asian and African countries will notice what is underlying the situation, as David Henley does:

> In South-East Asia, elite attitudes to village life, although condescending, are often also marked by nostalgia and a degree of admiration. Although Africa has had no lack of rulers with rural origins, their attitude to rural life has mostly been much less positive. Consequently they have tended to see development not as a matter of improving the living conditions of the

> peasant masses in situ, but rather as a question of accelerating the transition from rural backwardness to urban modernity, of which their own lives have been a microcosm. This has led them to favour elitist development strategies aimed at acquiring symbols of developed-country status (universities, steelworks, information technology, human rights) rather than meeting the urgent practical challenge of making poor people richer by whatever means lie immediately at hand.[11]

It is understandable that in Africa, frustrations are vented by those who follow the news on global trends like 'the fourth industrial revolution'. A Ugandan intellect asks:

> Why Sub-Saharan Africa has never undergone an industrial and manufacturing revolution, despite repeated declarations and summit communiqués by heads of state during the past 50 years? … we must try to look for the root causes, while acknowledging that the failure to industrialise is not due to absence of blue prints or elaborate government policy documents in the ministries, like that of industry. Today, we live in an era of national visions, with target dates, to which we add international blue prints issued by the United Nations.[12]

He went on to admit that the role of the government is central for industrialization, but blamed the dictates of the World Bank and the IMF's liberalization for greatly undermining the role of the state.

The tasks for latecomers to industrialization were to learn, emulate and adopt the know-how and technology of advanced industrial economies. Under the circumstances, Sub-Saharan African countries need a combination of technologies: hi-tech, modern, conventional and appropriate. The benefit of being developing countries is that it is easy to get technical transfers from other countries. These and so many other things should have already been done by African countries. And let us not forget that before contemplating the 'industrial revolution' and developing the manufacturing sector, rural-agricultural development initiatives should have been undertaken.

Speaking of the capitalist economic system, there were a number of different types of capitalism in the world history. A crude form of market economy had existed since the beginning of world civilization, and agrarian capitalism, mercantilism and industrial capitalism existed well before modern free-market capitalism.[13] What should be noted is that nearly all the currently existing capitalist economies are mixed economies, which combine elements of free markets with state intervention and, surely in some cases, economic planning. There is no such thing as a 100% liberal market economy in our reality, as pointed out by Ha-Joon Chang (2002, 2008, 2010). On 'transformative industrial policy for Africa', Chang stressed that industrialization must remain at the centre of African development, despite the prevailing economic orthodoxy, and that manufacturing and agriculture can work to support each other. He saw that African countries can still find room amid World Trade Organization regulations and the penetration of monopoly producers to achieve high levels of development through industrialization.[14]

No doubt, as was argued by Joseph Schumpeter, capitalism is the most effective economic system that the world has seen, as it creates wealth through the continuous process of advancing levels of productivity and technological sophistication. Therefore, in order to advance the state of economic development of African countries, due attention must be paid to advancing their 'capitalistic system' in terms of economic performance. However, amid vague expectations that somehow the free market will get things working, the fundamentals have been ignored. And what happened to innovations and 'creative destruction' that are supposed to come about following the progression of capitalism in Africa?

For decades, the Washington Consensus, the imposition of the neo-liberalist approach and even the giving of foreign aid itself were frequently cited by Africans and others as obstacles to Africa's development. But irrespective of the extent to which these have actually had an impact on African countries, these countries cannot be 'exonerated' from failing to carry out their innate responsibilities. The case of Korea is a sobering reminder of what needs to be done for a poor nation to move up the ladder of development, and its lesson is that aid, whether in the form of grants or financial loans, will be helpful when properly utilized. Foreign assistance itself is not the problem, as it is simply a means to an end. One can use it usefully or render it useless, and aid would not necessarily root out resources for the private sector or inhibit its growth. Business and the economy fail not flourish in the region not because there is too much aid, but because there is a lack of economic activities in the first place: modest entrepreneurship, a non-committal attitude when it comes to economic activities and investing their resources for future gains, etc.

Successful and creative entrepreneurs have certainly emerged in Sub-Saharan Africa, but they are too few in number and it takes much more than talented businessmen to turn around the economy. Recent reports confirm that Africa is still the most commodity-dependent continent in the world. In order to uplift and invigorate the economy, African countries need to have manufacturing industries that can export to create jobs and generate income for the rapidly growing population. Of course, it has become harder to industrialize. When developed countries and Asian countries industrialized, they did so in a different international setting from that in which African countries now find themselves. However, we should ask why Africa has not been able to build up a manufacturing industry when many others have been able to do so. As even African Development Bank experts point out, regardless of the hurdles facing Africa today, 'manufacturing remains the best hope for SSA to generate a large number of good jobs and reduce the prospects of political and social instability'.[15]

Achieving successful economic transformation would be unthinkable without an evolution in the manufacturing sector. Yes, there has been a lot of talk of entrepreneurship and buzz about business start-ups in many Sub-Saharan African countries, encouraged by the likes of CNN's *African Start Up* and *Africa Marketplace* programmes. While this is to be commended as positive, there is also some cause for worry. Leaving the vast segment of the populace in the private sector to survive in the wilderness of open markets by virtue of their creativity may be not the most responsible thing to do. Even in one of the most innovative countries like Korea, today about 70% of all start-up businesses fail within a few years. We should heed the warnings that premature deindustrialization is neither a desirable nor an inevitable trend for developing countries.

Many prominent scholars like Dani Rodrik, Ha-Joon Chang and Joseph Stiglitz have stressed the importance of realizing and deepening industrialization for developing countries. As noted earlier, Rodrik has written about the 'perils of premature deindustrialization'. Chang stressed that the idea put forward by neo-liberalists that countries can skip the industrialization phase and move on to the deindustrialization stage is simply an illusion; since the service industry is inherently small-scale and has limitations in terms of its production capacity, it cannot be a sufficient driving force for economic growth. Furthermore, service goods are not easily traded, so service sector-based economies lack exporting capabilities; according to Chang, this in turn curtails export earnings and the ability to purchase foreign technologies, jeopardizing economic growth.[16]

Joseph Stiglitz has lately expressed that the government plays a central role in shaping the economy, not only through formal policies (industrial, and expenditure and tax), but also in writing the rules of the game, and the economic structure is inevitably affected by the way in which the government structures markets.[17] In that sense, Stiglitz mentions that every country has an industrial policy, but some countries do not know it, and when governments are not self-conscious in their direction of the economy, this opens up the possibility of special interests greatly influencing the economy, leading to pervasive inefficiencies, lower growth and more inequality.[18]

One would think that Korea has already achieved a full cycle of industrialization, but in his recent book *There Is No Korea After 3 Years*, Byeong Ho Gong warns Korea against deprioritizing the manufacturing sector.[19] If the manufacturing industry is still vital for countries like Korea, which is the sixth-largest exporting nation in the world, what does this say about other developing countries?

Building an industrial economy for Sub-Saharan African countries should begin in the agricultural sector. In fact, on many occasions, African heads of state have convened to be reminded of, and recommit to, this need. For instance, they recommitted themselves to the Comprehensive Africa Agriculture Development Programme (CAADP) in Malabo in 2014. The CAADP is a continental framework with a 2025 vision for promoting inclusive growth and prosperity through investment in the agricultural sector. African countries are said to have taken the lead and put in place their own National Agriculture Investment Plans (NAIPs). Once again, there is no lack of expression, but the problem always lies in the implementation. The commissioner for the rural economy and agriculture at the African Union Commission writes:

> According to World Bank, evidence shows that in sub-Saharan Africa (SSA), investing in agriculture is 11 times more rewarding in reducing poverty than investment in other sectors. Data show that 80% of marketed agricultural production in SSA comes from smallholders, 60% being women. The issue, therefore, is no longer whether the agriculture sector is important; it is rather how Africa should invest boldly in its agri-food systems so as to leapfrog the structural transformation of the overall African economies ... In order to sustain the achievement and to accelerate the implementation of agricultural plans, countries will need to invest in systemic capacity building. The youth should be equipped with knowledge, if we want our agriculture to go the extra mile. African countries should rethink their capacity building strategies by focusing more on vocational training.[20]

A collective awareness that agriculture must be the priority sector to target for Africa's development seems to have materialized and gathered momentum among African leaders and experts, as well as international organizations like the World Bank. Without any doubt, the establishment of a sound agricultural industry will form the bedrock of economic transformation in Sub-Saharan African countries.

As much as rural-agricultural development is strategic for Sub-Saharan Africa, its realization cannot be expected to happen overnight either. However challenging the task may be, African governments and peoples must be patient and persist in their efforts. To begin with, while it would be desirable to add value to agricultural products and enhance the value chain, it is also crucial, in the meantime, to boost the production of crops. People were inclined to believe that because there is no market and poor infrastructure to transport agricultural goods in Africa, there is no use producing in mass quantities. But more and more African farmers are realizing that good production, in terms of both quantity and quality, is paying off. The stable production of large amounts of commodities of consistent quality are what everybody—the government, investors, private firms, donors and international organizations—is looking for, and the demand for these seems to be on the rise.

Korea's experience underscores the importance of the agricultural sector. Korea realized its Green Revolution and White Revolution during the period of the modernization drive in 1970s and 1980s. Throughout Korea's history, for the sake of stability and security amid external threats and invasions, increasing food production was a long-cherished desire of the nation. From the early 1960s, Korea set out its first National Economic Development Plan to pursue self-sufficiency in food production, making it a priority on the national agenda. As the government actively pursued various policies to increase food productivity, by the latter half of 1970s, Korea was able to achieve 100% self-sufficiency in rice production, which is the main national staple.[21] The achievement of self-sufficiency in rice production in Korea is referred to as the Green Revolution. This was accomplished through R&D efforts in the agricultural sector and a new technology transfer system, such as increased rice productivity through improved rice varieties, as well as the development of cultivation technologies and the swift dissemination of new technologies to farmers.

This process was also driven by the government's commitment through its policies and practices on building infrastructure related to rice production, flexible production and supply chains for materials such as fertilizers and chemical pesticides. Self-sufficiency in rice production became a cornerstone for strengthening the basis of national economic development not only for procuring food security and boosting incomes of farm households, but also for saving foreign currency required to import foreign rice.

The White Revolution refers to the modernization of the structure, material and technology of greenhouses in Korea needed to achieve the rapid expansion of protected cultivation areas and to produce a stable supply of vegetables from the 1970s to the 1990s. The name derives from the extensive use of white-coloured plastic or polyethylene films for greenhouses. Before the 1970s, all plastic films were imported into

Korea, but greenhouse vegetable production became popular from the 1970s onwards, when Korea built up its petrochemical industry. In this respect, industrialization greatly benefited the agricultural sector.

Before vinyl houses or greenhouses were used in Korea, vegetables could not be grown in winter, but once they became available, farmers were able to produce them all year round, which also benefited consumers, who could enjoy fresh vegetables all the time. In the 1980s, flower growing became possible, and now even fruits (including some tropical fruits) are being produced in greenhouses in Korea. Nowadays, 'smart greenhouses' with remote control technology are being developed. The White Revolution greatly contributed to Korea's rural employment and income generation, which in turn helped support the national economy. Economic growth as well as government plans and policies enabled the rapid expansion of protected cultivation using greenhouses in a very short period of time.[22]

Another critical element in Korea's successful development is the land reform that has been mentioned earlier. In many African countries, the system of ownership of land is managed in a 'flexible' but 'random' manner. While there is a need not to disrupt the status quo in land rights for the sake of social stability, a systematic and universal designation of land ownership must be enacted in the longer run for the efficient use of land for economic purposes.

Relevance of the Korean Development Model or Experience

South Korea's development experience and 'model' has many implications for Sub-Saharan African countries and it should be heeded from a practical as well as an academic viewpoint. Having come across a wide range of works on Africa's development conducted by a multitude of entities and having attended so many meetings, seminars and lectures on the topic, I cannot shrug off the impression that today's business in development has become too technical and routine, without being substantive. We seem to be lost in a world of logic and science, as if sharing rational and sophisticated thinking is the solution to problems. However, the essence of development is about *doing*, often needing to touch base with people at the grassroots level.

Africa's development programmes have failed to bear fruit not because the methods were wrong, but because people were not enacting them. Hence, the task is twofold: to basically 'adapt' to local conditions, but at the same time to 'challenge' the locals to change their attitudes and behaviour for the better. Thus, how to bring about change is key, and shaping perceptions, incentives and disincentives (or 'punishments') are of great importance. In this respect, Korea's development experience can provide useful food for thought as the Korean model is, in itself, an epitome of 'development as practice'.

In this respect, so much needs to be done, and one part of this is strengthening the social capital in African communities and society at large from the standpoint of practicality. However, albeit slowly, a certain level of awareness and endeavours to this end seem to be materializing in the region. For instance, Amin Mawji, who is the Representative of the Aga Khan Development Network (AKDN) in Uganda, has compiled best practice ideas of civil society in Africa in his book *Poverty to Prosperity*, in which he emphasizes values and ethics besides highlighting the best practices, and notes that 'an interesting challenge facing society today is how to motivate people from a cross-section of society – across tribe, colour, creed – to collaborate, to work together, to share'.[23]

The success of Sub-Saharan African countries is not assured even if they all adopt the same model of development, but their performance will depend not only on how they work on the basics, but also on how they compete and collaborate among themselves. And in the end, each nation has to figure out and pursue the best strategy for it to be competitive. And there is no need to prejudge or presume what is appropriate for the countries on their behalf. The value of the development model and examples should be gauged not on how much they can be easily replicated, but rather on how much motivation and positive impact they can bring to the countries.

Some experts are dismissive of the Korean case, claiming that it is an exceptional case and one which cannot have much relevance for developing countries. But there is strong merit in the Korean case being dramatic, forceful and clear-cut, and thus it should not be dismissed. In terms of an educated population, a skilled workforce and a sense of national unity, Korea may have been ahead of Sub-Saharan African countries at the time of its independence, but it was at a greater disadvantage in other areas. Also, many developing countries at that time surpassed Korea in various categories.

One could point out the different international setting for Korea at the time, which might have been more favourable for it compared to what African countries faced then and now. But on the flip side, it could be argued than some African countries as well as many other non-African developing countries may have had many more advantages than Korea in different ways. Generally, there are always many different ways to undertake personal, organizational, social and national tasks. If people make it a habit to think ahead and learn from previous experiences, the assignments they assume can be more easily and routinely carried out. This will enable more activity, output and speed.

People who harbour pessimistic realism or classist ideology may think that African leaders and elites, and foreign governments and companies, want the maintenance of the status quo in Africa—that is, continued underdevelopment—in order to safeguard their vested interests. And I also have heard from ordinary Africans that their leaders and ruling elites seem to not want the people to become enlightened or empowered because they fear that this might endanger their privileged status and interests. Some even suggest that African leaders are now themselves practising colonialism by exploiting their own people.

Resorting to tribalism, ethnic-regional division, taking advantage or fomenting security threats and conflicts, abusing security-military apparatus, etc. are traditional methods of ruling and maintaining power in many parts of the developing world, especially Africa. And unfortunately, in most instances, electoral democracy has degenerated into unwholesome contests to maintain power, influence and wealth. But the reality holds many truths. Normally, political leaders would neither be totally exploitive nor benign, but would fall somewhere in between these extremes. And no African leader would be able to fully manipulate and suppress their people. By all indications, the current rulers of Sub-Saharan

African countries are nowhere near the position of wielding complete control over their people without also jeopardizing their own status.

African leaders, from their perspective, could be apprehensive of the rise of public disgruntlement towards them, which can lead to social unrest. Internet usage and social media have also become widespread in Africa, and regional and international pressures are also significant, so that African rulers also have to watch their backs. All in all, Africa's persistent problems are primarily due not to the monolithic power of governments suppressing their people, but to a lack of coherence and unity in the nation, and a weak sense of purpose and commitment for development among leaders and people in general. The crux of the matter is that the nature of Africa's problems is portrayed mostly in terms of people's 'rights' (through the political prism), when in fact it is really about 'work ethics' or social conduct (functional, economic attributes). Today, just about everything is seen in a political light, and Africa's development is perhaps the greatest victim of this.

When the priority of African countries should be placed on finding human solutions to what are obviously problems of human nature, whether superficial or deep-seated, the trend of our times is moving away from this, following business, technical and educational sophistication, and the fanfare of innovation. So, there can be a misplaced 'conviction that progress can only be achieved by a quantum leap from (rural) backwardness to (urban) modernity'.[24] And what is also concerning is that the gap between the 'two worlds' inside African countries seems to be widening instead of narrowing.

Pursuing the trend of the times is a natural and smart thing to do. But such efforts will be hollow if the more fundamental tasks facing a nation are skipped over or forgotten altogether. South Korea was able to transform itself into a developed economy in such a short time not because it merely exerted itself in terms of adopting to the trend of the times, but, more importantly, because it focused vigorously in closing the 'development gap' by means of expeditiously tackling the innate basic obstacles that are characteristic of poor countries.

Who can refute that a nation has to be diligent for it to be successful in all aspects of life? This is self-evident, but I can hardly see any utterance of the word 'diligence' or 'hard work' in today's world, as if this is a thing of the past. Now and then, I see African leaders scolding their officials for being negligent and failing to get the job done, but I have rarely heard them enunciating the value of diligence as a norm that the civil servants or people should practise. Korea's turnaround required extraordinary work on the part of the people. If the Korean people were not supportive of the government's policies and did not actively take part in the development process, the nation would not have achieved such progress.

Many people seem to misunderstand that development or transformation will somehow occur over time and can be prompted by 'transfers' of capitals, know-how, technology, etc. But development is not about 'knowing', 'getting' or just desiring; rather, it is essentially about 'doing' things. Unfortunately for African countries, the world is becoming increasingly competitive and the human capital gaps are widening. This is why a dramatic turnaround in the mindset of the African population is necessary sooner rather than later. This is because development or transformation is equivalent to 'change', and the scale and depth of positive change over time matters. 'Speed' is also critical because if the changes take too long, it will offset any gains and might lead to other problems and even to regression. When you are nimble, there are advantages because you not only can go faster, but you can also have more time to fix things or turn back to find other routes when things are not right. A good example of this is Korea's response to the 1997 IMF bailout crisis.

Another crucial factor is the role of the government. South Korea is just one of many cases throughout history attesting to the importance of active government intervention to induce economic transformation and growth. We do not need to go back hundreds of years to the likes of Frederick List, Benjamin Franklin and Alexander Hamilton to be reminded of the genesis and tradition of government intervention to support the industry and economy. Today, governments of the developed world play expansive roles, albeit in a more intricate and technical fashion than in the past.

I have yet to see a businessman who has not admitted that the government's assistance is vital for his business. This holds true for all businessmen, regardless of their nationality and location. When it comes to doing business overseas, especially in new markets and in unfamiliar territories like Africa, businessmen say that the government's intervention is all the more crucial. Many advanced countries, including the US, are very regulatory in nature. The consequences of the 2008 global financial crisis give the case in point, proving the necessity of this stance. As for developing countries, governments can and should promote economic growth by playing an active role of facilitator and taking vigorous pro-capitalistic measures. Most importantly, the states should focus their energies on pushing for industrialization alongside the development of the rural-agricultural sector.

This is where the logic of 'economic discrimination' comes in. The word 'competition' is of essence in the economic world. And the forces that promote positive competition are incentives and disincentives or 'punishments'. If governments can be instrumental in encouraging many winners to emerge, this will spur economic growth. The economic history of the world is about winners. The rise and fall of powers, the surge of Western economies and the new rivalry unfolding among major economic powers today can all be seen in the context of who emerges triumphant over others. Hence, the future of the economies of Sub-Saharan African countries will hinge on whether and to what extent they espouse the rule of competitive economy and society.

There is an opportunity for change in the midst of challenges in Sub-Saharan Africa. The dissatisfaction of the masses in relation to their livelihood and the performance of states can remain latent and subdued, or can accumulate to generate pressure for reform, or cause unrest and chaos. But the leaders cannot remain complacent and idle because in order to stay in power, they have to be able to mobilize the resources to meet the minimum public demands. Most of all, the population explosion and the growing unemployed youth phenomenon must be dealt with before it reaches an untenable level.

What African leaders and governments have been doing is not working, nor is it desirable in terms of development. There are clear limitations on what foreign entities like foreign businesses, development partners, international organizations and NGOs can do for African countries, and whatever measures they take, it will revert to how African nations respond and what actions they take.

Therefore, the solution lies in breaking the psychological yoke—that they do not have the capability and are destined for underdevelopment—that has inhibited Africa from moving forward with confidence. As Ha-Joon Chang (2010) pointed out, Africa is not destined for underdevelopment: Africans are not poor because of any mysterious or immutable factors; they are poor for the same reasons other nations were once poor, which means that their poverty can be fixed if they apply the same solutions that other nations have applied. But before the right policies can be pursued, the psychological barrier that is at the heart of Africa's problem must be overcome.

Notes

1. IMF, *Regional Economic Outlook—Sub-Saharan Africa Restarting the Growth Engine* (April, 2017), p. 3. For 2016, most oil-exporting nations were in recession (with a contraction in GDP growth), while conditions in many other resource-rich countries also faced difficulties: continued political uncertainty (South Africa), weak fundamentals (Ghana) and acute droughts (Lesotho, Malawi, Zambia, Zimbabwe).
2. Jakkie Cilliers, 'Made in Africa-Manufacturing and the Fourth Industrial Revolution', *Africa in the World Report 8*, Institute for Security Studies, April 2018, pp. 7, 11.
3. A. Gelb, C. Meyer, V. Ramachandran, and D. Wadhwa, 'Can Africa Be a Manufacturing Destination? Labour Costs in Comparative Perspective', Centre for Global Development, Working Paper 466, 15 October 2017. Jakkie Cilliers, 'Made in Africa-Manufacturing and the Fourth Industrial Revolution', *Africa in the World Report 8*, Institute for Security Studies, April 2018, p. 11.
4. Ramathan Goobi, discussing 'IMF Regional Economic Outlook for Sub-Saharan Africa', presentation by Clara Mira, Country Representative of the IMF for Uganda, at ESAMI, Kampala, 15 June 2017.
5. 'How the Taxman Slows the Spread of Technology in Africa', *The Economist*, Middle East and Africa, 9 November 2017.
6. The first Industrial Revolution used water and steam power to mechanize production; the second used electric power to create

mass production; the third used electronics and information technology to automate production; the fourth is building on the third, the digital revolution that has been occurring since the middle of the last century. It is characterized by a fusion of technologies that is blurring the lines between the physical, digital and biological spheres. See http://www.weforum.org/agenda/2016/01/the-fourth-industrial-revolution-what-it-means-and-how-to-respond.

7. Continued globalization and technological progress (the fourth Industrial Revolution), an increasingly competitive international market amid the rise of emerging economies, among other factors, make the prospects of Sub-Saharan Africa's industrialization and structural transformation uncertain. The age of linear economic/industrial transformation may not be easy or sensible to pursue. In certain cases and areas, 'leap-frogging' might be both practical and inevitable because, for instance, ICT technology has already pervaded widely in the societies and economies of Sub-Saharan Africa.
8. Rafiq Raji, 'Additive Manufacturing: Implications for African Economies', *How We Made It in Africa*, 25 October 2017, https://www.howwemadeitinafrica.com/additive-manufacturing-implications-african-economies/60103.
9. Baldwin, *The Great Convergence: Information Technology and the New Globalization* (Cambridge, MA: Harvard University Press, 2016).
10. McKinsey Global Institute, 'Digital Globalization: The New Era of Global Flows', March 2016, https://www.mckinsey.com/business-functions/digital-mckinsey/our-nsights/digital-globalization-the-new-era-of-global-flows.
11. David Henley, *Asia-Pacific Development Divergence—A Question of Intent* (London: Zed Books, 2015), p. 25.
12. Semakula Kiwanuka, 'Why Has Sub-Saharan Africa Never Undergone Industrial Revolution?', *New Vision* (Ugandan daily), 24 March 2016.
13. See Ellen Meiksins Wood, 'The Agrarian Origins of Capitalism', *Monthly Review* 50, no. 3 (July–August 1998); Robert A. Degen, *The Triumph of Capitalism* (New Brunswick: Transaction Publishers, 2011), p. 12.
14. Ha Joon Chang, 'Transformative Industrial Policy for Africa: Put Manufacturing at the Centre of Development', speech given at the Second Annual Adebayo Adedeji Lecture, 3 April 2016, Addis Abbaba, provided by UNECA.
15. Haroon Bhorat, Ravi Kanbr, Christopher Rooney, and Francois Steenkamp, 'Sub-Saharan Africa's Manufacturing Sector: Building

Complexity', *Working Paper Series* No. 256, May 2017. African Development Bank, pp. 9–10.
16. Ha Joon Chang, *23 Things They Don't Tell You About Capitalism* (London: Penguin Books, 2010). The points made regarding markets and role of government are: (1) 'There is no such thing as a free market'; (7) 'Free-market policies rarely make poor countries rich'; (12) 'Governments can pick winners'; (16) 'We are not smart enough to leave things to the market'; (21) 'Big government makes people more open to change'; (23) 'Good economic policy does not require good economists.'
17. Joseph Stiglitz, *Rewriting the Rules of the American Economy: An Agenda for Growth and Shared Prosperity* (New York: W.W. Norton, 2015).
18. Joseph Stiglitz, 'Industrial Policy, Learning and Development', in John Page and Finn Tarp (eds), *The Practice of Industrial Policy: Government-Business Coordination in Africa and East Asia* (Oxford: Oxford University Press, 2015), pp. 23–39; WIDER Working Paper 2015/149, published by UNU-WIDER and the Korean International Cooperation Agency, Helsinki, Finland, December 2015.
19. Byeong Ho Gong, *There Is No Korea After 3 Years* (Seoul: Ishipilsegibooks, 2016) (Korean).
20. 'Why Strong Leadership Is Necessary to Transform African Agriculture', article written by Rhoda Peace Tumusiime, the Commissioner for Rural Economy and Agriculture of African Union (AU) Commission, appeared in *New Vision* (Uganda), 28 March 2016, p. 16.
21. Sok-Dong Kim et al., *The Green Revolution in Korea—Development and Dissemination of Tongil-Type Rice Varieties* (Seoul: KDI, 2012).
22. Rural Development Administration (http://www.rda.go.kr/foreign/ten). See also Hyo-duk Seo et al., *White Revolution of Agriculture in Korea: The Achievement of Year-Round Production and Distribution of Horticultural Crops by the Expansion of Greenhouse Cultivation* (Sejong: RDA, 2013) (Korean), pp. 15–18.
23. Amin Mawji, *Poverty to Prosperity: Empowering the Future, Best Practice Ideas from Civil Society* (Kampala: Graphic Systems Uganda Limited, 2017).
24. David Henley and Ahmad Helm Fuady, 'Sources of Developmental Ambition in Southeast Asia and Sub-Saharan Africa', *Developmental Regimes in Africa*—a joint initiative between *Africa Power and Politics* (APPP) and *Tracking Development*—Policy Brief no. 4, January 2014, p. 3.

10

Policy Recommendations for Africa

The Need for a Drastic Turnaround

In Chapter 5, I talked about the 'missing links' in Africa's development. The three things that I highlighted are the sense of nation, development-mindedness and the active role of the state. Mystified as to why so many things appeared not be working properly in the region, I pondered at great length as to what might be the reason for this. Over time, it occurred to me that basically these three things were fundamentally lacking.

Attaining these missing links expeditiously may not be easy but they are achievable, just as the Western and Asian countries, as well as others, have been able to do. Perhaps too many people, both Africans and outsiders, have come to have a fixed idea that African people cannot develop on their own and have to be helped continuously. But there can be nothing more detrimental for development than such thinking. No meaningful development can take place with outside assistance alone, regardless of how much assistance one can get from others. External supports can be of value only if they are used as instruments for bigger purposes than as short-term ends in themselves.

J.-D. Park, *Re-Inventing Africa's Development*,
https://doi.org/10.1007/978-3-030-03946-2_10

It is not enough simply to lay out national visions and express aspirations. Elaborate road maps and master plans that you see so often in many countries in the region have no bearing on development if proper and intensive actions are not taken in a methodical and sustained way. And there is no question that a nation will fare much better if it has a stronger sense of purpose and inclination to act in order to achieve whatever goals they might pursue as a nation. There have been no shortage of verbal expressions and written works stressing what must be done, but everybody seems to be waiting for someone else to take action. So, why is it that people are reluctant to take action?

Maybe a better question to ask would be: 'What induces people to act?' Here, the concept of *sinsangpilbhur*—the rule of incentives and sanctions (punishment) or economic discrimination—may come in handy. In the absence of incentives for good deeds, people will be less inclined to take positive action than otherwise would have been the case; equally, if there were no sanctions for misdeeds, people will be more inclined to repeat them than if there were sanctions. Hence, it will be an ideal proposition for a society to have in place a strong mechanism of incentives and sanctions for the maintenance of social order and productivity. The logic of 'doing' (being functional) should prevail over the logic of 'being' (being overly fixated on rights).

Regarding incentives, there is a general theory in psychology conceived by Abraham Maslow called 'the hierarchy of human needs', which is described in a pyramid structure. According to Maslow, human motivations follow a general pattern of movement up the ladder from basic needs to sophisticated needs: 'physiological needs' → 'safety and security' → 'social needs' → 'esteem' → 'self-actualization' → 'self-transcendence'. Originally, this comprised five stages, but Maslow later added 'self-transcendence' to his hierarchy. 'Physiological needs' refers to survival or basic instincts like wanting air, shelter, water, sleep, sex, etc. 'Safety and security' means individuals wanting to avoid immediate threads and dangers to their lives. 'Social needs' means love and belonging, like having friendship and family. 'Esteem' is about self-respect, confidence and achievement; 'self-actualization' means the realization of a person's full potential; and 'self-transcendence' is the achievement of one's 'highest' goal outside of regular dimensions in altruism and spirituality.[1]

Where there are human needs, there are incentives. Hence, the secret to success in achieving development may lie in inducing positive actions amongst the people using incentives that conform to their needs. But what are the incentives? This is essentially a relative and variable term, and their value or appeal depends on the perception of the people. For instance, all human beings would seek basic needs, but not necessarily everyone would pursue 'esteem' or 'self-transcendence', or at least not to the same degree. The meaning and importance of 'self-actualization' may vary greatly depending on the individual's social, cultural, economic background, and it also depends on personal traits and the level of ambitions of individuals.

So, what shapes human incentives? And how can they be structured? Can society and the state, together with the private sector, shape the structure of incentives for people in a way that can enhance national development? The answer is yes, and they should do so. These questions are related to perceptions, and therefore to mindsets. Along with incentives, punishments or sanctions can be a powerful and effective motive which can be conducive to development. But their value and effectiveness are only good insofar as they are perceived as such. This is why mindset change campaign is crucial, and the necessary interventions should be sought right away. Below is an illustration of how these are structured to meet national developmental goals.

The following figure illustrates incentives and punishments from the short-, mid- and long-term perspective. Short-term incentives for individuals would correspond to basic human needs or instincts for physical survival, like getting food and money. Mid-term incentives correspond to needs like securing a job, earning income and being recognized. Long-term incentives are the desires to realize self-fulfilment or gratification from the perspective of life accomplishment (Fig. 10.1).

Punishments are 'negative' incentives or disincentives. Punishments are applied for various acts—violations, misconduct, failures, crimes, etc.—that are censured by society. Short-term punishments are applied rightly and expeditiously, like when one is caught stealing. Mid-term punishments can be brought about by incompetence, under-performance, misjudgement, maladjustment, etc. and manifest themselves in the form of loss of trust, job, business opportunities, etc.

	short-term	mid-term	long-term
Incentives	**survival** (food, money, physical needs)	**stability** (job, income, recognition)	**self-fulfilment** (social status, career management, respect)
Punishments	immediate sanctions, penalties	instability, lost opportunities	deprivation, alienation, dishonour, life-failure

Fig. 10.1 The basic structure of incentives and punishments

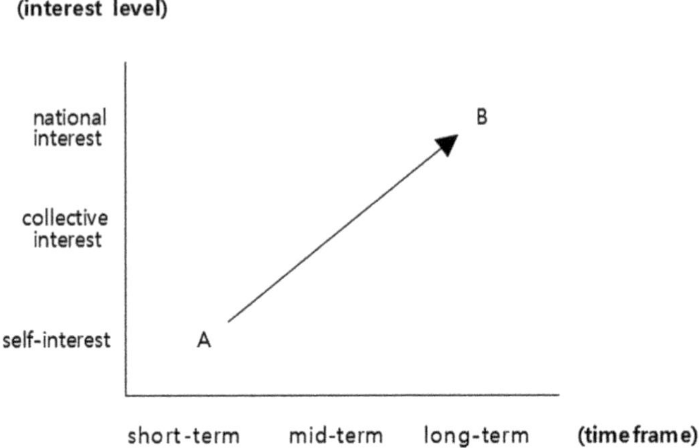

Fig. 10.2 The desired trajectory of pursuit of interest (incentives)

Long-term punishments would include more serious sanctions like long-term imprisonment, public censure and stigmatization, being banned for life from a profession, etc.

Once we recognize the basic elements of the incentive-punishment structure existing in the society, we may ask, how can they be applied? Figure 10.2 should be easy to understand. The vertical axis indicates different levels of interest that people seek, ranging from personal to national: self-interest, broader interest beyond individuals that can be called collective interest, and the national interest. The horizontal axis shows the timeframe: short-term, mid-term and long-term. If we can indeed engineer people's interest or incentive structure to evolve for the better, the desired path would be from point A to point B. People's pursuit of their personal interests is a matter of course. But people should always try to see the bigger picture of their environment and society because the 'inordinate' pursuit of personal interest by everybody will fundamentally deteriorate the conditions of their organization or society and make them unhealthy, which will, in turn, have detrimental effects on their personal interests—hence the importance of social order, social capital and collective/social interest. The same holds true for the national interest, and national development can be achieved only if national interests are promoted.

Figure 10.3 illustrates the missing links to achieving transformative and sustainable development in Sub-Saharan Africa: a sense of nation or national identity, a strong and proactive role played by the government and development-mindedness (knowing, practising, owning, passion: KPOP). 'Sense of nation' corresponds to 'social fabric'; 'active role of government' represents 'effective governance'; and 'development-mindedness' translates into 'productivity'. The pyramid shows in what order these three elements were put to work in realizing the economic (and to a certain degree political) transformation of South Korea.

Korea is a good case study highlighting the typical features of East Asian developmental states. Koreans developed a strong sense of national identity and unity during their struggle against Japan's colonial rule, the fight for independence and the push for post-war national

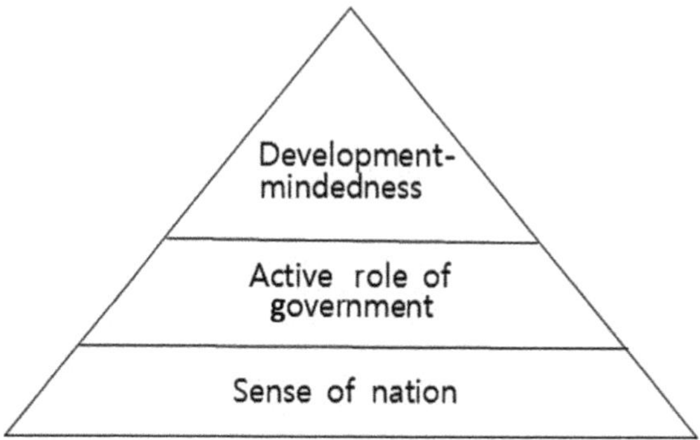

Fig. 10.3 The missing links to development

reconstruction.[2] In fact, throughout its history, Korea has been constantly subjected to aggression or threats by its neighbours and in the late nineteenth century, it became the arena of geopolitical rivalry among foreign powers.

Immediately after achieving independence in the aftermath of the Second World War, Korea was divided and subsequently engulfed in a civil war that devastated the entire nation.

Overcoming incessant adversities and challenges was at the core of the Korea's story of survival, modernization and full-fledged development. In the midst of despair and disorientation, the government's role was paramount in spearheading the nation forward on the path to modernization, particularly in the early stages of economic take-off. The government was the standard-bearer and initiated the empowerment of the people by instilling development-mindedness in them. The people positively complied, producing an extraordinary synergistic effect of government–people–business collaboration.

While this is not illustrated here, there can be alternative paths (in terms of sequence) for countries where a sense of nation, national identity and unity are still weak. For example, a strong government initiative bringing on board various political, social and regional leaders and groups could foster a sense of nation and development-mindedness. This could be done by national campaigns spearheaded by political leaders.

Before we deduce a development formula or model, which is an important aim of this book, it will be informative to also try to illustrate what is the basic structure of development of Sub-Saharan African countries. This is shown in Fig. 10.4. You can see that 'government' and 'firms' are marked much smaller relative to 'market' and 'foreign assistance', and that the area of overlap of these components is also small. This means that the role of or dependency on the market and foreign aid is relatively much higher. And often it is difficult to make distinctions between business and development activities.

Here, a widespread market liberalization is a common feature and the economy is left to the market system to take care of itself. There is little government intervention or role played to promote and stimulate the economy. Naturally, foreign assistance or donors' support is substantial,

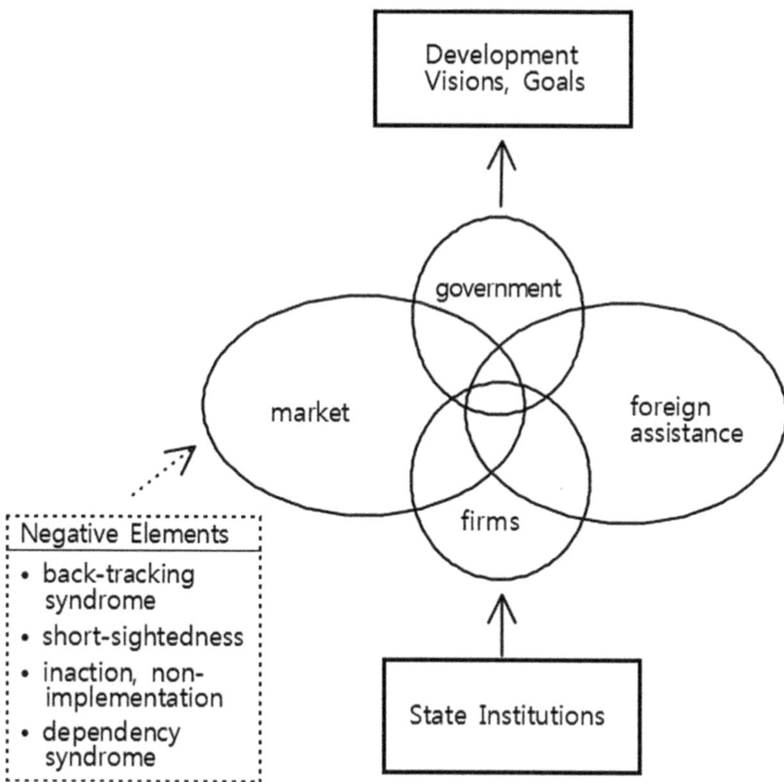

Fig. 10.4 The basic economic development structure of Sub-Saharan Africa

but this is not well integrated or converted into real economic growth. Businesses are lacklustre in terms of their numbers, scale, activities and contribution to national income. If we exclude foreign companies and multi-national corporations, it is further reduced. There is little fusion and synergy among these four economic elements, as the figure shows. I have indicated 'negative elements' because these are also substantial impediments to the attainment of development visions. Evidently, for most Sub-Saharan African countries, they seem to have 'sound' state institutions, superficially, that is, in statutory terms.

But there are many negative elements as well as shortcomings at various levels and stages of policy formation and implementation.

Enough has been said of corruption, lack of transparency and accountability, bad governance, disregard for the rule of law, etc. and these are not only the causes of problems, but also the reflections and outcomes of more deep-seated problems. Simply denouncing and wishing these away will not be helpful; what is more important is to tackle the underlying causes of these problems. The fundamental way to do so would be through a mindset change geared towards development.

Figure 10.5 depicts the 'holy trinity of economics' and 'economic discrimination', the terms coined by Sung-Hee Jwa.[3] He stresses that the market is not the sole entity in the capitalist economy and that the government and firms are also very important players. The picture shows that the market, the government and firms, the 'holy trinity' of economics, can be closely intertwined and can interact with one another to produce sustainable and dynamic economic growth, with 'economic discrimination'—the rule of incentives and punishments—playing a pivotal role at the centre, as was the case in South Korea. This will be addressed again later. Figure 10.6 shows a proposed model of development for Sub-Saharan Africa, which also provides a summary of the theme of this chapter.

The Sub-Saharan African nations have for so long underperformed and under-achieved in terms of their potential, while being unable to take advantage of opportunities, because they have not come to terms

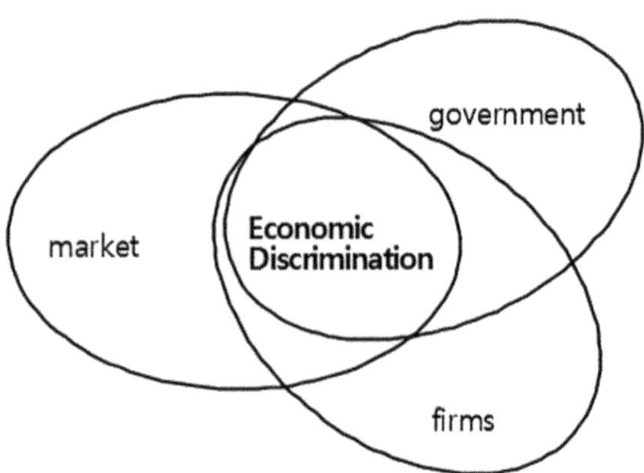

Fig. 10.5 The holy trinity of economics and 'economic discrimination' (*Source* Sung-Hee Jwa (2017))

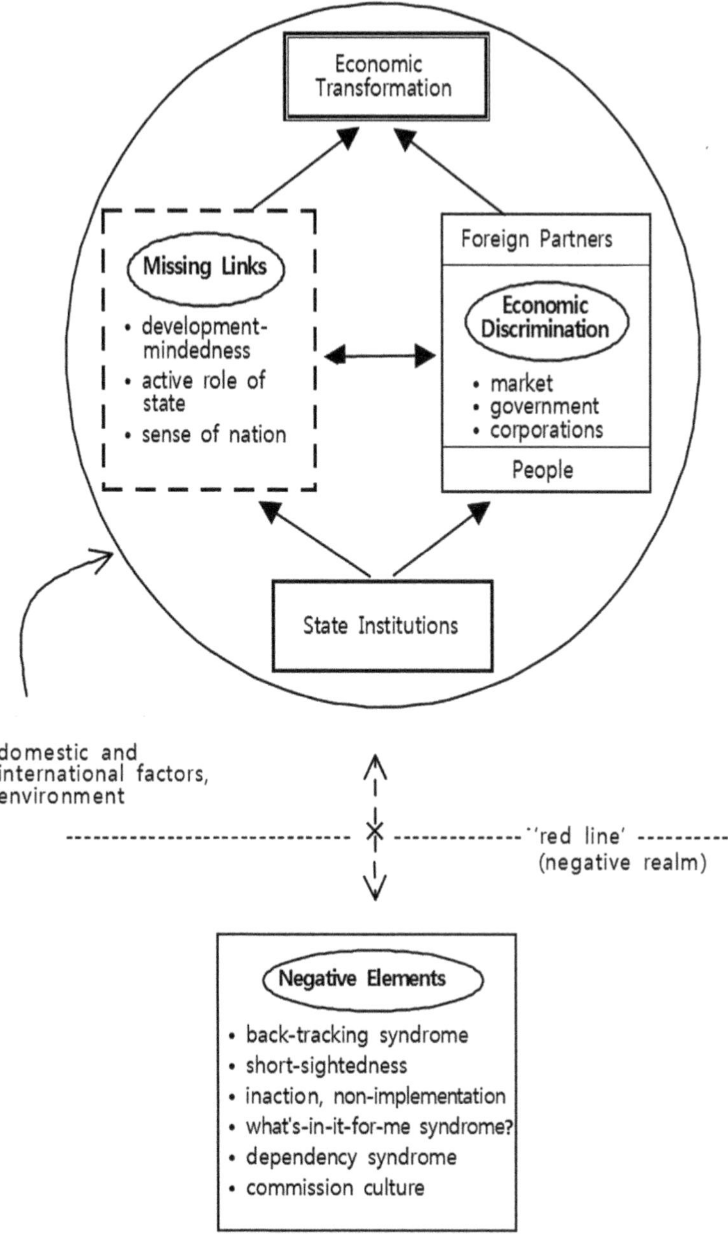

Fig. 10.6 The new development formula for Africa

with what must be done to enable real progress in relation to economic livelihood and status. But people may not fully grasp what they have been missing and can even be misled by unfounded praise. It was fashionable to talk about 'Africa-rising' and the continent has been touted as the last frontier of the global market. Citing the fast and sustained economic growth registered in Sub-Saharan African countries, some wondered whether African development has indeed turned the corner. However, Africa's growth started to dip in 2011, hitting a low in 2016. The region's economic growth has been picking up again from 2017, helped by the global economic recovery, but the trajectory seems to be a very moderate recovery, as projected by the African Development Bank (2018).

The lessons learned dictate that we need to be cautious. Many point out that the recent economic growth in Africa has serious shortcomings. For example, David Booth and Diana Gammack point out that the pattern of economic growth of Sub-Saharan Africa is not leading to the structural transformation that is needed because it:

> is not having a large impact on mass poverty, mainly because it is not rooted in agricultural productivity gains. It is not leading to a diversification of production and exports or to the acquisition of technological capabilities by new generations of productive enterprises. Much of the current growth is jobless growth, a fatal feature given that sub-Saharan Africa's population is expected to rise from 800 million today to 2.5 billion with a generation, with over one half of the total living in cities. (Mills and Herbst 2012: 18–19)[4]

Likewise, Kingsley Chiedu Moghalu poses a question: 'But let us pause and ponder. Is this development, in which Africa has come to be regarded as the "last frontier" of the global economy – an inevitable outcome of globalization – really a cause for celebration? Will it lead to the real rise of the continent as an economic power house in the mould of Asia or the West? Is Africa engaging the world – and globalization – on its own terms?'[5] And he adds that Africa's economic growth is not transformative, considering that its economic growth statistics are derived mostly from cyclical benefits from a structural dependence on primary commodity products.[6]

It seems that African countries and the international development community alike have stayed too long in a state of blindness. Many of them are likely to have fixed views on Africa, taking Africa's situation as a *given* and trying to get things done under the premise of the *given* circumstances. The fatal mistake was trying to do everything from one end—donors—while very little was done from the receiving end, the end where change needs to take place. Although foreign assistance did not 'fit' Africa because of a fundamental mismatch between the two, both sides stuck to doing the same thing for too long.

This compatibility matter is not confined to development assistance; it also applies to regular business, trade and investment, and other exchanges in various fields. The continued mismatch occurs because there is no proper process of 'incorporation' or internalization on the part of the protagonists. An African observer states: 'Many still blame colonialists, but more than 50 years of independence, is Africa where it ought to be? Aren't we also to blame for our continent's delayed transformation? A lot, if not all of our crude transformation impeding mentalities come from our culture–families which form our foundational perceptions, and interactions with the wider society … Who do we expect to perform magic of correcting these erroneous mentalities?'[7]

As shown in Fig. 10.6, I have 'remodelled' the 'holy trinity' formula to fit the Sub-Saharan African countries by adding two more elements to it: people and development partners. This reflects the different environment African countries are facing compared to those that Korea and East Asian countries faced during their high growth period. First, Sub-Saharan Africa is heavily dependent on foreign aid and funding. Second, the 'people' factor needs to be gauged because African governments are confronted with additional challenges in terms of garnering popular support due to intrinsic socio-cultural dynamics as well as the influence of democracy and globalization.

The merits of the 'holy trinity' model need to be mentioned. For developing countries, a move towards privatization and liberalization is a positive step forward and should be commended. As was the case in some African countries, reforming the economy to undo the government's ownership of business and wealth concentration that stifles incentives for private sector was a good thing. But government actions that fuel inefficiencies by excessive, improper government controls, uncompetitive policies and managerial incompetence are a very different thing from the government's positive intervention to facilitate the market mechanism, even correcting 'market failures' and generating economic dynamism. It is a grave mistake to confuse these two. Privatization and liberalization will not solve all the problems and will not be sufficient in themselves.

This is where disciplined, responsible and competent government leadership can make all the difference. While this seems to be a far cry from Africa's reality, it must be worked on, otherwise there is little chance that African countries will escape the trap of bad governance, inefficiencies and poverty.

The problems African states are faced with today mostly stem from inaction or non-implementation. And many African experts acknowledge this: 'The real challenge is to just get on with "doing it" … Most Africans understand that factors such as ethnicity or corruption have been big problems for the continent. But the real problems are at a full level below. They are foundational, and can only be addressed by a transformation that begins in the mind, in the way Africans *think*. Thinking is often more important than we think.'[8] The task of taking up the 'missing links' is all about genuinely committing to mindset change.

In the process of implementing the aforementioned formula for development, it is also important to keep things from reverting back to the negative realm. Progress made in this endeavour will have positive repercussions on the whole mechanism. It is no coincidence that Korea's development model reaped success, as it had the advantage of being action-oriented, pragmatic and strictly incentives-oriented.

Below, I will elaborate on the three important areas in the context of policy recommendations: the role of government and governance, education, and economic policy. So many recommendations, policy blueprints or technical studies, etc. have already been presented to Africa, and this is yet another. But the explanations and examples given here, which are easy to digest, do provide a valuable glimpse into Korea's experience and highlights some fundamentals that are integral to national development and therefore that should be put to work in unison with each other.

The Role of the Government

For any country, the importance of the role of the government cannot be emphasized enough, particularly in the case of developing countries. The general characteristic or the strength of government bureaucracy is being 'impersonal' and 'rationalistic' in the way in which it functions. But the routinization of the work of government organizations tends to entail unintended problems if the people who run them become forgetful of the purpose they are supposed to serve. Government bodies will deviate from the public's expectations over time if conscientious efforts to 'humanize' and invigorate the bureaucracy are not made. That is why even in developed countries, there are constant calls for reforming and reinvigorating the government.

As for most of African states, considering their areas of weaknesses, the government mode must shift gears towards: (1) performance; (2) a rigorous disciplinary regime for civil servants; and (3) the introduction of a practical and comprehensive e-government system to enhance service and transparency, and to curb irregularities and corruption. For these, a sensible and practical evaluation system must be put in place. And it is important not to fall into 'legislature-institutional traps'; it is equally important to maintain a sense of balance as well as some degree of flexibility in upholding norms and regulations on the one hand and making things work on the other hand. Figure 10.7 provides an illustration of this.

Returning to the question of balance and flexibility, as is often the case in developing countries where certain regulations are non-existent or weak, they tend to 'copy and paste' or combine various regulations of developed countries to fill the void. But the problem is that these provisions can be too stringent or unrealistic for developing countries that do not yet have the necessary conditions or level of governance to match them.

Fig. 10.7 The desired mode of governmental reform for Sub-Saharan Africa

A case in point is that we see elaborate procurement laws in place in the Sub-Saharan African region, but because of their complex conditionality, this leads to delays in public projects, along with increases in costs, inefficiency and corruption. An example of this is Uganda's procurement regulation for public construction works, which requires at least nine months before the funds can be dispersed for the projects.[9] People are either stuck in the regulations and waste so much time over technicalities, or they try to short-circuit the process by forging documents. A simple problem like potholes that should be repaired instantly is abandoned because of irrational procurement regulations. Laws and regulations in themselves do not prevent shoddy work; rather, it is the supervision on the ground, work ethics and discipline that actually count in terms of getting things done.

Regarding the functioning of the state organization, the goal should be 'incremental progress'. While the mindset change and commitment for renovation in bureaucratic circles ought to be sought rigorously and promptly, the goals pursued should be realistic, continuous and long-term. The optimal outcome would be 'incremental progress'. Given the circumstances of Sub-Saharan African countries, setting overly ambitious targets for governmental transformation is most likely to fail. To gather momentum for such drive would require a strong political will and a national campaign supported by the people.

The 'back-tracking syndrome' that I have already mentioned is also prevalent in Sub-Saharan Africa's bureaucratic society. This is the result of the penchant of government officials for their personal interests vis-à-vis the public interest, a lack of discipline (such as negligence in their duties and absenteeism), a failure to report and follow through, etc.

Performance, discipline and e-governance should be considered as the 'tripod' for the governmental reform in Africa. The lessons of countries that industrialized early and 'developmental states' justify the need for well-functioning and credible government in Sub-Saharan African countries, and political leadership and consensus must gather force to push reform in this respect.

Basically, we can categorize governmental roles into three types: 'state-dominant', 'citizen-dominant' and 'diffused-dependent': The state-dominant type refers to the transformational states playing a strong role as 'facilitators' of development, prioritizing performance; the citizen-dominant type means the advanced and mature state of nations where citizens and the private sector have an important bearing on the output and quality of the state's functions, ensuring stability; and the diffused-dependent type refers to the case in which most Sub-Saharan African countries find themselves i.e. being neither state-dominant nor citizen-dominant, which literally means there is a weakness in both the government's role and the people's participation and contribution with respect to development. So, in comparison to the first two types, the last type does not have apparent advantages, showing a variety of weaknesses like a tendency towards dependence on outside forces, continued poverty and the government's underperformance.

From this, we can deduce three different government orientations: politically oriented, performance-oriented and governance-oriented. The politically oriented kind is typical in most Sub-Saharan African countries: the government's attitude, engagement and day-to-day activities are driven more by political considerations and personal interests than by a true sense of duty to perform and deliver for the sake of the public interest. Executive functions are so closely knit to ruling party politics as well as the personal agendas of the powerful so that one can sense there is 'too much politics'; government departments conveniently serve as tools for politics in every way. The performance-oriented type is geared towards government output and is the hallmark of developmental states. The governance-oriented type, which is characteristic of developed countries, places priority on policy implementation and public service delivery in conformity with regulations and norms. Consistency, transparency and rationality, among other factors, are key measurements of success.

In reality, such distinctions would not be easy to make in a equally simple, clear-cut manner, and states will likely have to embody a mixture of different features. For the countries that need to catch up with the more developed countries, the primary role of the government should be spearheading development rather than maintaining the status quo. The prevailing thinking of established economies tends to view big governments and government interventions as something negative, causing distortions and inefficiencies in the economy. While this may be valid from the viewpoint of developed economies, it may not address the circumstances of developing countries.

Figure 10.8 shows various combinations of the intensity and orientations of the governmental role: on the *y*-axis, three different levels of government intervention—high, medium and low—are marked, while the horizontal axis indicates three types of government role orientation (political, performance and governance-oriented). A vast majority of Sub-Saharan African countries would belong to this category. As to whether or what countries in the region can be called developmental

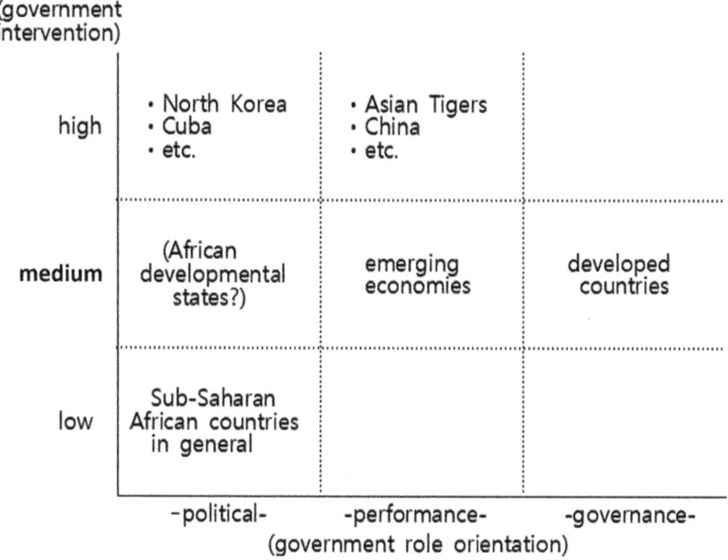

Fig. 10.8 Combinations of government intensity and orientation

states (the candidates can be such countries as South Africa, Rwanda and Botswana), the situation is unclear and debatable.

Also, what areas of government intervention we are talking about matters—it can be about only industrialization or the whole array of administrative tasks. Among the states with the highest levels of state intervention are countries like North Korea and Cuba. The actual placement of the countries in the matrix may vary when different criteria are applied. The same goes for governmental orientation. For instance, the orientation of a state's role can vary from sector to sector, and multiple orientations can concurrently exist. An example is Rwanda: the government's motivation is frequently seen to be political, economic, performance-oriented and governance-striving at the same time.

Given the necessity for African states to make their governments more functional, that is, being action-oriented, meeting the public's demands and policy goals, how to overhaul the structure and activities of government to make this possible needs to be considered. Once again, incentives and sanctions, sticks and carrots must be applied.

This requires a strong governing body or mechanism to supervise and enforce civil servants' compliance and delivery. We can start with the introduction of a regular 'mindset change' training of public officials and a tight regime of monitoring their performance.

Upgrading performance needs many things, like being focused, diligent and committed, while simple, routine administrative duties would only require steady work. But routine work is by no means a given in Sub-Saharan Africa, where civil servants' absenteeism and undertaking of multiple jobs is commonplace. But such behaviour on a broad scale should not be allowed to continue as it will only add to the vicious cycle of poverty and underperformance. Because of the widespread practice of negligence and corruption at the organizational level, if left unchecked, government institutions, especially those in the public service sector, will continue to deteriorate over time, becoming in themselves a serious problem for the nation.

For African countries that are in great need of transformational policy planning and execution across the board, the role of policy-makers and bureaucrats having the authority to carry out the necessary changes assumes particular importance. Institutions are weak in Africa, but the institutions themselves are moulded through the long-term accumulative practices of the nation. As such, the best way in which the development of African countries can be effectively driven is by starting with conscientious and calculated reforms within the government.

The government elites should be held to the highest standards in terms of upholding public interests. Officials undertaking the assignments must have pride, devotion and responsibility in serving their nation. The embedded 'sense of mission' to serve their nation ought to be the key attribute of bureaucratic elites, but unfortunately, this does not seem to be the case in Africa, as the majority of African elites are seen to have a weak sense of duty and responsibility, and often don't seem to know very well what they are supposed to do.

On the other hand, it might be unfair to denounce African elites for all of Africa's ills. The 'culture' and the demands of the people also undoubtedly play an important part in this. While the effectiveness of government rests with the ability of its officials, it is ultimately the people and public opinion that shape the outcome of governance. That is to say, bureaucratic society does not function in a vacuum, but constantly interacts with, and is affected by, the environment and various entities, the most important of these being the people.

I have heard many African political, bureaucratic and business elites admitting dissatisfaction and frustration with their people. On their part, they complain that their constituents or their relatives back home expect too much from them and that this is unsustainable. Realistically, a certain balance should be sought between simply trying to 'conform' to the demands of the people and informing or educating them that not only is this not sustainable, but that is also detrimental to society. But the African elites are giving in and are opting for the former, while failing to challenge the public with respect to what is right, rational and beneficial from the long-term perspective.

'Cultural pressures' that have detrimental impacts on society need to be tackled responsibly and persistently. It is only fitting that the wealthy and privileged class of Africa, rather than being detached from their own environment, must assume greater social and moral responsibility for their nations. If the elites and intellectuals fail to take a stand and lead society forward in a positive fashion, society will likely remain stagnant.

Only when the government and the people look squarely at each other and share common ideas and objectives can the state function properly in the long term. It could be said that the political leaders are only as good as the people who chose them. Hence, it is crucial to empower the people to take genuine ownership of their lives and nationhood. This means cultivating people to be not only assertive of their rights and vigilant against government's exercise of power, but also to have a strong sense of the common good, social and moral values, and collective interests.

In developing countries in particular, and even in some Western countries, democracy is often being stretched to its limits. In some cases, it is 'abused' in such a way that people think they can do anything in the name of freedom and democracy. When the society's dominant pattern becomes too transactional and everyone is bent on immediate personal gains without some counterbalance of a broader, collective restraining social mechanism in place, 'freedom' is much more vulnerable. In the extreme case, this can entail a deep turmoil and national crisis. Freedom and democracy are being stressed without equal emphasis on social and moral values and the maturity of the society to uphold civic standards and norms. In this respect, education, particularly in relation to civic duties, work ethics and development-mindedness, is of paramount importance.

The performance of government and the discipline of bureaucratic organization go hand in hand. In order for the government to deliver what the public requires, civil servants should be both motivated and disciplined with a sense that their goal and duty is to serve the public. To ensure this on a broader level, the general public should act as the ultimate vanguards to preserve and uphold the integrity, stability and prosperity of their nation. Parliament is expected to act as a check and balance vis-à-vis the executive body, but Parliament's competence and credibility is again dependent on the engagement and will of the people. It is on such grounds that I have gone to great lengths in this book to stress the need to build the social fabric, social capital, sense of nation and patriotism, and 'development-mindedness' in Sub-Saharan Africa.

In addition to the reorientation geared towards greater performance and discipline, e-governance can be added as the third pillar of governmental reform. The logic behind e-governance is that there is an enormous value in it for enhancing efficiency and transparency in administration and public services: it promotes discipline in government officials as the room for human error, irregularities or manipulation is greatly reduced, and illicit transactions in particular can be substantially curbed.

Korea has energetically promoted e-government as a central tool to make its government more competitive by capitalizing on its world's leading information and communications technology (ICT), including broadband Internet. The Korean government laid the groundwork for e-government schemes, such as the National Basic Information System (NBIS) computer networks in the 1980s, and streamlined applicable laws and institutions in the 1990s. It then made the implementation of e-government a major national agenda for the 2000s, concentrating on 11 major tasks for e-government (2001–2002) and 31 major tasks for the e-government roadmap (2003–2007). With such proactive measures, e-government has become firmly established in all areas of the Korean government.[10]

The benefits of Korean e-government were visible and manifold: the efficiency and transparency of administrative work have both greatly improved; administrative civil services have been substantially enhanced; and people's access to and participation in the policy-making process has expanded. Korea's e-government initiative has become a success story of its own, and the effectiveness of its e-government is now acknowledged worldwide so that its various e-government systems are being exported to foreign countries. The UN Global E-Government Survey, held in 2010 and 2012, ranked Korea first among all the member countries, with the highest possible scores given in the categories of the Online Service Index and the e-Participation Index.[11]

In Korea, what started as computerization of administrative work to reduce the workload (like handwriting) of civil servants in the context of the simplification of public documentation, developed into the overall informatization of the national administration and public service, after going through many different stages of informational platforms. Today, almost all work in government, both central and local, is computerized. The relative information is shared within the government and this is used to enhance the work efficiency of civil servants.

The ultimate goal of e-government or e-governance should be to realize a deepening of democracy through the enhancement of public service and the efficiency of public administration against the backdrop of the evolution of an information society. That is why the proliferation of e-government is regarded as synonymous with progress in governance. The technical advantage of e-government is that it can instantly carry out a number of tasks simultaneously with the least amount of effort and the lowest cost. This is evident in such a case as where a client does not need to visit a government office to get whatever service is required, but can instead use the Internet or visit portal sites to do the same. This makes personal contacts between civil servants and the public unnecessary, providing convenience to people while curtailing the possibility of corruption that is likely to take place in face-to-face encounters. The openness and transparency with which communication and service are carried out promotes a positive atmosphere and outcomes.

The City of Seoul adopted the Online Procedures Enhancement for the Civil Application (OPEN) system, which is the digitalization of the process of producing authorizations and permits for citizens from the stage of application to issuance. The OPEN system is used for such areas as construction and sales, which are prone to solicitations, delays, irregularities, etc. By removing the necessity of personal contacts between city officials and the general public, the OPEN system effectively curtails the roots of corruption while promoting the transparency of the public administration. The public's satisfaction with the OPEN system service and civil servants is exceptionally high.[12]

Most developing countries do not seem to be ready to fully embrace a comprehensive program of e-government. Rather than wait for total readiness, an approach of learning by doing and consolidating small gains is recommended. But it is really up to African leaders and the people to make strategic decisions as to where they want to be heading. They should realize by now that e-governance is more than a technological trend and that it represents a genuine opportunity to attain qualitative, cost-effective government services and a better relationship between the government and the public. Its benefits can go beyond the efficiency of public service and administration to enhance good governance and empower citizens. Online systems for users have not only cut the time spent on processing applications and thereby increased the efficiency of transactions, but have also made them transparent, easily traceable and accessible.

The benefits that Sub-Saharan African countries can reap from e-government are deemed to be huge. E-government promotes efficiency and also helps people to break away from unwholesome temptations. While the fundamental way to do this is through the 'mindset change' of the people, a much simpler but practical means that can be employed alongside this endeavour is digitalization, or 'impersonal transactions' of public service. The positive effects of e-government can be immediate and far-reaching.

But corrupt rulers and the privileged class enjoying vested interests are likely to resist the full-scale application of this tool. There is an interesting story coming out of donor circles that a fragile African country that has become another sad story of state failure in the region had refused an offer by a donor country to have an e-government system installed for it. At first, the government welcomed this offer, but after it learned that the system was designed to curb illicit financial transactions by making everything transparent, which it did not want to happen, it apparently rejected it.

To install an e-government system throughout government departments and agencies that would have a palpable impact on the nation would require considerable resources and capacity. But this can be done even in poor countries with the will of the government. Rwanda is an example that is moving in this direction and is yielding actual results.

The three key ingredients mentioned that Sub-Saharan African countries need to adopt to strengthen and reform the government are performance, discipline and e-government. In pursuing these measures, it is also important to retain some degree of flexibility to make this possible in practice. Regulations should be observed, but the emphasis should be placed on how to get things done rather than on the formality and technical correctness. An appropriate outcome of such government 'reorientation' or reform will be 'incremental progress', because gradual, steady progress is the most realistic goal to achieve under the existing constraints. Setting an over-ambitious goal can easily derail well-intentioned efforts from the initial stages, and the key is to keep the momentum alive and avoid stalling which most often happens in Africa.

Making e-government work requires commitment, devotion, resources and the right mindset. And this boils down to mindset change. Nonetheless, investing in e-government can only have beneficial results in terms of enhancing governance, public services and the efficiency of administrations. For African countries, it is all the more advisable to pursue e-government as aggressively as possible, as it is the most practical and effective way to tackle the kind of widespread irregularities that the region suffers from.

Economic Policy

For any country, navigating the economy towards stability and growth is front and centre of all government policies and is the greatest pre-occupation of the state leaders. But sound management of economic affairs is all the more imperative for African countries that have wide-spread irregularities to contend with alongside the formidable task of overcoming poverty and achieving economic prosperity. But the reality is that serious, in-depth discussions and analysis in relation to African countries' economic policies have been driven mostly by international development organizations and donors.

Africa's economic growth was a mere 1.7% in 2016, lower than all other developing regions except Latin America and the Caribbean, placing the narrative of 'Africa Rising' into question (UNECA 2017). The joint report of the African Development Bank, the OECD and the UNDP, *African Economy Outlook 2017*, attributed this to low commodity prices, the sluggish performance of the global economy, the slowdown of growth in emerging economies like China, second-order effects of the Arab Spring, amplified by the prolonged conflict in Libya, and bad weather conditions such as droughts in some African countries.[13] But African countries were expected to recover in the coming years thanks to a gradual rise in commodity prices, increasing private demand, including in domestic markets, sound macroeconomic policy management adopted by many countries, a generally improving business environment, etc.[14] Also, Africa's advances in trade and regional integration were noted: over the last two decades, Africa's trade with the world has quadrupled; the continent's trading partners are more geographically diverse; and regional cooperation is gaining momentum. This is possible 'because African countries have adopted more open policies, invested in infrastructure and continued to pursue regional integration'.[15]

The report recommended that Africa diversify its exports to reduce exposure to commodity price shocks, improve the capacity of intra-Africa trade and focus on regional integration. While recognizing that human development is slow and uneven, political and economic governance has shown some encouraging signs. According to the report: 'the most recent data show improvements in Africa but also challenges to overcome. Governments are using public resources more efficiently and delivering more social services, thanks to regulatory reforms and digital innovations. They are also working to enhance the quality of the business environment to catalyse private sector investment'.[16]

The report also mentions that 'promoting industrialization is back on Africa's economic policy agenda, with renewed impetus and vigour', but the strategy that about half of African countries are pursuing—which is to create labour-intensive industries to enhance job growth—does not address the needs of firms that have high growth potential. Governments should design strategies that remove the existing binding constraints on high-potential entrepreneurs; implementing productivity strategies requires full commitment, strong and far-sighted political leadership, efficient government coordination and active private-sector participation.[17]

UNECA's *Economic Report on Africa 2017* offers a more straightforward and sobering look into the state of Africa's economy that declined to a decade-low of 1.7% (1.4% for Sub-Saharan Africa) in 2016 from 3.7% in 2015, below the global average of 2.3%. It points out that African countries' reorientation from an investment-led to a consumption-based economy has hit them through a fall in demand and also indirectly through lower global commodity prices. To make matters worse, African inflation rose from 7.5 to 10%, due to supply-side factors, rising electricity prices and falling values of currencies.[18] Such weakness in both the supply and demand side of the economy, along with weaknesses in other economic fundamentals, make Africa's transformational development that much more difficult to attain and place Africa into a position of greater dependence on its development partners and foreign investors.

Among many aspects of Africa's social economy, what is of particular concern is a set of human elements: high population growth, low and subdued labour productivity, and rapid urbanization. It is projected that by 2035, Africa's urban population rate will reach 49%, and 'this shift has profound implications for achieving the continental and global targets for inclusive growth and transformation, including Agenda

2063 and the 2030 Agenda on Sustainable Development. Theory and global experience show that urbanization and structural transformation are closely linked – but less so in Africa, which has largely followed its own urbanizing path weakly tied to structural transformation, including industrialization'.[19]

Sub-Saharan African countries have many challenges and obstacles to confront and overcome, and a long way to go to reach the position of a transformed economy free from poverty and enjoying sustainability, stability and prosperity. The issue with the economies of Sub-Saharan Africa is that there is no lack of policy vision and identification of their problems, as many policy recommendations have been made by various international and regional development organizations, often in conjunction with African states.

Coming up with fresh new recommendations on economic policy for Africa may not be easy. As Joong-Kyung Choi suggests, applying a 'one-size-fits-all' approach will be very difficult and unrealistic, while on the other hand, a 'Christmas tree' approach that suggests 'every challenge in every field should be solved at once … is difficult to be implemented taking the government's capacity of the developing country into account'.[20] Choi points out that the desirable thing is to set priorities among the agenda items and then deal with them one by one. In Sub-Saharan Africa, there is the extra burden of pushing forward with multiple tasks at the same time to avoid regression or fall-back.

Economic policy recommendations for African countries in light of their reality, the lessons of Korean development and the global regime of economic governance can be classified into four categories: (1) macroeconomic stability; (2) effective industrialization; (3) human capacity development; and (4) reinvigoration of the market mechanism (economic principles having precedence over political considerations). In order for these recommendations to yield results, it should be matched by unrelenting determination and deeds. This all seems simple and clear, but contemplating on the grand scheme of inter-connecting and implementing these objectives, and actually delivering them are the hurdles that demand extraordinary efforts in order to be overcome.

Basically, I think that the countries can choose from the three options of 'low intensity', 'medium intensity', and 'high intensity' approaches:

the 'low intensity' option is more or less following the existing regime with improved efforts in basic areas like macroeconomic stability and good governance. The 'medium intensity' option is sort of a middle ground, while the 'high intensity' option is tantamount to vigorously pushing for full-scale transformational development similar to that which South Korea was able to do. The 'medium intensity' option can be described as that which in principle prescribes to the 'high intensity' approach, but, being 'restrained' by various conditions and limited in terms of national capacity, settles for the 'second-best' option.

These three options represents different levels of 'costs and benefits' or 'risks and rewards': the 'low intensity' approach is rather easy to pursue, without having to go through 'great pains', but its downside is that the 'benefits' or 'returns' will be modest, and the resulting change will be limited at best. On the other hand, the 'high intensity' alternative would be very demanding on nations, imposing a heavy burden on them on all fronts, but it could produce many great benefits if properly enacted.

The mainstream donor community and international organizations have not been avid champions of industrial policy for developing countries. Today, what is most frequently and widely stressed are macroeconomic stability, free markets and an open economy, a business-friendly environment, entrepreneurship, good governance, etc. Of course, macroeconomic stability is important for every country, but this and the free market system alone cannot ensure the substantive economic transformation of poor economies. Effective allocation of resources or production factors is a most basic condition for a well-functioning economy. But the more fundamental task for the poorest countries is how to achieve economic dynamism to broaden the economy in an expeditious manner.

In all fairness, the 'low intensity' approach is essentially a recipe for the status quo rather than evolution. Macroeconomic stability is the outcome of the accumulative work of managing inflation, interest rates, currency rates, deficits and the debt burden. It is what can be achieved by continued vigilance and prudent engagement by the authorities. With globalization and the high level of dependence of African countries on foreign resources, companies and markets,

African governments must have an equally high level of discipline in terms of managing macroeconomic stability.

Compared to the 1960s, 1970s and 1980s, when Korea was able to achieve phenomenal economic growth, the international economy nowadays is more competitive, interdependent and inter-linked, while the global financial and trade regimes have become more binding on national governments, making the 'autonomous' pursuit of economic policies considerably more difficult for developing countries. Moreover, African countries now face less lenient international trade regimes than was previously the case. How much leeway African countries can have under the current economic regimes if they decided to push ahead aggressively with industrial policy and export promotion is unclear and would require a more detailed examination. And there can be a grey area between what is stipulated in theory and allowed in practice. But for the poor economies in the region, there should still be quite a number of possibilities of which to take advantage and many ways to navigate through the situation if they are seriously committed to doing so.

Perhaps there is a fourth option: the 'incremental change' approach. The goal here would be to first reach the 'low intensity' target of macroeconomic stability and sound governance, but rather than stopping there, moving on to the next phase of meaningful industrialization and then to high-end industrialization and a service sector economy. The goal for every nation would be to enjoy growth and stability at the same time.

Korea started out in the early 1960s with an aggressive export promotion and economic growth policy, followed by a policy of gearing-up HCIs in the 1970s. But Korea had to pay more attention to economic stability during the process of economic development. Overall, Korea's 'high intensity' development approach was about growth first and then stabilization afterwards. Since the 1990s, Korea has been trying to balance the two, with special lessons learned from the 1997 IMF financial crisis and the 2008 global financial crisis on the need to manage financial transactions and markets.

In relation to industrial policy, Korea provides an example of fundamental but long-forgotten lessons of industrialization: that an economy has to undergo different stages of policy orientations in order to attain full-scale development. For Korea, each phase was extraordinarily clear-cut: (1) post-war national rehabilitation (the 1950s); (2) laying the foundations for a 'self-supporting' economy (the 1960s); (3) upgrading the industrial structure and modernizing the rural sector (the 1970s); (4) shifting towards openness and liberalization (the 1980s); and (5) espousing globalization and structural reforms (the 1990s).

Korea's situation in the aftermath of independence and the Korean War was not very different from that which Sub-Saharan African countries faced upon their independence. But what sets Korea apart from African countries is that Korea was able to fulfil all the stages of economic development following the path of industrialization of developed economies, albeit in a very compressed manner.

In the case of Sub-Saharan African countries, it seems evident that of these five phases, phase 2 and phase 3 have not properly taken place. The relevant policies have not been effectively pursued in a timely and systemic manner, and the countries have thereby missed many opportunities. African countries have opened up their economy, liberalized the market and privatized companies without fully understanding the implications of doing so. Without taking up crucial tasks of laying the foundations for a 'self-supportive' economy and pushing for industrialization and rural development, they have opted for an easier solution of opening up and liberalizing. In so doing, they have essentially outsourced most of the components needed for a successful national economy.

As a consequence, all kinds of policy goals are pursued in juxtaposition, complicating efforts and compounding the already challenging tasks. Still, many African countries have not completed laying the groundwork for statehood and economic development. Korea achieved rapid growth based on the solid cornerstones of development: land reform, socio-economic mobilization and empowerment of the people, the creation of various agencies, proactive government initiatives, etc., and these turned out to be vital 'building blocks'. More important was the actual follow-up actions to these plans.

But instead of exercising true ownership of their economy, Sub-Saharan African countries have frequently taken a regressive and deleterious stance. After a half-century of independence, many African leaders are still blaming the influence of colonialism and international environment for their economic failures. Apart from the lack of grand economic schemes, the post-independence African economy suffered severely from a deficiency of participation and support from various indigenous players and sectors. Unlike Korea, which made the most of what little resources it had in laying the groundwork and setting up bodies for national development, African states wasted their precious resources and opportunities through inaction, misconduct and missteps.

Sub-Saharan African nations received more financial inflows and aid grants in the context of development assistance than any other region in the world. The tasks they faced—uniting the nation, providing security, achieving economic growth and welfare, democratization and good governance, etc.—are the basic things that the leaders and people of every country have to assume as their own responsibility. The African problems have been caused not by acts of nature and irresistible forces, but by human failings. African leaders readily invoke sovereignty or non-interference in domestic matters, but when it comes to economic problems, they are quick to put responsibility on external causes and colonial legacies, Western imperial designs and so on.

On the flip side of Africa's energetic open-arms policy towards foreign investors, there is a disquieting reality of dependency and opportunism by the 'well-connected' for rent-seeking. 'Upper-echelon' African business circles seem to be have evolved in an unwholesome manner. Rather than trying to be entrepreneurial and competitive in their own right by showing commitment, making investments and taking risks on their own, many seem to want to act as 'middlemen' in order to gain short-term profits or windfall gains.

The common challenges facing Sub-Saharan African countries are rapid urbanization amid a population explosion, acute unemployment for the youth and college graduates, etc. But the overarching problem is the myopic thinking when it comes to business, often being seriously blindsided and, worse still, not really doing the things that need to be done. Sub-Saharan African countries have no shortage of policy papers, road maps and master plans laying out 'what is lacking', 'what is to be achieved' and 'what is the way forward'. But the persistent problem is always the implementation, and it reverts back to intent, commitment and practice. The question is: how much are elites and the privileged class conscious of public interests, and how patriotic and devoted are they to contributing to the improvement of lives of their compatriots beyond their own personal gains?

Jennifer Blake compared Africa and the Association of Southeast Asian Nations (ASEAN), and pointed out that there are three aspects of the ASEAN growth experience that can provide useful lessons for Africa. First, ASEAN countries have made many of the reforms and investments needed to ensure longer-term prosperity; measurable progress has been achieved across the region in terms of tearing down red tape and putting in place institutions, educational systems and infrastructure. Over the past four decades, they have improved their productivity by diversifying their economies rather than depending on volatile commodity prices. Second, they have been much more successful in regional integration compared to African countries, recognizing that in a rapidly evolving global context, they must join forces to reap the economies of scale. Third, economic outcomes are driven by positive expectations: 'In much of Asia there is an inherent belief that countries will experience rapid economic progress – of course driven by past experience but also a general confidence in the future – and this tends to reinforce a positive self-fulfilling prophecy. Greater confidence in the future would be a boon in Africa, which is particularly at risk due to the present slowdown.'[21]

When all approaches stumble time after time, then it is likely that something simple and basic rather than something very complex and technical has gone wrong. When everybody, including development experts, is looking everywhere to find reasons, the ultimate answer may lie in the fundamentals, like being steady and consistent. I concur with David Henley's view that what successful development strategies aim to do is 'to alleviate poverty on a massive scale (outreach), with great *speed* (urgency), and with a pragmatic and sometimes ruthless eye for *simplicity* (expediency)'.[22]

Returning to the development path of Korea, post-war national rehabilitation self-supporting' economy most Sub-Saharan African countries have barely fulfilled even a few of them. African countries have seemingly 'jumped' to phases (4) and (5) without properly fulfilling steps (1), (2) and (3). And the steps taken ((4) and (5)) are not perfect either. The first three stages indeed require arduous work and are by no means rudimentary. The post-war national rehabilitation era of Korea should approximate the early period of post-independence of African countries. All-out efforts in nation-building should have been made at this time, with a renewed sense of national identity and unity translated into a vigorous institutionalization of state structures and a push for modernization, but apparently this has not happened in Sub-Saharan Africa.

Most Sub-Saharan African countries have not completed nation-building and laying the foundations for economic development, hence, the next step—upgrading the industrial structure and modernizing the rural sector—is still far from reach. When the countries under this 'pre-mature' state merely open up markets, they can drift further away from the desired path of development, with the outcome that we see today: a commodity-dependent economy, the domination of multi-national corporations and foreign companies, the underdevelopment of the agricultural sector, a meagre manufacturing industry, a huge informal economy, snowballing youth unemployment, rising debt, widespread corruption, etc.

There is still a tendency for African rulers to complain about the 'unfair treatment' of Africa by the West. They do so when they benefit vastly from, and rely so heavily on, aid, funds, investments and business operations from rich nations. An East African state leader pointed out that Africa is on the rise and 'even as we rise, the international system maintains an irrational unjust structure that relegates Africa to [the] periphery, that defends injustice and double standards as a matter of course, and, which impoverishes us'. He questioned the dividends of globalization and implored African leaders to look more inwardly by promoting intra-African trade for its people's prosperity in a 'rigged international system', adding that 'even in the face of an international order stacked against us, built on our backs, Africans have made painful progress'.[23]

Besides pointing out the need for African regional integration, it has also become fashionable for African countries to create industrial parks in a bid to attract investments and form industrialization hubs. But due to poor infrastructure, administrative hurdles, a lack of available materials and skilled labour, corruption, a lack of capable local partners, etc., this has mostly not materialized in any satisfactory way.

We have discussed macroeconomic stability and industrialization. Now we turn to human capacity, which includes entrepreneurial skill with the emphasis on management capacity, as well as the quality of the workforce in general. The surest way to move towards an industrialized economy is to have local, home-grown companies flourish and expand, with local businessmen having true ownership of their business. For this to occur, a major increase in skilled workforce and competent management that will support the expanding businesses and economic growth is necessary. But what is clearly the weakness is 'management capacity'. There is a very good chance that the threshold of transformation will be reached when the overall managerial capability of the people is enhanced. Figuring out what holds this capacity backs and how it can be substantially raised will be a game changer for sure.

Sung-Hee Jwa stresses that it is not the market but enterprises that are the most important driving force for economic growth in developing countries. He rebukes the theory of the 'invisible hand' of the free market mechanism, arguing that thriving companies are the answer to successful industrialization and that, without them, developing countries will remain as agrarian societies.[24]

So, what are the conditions for indigenous or local companies to successfully emerge as competitive and sustainable businesses? The productivity which allows the quantity and quality of commodities and services, as well as the managerial skills that render this possible, readily comes to mind. The reason why there are so few prominent 'native' enterprises in the region is because of the lack of such capabilities. In this regard, what African governments can take away from Korea's experience is that the government must do much more and must fundamentally reposition itself from being an 'onlooker' to taking the helm in relation to industrial planning and the promotion of business and economic growth.

The restraints on the competitiveness of Sub-Saharan African countries are mostly human factors, and hence they can be tackled. A prevalent problem is the poor work or low credibility of the workforce. Supervision is a very demanding and arduous task, and this pushes up costs in terms of extra time, labour and money spent. Basically, it is an innate issue of individuals rather than being structural or externally influenced, but the accumulative impact on the economy is huge. At the institutional or organizational level, rampant corruption and unhealthy practices, such as public officials openly engaging in private business, further undermines the overall economic efficiency of the countries in the region.

To put things into perspective, the opportunities were always there for the taking. I have heard political leaders in the region citing successes that the Indian business communities have been able to reap in eastern and southern Africa over so many decades, while deploring the fact that their own people do not exert themselves in the same way; others have pointed out that the Lebanese expatriates have been doing the same all over western Africa. It is not mere commercial savvy, but, more importantly, hard work, commitment, discipline and perseverance that determine the outcome of business. Ideas and plans are only as good as their implementation. And implementation hinges on what I have termed 'development-mindedness': knowledge, practising, ownership and passion (KPOP).

Education in Ethics and Mindset Change

When we are dealing with a magnanimous goal like changing the course of a nation, people should embrace it wholeheartedly, and it is always good to begin with a sound education. The progress of Sub-Saharan African countries thus far is disappointing, considering how much potential they have, but how little they have advanced over the decades in terms of strengthening their social, economic and political fabric. The international community which has struggled in terms of its development endeavours on Africa, should also reflect on whether there had not been blind-spots in its methods rather than just go about doing business the same way.

This calls for objective, cool-headed reassessment of Africa's problems. And it should begin with a recognition of the nature of the problems. What kind of a response is needed would depend on the nature of the problem. If the problem is technical, it would require a technical approach. If it is more fundamental and deep-seated, it should be approached differently, in the context of 'tailored response'. But in order to be able to do this, countries must recognize their problem as such and also accept the required means.

Anyone who has worked on African development ought to understand that what is required in terms of addressing the nature of the challenges facing Africa is not simply distributive, welfare or poverty-relief types of responses. It is not only about a 'lack of capacity' either. Rather, the answer lies elsewhere, at a different level: *the mindset and behaviour of the people.* There seems to be a big gap between what is desired and what is necessary. Changes will come when people understand how wealth is created and through what process it can be reproduced and sustained. The blind-sights or negligence have continued for so long because no meaningful evolution in terms of the mindset has occurred.

From the development partners' perspective, there can be an issue of 'short-memory', a short cycle and turnover of projects, frequent shifts in the officials in charge, etc. They could also be 'captured' or entrenched in their own systems, without themselves knowing that this is the case. People could make the mistake of treating such subjects like people's mindset and culture as taboos on the premise that these are intrinsically unchangeable. But as I have already pointed out, cultural heritage, identity and traditions that are objects of national pride and hence need be cherished should not be confused with 'social behaviourism' that can and should evolve over time when necessary. Development itself is about evolution, and hence sticking rigidly to old habits is counter-productive in terms of development and is tantamount to self-denial of improvement. People cannot have it both ways: 'comfort' and 'progress' are mutually exclusive. I deplore it when I see people complaining and even indulging in self-pity when they are willing to do so little to help themselves.

Development means changing for the better. That is why we have education, public campaigns, activist movements and so on. Today's degradation of the natural environment, increasing security threats and growing competition in business, among other factors, demand change on the part of the people, even if only for their survival, let alone from the perspective of development. The logic of social development, people's empowerment, as well as economic principles, should serve as the basis for healthy politics; it should not be the other way round, where everything is being driven by political considerations.

In Sub-Saharan Africa, so many things break down and deteriorate in everyday life that such phenomena are accepted as normal. Self-regulating or correcting mechanisms in society are feeble, and responses to public requirements, accidents, crimes, natural disasters and contingencies are not swiftly and effectively taken, and are sometimes grossly neglected. Expectations of and trust in the public service is very low, and the general sense of people's powerlessness and detachment from the country's centres is perceived to be widespread. Even the elites and the privileged class have their fair share of frustrations and uneasiness in relation to their society.

But the vast majority of people seem to accept the reality with a 'subsistence' mindset and, as a result, society is bogged down in a languid state. You rarely see any expressions of social outrage or calls for fundamental change in the form of large-scale public demonstrations and campaigns. In certain countries, we see demonstrations and strikes all too often, but these are almost entirely protests against poor public services, labour unions demanding better wages and the poor demanding more welfare.

Moreover, activist movements that are energetically pursued are not in evidence either. Under the circumstances, Africa's politics have managed to adapt to the reality in their own way, not in strengthening governance and fabric of the society, and empowering the people, but by following a 'minimalist' strategy and catering to the people's needs that remain largely subsistence-oriented.

Problems stemming from the weak fundamentals of civil society, like people's sense of themselves and their community, civic values, work ethics, etc., that pertain to the realm of human development should be recognized and dealt with in a serious fashion and should not be left to be addressed in the political context or politicized. The international community also has to be careful of the traps of taking a political approach from their end. Mainstream partners sometimes make the mistake of focusing on what is nominal and lose sight of the issues that plagues Africa's development.

The ills of an overdose of politics are consequential: diversion of attention to politics; loss of opportunities to engage in issues of more substance, like work culture and work ethics; dependency on politics and political figureheads; division and fragmentation of society stemming from politics, etc. The profound harm done is that the people, especially the rural population and the youth, become so dependent on politicians and assistance from the state that they lose any motivation to work and take ownership of their lives.

The workings of the elite class, entrepreneurs and foreign partners, under the given circumstances, will not be sufficient in themselves for the countries to overcome poverty in a transformative fashion, regardless of how many resources may be injected. It is the broad section of the masses, the ordinary people that have to be empowered and enlightened. Only then will African societies be able to enjoy sustainable development and prosperity. In order for this to occur, the expectations and ambitions of individuals for their lives must also be raised substantially. Without people's sense of self-esteem and pride, expectations for a better tomorrow and, most importantly, the willingness to take on responsibilities, all the endeavours made will most likely end up achieving little.

So, how can countries turn around the degradation of people's values and the sense of ownership in their lives and work ethics? The only logical answer that I can find is through education in ethics, human and social development emphasizing the need for dynamic change. There should be a boldness to include in the curriculum the resocialization or reorientation of existing modes. African nations ought to take this matter very seriously and wholeheartedly and carry out the entire task forcefully. This is the field where the role of donors can be vague and limited, as it will be an uncharted territory for the traditional donor community.

Korea provides a good set of examples of mindset change initiatives that Africans may find relevant and appealing. In a sense, such endeavours can be considered as the nation-building process, and hence for developing countries, there is great value in conscientiously launching them in a campaign-like fashion. Development is about changing for the better and people cannot expect positive things to happen when they are not willing to change themselves. Korea's experience in this field offers a worthy example from which countries can readily take inspiration.

Ethics has been taught in Korean schools as a regular subject on the curriculum since 1955, when the relevant provision was enacted. Along with ethics, an early vocational course called 'practical arts' (*shilkwa*) was also established in the same year. Both of these are still taught in Korean schools. The subject of ethics in primary schools is called *barunsenghwal* or 'right habits of life', in secondary schools *dodeok* or 'ethics' and in universities it was called *kokminyoonli* or 'national ethics' up to the mid-1990s, but later changed to 'ethics'. It started with the purpose of teaching the basic morals like attitudes of individuals befitting dutiful members of society, patriotism and a law-abiding spirit, responsibility towards one's family members, etc.[25]

Furthermore, in 1968, in an effort to solidify the foundation of a national ethics and ethos, the Charter of National Education was promulgated by the Korean President. The reason for its promulgation was because of the need to address various shortcomings of the nation: Korea's valuable traditions and heritage were not being followed and advanced; there were imbalances or disharmony between material development and people's value systems, the latter lagging behind the former; people lacked a sense of state, society and national identity; and national education indicators were ambiguous, while spiritual and ethical education was being neglected.

The Charter's main body is broken down into three parts emphasizing: the pride and duty of the Korean nation; norms and virtues in everyday life; and national unification and evolution of democracy. The sentiments underpinning the charter are: (1) the establishment of a national identity; (2) the creation of a new national culture through harmony between tradition and progress; and (3) the development of democracy by means of harmonization of individuals and the state.[26]

In the 1990s, the Charter was removed from Korean textbooks. As for the ethics course, although it has been maintained for a long time, it is gradually being phased out, reflecting political and social changes in Korea. For example, 'national ethics' was dropped from exams to recruit civil servants in 1994. In more recent years, since 2014, ethics is no longer taught in high schools. Although the economic achievements of Korea during the 'developmental dictatorship' era are undeniable, Korean people living in a different era of democratization, a pluralistic society and in a situation of economic prosperity tend to hold a more sophisticated or critical view of past events and legacies.

But the mindset change, moral and work ethics-oriented initiatives that Korea undertook should not be dismissed easily as being out of touch with today's reality. These can be all the more relevant in developing countries. In fact, Korea's public or state-led mindset change and ethics campaign did not come out of nowhere, but had deep roots in Korea's history and society. Korea, having undergone a process of economic, political and social evolution, has placed greater emphasis on public service and ethics codes for civil servants and politicians.

The Canaan Farmers School is reputed to have positively contributed to development by spearheading changes in its own way. Founded in 1931, the Canaan Farmers School methodology is said to have been adopted later in the model of the New Village Movement, the *Saemaul Undong*, which was launched in 1970.

This school's ideas are about making people disciplined, voluntary, active, hard-working, forthright, ethical, frugal and responsible as individuals and community members. It tries to instil the 'I work first, I serve first, I sacrifice first' mentality in people, with the motto of 'let's learn until we know, let's devote ourselves to work, let's serve in humility'. It has an eye-catching slogan that is emblematic of its ethos: 'do not eat to eat, but eat to work. If you don't like to work, do not eat. Work at least four hours for each meal'.[27]

The school also teaches 'mindset pioneering': that it is all up to the people to get things done, so they should have a positive 'can-do' spirit. Individuals are urged to wake up early before dawn to start the day, and changing oneself for the better, being passionate and faithful pioneers and the need to maintain one's own good health are also emphasized.[28]

The logic of the school's approach is that while various projects for poverty eradication and sustainable development are necessary, it is more important to educate leaders who will effectively drive these projects forward and have the ability to lead others. The basic component of leadership training is mindset transformation based on the belief that a person can change only when his or her mind changes. The task here is to make the changes in mindset embedded in the personality of trainees so that they will act differently, in a more positive manner. The expected benefits are twofold: the creation of model communities of poverty eradication based on mindset transformation and raising leaders who practise and live out the changed mindset.[29]

The founder of the Canaan movement, Kim Yong-ki (1909–1988), spent his whole life cultivating barren land and enlightening farmers during Korea's most difficult times of Japanese occupation and the post-war periods when the nation was suffering from extreme poverty and hunger. He said:

> For a country like ours, learned people must get involved in agriculture. Agriculture is the core of all industries. But on the contrary, learned people are avoiding agriculture and only ignorant rural people have been working as farmers. This has kept our nation's economy and civilization primitive, resulting in loss of our sovereignty to Japan. To recover our sovereignty, we must gain economic independence. And for that, there is no other way but for the learned to get involved in agriculture and increase food production.[30]

He would also say: 'Don't tell people to work but be the one to work first', 'Don't just keep your appearance clean but keep your heart clean', 'If you don't like to work, do not eat', 'Take courage, my country', 'You will reap as you sow', 'Young men, go to the countryside', 'Do good and do not lose hope' and 'Be the pioneer to change your fate'.

Kim Yong-ki's extraordinary passion to fight against the odds and break 'the status quo' by tackling head-on what could be extremely onerous and almost impossible, but essential undertakings for transformative development—changing the mindset of people—is remarkable. It is said that his thoughts and conviction on the Canaan Farmers movement were rooted in his Christian faith. In any case, from the perspective of development, I think that 'his thoughts and deeds form imperative basis for mindset transformation of leaders in developing nations'.[31]

According to the Canaan Farmers School, immediately after General Park Chung-Hee took power following a military coup in 1961, he visited the school. When he visited the school again in March 1962, he is said to have remarked 'we led a political revolution, but you led a lifestyle revolution'. In April 1962, hundreds of district leaders led by the Vice Minister of Home Affairs came to the school for training.[32]

The Canaan Farmers School seems to have strongly inspired President Park to envision and launch the *Saemaul Undong*, the New Village Movement, in 1970.[33] As the school was increasingly recognized at the start of the 1970s, it attracted not only farmers but increasingly people from all walks of life, including soldiers, civil servants, businessmen, professionals, college and high school students. As a result, the school's facilities and training courses were also expanded. Over time, the curriculum went through some changes in its content to reflect the changes in reality of Korea, but the mindset-change approach and the heritage of farmers' education continued to be its central component.

Notes

1. Abraham Maslow, *The Farther Reaches of Human Nature* (New York: Viking Press, 1971).
2. In this sense, it could be said that South Korea's sense of nation and national identity was a 'pre-existing condition' at the time that the 'modernization of motherland' drive was launched in the early 1960s.
3. Sung-Hee Jwa (2015).

4. David Booth and Diana Gammack, *Governance for Development in Africa* (London: Zed Books, 2013), pp. 3–4.
5. Kingsley Chiedu Moghalu, *Emerging Africa* (London: Penguin Books, 2014), p. 6.
6. Ibid., pp. 6–7.
7. Patrick Katagata, 'Why Africa Has Failed 50 Years After Independence', *Daily Monitor* (Uganda), 9 May 2017, p. 14.
8. Kingsley Chiedu Moghalu (2014), p. 305.
9. Allen Kagina, the Executive Director of Uganda National Road Authority, was commenting, as a discussant, on Uganda's problems during the 25th Joseph Mubiru Memorial Lecture with Keynote Speaker Ha-Joon Chang on 1 December 2017, Serena Hotel, Kampala, Uganda.
10. National Information Society Agency (NIA), e-Government of Korea: Best Practices (Seoul: NIA, 2012), p. 4, http://unpan1.un.org/intradoc/groups/public/documents/UNGC/UNPAN043625.pdf; see also Special Committee for e-Government, Republic of Korea, *Korea's e-Government: Completion of e-Government Framework* (e-Government White Paper) (2003), pp. 8–16.
11. Ibid.
12. MOK Jin-hue, 'E-Government and Transparency of Public Administration', 28 April 2008, http://humanarchive.tistory.com/295.
13. Africa Development Bank, OECD Development Centre, UNDP, *African Economic Outlook 2017, Special Theme: Entrepreneurship and Industrialization* (Paris: OECD Publishing, 2007), pp. 23–25.
14. Ibid., pp. 27–29.
15. African countries' more open policies, investment in infrastructure and continued pursuit of regional integration have eased business activities and also increased the continent's appeal as a partner in global trade, according to *African Economic Outlook 2017*.
16. Ibid., p. 18.
17. *African Economic Outlook 2017* offers three suggestions for easing the constraints that most entrepreneurs in Africa are confronted with: first, to strengthen skills and meet the needs of labour market, it is necessary to implement public policies that prioritize formal education, apprenticeships, vocational training and managerial capabilities; second, policies that support business clusters can help raise the productivity and growth of firms, including smaller ones; and, third, financial market policies can increase firms' access to innovative and tailored sources of finance.

18. United Nations Economic Commission for Africa (UNECA), *Economic Report on Africa 2017: Urbanization and Industrialization for Africa's Transformation* (Addis Ababa: ECA, 2017) pp.2–3.
19. Ibid., executive summary xx.
20. Joon-Kyung Choi, *Upside-Down Success Story of Korea's Economic Development* (Seoul: Daewon Publishing, 2013), translated by Christy Hyun-Joo Lee, p. 180.
21. Jennifer Blanke, Chief Economist, World Economic Forum, 'From Kigali to Kuala Lumpur: What Will It Take for Africa to Follow South-East Asia's Development Path?', 31 May 2016, https://www.weforum.org/agenda/2016/05/from-kigali-to-kuala-lumpur-what-will-it-take-for-africa-to-follow-southeast-asia-s-development-path/.
22. David Henley (2015), p. 178.
23. Statement by Kenyan President Uhuru Kenyatta on 19 November 2016 during the 2nd annual Diplomatic Black Tie dinner in Kampala (reports by *New Vision* and *Daily Monitor* on 21 November 2016).
24. Sung-Hee Jwa's paper 'Korea in Crisis Asking Park Chung-Hee for Answers' (Korean), presented at the symposium held by the Park Chung-Hee Foundation on 15 June 2016.
25. *Doosan Encyclopedia* (Korean), http://terms.naver.com/entry.nhn?docId=1082774&cid=40942&categoryId=31723.
26. The Academy of Korean Studies—Research Information Service of Korean Studies (RINKS).
27. The slogans of the Canaan Farmers School are as follows: (School ideas) I work first. I serve first. I sacrifice first; (School motto) Let's learn until we know. Let's devote ourselves to work. Let's serve in humility; (Table manners) Do not eat to eat, but eat to work. If you don't like to work, do not eat. Work at least four hours for each meal; (Mindset) Mindset Pioneering! Pioneering Mindset! We are still young. Much work to do. Let's make it done. It can be done. Wake up the dawn. The people are calling for us. Let's go to Canaan; (Change) Change myself first. Change now first. Change here first. Change small things first. Change doable things first. Change until the end; (Pioneers) Pioneers must be dreamers. Pioneers must be confident. Pioneers must be strong-willed and patient. Pioneers must be brave and decisive. Pioneers must sweat and weep. Pioneers must be knowledgeable. Pioneers must be committed. Pioneers must be dedicated. Pioneers must be devoted. Pioneers must run. Pioneers must maintain a peaceful family. Pioneers are not born overnight. Pioneers must be passionate and faithful; (Sweat) I

have seen my sweat on the forehead. I confirmed my sweat. The less I sweat, the more I weep; The more I sweat, the less I weep; (Health) If I lose money, I lose a little; If I lose honour and credit, I lose much; If I lose health, I lose all. Health is the only thing I cannot borrow from others. The failure, frustration, and hopelessness I suffer today is the result of the time I spent badly yesterday; The success, joy, and hope I enjoy today is the reward of the time I spent well yesterday; (Today) Today is the first day of the rest of the days left. Today is the first day of the rest of my life; (Wake up) Let's wake up the dawn. Let's start the dawn. Let's welcome the dawn; (Take courage) Take courage, my country. Take courage, my people.

28. Canaan Farmers School (Wonju) website http://www.canaanin.or.kr; KIM Bum II, *Achievers Are Believers* (Seoul: Kyujangmunwha, 2008) (Korean), pp. 12–20.
29. Introductory briefings from Canaan School of Farming (Wonju) during the author's visit to the school on 12 May 2011.
30. Canaan Global Leadership Centre, 'Introduction to Canaan Global Leadership Centre', 29 May 2010, https://sites.google.com/site/canaangloballeadership.
31. Ibid. The Canaan Farmers School is now engaged in projects for many developing countries.
32. Ibid.
33. According to the Canaan Farmers School, 66,000 male and female leaders were appointed to represent 33,000 villages around the nation and work diligently for their villages without any monetary reward. The one-week-long camp training for these leaders first took place in the end of January 1972 at the Saemaul Leadership Institute, which adopted the curriculum from the Canaan Farmers School. While the programme helped the trainees with new knowledge for agriculture, the Canaan Farmers School noted that most testified that the Canaan-style mindset training was most helpful. Initially targeted at rural leaders, the *Saemaul Undong* training was expanded to include urban area projects in 1973 and male and female *Saemaul* leaders from cities were sent to one-week-long *Saemaul Undong* training programmes as well. Later in 1974, further expansion of the programme included the training of high-level central government officials, administrative ministers, university professors, members of the media, entrepreneurs, artists, religious leaders, etc. The Canaan Farmers School observed that the *Saemaul Undong* training played a crucial role as a means of national mindset training.

11
Engineering Rural Development for Africa

The Need for a Success Story

In view of the nature of the task of Africa's development, the key word to be used is 'change'. This is because development itself implies change, while in Sub-Saharan Africa, so many things remain unchanged. In a fast-moving society like Korea, 'change' is almost synonymous with 'survival'. 'Change' could mean many things: improvement, adaptation, progress, achievement, innovation, etc. In Korea, the fervour for 'change' was evident during its rapid growth era, but even now it is regarded as a virtue and a necessity. I recall that even in around 2005, when Korea was already well underway in terms of innovations, there was a boom in demand for innovative leadership training sessions all over Korea. These sessions would stress that 'change' is innovation. Increased competition under globalization and technological innovations requires people to become more nimble.

But what is surprising is that in spite of this necessity, Sub-Saharan Africa has been so silent on 'change'. Basically, it is perceived that the political leaders and elites with vested rights want to maintain the status quo. But, in addition, the masses who should be outraged and yearning

J.-D. Park, *Re-Inventing Africa's Development*,
https://doi.org/10.1007/978-3-030-03946-2_11

for change have chosen the status quo by adhering to their subsistence way of life. Add to this the dependency syndrome or the welfare-oriented policies and mindset, and you get the picture of Africa that we see today. Breaking old habits is as important as having a rejuvenated and committed governmental leadership.

I have come across a number of foreign professionals, both Western and Asian, working in Africa who expressed that after having spent many years in Africa, they have become convinced that Africa's fundamental obstacle is 'cultural' in nature. Some believe that the 'yoke' of the 'traditional way of life' of the locals is far stronger than anything else and supersedes even their professed religion.

But we can understand this from a different angle. It is not necessarily the cultures impeding development, but rather that development efforts failing to have an impact so that the cultures remain intact. Transforming various aspects of life is the very aim of development. Experts can be burdened by the connotations of the word 'culture', but this should be approached in a practical manner. As I have mentioned, 'culture' can be broken down into two categories: (1) cultural heritage; and (2) behavioural modes. Needless to say, the former, in the form of arts, languages, food, lifestyles, traditions, etc., are to be cherished and upheld, but the latter, when necessary, can and should be modified or ameliorated. This is where education can be instrumental. An appropriate synthesis of civic values, education and development projects can yield positive outcomes in this respect. Since development is about changing, why shouldn't behaviour modes that impede the improvement of lives not be targeted for change? Once this necessity is recognized, then the next logical step would be to find and apply an 'antithesis' to the problem at hand.

Korea's *Saemaul Undong* campaign is a resounding success story of turning around the mindset of the people to realize transformative development. In every respect, the *Saemaul Undong*, which was based on the spirit of diligence, self-help and cooperation, is deemed an ideal model of development for Sub-Saharan African countries because it invokes voluntarism and hard work in the people.

While the *Saemaul Undong* was a national campaign carried out ambitiously in the 1970s and continued afterwards in Korea, as the

Korean economy and society became increasingly sophisticated, it began to be viewed as a 'relic' which had merits when Korea was poor but was not so relevant to the current situation. People became less communal, more urban life-oriented and individualistic, and the attention has shifted towards undertaking *Saemaul Undong* programmes overseas in view of its popularity among developing countries that continue to struggle with poverty and underdevelopment.

It is against such a backdrop that Korea's development agency KOICA launched Smart *Saemaul Undong* in September 2015, which coincided with the adoption of the SDGs. It refers to a holistic community development initiative capturing the partnering government's willingness for development and the people's voluntary participation. Its strategy is to implement an integrative programme utilizing appropriate technology, creating value chains and strengthening partnership, based on the foundation of governance and social capital. This includes embedding the *Saemaul Undong* into partner countries' community development policy, promoting the spirit of the *Saemaul Undong*, and establishing sound governance. Detailed components of this strategy involve: (1) a sector-integrative programme; (2) the appropriate technology; (3) a value chain; (4) competition and incentives; (5) village-level development; (6) *Saemaul Undong* education tailored to the needs of each community; and (7) partnership with the private sector.[1]

Regarding sector-integrative programmes, it is argued that the *Saemaul Undong* has great potential to contribute to the achievement of SDGs as an integrative community development model that encompasses agricultural sectors such as livestock and fisheries, social sectors such as education, health, hygiene and gender, and technology sectors such as ICT, energy and the environment.

With respect to appropriate technology, the *Saemaul Undong* aims to drastically raise performance in improving the level of income within a short period of time by identifying and mobilizing technologies that are the most appropriate in specific settings of partner countries. As for improving value chains, including production (land, seeds, equipment, micro-financing and cultivation technology), harvesting, storage, processing, distribution, marketing and sales are important if income is to be increased on a sustained basis. Thus, the value chain is taken into consideration in planning what activities to carry out in order to generate income.

'Competition' fuelled by incentives (and disincentives) constitutes another key aspect of the *Saemaul Undong*. Without the willingness and commitment of the beneficiaries, real and sustainable development cannot happen. Thus, places in which a *Saemaul Undong* project is to be undertaken are carefully examined to confirm whether the targeted community or entity has sufficient willingness to change. To measure the outcomes of projects, performance indicators are devised and reviewed on an annual basis to identify and reward high-performing communities.

The *Saemaul Undong* is undertaken at a village level. However, in Korea, this turned into a pan-national movement, so while villages were the main implementers of various projects, other networking bodies existed as well. The *Saemaul Undong* was an integrative work in itself and in the process of actively promoting this movement, an enhanced governance structure in the form of a newly integrated local administrative system emerged.

'*Saemaul Undong* education tailored to the needs of each community' means that the local community must provide training to its members, which can be done through the collaboration of village leaders learning from each other and coming up with *Saemaul Undong* textbooks developed following internal discussions. This is important because the learning process is internally driven, making the villagers self-serving with a true sense of ownership, in contrast to 'outside experts' seemingly dictating everything, as is the case in many development projects. Local problems should be solved through locals' understanding and participation, and by mobilizing local resources.

The KOICA President expressed that 'KOICA is currently receiving requests from 50 developing countries to share knowledge in *Saemaul Undong* or community development. In addition, international organizations such as [the] World Food Program (WFP), United Nations Development Programme (UNDP) and United Nations Economic and Social Commission for Asia and the Pacific (UNESCAP), and world-renowned scholars, including Professor Jeffrey Sachs, have lauded *Saemaul Undong* as an excellent development model'.[2]

The Korea *Saemaul Undong* Centre was created in 1980 with sub-regional organizations at the national level, along with five member associations, including the Central Council of *Saemaul* Leaders, the Central Council of *Saemaul* Women's Club, the Central Council of Corporation and Factory *Saemaul Undong*, the Federation of *Saemaul* Mini-libraries and the Federation of *Saemaul* Credit Unions. These organizations, like the *Saemaul Undong* Centre, all have vertical sub-regional networks. While this centre has been in existence for a long time, it is only recently that it has started to embark on the Global *Saemaul Undong* programme in around 2009.

In order for the *Saemaul Undong* to have any real impact on African countries, a pragmatic scenario would be having success stories of the *Saemaul Undong* emerge in Africa so that they can be replicated and expanded over the region. The *Saemaul Undong* will not be met with the same degree of enthusiasm in all countries, so the programme needs to be strategically focused.

Saemaul Undong in Uganda

Although the Ugandan example may not be the representative case for the whole Sub-Saharan African region, it should provide an informative case in understanding what can be possible in this region. The *Saemaul Undong* in Uganda is in a burgeoning stage, making it an interesting and valuable testing ground for its African and international programme. The *Saemaul Undong* was formally introduced in 2009 when the Korea *Saemaul* Undong Centre collaborated with Korea Africa Investment and Development (KAID) that was established by a Korean missionary body to conduct model *Saemaul Undong* village projects in Kitemu and Katereke in Nsangi sub-county, Wakiso District.

Around this time, or actually a little earlier, the Canaan Farmers School also began its activity in Uganda. Government leaders in Uganda had shown a keen interest in many aspects of Korea's development, and in 2009, some 20 Ugandan governmental leaders and officials, including the Vice President, visited Korea to attend the Canaan Farmers School's training course. The idea to train these government officials in the school came from President Museveni, and the Ugandan government paid for their travel costs.

Until a few years ago, the *Saemaul Undong* village pilot project in Uganda, which was sponsored by the Korea *Saemaul Undong* Centre, was largely unknown in Uganda due to the low-profile approach that the Centre followed. On the other hand, the Canaan Farmers School was quite popular, as President Museveni himself was fond of this institution.

It was on 31 May 2013, when President Museveni visited the Korea *Saemaul Undong* Centre in Sungnam, that he understood the difference between the Canaan Farmers School training and the *Saemaul Undong*. He learned that the school focused on mindset change training by emphasizing hard work, frugality, a disciplined life, etc., along with farming skills, whereas the *Saemaul Undong* was a more extensive and systematic community development movement based on the spirit of diligence, self-help and cooperation. The latter was a national movement involving the government, while the former was a private organization for training.

There are three main entities carrying out *Saemaul Undong* programmes in Uganda: KOICA, the UNDP and the Korea *Saemaul Undong* Centre. The earliest to arrive in Uganda was the Korea *Saemaul Undong* Centre's programme mentioned above. KOICA followed suit with the launch of the Mpigi Saemaul model village project in December 2015. Also, KOICA's National Farmers Leadership Centre (NFLC) in Kampiringisa, Mpigi, was officially launched in May 2016. The third entity is the UNDP, which launched the 'inclusive and sustainable new communities (ISNC) in Uganda' project adopting the *Saemaul Undong* model in July 2015. This project was an outcome of the Memorandum of Understanding signed between KOICA and the UNDP on the *Saemaul Undong* in 2013. Meanwhile, the Canaan Farmers School continues to train Ugandans in Korea. The school's programme may not be considered as *Saemaul Undong* per se, but is seen as complementing the *Saemaul Undong* through its mindset change training.

As already mentioned, Korea has announced the four key areas it will engage in to implement the SDGs, and the Project to Establish *Saemaul* Model Villages (ESMV) in Uganda, which was launched in December

2015 in Mpigi District by KOICA, falls into the first category of Inclusive and Sustainable Rural Development.[3]

Mpigi was chosen as the project site because KOICA wanted the NFLC, which was being located nearby, to have a synergistic effect with this project. The objective was to apply the new paradigm of the *Saemaul Undong* to achieve sustainable and integrated rural development. The activities involves the following: enhancing villages' agricultural productivity and income, improving the living environment and the rural community infrastructure; strengthening social capital by instilling a spirit of diligence, self-help and cooperation; strengthening the capacity of farmers' cooperatives and local central government. This was a three-year project (2015–2018) worth a total of USD 3 million.

As the beneficiaries of this project, seven villages were chosen by based on a baseline survey: Tiribogo village (Muduuma sub-county, 224 families, population 856), Kololo village (Kiringente sub-county, 249 families, population 1023), Nsamu village (Mpigi Town Council, 171 families, population 682), Kiwumu(A) village (Kammengo sub-county, 97 families, population 441), Kumbya village (Buwama sub-country, 131 families, population 671), Lwaweeba village (Kituntu sub-county, 129 families, population 666) and Lukonge village (Nkozi sub-county, 1078 families, population 4765). An important point to note is that these villages are not just beneficiaries, but are in competition with one another. Competition and motivation through incentives are central elements of the *Saemaul Undong*. The level of assistance they receive will depend on the results (KOICA Office Uganda).

The expected outcomes of the project are: (1) strengthening social capital—earning higher credibility, nurturing a sense of community and an increase in the frequency of town hall meetings; (2) increasing agricultural productivity and rural income—an increase in both agricultural and non-agricultural income and improvement in product of crops and livestock; (3) improving infrastructure and the living environment—the supply of clean water, better access to medical services, improving living quarters, better access to markets and improvement of the students-per-class ratio; and (4) improving governance in model villages—an increase in the number of projects carried out, enhancing the quality of project planning and reducing the time taken to resolve village issues.

The history of this project can be traced back to May 2013, when President Museveni visited the Korea *Saemaul Undong* Centre and appreciated the *Saemaul Undong* programmes. He said that Ugandans have gotten used to welfare policies and foreign aid since independence, and in the process Uganda's communal tradition like *Bulungi bwansi* had been lost, and thanked the Centre for refocusing on the lost traditions of Uganda.

The Ministry of Agriculture, Fisheries and Livestock of Uganda submitted a formal request for the project on September 2013, which led to the dispatch of a KOICA site survey team the following year. Consultations and the signing of a MOU took place in April 2015. Then in November 2015, the project office was set up and the steering committee leaders were trained in Korea, and seven model project villages were selected. The official launching ceremony took place in December 2015. In March 2016, members of the committees and sub-committees of these model villages were appointed, and rules on competition and incentives were finalized. It was decided that project funds would be allotted to each village, taking into account their performance. In April 2016, training in *Saemaul* leadership and general development issues for the committee members was conducted. A baseline survey on the villagers' feedback and the progress of projects as well as the formulation of a *Saemaul* action plan was completed in May 2016.

From the perspective of KOICA project management (PM), the four main tasks are: dispatch of experts; supply of logistics/materials; performance management; and public relations. KOICA sent two Korean experts to oversee the project on the ground, while setting up a project team with local employees, as well as drawing up the project scheme. The KOICA Office supplied the necessary logistics, like an office facility, official vehicles and various kinds of materials. Performance management entails using baseline surveys, mid-term appraisal and final assessment to measure performance and draw lessons from the standpoint of the *Saemaul Undong*. Public relations activities include regular press briefings, distribution of brochures, etc.

The flagship of the Korean development project in Uganda is the NFLC, which was built in Kampirignisa, Mpigi District, to showcase a comprehensive Korean model of rural-agricultural development. As the then Korean President pointed out in her speech during the opening ceremony of the centre, this is the first of its kind in Africa. President Museveni had expressed his desire to the Korean side in March 2010 to have such an institution (modelled on the Canaan Farmers School) built in Uganda so that Ugandans could be trained in Korean-style mindset change programmes.

This project to establish the NFLC was carried out from April 2011 to May 2016 with a budget of USD 4.4 million. While the centre was formally opened in 30 May 2016, the project was extended for a year in order to place it on a stronger footing in terms of operational capacity and financial sustainability before its handover to the Ugandan side, which took place in May 2017. The NFLC project's vision is the establishment of a 'top-notch' leadership centre in Uganda and East Africa that will lead to the development of the rural community and the country. Its mission is: (1) to transform mindset and empower farm leaders, civic and political leadership at all levels of government; (2) to train leaders who will be a role model to others by working, serving and sacrificing first; and (3) to impart agricultural technologies to transform from subsistence to commercial farming for wealth.

This NFLC's basic approach is combining the *Saemaul Undong* spirit and agro-technologies. The expectations of the NFLC were very high indeed in Uganda, and hence there was considerable pressure on the key stakeholders to deliver the expected outcomes. The project has three facets: physical infrastructure, a 'delivery system' or operation and the contents or substance. But making these three things happen or work is no easy task and poses big challenges. The physical construction of the NFLC entailed a prolonged and laborious process due to the various obstacles that face construction projects in Africa. Here, the 'contents' are the Korean model of rural-agricultural development, including the *Saemaul Undong*. No matter how good the infrastructure and the contents, these will be worthless if the delivery—the project operation—does not match up.

Hence, KOICA focused on making the NFLC operation efficient and sustainable before it handed over this project to the Ugandan side. The devil is in the detail and the technical aspect of the project—the question of how to make it sustainable—is a major challenge, especially in Sub-Saharan Africa. KOICA's work plan for the operation of the NFLC had the goal of setting up a sustainable operation system of the NFLC through capacity-building.[4]

Before the NFLC was officiated in May 2016, it conducted test operations for more than a year, and over 400 people were trained in *Saemaul Undong* and agricultural skills. Since the official opening, the NFLC has collaborated with the *Saemaul* model village project (ESMV) in Mpigi District, providing training for the latter.

The NFLC had an operational structure of cooperative links between the KOICA Uganda Office and the Ministry of Agriculture, Animal Industry and Fisheries (MAAIF). They signed a MOU on co-management of the NFLC on 25 May 2016. The project management consultant (PMC) led by the Chonbuk National University consortium worked under the KOICA Office. Within this PMC, there was a project manager (PM) who worked as the Cooperation Head of the NFLC to conduct operation of the NFLC, develop modules and a master plan, and run training programmes and farms with his team of Korean experts. On the Ugandan side, a steering committee composed of various officials concerned was placed under the Ministry, while the principal was tasked with contacting the Ministry, securing a governmental budget, legalizing the status of the NFLC, organizing a steering committee and recruiting staff.

The UNDP *Saemaul Undong* project, the Inclusive and Sustainable New Communities (ISNC) Project in Uganda, is the first *Saemaul Undong* programme that the UNDP has launched in Sub-Saharan Africa. In September 2014, Uganda's Ministry of Local Government officials met UNDP officials in New York and learned from them that the UNDP was planning to pilot the *Saemaul Undong* model in some developing countries, particularly in Africa. The Uganda officials persuaded the UNDP officials to include Uganda in this programme. Then, in October 2014, a team from the UNDP headquarters visited

Uganda to work with the Ministry to start putting together the project document for the ISNC programme.

The Ugandan Ministry of Local Government appreciated the follow-up actions of the UNDP as appropriate and timely, as Uganda was re-examining its development agenda through the National Development Plan II with a vision to becoming a middle-income country by the year 2030. It recognized that the project, which would activate the *Saemaul Undong* principles of diligence, self-help and cooperation, would provide the much-needed result-oriented development impetus that is poised to pull the country out of poverty.

This ISNC project is based on the rural development model of the *Saemaul Undong* with the goal of transforming communities with a long-term shared vision of a better life for all, and an infectious enthusiasm for local development, sustained by volunteerism at the community level. The project ran for two and half years (July 2015–December 2017) with funding of USD 1 million provided by Korea. It was implemented in the three districts of Kabarole, Maracha and Luuka, targeting a total of 15 communities. The envisioned results were: (1) a strengthened institutional system of local development; (2) enhanced cohesiveness and inclusiveness in community development; (3) improved and increased local resources and financing mechanisms; (4) scaled up of proven sustainability innovations; and (5) the documentation and dissemination of generated knowledge.

The Minister of Local Government of Uganda spoke about the *Saemaul Undong* model on the occasion of the launching of the ISNC in July 2015:

> During my visit to South Korea in October 2014, I witnessed the transformation that the country underwent over the years and was mesmerized by the impact that was caused by the model. I was particularly intrigued to learn that the model was premised on the platform of spirit of diligence, self-help and cooperation among the rural communities. In Korea, this led to improved livelihoods, but more significantly, transformed communities to develop a long term shared vision of a better life for all, and an infectious enthusiasm for local development, sustained by volunteerism at community level.[5]

The Korea *Saemaul Undong* Centre started its project in Uganda in 2009 with the two model villages of Kitemu (500 households, population 2500) and Katereke (250 households, population 1500) of Nsagni sub-county, Wakiso District, over a five-year period. Then in 2015, it newly designated six model villages in Mityana District: Bbanda (110 households, population 480); Nabaale (105 households, population 450); Kyabombo (110 households, population 390); Mawanga (100 households, population 490); Ndirabweru (96 households, population 470); and Buwala (98 households, population 440). Besides these model villages that are officially supported by the Korea *Saemaul Undong* Centre, 'autonomous' *Saemaul* villages (estimated to be more than 40 as of July 2016) that have adopted the *Saemaul Undong* voluntarily are growing at a fast pace in Uganda.[6]

The typical *Saemaul Undong* programmes for these villages fall into three categories: improvement of the living environment, increase in agricultural production and household incomes, and education. All the work is done by the village residents collectively. Improving the living environment includes constructing *Saemaul Undong* halls, public toilets, public wells, *boda-boda* (motorcycle taxis) shelters, improving kitchens, and cleaning up villages and flattening out dirt roads. Examples of activities to increase agricultural production and incomes are operating cooperative farms (to produce mushrooms, vegetables, maize, bananas, ground-nuts, etc.), factories (to produce feed, blocks, candles, soaps, slippers, furniture, etc.), fish-ponds, piggeries, goat banks, pig banks, sewing schools, beauty parlour schools, *Saemaul* banks, etc. Lastly, the education programme involves training Ugandans in the Korea *Saemaul Undong* Centre and operating a 'mobile *Saemaul* School' in Uganda. Around 170 Ugandans were trained in Korea from 2009 to 2015, and the mobile school has been in operation since 2014.

The Uganda *Saemaul Undong* Centre was formed to undertake *Saemaul Undong* programmes in Uganda supported by Korea's *Saemaul Undong* Centre. Its activities have been steady and engaging, but there is a room for greater expansion. The irony is that the first-term model village assistance for five years by the Korea *Saemaul Undong* Centre showed a rather mediocre performance, while the voluntary *Saemaul* villages like Busanza and Kiboba, which received no direct support from Korea, did markedly better and their mode more closely resembled the typical model practised by Korean villages. It could be that Kitemu and Katereke villages are located near the Capitol Kampala and have semi-urban features. Also, because many leaders and members of this sub-county have had the chance to visit Korea to be trained there, and received some sort of support on a continuous basis, this probably made them 'dependent' without being really motivated. Of course, the assistance provided by the Korean centre was modest in amount, and in many cases it came in the form of matching funds. But, overall, the two villages did not meet the expectations of being pioneering *Saemaul Undong* villages in Uganda. The leaders and officials became familiar with the *Saemaul Undong* skills and approach, and did well in presentations, but fell short in terms of energizing, expanding and promoting this movement in their region. This turned out to be a very important lesson in itself.

The strength of the Uganda *Saemaul Undong* Centre lies in its local presence and local networking. While Korean experts, volunteers or officials come and go, the Uganda *Saemaul Undong* Centre run by Ugandans has accumulated expertise on the ground and through its contacts with Korean side. Its activities have been widened as it started to provide mobile *Saemaul Undong* clinic services and collaborate with the NFLC, ESMV and ISNC projects. The Korean Embassy in Kampala, working closely with the KOICA Office, has provided oversight for *Saemaul Undong*-related programmes and activities for Uganda. Communications with the host government and relevant entities, and public diplomacy, among other activities, comprise the embassy's regular work.

To help promote the *Saemaul Undong* in Uganda, the embassy itself has held related events. First, it held a *Saemaul Undong* demonstration day event on four occasions between December 2013 and December 2014 in Kampala and Wakiso District. This was a simple cleaning-up exercise designed to draw public attention to the *Saemaul Undong* and to enhance awareness of and support for this movement. Later on, it organized annual the Uganda National *Saemaul Undong* Competition, which started in 2015. The competition plan was announced to interested village leaders, religious leaders, civil society representatives and journalists who gathered at the embassy. The next step was communicating with competition participants. The embassy responded to inquiries and applications, explaining the guidelines of the competition. Then, an evaluation process was carried out on the work schemes submitted by each village. Participants were also required to present implementation reports with photos of the proposed project sites before and after the execution of the work. Subsequently, an on-site evaluation was conducted, and after going through each committee assessment, the winners were chosen and awards were presented at the end of the year. A total of 190 villages applied for the competition in 2015.

The evaluation criteria basically comprised four elements: (1) the creation or amelioration of the village's common properties (wells, expansion of village roads, etc.); (2) the enhancement of the village environment and living conditions (how much cleaner the village became after entering the competition); (3) organizational capacity (how efficiently structured the village leadership and organization had become for the implementation of *Saemaul Undong* activities); and (4) voluntariness (how much did the people contribute in terms of labour and funds, how regularly did the villagers gather to conduct joint projects, etc.)

The awards, comprising certificates of recognition and a prize, were given to the top seven villages. The awards ceremony, the finale of this competition, was filled with the joy and excitement of the participants, and attracted media attention. The prizes given were not cash, but in-kind materials that the villages were in need of and had asked for. The purpose of the awards was to instil a sense of accomplishment and honour in the practitioners and to encourage them further, in line with the 'incentives and punishment' principle. The embassy also held stakeholder meetings to inform Ugandan and international partners about *Saemaul Undong* projects and to seek their collaboration. On 30 June 2015, it hosted the High Level Seminar on the *Saemaul Undong*, with participants including the Minister of Local Government, the Chairman of the National Planning Authority, the Permanent Secretaries of the Ministry of Agriculture and the Ministry of Local Government, the Vice President's senior assistant, the UNDP Resident Coordinator, the KOICA Office and the KOPIA Centre heads.

On 15 December 2015, the embassy organized with the UNDP a seminar on implementing SDGs in Uganda. The Senior Advisor to the President on Economic Planning and representatives of various organizations like the UNDP, USAID, the EU, the World Bank, KOICA, KOPIA and civil society attended this meeting. An important subject on the agenda was sustainable rural development, and naturally the *Saemaul Undong* model was discussed.

One of the most memorable moments was when I participated, together with the visiting Secretary General of the Korea *Saemaul Undong* Centre, in the third National *Saemaul Undong* Convention organized by the Uganda *Saemaul Undong* Centre on 23 October 2015 in Kampala. Vice President Edward Ssekandi, other high-level government officials, UNDP representatives and over 1000 *Saemaul Undong* practitioners representing various districts gathered together. The Secretary General was in awe at seeing with his own eyes the fervour of the participants. The Vice President stressed that the dependency syndrome was seriously impairing Uganda's development and that the *Saemaul Undong* emphasizing diligence, self-help and cooperation was the 'best approach' to overcoming Uganda's problems.

The Proposed Scheme for Africa

I have cited Uganda's example of the *Saemaul Undong* to highlight its possibilities, challenges and applicability in Sub-Saharan Africa. Uganda is considered to be a notable case of the *Saemaul Undong* taking root in Africa. There are other candidates like Rwanda and Ethiopia, but Uganda could be the best testing ground for the *Saemaul Undong* in terms of its application to the region as a whole.

Many Sub-Saharan African countries have a tradition of communal self-help similar to the *Saemaul Undong*. As far as I know, these include Rwanda, Uganda, Burundi, Ethiopia and Tanzania, but there must be many more. Also in South Africa, a similar tradition exists, the *Ubuntu*, an obscured legacy that needs to be revived. *Ubuntu* spirits are *enhlonipho* (respect), *abantu* (fellowship), *illlima-letsema* (working together), *stokvel* and *lekgotla* (community dialogue). But a very meaningful development is unfolding: the *Saemaul Undong* programme entitled the '*Saemaul* Mindset DEEP (Development Experience Exchange Partnership) programme', a joint project between KOICA and the Ministry of Rural Development and Land Reform of South Africa, was launched on 16 July 2018 in Pretoria.

Over the years, various Korean organizations have been actively collaborating with Uganda, Ethiopia and Rwanda in the *Saemaul Undong*. There are also other countries in western and southern Africa that are interested in the *Saemaul Undong*, but East Africa is deemed to be the most active and successful thus far in this endeavour. South Africa is the latest addition. Overall, *Saemaul Undong* programmes are in a fledgling stage in Africa.

Rwanda tops the region when it comes to the level of governance and its *Saemaul Undong* project seems to be undertaken in a most organized manner in Africa. But the general features of Rwanda make it somewhat 'atypical' in the region. The nation has a very small territory, while having one of the lowest levels of ethnic diversity in Sub-Saharan Africa. In contrast, Uganda is considered to be ethnically the most diverse nation in the world, with a territory nearly ten times larger than that of Rwanda. Ethiopia is also a much bigger country facing greater challenges for expanding and managing development projects like the *Saemaul Undong*.

All in all, Uganda provides an interesting case study to test the viability of the *Saemaul Undong* in Sub-Saharan Africa. There are several major players involved in Uganda: KOICA, the Korea *Saemaul Undong* Centre, the UNDP and the Canaan Farmers School, as well as other various institutions on rural-agriculture development. Hopefully, in due course, when enough information and records have been accumulated on the progress of *Saemaul Undong* projects in the African region, a comprehensive and systematic analysis of the impact of the *Saemaul Undong* on the region will be possible. But for the time being, strenuous efforts need to be made both in terms of the application and in the studies of the *Saemaul Undong* to keep the momentum going.

In light of what has transpired in Sub-Saharan Africa over many decades, we might as well try things differently and more aggressively in relation to development projects for the region. Most of the development projects that have been carried out in Africa were repetitions of what was done in the past. It is true that capacity-building or educational programmes, and rights-oriented programmes to promote social justice or peace, to protect and empower people, etc. also share a common goal of trying to change people's attitudes and behaviour. But there is a major difference between these approaches and the *Saemaul Undong*. In terms of substance, the established programmes are either theorectial or technical in nature but the *Saemaul Undong* is all about practicality, directly and firmly anchored in the mindset change scheme.

A textbook form of generalized education as well as overly specialized programmes might not yield the desired results. Rather, vocational, technical training is far more desirable for Africa, but this needs to be supplemented by mindset change or 'resocialization' programmes underscoring work ethics to have the necessary actual ripple effects. The advantage of the *Saemaul Undong* is that it encompasses and inter-links players at different levels—individual, village or community, regional and society at large—to produce immediate and palpable benefits to those who practise it. It is a pragmatic approach that goes 'with the grain' of local traditions in African countries. And the practice of 'doing things' with a 'can-do spirit' that the *Saemaul Undong* promotes is what African countries desperately need.

There are elements conducive to the *Saemaul Undong* as well as many challenges in Uganda. What is definitely positive is that there is wide support among Uganda's leaders and people for the *Saemaul Undong*. The level of enthusiasm may vary depending on people's background, but they seem to all see the necessity to pursue such an action-oriented initiative as a rational alternative to the existing modes.

For those who are more insightful and practical-minded, the *Saemaul Undong* is even more appealing. Many Ugandan politicians, officials, civil society and religious leaders have expressed a strong desire to have the *Saemaul Undong* introduced to their districts. Because African rural areas are largely in a state of destitution, they welcome any support programmes they can get, and it is understandable for Ugandan's interest in the *Saemaul Undong*. But there are also many who genuinely like the movement, knowing it is something very different and that can have more substantive impact on them.

Another merit of the *Saemaul Undong* is that it has a strong appeal from the perspective of national development policy and the availability of state resources. Sub-Saharan Africa's number one priority is arguably rural-agricultural development, as the majority of population reside in rural areas. How to effectively achieve rural-agricultural development on a national scale should be the ultimate task of the leaders. In Africa, successful industrialization is likely to emerge from the agricultural sector, making such an approach all the more worthwhile. It is argued that in Korea, the *Saemaul Undong* served as 'the second economic movement' supporting the government-led economic growth policy.[7]

Political stability and security are also important factors for the success of the *Saemaul Undong*. In this respect, Uganda enjoys a rather favourable politico-security environment compared to other Sub-Saharan countries, making it a good testing ground. Also, the fact that Uganda is blessed in terms of rich natural endowments and favourable agricultural conditions, but is experiencing persistent poverty can prompt people to rethink their existing methods and espouse a new approach such as the *Saemaul Undong*.

Thus, there are good reasons for countries to embrace the *Saemaul Undong* if they know what it is about. But then again, even with all the good intentions and enthusiastic support of stakeholders, various barriers remain. These challenges are what the proponents of the *Saemaul Undong* must continuously fight against and which also demand a different mindset on the part of the Korean development partners. The reason why most development projects do not live up to expectations and wither shortly after donors have completed their mission and hand them over is because the recipients have inherently little zeal to take ownership of and responsibility for them. Hence, it is important for donors to conduct post-management of projects in whatever fashion possible and not to totally terminate engagement for a certain period.

Foreign development partners in the field are faced with double jeopardy. Not only do they have to follow very tough guidelines and regulations of their home country, but they also have to deal with everyday hardships on the ground and worry about the possibility of the failure of their projects due to problems beyond their control. But knowing all too well how things will likely to unfold given the practices and conditions of the country they are assigned to, it would almost seem irresponsible for foreign aid workers to ignore reality altogether. Hence, regardless of how difficult it may be, development partners should be more demanding, proactive and straightforward in 'pushing' locals to comply and carry out their necessary part in the process. What is required is much more intrusive enforcement of disciplined work standards, supervision and the rule of 'incentives and punishment'.

This vindicates the adoption of a stringent mindset change approach like the *Saemaul Undong* in the Sub-Saharan African region. What came to me as an important reckoning was that serious self-reflection must come from within Africans themselves, and it should not be the job of the development partners to spell out the problems of which the African people should be all too aware. A first meaningful step forward would be to recognize that 'something is wrong' and that it needs to be dealt with. I have seen people blaming others, so often but rarely do they put blame on themselves.

There is a delicate balance between the need for the *Saemaul Undong* to be welcomed and voluntarily espoused by the locals on the one hand, and the need to be strict and really be 'pushy' so that it can produce the desired outcome on the other. For foreign workers, making the locals change their attitude and behaviour is a very difficult as well as a sensitive task. Therefore, *Saemaul Undong* programme managers or instructors need to have extra passion, perseverance and devotion to their duties. They themselves should have strong communication and leadership skills.

In the case of poor countries, there is no choice for them other than to rely on a labour-intensive sector to build and grow the economy. But the socio-economic dynamics of the world have changed and people's work ethic in general is deemed to have deteriorated. Even in the poorest countries, it cannot be taken for granted that ordinary people would be willing to undergo toil and hardships in order to make it in life. A virtue like the Protestant work ethic, which, by the way, has similar features to the teachings of the Canaan Farmers School, may be dissipating fast. There are signs that even the poor and jobless in Africa are increasingly shunning laborious work and are instead aspiring for easy-going, high-paid jobs that are out of their reach. But there is not much to hope for when the population continues to be neither productive nor diligent.

Other unwholesome trait that I have discovered to be prevalent even among African elites is a lack of confidence which can turn into a more serious form of defeatism. Lack of confidence and motivation breeds inaction, dependence and loss of self-esteem, which in turn can lead to expediency, deviation, irregularities and abandonment of one's responsibilities. Lack of confidence and commitment is reflected in the tendency to 'regress' or 'give up early and have other thoughts'.

The lessons learned from the operation of the *Saemaul Undong* in Uganda over the past six years or so can be summed up as follows: (1) poverty is opportunity; (2) competence and drive in grassroots leaders makes all the difference; (3) flexibility and incremental scaling up of governance is required; (4) apply Goldilocks principle in assistance; and (5) an 'organically' interlinked system of support should be developed.

In Korea, the *Saemaul Undong* was successfully implemented because so many people took an active part in it, and the ultimate factor behind this was poverty: people were united in terms of wanting to get out of poverty and improve their livelihood. And the confidence that was bred into them only made them more passionate. It is believed that the Korean rural population complied actively with this movement because they were hopeful in light of the success of the government's export promotion in the 1960s.

In Uganda, as in other Sub-Saharan African countries in general, rural regions remain poor without much, if any, change taking placing, despite the evolution of the times and technological advances. For those people who are conscious of their situation, who know very well their limitations in the means (and the limited support they can get from their government or donors), but who desire a better life, the *Saemual Undong* can be appealing. But there is variation in the responsiveness to this according to the type of communities: (1) communities near urban or commercial centres, having easily access to business, economic activities; (2) 'communal' villages in provincial districts; and (3) hard-to-access, very remote and isolated 'troubled regions' (with a weak social fabric and dire poverty). The type that is most likely to have the best chance for the *Saemaul Undong* is communal villages. In sum, poor 'communal' villages having a certain level of yearning for a better life and hope have been found to be most suitable for the *Saemaul Undong*.

Since the *Saemaul Undong* is undertaken at the grassroots community level, no matter how organized and buffed up the external support system may be, if there is no interest, commitment and implementation on the part of the villagers themselves, then there is no point in pursuing the programme. Villages with certain people or a group of people with exceptional vigour in this regard can make a big difference. Thus, it is crucial to identify and assign such leaders during the early stages of planning and launching of the *Saemaul Undong*. A good example is the 'Greater Masaka Mindset Change Agents Club' of Uganda. This youth group that underwent training in the NFLC in April 2017, formed this club during the training and returned to their villages to implement the *Saemaul Undong* in an energetic manner.[8]

For the *Saemaul Undong* to take root and expand successfully in African countries, and not end up as merely a banal project, the government, both at the local and the central levels, must be engaged in a meaningful fashion. Hence, there is a need for a matching administrative system or governance to be put in place. Regarding the governance of the *Saemaul Undong*, it would be unrealistic to expect the African countries to form a strong system of the *Saemaul Undong* governance, even if it is espoused at the state level, because the state of governance in African countries itself is weak in the first place. Endorsement by the head of state and the support of the relevant ministry are definitely encouraging and helpful, but these are not enough. Rather than making this a task in itself, it would be practical to start with a flexible approach of focusing on a grassroots movement to prove the usefulness of the *Saemaul Undong* with concrete outcomes. This will bring about the government's involvement in a natural way.

The fourth lesson is about applying the Goldilocks principle ('just right') in terms of providing assistance for Saemaul Undong. Neither indifference nor 'full support' is desirable. The 'just right' thing is to be moderate and deliberate in *Saemaul Undong* projects: provide intensive training at the initiative stage, but allow the local leaders and residents to take up on their own in the spirit of diligence, self-help and cooperation. Encouragement and appreciation of their efforts are important, but direct material support should be very limited and measured, only being provided as an incentive in consideration of their actual performance. It is much better and more effective to enhance people's pride and inspire them further through face-to-face communications and 'symbolic' rewards rather than assisting them with material means, otherwise they will simply remain dependent.

What is also important is to nurture an environment of openness and possibilities of collaboration. Motivation, passion and optimism are what drive the *Saemaul Undong*. These can only be sustained when people see the benefits of the *Saemaul Undong* and the positive links it has for their income generation in the longer run. And as a matter of course, this is the area where African governments should play their necessary part. But the *Saemaul Undong* can collaborate with other relevant Korean projects, the host country's projects and other foreign development partners as well. The purpose here is to provide synergistic effects and prevent duplication of efforts through coordination. For example, a network comprising the NFLC, the KOPIA Centre, various *Saemaul Undong* activities and UNDP programmes is being fostered in Uganda. Also, the relevant *Saemaul Undong* bodies can team up with the Ugandan government's Operation Wealth Creation (OWC) that is being implemented to support rural households' agricultural production. I realized that in order for all this arrangement to succeed, a central oversight authority was still very much necessary.

Then how should we engineer the *Saemaul Undong* for Sub-Saharan Africa? Coming up with a blueprint that is applicable for the whole region in a detailed fashion will be almost impossible because not only does the situation vary from country to country, but each provincial region within a given country would have its own unique features. The practical thing to do would be to set some kind of general criteria or benchmarks to start with.

Under the principles or core values of the *Saemaul Undong*—diligence, self-help and cooperation—we can deduce 'three targets' and 'six measures' that are deemed pertinent to Africa. The three targets are: (1) income generation; (2) contribution or burden-sharing by the locals; and (3) formation of economic links for value chains and market access. The six measures required to achieve them are: (1) maintaining openness and outreach to other initiatives/programmes; (2) adopting and teaching national, social and work ethics at schools, in government circles and in local communities; (3) forming an interactive network among central government, local government and communities; (4) fostering competent and dedicated *Saemaul Undong* leaders; (5) promoting a strong community-centred mechanism like town hall meetings; and (6) developing cooperative business arrangements for increased value addition and access to markets.

Moreover, agents serving as a medium between these targets on the one hand and the relevant measures on the other are mindset change, skills/know-how and financial ownership, which I will refer to as 'MSF' ('M' standing for mindset change, 'S' for skills/know-how and 'F' for financial ownership of the locals). An important thing to note is that these three agents or components need to occur simultaneously and to be synchronized. Figure 11.1 below illustrates this. At the very top you can see the guiding principles of the *Saemaul Undong*: diligence, self-help and cooperation. The three targets that are placed under these principles are income generation, burden-sharing by the locals, and forming value-chains and economic linkage.

To simplify things, the basic goals of Korea's *Saemaul Undong* were twofold: first, improving living quarters and community infrastructure; and, second, increasing household and community incomes through various agricultural and manufacturing activities. In order for economic development to be felt by the ordinary people, it should take place where the majority of the population live—in the rural regions. Thus, improving the basic living environment for rural residents is an important step in realizing national wellbeing.

This is important not only in terms of cleanliness, sanitation and order of rural communities, but also for people's healthiness of mind, which is conducive to socio-economic development. It also helps strengthen the social capital. Not only does one feel much better living in a clean and orderly neighbourhood, but it also makes one more motivated and responsible to maintain that level of living. The work went beyond cleaning up, fixing and building living quarters, like upgrading

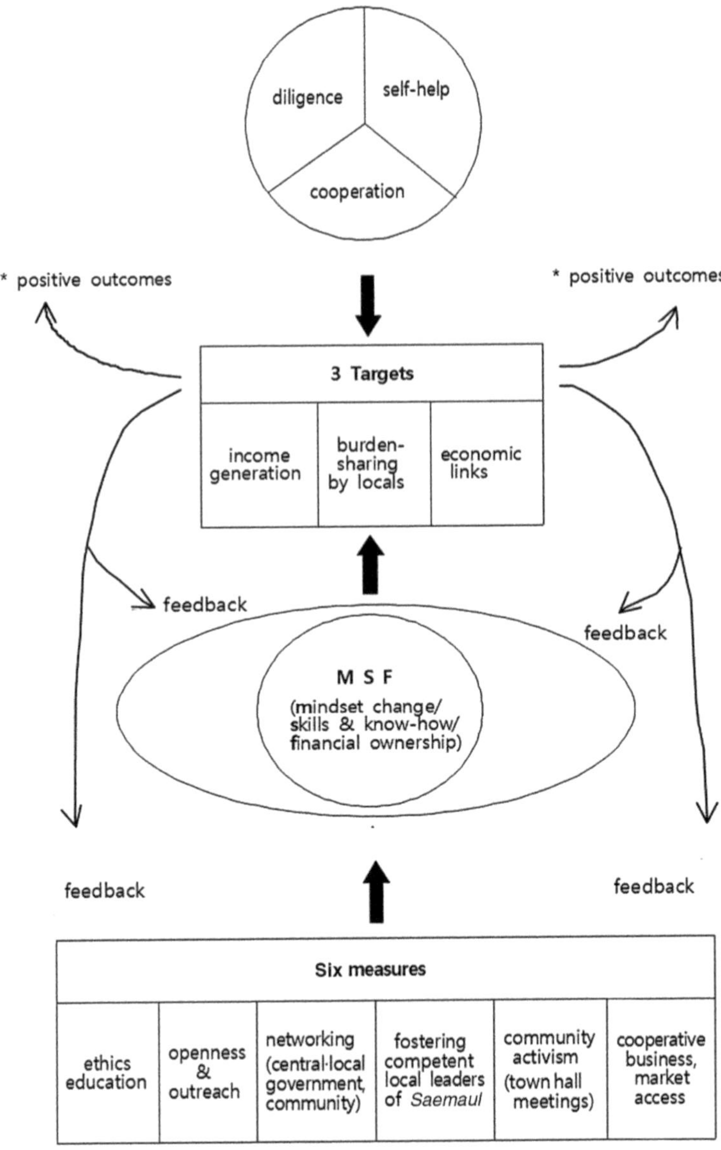

Fig. 11.1 The *Saemaul Undong* scheme for Sub-Saharan Africa

and expanding various forms of physical infrastructure in the community: improving and enlarging roads, constructing bridges, flood-prevention structures, etc. This not only made living in rural areas much more convenient, but also created a beneficial environment for commercial activities and opportunities for locals. The appearance of orderliness reflects the state of mind of the people and says a lot of about the possibility of development.

The second category I mentioned is the enhancement of rural income through improved agricultural production and other income-generating activities. Income generation for rural areas is the ultimate goal as well as the benchmark of success of the *Saemaul Undong* in Africa. So, in order for the *Saemaul Undong* to prove its worth and hence be able to flourish as a relevant development model in the region, there must be a marked positive outcome—income generation—derived from it.

Another target is people's contribution or burden-sharing. This cannot be over-emphasized, as the *Saemaul Undong* is about empowering the people by instilling a 'can-do' spirit and a sense of ownership in them. People will feel true ownership if they invest and have a stake in the work they undertake. Many existing development projects involve only the one-way provision of assistance or delivery of facilities or equipment to beneficiaries. In other words, they do not directly invoke positive change in recipients by making people act or contribute immediately. The important thing is to strictly uphold the rule that 'nothing is free' and that the locals should play their due part in return for the benefits they receive.

The third target is the formation of economic links in terms of value chains and market access. For *Saemaul Undong* villages, being connected to markets and business or industrial centres is crucial to their viability and welfare as communities. Without such economic connectivity, communities will not be able to achieve autonomous and sustainable development. In Sub-Saharan Africa, most villages in rural areas are remote from economic centres, main roads and markets, and these largely 'isolated' areas are cut off from even what little commercial opportunities are available in provincial regions. A severe shortage of road networks, poor condition of roads and poor means of transportation limit economic and social spill-over effects and exacerbate the divide that exists between the capital city and the rest of the country. When left unchecked, a vicious cycle in the form of double dipping—the growth of slums and over-population in cities, and the marginalization and deprivation of rural areas—will continue. So, the pursuit of regional economic links should be especially underscored in Sub-Saharan Africa.

As a means of reaching these three targets, I have laid out six measures, which, in turn, have to be driven by the three elements of MSF in a concurrent fashion: mindset change, skills and know-how, and financial ownership. First, if people go about doing business with the same frame of mind, this will not make a difference in terms of speed and quality of work. Second, having a strong and positive mindset is critical for individuals to be self-serving and become more adept in their work and training. In African urban areas and rural regions, there is a great gap in education and knowledge. Hence, conscientious efforts must be made to enlighten, train and educate the rural population, but the desire to learn must come from the residents themselves. And the embodiment and application of mindset change and skills will not be sufficient if this is not accompanied by 'financial ownership'. Having financial ownership means that people have to put their own resources in the project from which they wish to benefit. This makes everybody a worthy member of the community, each contributing to, and having a stake in, the success of the work carried out in their community. It is also good for nurturing civic values.

Learning that 'nothing is free' is a big part of the *Saemaul Undong*, particularly in Sub-Saharan Africa. A government official and politician from northern Uganda told me that no matter how much he helps his constituents, 'no one is willing to even contribute one dollar' to the community projects that they will be benefiting from. Practising financial ownership can also bring dividends in terms of encouraging badly needed savings in Africa.

With MSF as the driver of the *Saemaul Undong* in Africa, six measures should be taken to ensure the overall success and expansion of this rural development model: ethics/civil education; openness and outreach; networking; fostering local leaders; community decision-making and a consensus-building mechanism; and cooperatives. Of these, the first two seem particularly pertinent for Africa, while the others are more obvious and generally applicable to other regions of the developing world.

First on the list of measures to be taken is embarking on a programme of national education in ethics. The need for a major overhaul in national educational contents in Sub-Saharan Africa cannot be overemphasized. African countries must adopt more vocational, technical courses in schools as opposed to the current theoretical, academic subjects. But more importantly, they need to introduce and vigorously launch public education in ethics—social ethics, work ethics, national ethics, etc.—for all levels of students and also for adults.

The matter of ethics seems to be taken either too lightly or too seriously. First of all, the issue of ethics has many dimensions. We can break down ethics in three categories: (1) moral ethics; (2) collective ethics; and (3) functional ethics. The first of these is usually referred to as 'morals' or personal character. The word 'ethics', in comparison to 'morals', connotes a social context. And I think what is ignored in many developing countries is collective and functional ethics. While moral ethics or morality is innately personal and spiritual, collective ethics is more about one's attitude, beliefs and behaviour *in relation to* one's community, society and nation. While the former is 'inwardly oriented', the latter is 'outwardly oriented'. The former asks whether we are decent and rightful, while the latter asks what inclination we have towards various units of the society. Lastly, functional ethics is about how we 'do' things, or the tendency that we have in our actions and work.

It is crucial that we bring elements of behavioural science into the discourse of development in order for it to be more relevant in our search for answers or solutions. The problems in the first category—corruption, irregularity, bad governance, crimes, etc.—are tied to social and structural problems like poverty and underdevelopment, and they will not go away easily. The second category is more concerned with how to perceive things, to go about doing work, living one's daily life and contemplating one's situation and role in the society. We need to differentiate between these two and pursue them simultaneously, but on different tracks.

When I say that ethics is taken too lightly, it means that we are not realizing how much difference people's mindset and ethics can make in relation to development. On the contrary, taking the subject too seriously means that people become so fixated on the notion that nothing could be done about it. Neither of these two views is helpful and we need to find a happy medium where we clearly understand the gravity of the problem and act forcibly and continuously to root out the negative socio-psychological syndromes.

In Africa, there is no shortage of general teachings on personal morality. These come in the form of expressions of universal values, civil education and religious-moral teachings, etc. from various entities, including developing partners, government leaders, NGOs and rights groups, social and religious leaders, etc. But what is very much lacking in the discourse of development is the collective and functional ethics.

As for functional ethics, the word 'functional' may not seem very fitting to the realm of ethics as it implies the 'capacity' of people and how people work. But when this becomes problematic, it entails unnecessary cost—human toil, both in relation to time and financial—and the issue of responsibility. Keeping time for appointments and delivery of work, making things in a 'standardized' and acceptable manner, being focused on the job in hand so that things are done properly first time and do not have to be done all over again, etc. are standards are often not kept to the satisfaction in the region.

In this sense, the term 'functional ethics' is similar to 'work ethics'. But the term 'works ethics' implies a generalized meaning of desirable attitudes for work and fails to capture the innate characteristics and issues typical in Sub-Saharan African. That is why I have rephrased it as 'functional ethics' to signify a wide range of attitudinal tendencies—micro-, organizational and social—to explain the case in the region.

Particular emphasis should be placed on education on the collective ethics and functional ethics for Africa; a comprehensive education plan should be implemented to 'inculcate' students and the general populace on civil (or social or national) ethics, how to be rational, effective and successful in their daily work and jobs, and organizations or business. Functional ethics should also include technical and detailed ways of handling basic work.

'Morality' is synonymous with 'rightness' or 'goodness', but the term is subjective, being influenced by religious beliefs, a traditional social code of conduct or norms, cultures, philosophical orientations, etc. Enumerating what are evidently universally accepted *immoral* acts is much easier: stealing, cheating, lying, adultery, raping, murdering, etc. Then there are civility and virtues like being polite, responsible, honest, generous, diligent, indulgent, patient, helpful, selfless, etc. More lofty and abstract attributes include 'integrity', 'inspirational', 'visionary', 'saintly', etc. And there is a whole array of 'misdemeanours' or 'misconducts' construed as offences or improper and unlawful acts. And of course, acts of 'deviation' and crimes, whether simple, white-collar, organizational or collective, are committed everywhere all the time.

But such common forms of practice that people take for granted in the region, like failing to keep time for service deliveries, failing to be punctual for appointments, not keeping promises or following up, etc., should be also treated seriously. Such a matter lies somewhere in between moral norms and cultural practices or customs, but its accumulative effect leads to a fundamental curtailment of development.

Most of all, what appears to be the unending and unabating widespread practices of irregularities or corruption taking place every day at all levels of society needs to be addressed. The problem derives from a weak social fabric and a genuine lack of a 'culture of shame'. How to rectify this is really in the hands of Africans and something must be done about it.

Collective ethics is a different category. It is routine business for development partners, Africa's civil society and NGOs to raise human rights abuses and governance issues. But they will likely find collective ethics and, to a greater extent, functional ethics a bit odd. By collective ethics, I mean a sense of nation, patriotism and community; people recognizing the necessity and inevitability of their connection with the larger units of life outside their own. Western ideas of liberal democracy stress human rights and individual freedom, but this is premised on the existence of a potentially powerful state ('leviathan') that can infringe upon the rights of citizens.

What the people need is a stable but evolving environment in which to lead decent and better lives and build their society and economy. And it is basically through state-building and making the state to function properly that nations can prosper. Without having a well-functioning state mechanism in place and without a certain level of social capital being nurtured, development endeavours will be seriously jeopardized. The state or society needs to empower the people so that the people, in turn, will be able to develop their nation. This is a mutually reinforcing process. There needs to be a kind of binding social fabric conducive to the formation of a wholesome nationhood for long-term or sustainable development in Sub-Saharan Africa.

Countries lacking this essential foundation will continue to struggle with the challenges they face today. It will not be easy to engender a renewed national ethos or a sense of nation in the people, but it is certainly achievable, as many others have already done so. But of course, a special level of commitment is necessary.

The first step will be to embark on a national campaign of enlightenment or mindset renewal. Adversities can be turned into opportunities. There can be more harm than meets the eye in nations believing that all they need to do is to follow the trend of globalism and open up their economy, while adopting and emulating developed countries' institutions and values in a literal sense without understanding the prerequisites and underlying issues. Perhaps the greatest barrier to any attempt to overcome such limitations is African politics and populism. The leaders and elites seem to shun what is difficult but what is the right thing to do, and instead opt for what is unwholesome but is politically expedient or the easy thing to do.

Development partners should also pay attention to the issue of collective ethics. And while the initiative must come from within—from African people—it would do no harm if development partners also engage themselves in this endeavour to assist African nations in this process. This can be a new and challenging task for the development community, and would require extra sensitivity, patience and time, but it may pay off in the end.

What is hindering the formation of a healthy 'nationalism', patriotism or national identity in many African countries is party politics. Because of the divisive nature of politics and people's suspicion that there is a political agenda behind public campaigns led by government, it is become more difficult to win people's approval and support and mobilize them to get things moving. This is the irony of a contemporary electoral democracy that appears robust in Africa, but in reality in many instances is hindering much-needed real changes needed for national development.

An independent body along with civil society, joined by the government and even development partners, can drive the process forward. But politics should be avoided at all costs, otherwise it will be doomed from the start. It has to be collaborative work among various stakeholders, with the general public at the centre. It should be conducted through gathering public opinions, advice from social and religious leaders, education experts, intellectuals, etc., as well as benchmarking relevant cases in foreign countries. The process can be contentious and noisy, but this is how difficult things are done.

There is always the possibility that such an initiative, even if it were to be launched, will lose steam and wither quickly like so many others have done. But my response to this is that if you want transformative development, it has to be done because inherently, there is no quick fix and easy way out in relation to developmental challenges. Being intrinsically action-averse is the reason why Africa is struggling in this regard.

Functional ethics is another important area and it is all about going back to basics. 'Orderliness' is the key word. Among many things, a factor hindering development is the lack of a basic work ethic for observing 'orderliness'. There has been much talk about 'skilling' youth or the workforce, but the terms like 'skilling', 'capacity-building' and 'technical training' disguise what is the real underlying challenge—it is not so much the lack of 'knowledge' and information, but the attitude and pattern of behaviour that counts. There is much ado about 'creativity', 'innovation' and 'entrepreneurship' these days, but what is overlooked is the importance of being organized and conforming to 'standardization'. African products and services are less competitive and African workers are less frequently employed by foreign companies than they should be because of this.

Development can be achieved when individuals do their best with the tasks and the means given, and do not wait for everything to be right. In most parts of Sub-Saharan Africa, where so many basic needs are left uncared for and so much work needs to be done to get people out of a state of destitution, a sense of urgency to do something about the situation is largely absent. It appears that there is little, if any, appetite on the part of leaders and elites to really sound the alarm and spearhead campaigns to turn things around.

Orderliness and geometrical correctness are part and parcel of all the goodness and signs of advancement. They need to be observed and internalized by workers, businesses and society to make them competitive, viable or generically wholesome. Whether it is about simple manual work, the fabrication of goods, engineering or sophisticated tasks, the most basic rules or standards of work must be followed. While African people in general recognize and value manual dexterity, they sometimes fail to understand that the most basic element to observe at all times in work is geometrical correctness. In a larger context, this is the matter of 'standards' directly connected to economic competitiveness.

Cursory work done with a lack of focus and attention to detail, along with a lack of skills has many negative impacts on society and the economy. First, the direct outcome of the labour is poor-quality work. And costs—time and extra labour demands (including extra supervisory work)—go up, seriously curtailing the competitiveness and credibility of those workers. The typical work pattern of labourers is that they simply come in and do things without setting a proper work scheme and carefully conducting measurements.

Standardization, which is an essential prerequisite for manufacturing, engineering and industrialization, is also critical for social orderliness and quality of life. It is impossible to imagine achieving skills, technology and science while neglecting geometry. One of the reasons why many businesses in the region struggle to be competitive is because of shortcomings in their packaging skills as well as the quality for their products. Many decry the state of African trade that is driven by exporting raw commodities with low value addition, and they call for local processing and value addition of the products and the building of manufacturing industries. But again, it is only through a fundamental 'reorientation' of people's attitudes and behaviour that such progress can come about.

The second measure is 'openness and outreach'. What makes this necessary is because of the unique opportunity as well as the limitations existing in the region. There are community-oriented traditions or customs in Africa that the *Saemaul Undong* can utilize or collaborate with so that it is actually 'going with the grain' in relation to local practices. As I have mentioned, Sub-Saharan African people in general are very open-minded towards outsiders and in many cases there is a natural 'affinity' for movement such as the *Saemaul Undong* in Africa. Furthermore, rural-agricultural development is very high on the agenda in the minds of African leaders and the public.

Many leaders in Africa do appreciate and welcome the *Saemaul Undong*, and if African governments take this model seriously and follow it up with care, then there will be a much better chance for its success. But as we all know, in most cases Sub-Saharan African countries are not known for the efficient delivery of public services. In any case, the strong backing of central government is no doubt conducive to the success of the *Saemaul Undong*.

For the development partner overseeing the programme, in this case Korean agencies, executing *Saemaul Undong* projects in a well-coordinated, systematic manner will be quite a challenge. Therefore, the *Saemaul Undong* needs to be pragmatic and flexible in its approach and be open to collaboration with other similar initiatives. This means not only accommodating 'local variance' to the Korean prototype by taking local practices and conditions into account, but also working in conjunction with other ongoing programmes. There can be a trade-off between 'outreaching' and 'fine-tuning' of the *Saemaul Undong*, and which is more important is debatable. But considering the circumstances, a certain degree of flexibility and localization is both inevitable and practical to facilitate the 'replication' and expansion of the *Saemaul Undong* in the region. The important thing is to adhere to the core principles and modes of the *Saemaul Undong*; the rest can take different forms in varying situations.

Third on the list is networking. According to So, Jin Kwang, the former President of the Korea *Saemaul Undong* Centre and Professor of Gachon University, the benefits of the *Saemaul Undong* as a national movement can be summed up as follows: (1) governance; (2) social capital; and (3) sustainability.[9] Through the *Saemaul Undong*, a new 'governance' system linking central government, the provinces and grassroots communities emerged in Korea in the 1970s. This greatly enhanced central government's administrative capacity and efficiency vis-à-vis provinces. Previously, different ministries and agencies were dealing with provincial issues, but the *Saemaul Undong* streamlined and integrated communication and policy implementation channels between the government and local entities.

The essence of the *Saemaul Undong* is a bottom-up, voluntary movement by the local population. But the role of government was also critical in designing the *Saemaul Undong* as a national campaign, encouraging and stimulating the movement by offering incentives and awards. What makes the *Saemaul Undong* different from other programmes is that the government did not provide direct assistance to local communities. The Korean government had a grand vision for the *Saemaul Undong*, but it was the local population themselves that undertook the village projects.

The goal of *Saemaul Undong* projects for Sub-Saharan Africa is to churn up exemplary villages so that they can be emulated by other villages, with the expectation that this will lead to the expansion of the *Saemaul Undong* on a national scale. Undoubtedly, if this model underscoring diligence, self-help and cooperation can take root and expand in Africa, it will have many unexpected positive repercussions on the development of the region.

The viability of the *Saemaul Undong* will hinge on, among other things, the central government's continued engagement with and 'ownership' of this campaign. At least in the villages where the *Saemaul Undong* pilot projects are being conducted, there needs to be a close working relationship between the central government, local government and the villages. An ideal scenario would be that the central government officially endorses and incorporates *Saemaul Undong* programmes in its rural-agricultural development policies. This will ensure a favourable and stable environment in which *Saemaul Undong* proponents can pursue their activities.

Another essential measure is fostering competent local leaders who can inspire and lead people in the *Saemaul Undong*. Korea's success with the

Saemaul Undong came about because of passionate people who were led by passionate leaders. No matter how many resources the Korean government an provide for Africa's *Saemaul Undong* programmes, if the Africans themselves are not enthusiastic, it will be pointless pursuing them.

That is why it is critical that 'true believers' of the *Saemaul Undong* emerge continuously. Conventional development assistance methods are mostly about imparting knowledge and skills, and they are carried out in a matter-of-fact fashion. I have not seen a development programme in any other country that emphasizes such a level of passion, devotion, collective efforts and sacrifice of the people being targeted. But we have reached a point where the international development community should give serious thought to employing a value-oriented approach as a supplementary means to existing development endeavours for change. Outside the realm of religious or spiritual teachings, there clearly exists a domain of ethics that can be widely accepted and applied internationally. This should not be a job for religious and spiritual leaders, and moral activists only—it should be taken up by the mainstream players of development, including government circles and civil society in general.

In 2013, the *Saemaul Undong* archives were recorded in the United Nations Educational, Scientific and Cultural Organization's (UNESCO) Memory of the World Register. At the time, the UNESCO International Advisory Committee stated that 'the movement became the cornerstone of Korea's rapid growth from a poor country to one of the world's top ten economic powers and a precious asset to the history of mankind'. It added that 'since it gives the whole picture of how successfully the movement was carried out to modernize 34,000 selected rural villages across the nation, the archives are valuable resources to developing countries and international development agencies who seek to eliminate poverty and modernize rural areas'.[10]

The established international community does not hold back when speaking out against political, human and humanitarian rights abuses. But why is the community silent when it comes to the 'economic developmental rights' of poor nations? It is evident that negative practices, mindsets and syndromes that hinder development are preponderant in the region. So, if development partners care about the livelihood of African peoples, why are they not speaking out on the issue? Which is more evil: being diplomatically and politically correct or being honest and straightforward? The former is a case of being nice but hypocritical, while the latter is about being blunt but genuine. On development matters, our purpose should be to try to make a difference, even if we have to sometimes stray from our 'comfort zone' and that of others. I think it is actually immoral to keep silent or not speak out on fundamental matters that fundamentally impact the lives of people simply for the sake of avoiding discomfort (and likely criticism). Civility and sincerity must go hand in hand.

The word 'transformation' is popularly used in Africa to accentuate the goal of development. But transformation does not come about easily and is the outcome of an arduous and painful process. National transformation cannot take place with some instances of excellence displayed by a few, but through the mobilization and efforts of the masses. The people must come on board and this requires a substantial and growing number of 'agents of change', the leaders who will urge others to join the path towards development. Since the *Saemaul Undong* is basically a communal campaign (although it can be practised in factories, companies, schools, etc.), its success derives from the vitality of 'community activism', which in turn is dependent on the unity and enthusiasm shown by individual members in their communal work.

There are already similar rural development projects that have been undertaken by various international organizations and bilateral development partners, which all put forward 'sustainable rural development' as their goal. But they are overwhelmingly assistance-oriented programmes trying to help the locals in various fashions (skills training, provision of equipment and facilities, micro-financing, creating marketing opportunities, etc.) to engage in agricultural production or agribusiness. And they may have yielded some positive results, mostly modest and limited, but not to an extent that is 'transformative'.

So, there is an innate risk that *Saemaul Undong* programmes, if not properly understood and pursued, will follow the same fate as other aid programmes. This is particularly so if donor agencies as well as the locals carry out *Saemaul Undong* programmes without sufficient inputs by *Saemaul Undong* experts. But there is a major difference between the *Saemaul Undong* and other aid initiatives in that the former is essentially a self-reliant community movement that includes self-planning, self-decision-making, and the self-execution of work projects.

Community activism is a positive thing as it has many benefits: promotion of grassroots democracy, information-sharing, building and strengthening the 'social fabric', collective problem solving and education, etc. And economic spill-over effects in the rural regions can be far greater than expected when communities come together. It is so much easier to deal with community units, if they conform to a common cause, than belabouring to somehow win over all the people on an individual basis.

Another important measure to take for the success of the *Saemaul Undong* is taking advantage of cooperatives, which has many parallels with the *Saemaul Undong* and which has proven to be a very good tool to supplement the *Saemaul Undong* in the case of Korea. A cooperative is an autonomous association of people joined to own or operate enterprise for their mutual benefit. The association's characteristics are that it is formed voluntarily, operated democratically by those working for their own benefit (self-help), and managed autonomously. It has a long history and the current, modern form of cooperatives is said to have originated in Europe, but Korea also has a very old tradition that is similar to cooperatives.

While the *Saemaul Undong* was a national spiritual 'reform' movement as well as a driving force for economic growth, Korea's agricultural cooperatives greatly contributed to rural-agricultural development since its inception in 1961. Korea's agricultural cooperatives collaborated with the government in Korea's Green Revolution (involving the development of new rice varieties) and the *Saemaul Undong* in the 1970s. The major projects of Korean agricultural cooperatives include financial services like trust guarantees for farmers, agricultural technical training, protection of farmers' rights, improvement of rural livelihood, supporting agribusiness (the sale of products, the purchase and supply of agricultural equipment and basic necessities for farmers), etc. In Korea, the successful combination of the *Saemaul Undong* along with the dissemination and application of agricultural technology and cooperatives were instrumental in bringing about rapid development in the rural region. Cooperatives had significance as the final-stage guarantor of the agribusiness value chain. Many farmers found confidence, stability and security in their production activities because of the efficient cooperative system.[11]

Normally, cooperatives are economic associations formed by economically and socially underprivileged people who want to improve their situation and meet their needs. Therefore, if the cooperatives are operated properly, this can greatly benefit the vast majority of African villagers and farmers. In Uganda, cooperatives have failed in the past due to improper management or (political) abuses, but now the government is trying to revive the system, recognizing its merits.

Along with the introduction of cooperatives, enhancing market access for rural regions is considered crucial for the success of the *Saemaul Undong*. Naturally, in order to invigorate cooperatives, the market accessibility of rural regions needs to be continuously upscaled. Market access, in addition to the value-addition of farm products, is a fundamental challenge for Africa's rural regions, where the vast majority of the population resides.

To sum up, as was shown in Fig. 11.1, *Saemaul Undong* projects should be implemented with MSF as the driving force to achieve the three targets (income generation, burden-sharing and the formation of economic links) based on the six measures outlined above. Once this is achieved, it would have positive outcomes (spill-over, governance, social capital and sustainability) and feedbacks.

Notes

1. 'Smart Saemaul Undong Story', an information pamphlet published by KOICA in the autumn of 2015.
2. Ibid.
3. The four areas are: (1) Inclusive and Sustainable Rural Development; (2) Better Life for Girls; (3) Safe Life for All; and (4) Science, Technology and Innovation (STI) for Better Life.
4. JEE Hyeong-jin, the Co-Head of the NFLC, presented this plan on 20 July 2016 during the project launching workshop at the NFLC.

5. Speech by Adolf Mwesige, Uganda's Minister of Local Government, during the ISNC launching ceremony on 10 July 2015, in Kibiito Town Council, Kabarole District, Uganda.
6. SMU Uganda.
7. Choi Hae-suk, *Study of Canaan Farmers School from the Perspective of Life Time Education* (Seoul: Ajou University, 2006) (BA Thesis) (Korean), p. 25.
8. During the 'Program for the Launch of Greater Masaka Model Villages' on 3 August 2017, held at Kkindu Parish Community, Masaka District, the SMU Change Agents divulged that their biggest challenge was confronting the negative mindsets of the villagers.
9. Jin Kwang So, President of the Korea *Saemaul Undong* Centre, gave a lecture on the *Saemaul Undong* to Baanda village (*Saemaul* model village) in Mityana District on 18 August 2016 during his visit to Uganda.
10. UNESCO Memory of the World, 'Archives of Saemaul Undong New Community Movement', http://www.unesco.org.
11. National Agricultural Cooperatives Federation (www.nonghyup.com), Choi Byung-ik and others, *Saemaul Undong and ODA* (Chungyang: Kukjemunwha University, 2014), pp. 46–48.

Part VI

Africa on the New Path to Development

12
Re-setting the Priorities

Realizing the Nature of the Problem

Recollecting my memories when I first stepped on to African soil in 1973 and then returning back in 2001 and again in 2011, I found out that there are two clear trends taking place: one was urban growth, while the other was the levelling-up of freedom of expression and the means of communication. But the manner in which these were unfolding was quite different from what I expected or was used to seeing in my native country and other regions.

In most cases, I noticed deterioration rather than improvement in the overall orderliness, infrastructure management and environment of urban centres. An observer would note: 'Although Sub-Saharan Africa is the least urbanised continent, its rate of urbanisation is among the highest in the world. While urbanisation can be a welcome engine for socio-economic development, innovation, and employment creation, it can also bring about a number of challenges, most of which are manifest within the sphere of urban environment … [which are] crowded living conditions; poor disposal of wastes; inadequate basic infrastructure;

J.-D. Park, *Re-Inventing Africa's Development*,
https://doi.org/10.1007/978-3-030-03946-2_12

pollution of water and air; and the decline of the urban green frame.'[1] And I would add to this the unbelievable traffic congestion and chaos.

Another striking feature was a noticeably greater extent of freedom of expression enjoyed in the countries compared to the past. By and large, this is the effect of globalization and the spread of technology. The acceleration in usage of the Internet and mobile phones in the region is remarkable and the flourishing of mass media in terms of the number of outlets and variety available is something that was unimaginable in the old days. This is not to negate the reality that sometimes oppression of expression is exercised for political purposes by rulers, but largely such a liberal trend is evident.

As countries increasingly engage with the outside world, and managing public and economic affairs becomes as complex as ever, they need to have stronger capacity in this regard. But this not being the case, we see the unruliness, disorganization and mismanagement of affairs that is typical of Sub-Saharan Africa today. At the heart of the problem lies the tendency of 'right here, right now': people trying to merely 'adapt' to (rather than tame or overcome) the circumstances or environment in which they find themselves, or wanting to settle things now, opting for 'immediate' rather than 'delayed' gratification.[2]

Everything is relative and no society is perfect or doomed. But attitudinal orientations matter. No matter how far our times and technologies have evolved, and however old-fashioned it may sound, the importance of the human mind and determination cannot be emphasised enough. As the moral of Aesop's Fable on the turoise and the hare would tell us, individuals can beat seemingly formidable odds, while people can quickly end up as losers despite their physical or material advantage over others. There is a good chance that a society enjoying an abundance of natural resources and other means, but lacking sincerity and commitment would fare worse than a society which has the opposite traits.

Since people's actions are in the end derived from their perception, attitudinal orientations and goals, despite all the hoopla and excitement over new ideas, technologies and innovations, if any meaningful development is to occur, it has to be accompanied by a mindset change in the people. By development, we are talking about positive changes that are accountable and visible. It can take many forms that are discernible: the cleanliness and orderliness of living quarters and the neighbourhood and public facilities; the improvement of infrastructure and the delivery of service; improved education and health facilities; enhanced economic activity, productivity and income generation, etc. Hence, if such improvements do not happen, with or without foreign assistance, it means that people are not being responsive and something must be done about it.

There is plenty of blaming going on, but at least people are recognizing that there are problems. Many African leaders have their fair share of frustrations with the lack of progress being made in terms of development. For instance, as reasons for Africa's underdevelopment, Uganda's President Museveni has blamed poor education, underdeveloped human resources and skills, a lack of indigenous entrepreneurs, hindrance to private businesses, small markets and inadequate infrastructure, and a lack of energy resources. He also cites tribal, religious and gender ideological disorientations, a lack of industrialization and a lack of viable pillars in the judicial and defence sectors leading to a collapse in the state's authority.[3]

The African Peer Review Mechanism (APRM) meeting held on 26 August 2016 in Nairobi adopted, as Africa's development blueprint guide, President Museveni's paper on Africa's ten bottlenecks: ideological disorientation; a weak state exemplified by a weak army; human resource underdevelopment; poor infrastructure; a failure to industrialize; fragmented markets; underdevelopment of the service sector; undermining of the private sector; a laissez-faire attitude that is crippling the agriculture sector; and past shortcomings in democracy.[4] African leaders and elites seem to understand what their countries are lacking, but the obstacles that were identified can be seen largely as the outcome and not the causes of more deeper and fundamental problems.

Some mention that the top seven reasons why Africa is still poor are civil wars and terrorism, unending corruption, an education and knowledge gap, poor health and poverty, geographical disadvantages, international aid and unfair trade practices.[5] Greg Mills mentions in *Why Africa Is Poor* that the main reason why Africa's people are poor is because their leaders have made this choice, not because of all the things cited as lacking or being blamed for this: African rulers have externalized their problems, blaming donor countries and bodies for all their unaccomplished ills.[6]

Those who subscribe to mainstream economic liberalism tend to define the essence of economy too simply or narrowly: in terms of free market mechanism. But what is much more important to developing countries is 'effective capitalism'. 'Markets' existed since the beginning of human civilization and are nothing new or special. In theory, a market is nothing more than a supply-and-demand mechanism. It is of course the most basic means or medium for the exchange of goods and allocation of resources, but in order for wealth creation and economic prosperity in a society and nation to come about, so many more things are needed, like the robust entrepreneurship of business leaders, a skilled and devoted labour force, socio-political stability and security, capital mobilization, an appropriate role played by the government (like 'strategic oversight' or guidance in industrialization), a positive 'national ethos' or work ethic, technology, social capital, good governance, a favourable natural endowment, geographical conditions … and the list goes on.

The reality is that it is not that simple to treat everything in a dichotomic context: liberal (good) and protectionist (bad). And governments can indeed play a key role in economic development if they act as facilitators and drivers of effective capitalism. What matters is keeping politics out of the economic realm as much as possible. Fostering competent and disciplined bureaucracy insulated from political influences is a good way to start and it is never too late to do so. South Korea's case is a vindication of the 'holy trinity' of economics: markets, corporations and government. Reforming government is the way to go, not doing away with it.

There is no question that the national rulers are the ones most responsible for their country's state of development. But we should not underestimate or overestimate their ability. We can talk about the issue of too much 'political correctness', but we should also be aware of the flaws of 'intellectual correctness' or 'academic correctness', which places all the blame on the rulers and portrays the masses as victims. This can be more detrimental than meets the eye. We should also note Joseph de Maistre's quote that 'every nation has the government it deserves'. And the following observation has also makes a salient point: 'the leaders of any given society, club or country are just the picture of that society, club or country at large … People are trained by the society. The value system of that given society is what teaches them what to believe, how to behave, what to pursue with their lives and how to lead their people'.[7]

The leaders of states get their agendas implemented through their teams of elites and civil servants, and ultimately through the workings of the people. The rulers cannot control everything and cannot be effective in managing their economy and other affairs if they are not sufficiently supported by many layers of 'collaborators'. South Korea would not have achieved an economic miracle if it were not for the sacrifice of hardworking people and the enterprising private sector, as well as its bureaucrats.

The state leadership should be the key drivers of development as well as its last bastion. But still, many African leaders are corrupt and abusive of their power, and seek to maintain the status quo. It is also true that any leader with a reasonable mind would dearly want to prove their worth through economic performance, as the pressure is mounting on them to deliver whatever they can to satisfy the rising expectations of the masses. Therefore, economic performance is deemed to be the surest answer to achieving political success. In most cases, African leaders come short in terms of their goals because they are stuck in the comfort zone of compromising with reality even before earnestly attempting to produce results. Thus, it takes much more than the simple decisions of leaders.

While it is easy to destroy what was achieved in an instant, it would require mammoth efforts to rebuild whatever has been undone. Raila Odinga, the former Prime Minister of Kenya, spoke on the day of the Centenary of Nelson Mandela's birth that Africa's ills can no longer be blamed on the colonial legacy, but rather that Africa's deterioration has been brought about by bad politics and African leaders abusing their power. The main root cause of Africa's continued poverty is undoubtedly the mindset issue, which hinders positive action being taken. But the prospect of confronting the root causes may be daunting for political leaders, policy-makers and even civil society. Many African nations are by no means static. On the contrary, you see so much vibrancy in individuals when they *come together* in social life—cultural events, social gatherings, public celebrations, commemorations, etc. What is desirable (and it could be a strategic move) is to induce the people to show an equal level of liveliness and passion in their workplaces and businesses.

For this purpose, 'leaders' are always needed in every corner and level of society. When the people, especially the poor, are left on their own, they feel powerlessness and alienation, but when they come together as an entity, they form a sense of social belonging and can suddenly feel inclined to act. This holds true both in rural-communal areas and semi-rural urban localities. In such an environment, a 'communal' approach such as that adopted by the *Saemaul Undong* can be effective in driving people to act in the pursuit of shared goals. Motivation and confidence can be built up easily through associations. However, when their orientation is misplaced and becomes primarily 'transactional', and matters are settled in courts, the society is likely to further degenerate and it will be difficult to turn back the tide. That is why initiatives like mindset change campaigns need to be executed, with leaders setting examples.

Figure 12.1 below illustrates the persistent gap between the developed world and Sub-Saharan African countries. The y-axis represents the level (quality) of the social and institutional fabric, as well as the technical, productive skills. Since independence, the overall level of the social and institutional fabric of African countries in terms of social capital, civic values, governance, respect for norms and regulations, etc. has remained largely unchanged at a low level. Hence, there are still big gaps that need to be reduced. The curves are rough depiction of the estimations of the levels assessed.

Of the two gaps—that in the social and institutional fabric, and that in skills and technology—the latter can have particularly deep repercussions on African countries in the low end as having a competitive edge in terms of skills and technology on a global scale is of great importance today.

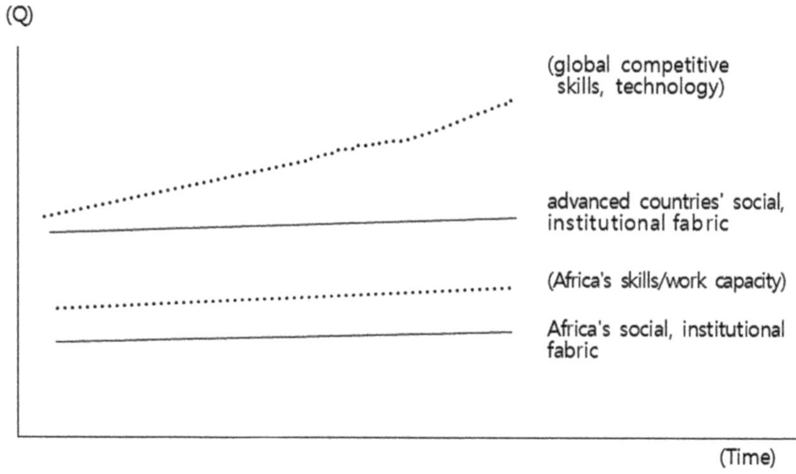

Fig. 12.1 Development gaps: the problem of being transfixed

The upper dotted line in Fig. 12.1 represents the global competitive skills and technology (mainly for business) level, which is much higher than that of Sub-Saharan Africa. The trend is that the gap between the world's and Africa's skills and work capacity is widening.

What this implies is that Sub-Saharan Africa, which is open for business, is exposed to and can partner with foreign and multi-national companies with the highest competitive capacity, skills and technology. And there is an increasing number of visits between Africa and the rest of the world. So, there seems to be good exposure and opportunities for Africa to make up for its weakness by way of opening up its markets.

However, this will not resolve the problem of poverty because the fundamental gap will continue to exist under the circumstances. Without a proper policy, governance and mindset in place, it will be difficult not only to 'harness' foreign businesses, but also to properly 'support' and utilize them so as to reap the maximum level of mutual benefits.

There is a good example in Latin American countries that missed the opportunity to achieve rapid economic growth and successful transformation in the early stages of development due to their unsuccessful import substitution policies, premature introduction of foreign direct investment and heavy reliance on multi-national corporations. Many of them are now paying the price for repeated missteps, like not being able to industrialize at auspicious moments, and giving into populism and the demand for welfare surpassing the means, as well as a failure to curb corruption.

Liberalization or globalization cannot be all bad for Africa. But when countries use these forces to forgo their own responsibility while trying to find solutions in foreign partners, the possibility of attaining economic viability in the context of self-empowerment will be diminished. Without addressing mindset and fundamental challenges, they will drift further away from the desired path of development.

Attitudes and Work Ethics

Attitudes and work ethics do matter—very much in fact—regardless of whether we are in a traditional working environment or high-tech sectors, and most likely also AI industries in the future. Basically, in the labour-intensive economic structure that characterizes Sub-Saharan Africa (only South Africa has a very capital-intensive industrial sector), the work ethic assumes a great significance. But even in capital- and technology-intensive sectors, where the cost of human failure in decision-making or management could be far greater, attitudes and ethics are deemed all the more crucial. People may not be amply aware that no matter how far machines, automation and artificial intelligence can be advanced, there is still room—and considerable room at that—for human interventions, as even the most sophisticated robots cannot replace humans (there are already troubles surfacing in relation to overmechanization).

As long as we choose to remain as 'humanity' irrespective of technological innovations, we cannot do away with norms like work ethics. Thus, many things depend on human attitudes and they can impede or stimulate progress. If people do not have the 'proper' set of attitudes, all the natural endowments available or all the technical and institutional support offered would quickly lose their value. Sub-Saharan Africa is an ironic case in that it probably has the largest 'untapped' and most 'concentrated' fertile land mass in the world, but its agricultural output is one of the lowest in the world.

And how are Africa and international organizations trying to cope with the situation? The common solutions that are sought seem to be mainly technical and material, and such a pattern of recourse seems to be stubbornly followed in spite of repeated setbacks. Acquiring 'knowledge' is crucial, and knowledge and attitude go together, but considering that the methods used have barely improved, there must have been a serious neglect or a blind-sight in the efforts. Or it may be that the international community, having not yet found a better alternative, has no other choice but to continue its course.

In 2015, the African Development Bank recommended that Africa can boost agricultural productivity by doing the following eight things: develop high-yielding crops; boost irrigation; increase the use of fertilizers; improve access, regulation and governance; make better use of technology; adopt genetically modified (GM) crops; reform land ownership with productivity and inclusiveness in mind; and step up integration into agricultural value chains (AVCs).[8] This all sounds fine in theory and would go down well with conference attendants, but from the perspective of policy-makers and farmers, how helpful will this be? Such a long shopping list of the things that ordinary people can hardly manage to undertake cannot be the best practical solutions.

An increasing number of experts seem to agree that natural endowments, physical resources or even technical know-how do not matter greatly in terms of making the difference in the absence of a positive attitude or mindset in the locals. For instance, Piet van Asten explains that an in-depth study shows how farmers in East Africa make decisions in farming is depended on how they percieve reality rather than the actualy conditions on the ground, and given that attitudes of farmers plays an important role, understanding their attitudes will provide insights into their actions, and thereby some clues as to what can be done to assist them.[9] But understanding attitudinal traits is one thing and deciding what to do about it is quite another.

Naturally, such an attitudinal issue is not confined to farmers, but affects the whole spectrum of society. In this book, I have tried to dissect the meaning of 'mindset', which is a broad and general concept. And I think it boils down to 'attitudes' and 'work ethics' from a developmental perspective. There are many nuances to the word 'attitude', but from the point of view of development, it can be defined as 'a manner of thinking, feeling, or behaving that reflects a state of mind or disposition the way a person views something or tends to behave towards it, often in an evaluative way'.[10] Different people see and respond to problems in different ways and for different reasons. The issue of being 'transfixed' is not only a problem for Africa, but is also a factor in the approach of the international community. Things will remain static when activities only touch upon what is on the surface, without going deeper to address the root causes. In just about everything, 'rationality' is assumed and the efforts to bridge the 'divide' have been dismal at best, so the 'parallel' continues.

Essentially, there are two dimensions to Africa's needs: first, the improvement of basic conditions and quality of life; and, second, sustainable economic development. The former concerns the basic human needs and rights of the people, while the latter concerns more mid- to long-term tasks of nations, like achieving structural change in the economy.

However, it is true that the mainstream donor community is seen to be principally focused on the former while 'neglecting' the latter. On the other hand, China, an emerging donor, literally confines itself to the 'hardware' sub-division of the latter, like infrastructure construction and energy development projects. What seems to be increasingly evident is that the promotion of the former (the fulfilment of human needs and rights) does not necessarily lead to progress in the latter (sustainable economic development). Equally, it is certainly the case that Sub-Saharan African countries are in dire need of physical infrastructure, but infrastructure constitutes just one of the many things necessary for national development, and the issues related to the construction of infrastructure, like corruption, rises in the cost and delays of work, poor management, etc., revert back to the question of governance, the ethics of individuals and the norms of society. As such, there is no quick fix or a means of circumventing the fundamentals.

Only the people of Africa can do what it takes to effectively close the perennial poverty gap, although the international community can certainly help. Without wasting more time and resources, we should come to terms with the fact that the principal root cause of Africa's poverty is the mindset issue, and therefore we should re-align our efforts to tackling this matter. Recently, I have discovered a casual way of getting my message across and starting a conversation without sounding too blunt or judgemental (or undiplomatic): I would say 'I think the reason why Africa remains poor is not necessarily because people lack the resources or the means, but rather, it's more due to the management problem'. No one objected and people could not agree with me more.

I was recently reminded, once again, that we too often take it for granted, or presume, that others' thoughts, behaviours and needs are the same as ours, when in fact they may not be. I heard from a number of experts from international aid agencies that in order to ensure effectiveness of aid programmes, donors must understand the culture and attitudes of the locals. I have had an opportunity to consult with the representatives of UN specialized agencies, who told me that the international development community makes the common mistake of pursuing an individual-oriented approach when the typical characteristic of African locals is familial or communal in nature—in other words, that people's actions are bound up with their kinship.

During the discourse, the head of the UNDP office in Uganda told me about some interesting episodes that occurred with a number of projects to assist women and girls in the rural region. They provided borehole pumps to the villages to save them from walking many kilometres a day just to fetch water. However, it turned out that the girls were not using the pumps in their villages, but instead were continuing to fetch water from the remote water sources. The explanation for this was that they wanted the privacy and 'free time' by themselves, to meet and chat with their friends, perhaps to escape boredom (or the shackles of their in-laws) or to refresh themselves. As such, the organization decided to provide bicycles to girls, but this did not work either, and men were using them instead. Another story was about young women shunning newly built latrines in or around their homes. It is said that women do not feel comfortable either sharing or being seen using the same latrine with other family members or relatives, especially the elderly; they would rather find remote places.

Therefore, the advice of these experts was that before we, the donors, embark on assistance programmes, we should consider the culture and attitudes of the beneficiaries to ensure that these programmes have the desired impact on them. They also suggested that mindset change takes time, and we should expect the results to come slowly and gradually. I was all ears and their arguments made good sense to me. I thanked them for enlightening me about what I have not known before.

But later that day, when I tried to figure out what lessons could be taken away from the meeting, I realized that the perceptions within the international development community can also be highly divergent. I could not brush off the feeling that what these international aid officials were suggesting implicitly was that their logic and methods were essentially geared towards maintaining the status quo. More agents of change, not less, are needed. There is every reason to acknowledge and take local cultures and practices into account, but there is also a danger that by doing so, we could fall into the trap of perpetuating the status quo, which is exactly what development efforts should fight against.

Currently, there are basically two different trains of thought underlying international aid and development with respect to Africa. As mentioned earlier, one is about prioritizing basic human needs and their rights; the other is about prioritizing the building of physical infrastructure. People might think that this covers the essentials, but it does not. In fact, there is a big blind-spot in the existing development architecture, a third arm which we can call mindset change or a 'power-of-the-mind' approach or empowering the people with a development mindset.

The benefit of this mindset change approach, when properly applied, can reap enormous results, as demonstrated by the South Korean case. The advantage of this mindset change approach is that while the first 'basic-human-needs-and-rights (BHNR)' approach and the second physical infrastructure building approach both breed strong dependency on the part of the recipients, this, on the contrary, promotes the attributes of self-reliance, independence and self-ownership. Not only can, and should, this approach be employed to complement the first and the second approaches, but when successfully pursued, it will make these two approaches redundant. For example, in the case of South Korea, the amount of aid it received for BHNR and physical infrastructure was minimal, and the duration of such assistance was far shorter compared to other countries.

Figure 12.2 below represents a proposed new formula of development assistance to Africa, the tripod of development assistance: the existing BHNR approach and physical infrastructure building projects, and the addition of the new mindset-change approach. The BHNR approach is what the traditional donors have mostly been engaged in, while physical infrastructure projects are what China and, to a lesser extent, other emerging donors have been mostly focusing on.[11]

The mindset-change approach is not unique to Korea, but is applied routinely in the everyday lives of all the people. Whether in films, dramas or novels, we almost always see someone taking the lead in uplifting others to fight on or rise to the occasion and not give up in despair. This does not happen only in dramatic scenes; even small words that touch our hearts and encourage us can unleash powerful forces in individuals. In schools, companies, factories, sports teams, hotels, hospitals, the military, government agencies, etc., people are repeatedly and persistently reminded of their 'code of conduct' and are urged to exert themselves in order to fulfil their duties.

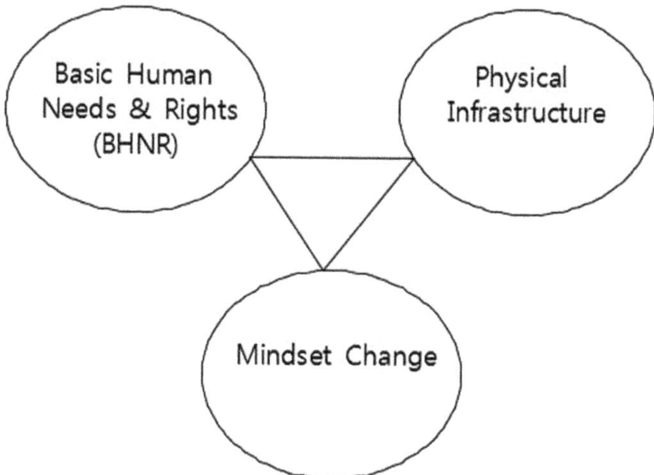

Fig. 12.2 The tripod of development assistance

In every society, there is a constant need to 'energize' people to act positively, and this is a vital part of the management process for any institution or organization. And the mechanism for motivating or energizing people is, of course, 'rewards (remuneration) and sanctions (punishments)', as mentioned earlier. The problem is that we have forgotten to do all this when it comes to Africa's development.

Going back to the term 'development-mindedness' or KPOP, all this seems to underscore the importance of the last 'P', which stands for 'passion'. I have pointed out that Korea's uniqueness of its mindset change approach can be found in the 'reverse engineering': the act of instilling passion in people first and letting the power unleash itself, which will take care of the rest.

The achievement or success of a nation is not assessed in terms of how the powerful and the privileged have amassed wealth and lead prosperous lives; instead, it is the overall level of living of the whole population that counts and matters. That is why when we are talking about national development, it is crucial to have a set of initiatives that connect with the people and are relevant at the national level. This is the area in which most Sub-Saharan Africa countries find themselves at the weakest point.

What Africa lacks most, and hence needs to assign the highest priority to, is none other than the software compartment of mindset change. Without an attitudinal change in the people and the leaders, and understanding what constitutes or enables development, all the assistance provided by the international community, and all the investments and other business opportunities that foreigners may offer will be to no avail, since Africans will not be the true drivers and owners of development.

The first thing to do is to be aware of the necessity of mindset change. The next challenge is how to focus on and implement this task. The mindset change campaign itself should come from Africans themselves. For donors, their role should be assisting such efforts in a supplementary and facilitating fashion.

Critics have pointed out the ills of continuous flows of aid to Africa. If a wise thing to do is not cut these drastically—and I do not see this happening anytime soon—then both donors and African countries should at least work closely together to foster a new environment of development partnership. It should start with the premise that people's attitudes are 'changeable'. And the practical way to launch this endeavour is to bring the locals, the leaders and the masses to the point where they comprehend the inevitability of change in their mindset and behaviour if they want to lead better lives. A strong community drive in which committed leaders from different backgrounds come together can be instrumental in this regard. People should be made to realize that relying on handouts from their government or aid organizations will get them nowhere and will only disempower and impoverish them further.

Such initiatives should not just target the 'development-mindedness' of the people in general, but should also involve concrete measures to curtail specific obstacles that undermine development. For example, a typical hindrance commonly experienced by donors are delaying and 'sabotaging' efforts by the officials in charge. Such acts are committed due to a lack of supervision and enforcement of disciplinary rules, as well as the overall weakness in the governance of the state. If African governments can put in place a more stringent administrative oversight and accountability enforcing mechanism in their system, it would considerably enhance the performance of development projects.

The continued gaps and discrepancies between what the development community is pursuing and what will actually take place are more attributable to 'attitudinal' factors than 'capacity gaps' and local conditions that the people on the receiving end often cite as the reason for such shortcomings.[12] By suggesting that a lack of capacity is the primary reason for failures, they are in fact asking for open-ended support from donors. They try to conveniently avoid responsibility by invoking their 'lack of capacity', when the real reason is their intent. Attitudes and capacity are two very different things, and attitudinal problems should not be masked by such terms as 'lack of capacity'.

The word 'capacity' implies the ability of someone to carry out certain assignments or demonstrate their skills, and is based on accumulated knowledge and training. So, when people say that the problem is due to a lack of capacity, they are insinuating that its nature is technical and what is needed is more investment for building capacity. But the reality is that the most egregious transgressions are often committed by those who know all too well the field of their expertise and hence should know better. The issue is far more profound than simply accumulating knowledge and capacity.

There is no denying that in the region, many people do lack the necessary education and technical skills training, and the illiteracy rate in Africa in general as a continent is probably the highest in the world. Of the top ten countries with the highest illiteracy rate in the world, nine are from Africa, with only one country coming from outside the continent (Afghanistan).[13] Fighting illiteracy and providing greater education opportunities to the population should be the rudimentary responsibility of the state. But what is necessary is moving beyond people's ability to read and write, as this is only the first step in the long process of human development.

The question is not only how we can fight widespread irregularities and corruption, but also how the people can be uplifted and empowered. The reason why Sub-Saharan African countries are not faring well compared to many other developing nations in Asia and other parts of the world is that the 'double drawbacks of underdevelopment'—corruption and poor work ethics—are markedly more serious here than elsewhere. And these will not take care of themselves in a social, economic and political environment that seeks to maintain the status quo. A 'shock-therapy' type of approach and an all-out campaign at a national level might be needed.

A Westerner once asked me why I thought when there is so much corruption in China, just like Africa, China still manages to reap economic success. I replied that it must be due to differences in the level of work ethics. Africans themselves know better than anyone else how much corruption there is in Africa, so they are curious to hear from foreigners how their countries were able to deal with corruption. A Dutch colleague of mine once told me that when he was asked by a Ugandan businessman whether there was corruption in the Netherlands just like in Uganda; he responded that corruption exists everywhere, but the difference is that in the Netherlands those who commit irregularties are likely to be held accountable for it while in Uganda they are not.

I have discussed the preponderance of the 'commission culture' and the 'allowance culture' in Sub-Saharan Africa that is eating away at the competitiveness and public interest of the nations in the region. The former is an unwritten practice, while the latter is institutionalized in the governmental sector. In any case, they reflect unwholesome opportunism, laxity or loopholes in supervision and disciplinary mechanisms, and the temptation to seek windfall gains whenever possible. Another widespread practice in governmental circles in Africa that I still do not understand is the failure on the part of the government to pay its employees' monthly salaries on time. The payment of regular salaries should be a predictable task and it is purely due to administrative laxity that this is not the case, so there cannot be any excuse for that.

Why governments and their public sectors seem to always fall short in terms of delivering public service and spurring economic dynamism in Africa is due not so much to bureaucratic bottlenecks and inefficiencies, but rather a lack of supervision and managerial negligence, in addition to the prevalence of irregularities and corruption. In most countries, the function of government falters not necessarily because of 'bureaucratization', but rather because the organization is deficient in 'life' and a sense of purpose. Generally, the merit of public service is the honour to serve one's nation, as well as job security. Since government officials' salaries and budgets come from taxpayers, they have the obligation to serve the public interest. If an employee wants to amass wealth, they should be in the private sector doing business. The same holds true for elected officials and parliamentarians in particular. Carrots and sticks are always necessary in the management of personnel and the operation of any organization. And, of course, the important thing is to enforce them vigorously. Most of all, 'sticks' or 'sanctioning mechanisms' are required to prevent civil servants from committing detrimental acts.

Frederick Herzberg, who studied employees' attitudes and motivations in order to come up with the 'motivation-hygiene theory', claims that there are satisfying and dissatisfying factors in employees' work environments. Satisfying factors, which he called 'motivators', include recognition, achievement and the challenge of work itself. Meanwhile, dissatisfying factors, which he termed 'hygiene factors' that do not give positive satisfaction or lead to higher levels of motivation (though dissatisfaction results from their absence), include status, job security, salary, fringe benefits, work conditions, good pay, paid insurance and holidays. The word 'hygiene' is used in the sense that these are maintenance factors.[14] The conclusions drawn from the case in the US, where the study was conducted, cannot be applicable to all other regions. But the most striking feature that is typical of Sub-Saharan Africa may be that the management system to effectively apply incentives and disincentives for employees is difficult to find.

If the employers or leaders of organizations were truly dedicated to enforcing carrots and sticks, exercising their powers in a constructive way, we would probably see a far different situation from the one we see today. The gross failure in management comes not from a lack of 'knowledge' or 'capacity', but from an unwillingness to take the trouble to see to it that things are working properly. It is basically an attitudinal rather than a technical problem. But then the same holds true for employees. Workers need to have an 'earning-one's-way-to-success' mentality and their catchphrases should be 'work ethics', 'devotion', 'consistency' etc.

Regarding methodology, it would be worthwhile if comprehensive and in-depth research on the mindset of the people could be conducted. A study of the mindset can become a field where many 'mysteries' or paradoxes can be unlocked, and hence solutions can be discovered. Confronting the matter of the mindset of people can be both a daunting and an onerous task, and there can be a disinclination to address the topic at all. But this is an opportunity to think creatively and enlarge our boundaries of engagement with respect to development. I hope this book spurs new interest in this field.

A famous phrase—'truth will set you free'—comes to my mind at this point. There are many issues around the world, and some seem to be simply too daunting to rein in. Fighting natural disasters and the effects of climate change, dealing with conflicts that are based on political, ethnical, and religious divides and that reflect direct conflict of interests or a stalemate in power dynamics are some examples. However, the truth is that lifting Africa out of poverty should by no means be an insurmountable task because there is no inherent conflict of interests or strategic stalemate involved here; that is, no intrinsic or intentional obstacle exists to discourage Africa's development. Thus, there is no point in shying away or refraining from 'searching' for the truth because the truth and the facts will only lead to ultimate solutions. As far as the development of Sub-Saharan Africa is concerned, there are no risks involved in assuming a bold, proactive posture in order to move forward.

As was the case in South Korea, the kind of mind transformational initiatives must come from within. This requires the courage to confront 'inconvenient truths' rather than hiding behind the cloak of political and academic correctness. Ethical and civic society can only be attained from the self-reflection of individuals through the embodiment of ethics, and this cannot be provided externally. People might be tempted to seek explanations and solutions to the problems outside of themselves, but this will do no good even in the short term. Being truthful to oneself or, to put it differently, 'internalizing' one's responsibilities is the entry point of *social correctness*. When individuals only blame others, they are choosing to become a mere 'dependent variable' of others.

Especially in development, the question of attitudes is a core issue and it should be recognized as such by all the stakeholders involved. For instance, being optimistic and having confidence is always a good trait. But having an empty sense of pride or being overly naive that somehow everything will turn out for the best or that someone else will take care of the problems will not help.

'Mindset' is a term encompassing 'attitudes' and 'work ethics'. There is no given definition of 'work ethics' and it could be defined simply as 'an ethical principle that places greatest value on hard work and diligence'.[15] Business etiquette expert Jacqueline Whitmore talks about seven elements of strong ethics: professionalism, respectfulness, dependability, dedication, determination, accountability and humility.[16] We can see how far in depth we can go with the term 'work ethics' and how much it is relevant in today's business and our livelihood in general. Hence, unless the work ethics of the people of developing nations are successfully targeted and changed, business, foreign aid or development projects will continue to have only a very limited output. What is in everybody's interests is to avoid turning material or financial support or resources into de facto handouts that have no visible impact on Africa's development.

People's work ethics make all the difference in the performance of a nation. I do not wish to be seen as biased, but there is such a thing as a typical work pattern of the local workers. To cite an example, this becomes evident when you are moving in and out of countries. I know that moving household goods out of your home and loading them into a 40-foot container truck takes half a day's work in Seoul. In Rome, it took a full day plus some extra hours the next day. In Abidjan (the capital of Cote d'Ivoire), it took two full days. In Uganda, three days were needed to get everything out.

Increasing economic efficiency and competitiveness does not happen easily over time and the most practical way of enhancing it is through strengthening the work ethics of workers. Whether it is simple manual work or a technical assignment, what must be done must be done, and cutting corners always has consequences.

In sociology, there are theories of social movements or revolutions explained in terms of 'relative deprivation', such as James C. Davis' J-curve theory (1962). According to this theory, revolution occurs when the gap between people's 'expected need satisfaction' and 'actual need satisfaction' widens to an intolerable level. But from the perspective of development, the correlation between people's level of 'desires' and level of 'work ethics' could be more meaningful.

In the economic sense, 'work ethics' has bearing on 'supply' aspect of market mechanism as work ethics affects productivity, output, competitiveness, quality of work, service delivery, etc.. The work ethic of a nation is deemed to be a fundamental determinant of its economic performance. And logically, people's demand (desires) should be matched by supply (work ethics) to ensure the stability, satisfaction and prosperity of society or nation. Needless to say, as in the case of J-curve theory, the growing discrepancy between people's expectations and reality can have a negative impact on society.

We should pay attention to what different combinations of desire and work ethics imply. A society showing both desire and work ethics on a steady rise is an ideal state for developing nations that need to escape poverty and attain sustainable development. When countries have achieved economic transformation and enter the phase of mature industrialization or post-industrialization, the overall level of the work ethic in the people measured in conventional terms (hours of work, labour intensity, etc.) will drop. When countries become wealthier, they can afford to provide better working environments for people, but the rich nations' desires, which are already high, may continue to rise. In such a case, the gap should be filled by innovative measures enhancing the efficiency and competitiveness of the workforce, institutions and policies.

When the levels of both desires and work ethics remain unchanged at low levels, this represents a stagnant society with an economy stuck in a state of underdevelopment. Meanwhile, when the work ethic stays sluggish, but desires continue to ride high, this means that a society cannot satisfy its own demands, possibly resulting in the public's dissatisfaction and distrust in the government and the system, increased dependency on outside assistance and investments, a deterioration in public services, corruption and irregularities, etc.

Notes

1. Thomas P.Z. Mpofu, 'Urbanization and Urban Environmental Challenges in Sub-Saharan Africa', *Research Journal of Agricultural and Environmental Management* 2, no. 6 (June 2013), pp. 127–134.
2. See the book *Don't Eat the Marshmallow Yet: The Secret to Sweet Success in Work and Life* written by Joachim de Posada, Berkeley, 2005.
3. The remarks made by President Museveni's during the ceremony of the 50th anniversary of Uganda's independence in 9 October 2013 and other occasions.
4. 'Africa: Museveni Paper Adopted as Africa's Dev't Blueprint Guide', *The Observer* (Uganda), 27 August 2016. Uganda's President Museveni elaborated on this earlier on 9 October 2013 during Uganda's Independence Day celebrations: (1) ideological disorientation, which manifested itself in the sectarianism of religion and tribes (failing to see that all groups in Uganda benefit from each other by buying products of the respective groups apart from the other historical, linguistic and cultural similarities or links); (2) the need to radically reform the state structure, especially the army, which was not only being sectarian but was also led and manned by people of little or no education; (3) attack

on the miniscule private sector based on the ideology of inadequately analysed nationalism (because all investments made in Uganda, being part of its GDP, strengthen Uganda's independence rather than weakening it); (4) human resources that was not educated or well catered for in terms of health; (5) inadequately developed infrastructure—especially electricity, roads, railways and piped water—all undermining the profitability of investments in the country on account of the high costs of doing business in this economy; (6) a small internal (regional) market on account of colonialism fragmenting the ancient pre-colonial market that used to stretch from the River Congo to Zanzibar on the Indian Ocean and to the swamps of South Sudan, the inconveniences caused by the greedy tribal chiefs; (7) a lack of industrialization, exporting only raw materials, thereby donating money and jobs to foreign economies; (8) an underdeveloped services sector (hotels, banks, insurance, transport, etc.); (9) an under developed agriculture with only a small portion of the economy being engaged in commercial agriculture, while the majority of the farmers were only engaged in subsistence farming using inferior seeds and breeding stock, not using fertilizers, no irrigation and not using improved agro-practices; and (10) a culture and history that lacked democracy.

5. Kajuju Murori, '7 Top Reasons Why Africa Is Still Poor, 2017', *The Africa Exponent* (Tanzania), https://www.africanexponent.com/post/billions-lost-in-profits-by-foreign-companies-tax-evasion-1953.
6. Greg Mills, *Why Africa Is Poor: And What Africans Can Do About It* (Johannesburg: Penguin, 2010).
7. Otoaye Godfrey Martins, '7 Reasons Why Africans Are Poor and How to Be Rich in Africa', *The Spirited Hub*, http://thespiritedhub.com/7-reasons-africans-poor-rich-africa.
8. Africa Development Bank, *Africa's Competitiveness Report 2015* in Mark Jones, '8 Ways Africa Can Raise Farm Productivity and Boost Growth', World Economic Forum Global Agenda, https://www.weforum.org/agenda/2015/06/8-ways-africa-can-raise-farm-productivity-and-boost-growth.
9. Piet van Asten made the remarks during his presentation at the 'Seminar on Uganda's Agricultural Development' at the Sheraton Hotel, Kampala on 5 December 2016. This seminar was organized by the Korean Embassy. The attitudes were broken down into four categories: 'pessimist', 'optimist', 'pragmatist' and 'trapped'. The International

Institute of Tropical Agriculture (IITA) is a member of the Consultative Group for International Agricultural Research (CGIAR) consortium.

10. *The Free Dictionary*, https://www.thefreedictionary.com/attitude.
11. It has been a general tendency for traditional bilateral donors, namely Western donors, not to focus on major physical infrastructure projects, while regional bodies and international organizations like the EU, the World Bank and the African Development Bank have been considerably more active in this field. China is the most conspicuous collaborator in infrastructure-building projects for Africa.
12. I have realized that often the locals, when talking to foreigners, purposefully avoid using words with negative connotations like 'corrupt', 'deceitful or 'unethical', but instead use more neutral terms like 'lacking capacity' to explain their problems.
13. *Which Country*, http://www.whichcountry.co. The information is said to be verified by authentic sources and collected from the CIA World Factbook (2011).
14. 'Summary of Herzberg's Motivation and Hygiene Factors. Abstract', *Value Based Management*. Retrieved on 6 January 2016, http://www.valuebasedmanagement.net/methods_herzberg_two_factor_theory.html.
15. *The Free Dictionary*, http://www.thefreedictionary.com/work+ethic.
16. Jacqueline Whitmore, '7 Elements of a Strong Work Ethic', *Entrepreneur*, https://www.entrepreneur.com/article/250114.

13

Enacting Bold but Harmonious Change

Recapping the Fundamentals

In this volume, I have laid out many issues that are pertinent to Sub-Saharan Africa and have stressed what are deemed to be the priorities for Sub-Saharan African countries in order to attain transformative development. Describing problems may be the easy part, but the root causes of the problems must be identified if they are to be tackled. The overall assessment is that Sub-Saharan Africa appears to have fallen further behind the rest of the world in terms of economic competitiveness, work capacity, industrialization, income equality and possibly the social fabric. But the tide can be turned and some countries are doing better. Africa's blessings in terms of its natural endowment and economic potential are undeniable, and hence the fundamentals should be worked on assiduously to reap the maximum dividends from such possibilities.

As I have mentioned, development should be a way of life. Indeed, national and political leaders, their vision, and government policies serve as signposts for this, but ultimately it all comes down to how people—the elites, civil servants, businessmen, workers, farmers, etc.—conduct

J.-D. Park, *Re-Inventing Africa's Development*,
https://doi.org/10.1007/978-3-030-03946-2_13

themselves in their everyday lives, which will have an accumulative effect as a nation. Perhaps the most deceptive caveat to development is the complexity of the development narrative or the 'professionalism' of this field: development is portrayed and pursued too much in technical terms aloof from reality.

The world is fast-moving and everybody is busy trying to catch up with the trends that are taking place. And in the process, people can lose sight of the bigger picture, which is the basics or the fundamentals of economic and social development that apply universally. In any field—and this is particularly evident in science and technology, and sports—the fundamentals are the most important factor. They are called 'fundamentals' not because they are rudimentary and easy, but because they are the most crucial elements. In science, for instance, 'applied technology' is derived from 'original technology', which is extremely difficult to acquire. No matter how elaborate the applied technology, if it is not based on original technology, it will not work. In sport, one cannot expect to become a top athlete without embodying all the sound fundamentals of the discipline.

Therefore, to treat the fundamentals of development as 'outdated and irrelevant' is a grave mistake. The world has long forgotten the fundamentals of development and in Africa they never seem to have been properly put in place. I believe that in development, there are fundamentals within fundamentals and it is crucial to understand and capture these. In this context, drawing on Korean development model (Fig. 8.1) can be most useful.

To simplify, and go straight to the crux of the matter, the two most essential principles of development that are universally applicable are economic discrimination in the economic realm and development-mindedness in the socio-political realm. But strictly speaking, these two are interactive and inter-connected. Korea's development was driven by these two principles, which acted as engines of development. This was particularly true during the decades of high growth, but their relevance is by no means lost today.

In the case of Korea, the 'four cornerstones' (land reform, empowerment of the people, educational reform and governmental reform), which now may seem rudimentary, constituted the crucial groundwork for development. The active role played by the government was another major ingredient of success. And what made economic discrimination and the strong development mindset work effectively was the 'egalitarian spirit' of Koreans. The development path was basically followed two tracks: economic discrimination propelled economic transformation while the strong development-mindedness led socio-political transformation.

A development formula for Sub-Saharan African countries (Fig. 10.6) was deduced from the Korean development model, i.e., lessons learned from the Korean development experience, taking into account Africa's circumstances. As was the case in Korea, African countries also need 'economic logic'—economic discrimination—to prevail for the sake of their business and economic growth. As was explained, economic discrimination works through the inter-play of the market, businesses and government. But in Sub-Saharan Africa, international donors or development partners have a big stake in the economy and hence I have included them in the equation. 'People' is also included in light of Africa's large, unorganized informal sector and the fast-growing youth population that can make a difference for the economy if they are properly targeted.

Running parallel alongside the economic track are the 'missing links', which comprise of sense of nation, development-mindedness and the active role of the state. These are deemed important for Sub-Saharan African countries to embrace and adopt. Last but not least, active measures to counter and ultimately stamp out various negative elements are considered crucial for the region's development. Countries must vigorously fight the negative elements—the back-tracking syndrome, short-sightedness, inaction, the 'what's-in-it-for-me' syndrome, the dependency syndrome and a commission culture—that can quickly offset various development endeavours made by the countries and international partners.

So the tasks confronting Sub-Saharan African countries are significant as already laid out. But since these are essentially human factors, they are achievable and the important thing is to work on multiple fronts at the same time. Here, speed is of the essence and a 'slow and piecemeal approach' should be avoided. There cannot be progress when any new gains made in a certain area are undone by lack of progress in another. It should be noted that Korea was successful because the reform was conducted expeditiously in many areas to produce synergistic effects.

Many economic aspects in the region have the characteristics of being 'static', when 'dynamism' is the trait that developing countries should be embracing. For example, in Africa, there seems to be too great a level of preoccupation with how to allocate the 'pie' (wealth or resources) when much greater emphasis should be placed on how fast they can enlarge the pie. So the key question for Africa is how the dynamism on the part of the people and the economy can be acquired and enhanced.

In fact, there are so many ways to make improvements and make them fast: working harder (faster and longer hours), becoming more focused and organized, reducing wastage, being more consistent and predictable, better conforming to norms and regulations, etc. It does not require extra skills, technology and resources to be able to do all these things; it concerns human factors like attitudes, work ethics, the level of determination and discipline, etc.

There is no hidden agenda or risks in such an attitudinal or mindset change approach. There is absolutely nothing to lose and everything to gain with this kind of approach as its merits are so evident. But working out how to effectively pursue this as a public or national initiative may not be so easy. The ability to enter this threshold of social mobilization will, in itself, represent a milestone. But we should ask who should be spearheading such an initiative and through what mechanisms it should be pursued.

Ideally, this could take the form of being a grassroots citizens' movement with the support of the state. But in reality, the role of national leaders will be central, at least at the launching stage. The vision, drive and wisdom of leaders will no doubt be important. The majority of African countries do not yet have credible and efficient political and governance systems in place, so the personal capability and traits of national leaders can be all the more important. Ideally, they should be fervent patriots and their ideas should be zealously followed and implemented by the nation's civil servants. But there is also the danger of the campaign being seen as politically motivated, which would greatly undermine its legitimacy. Hence, a national consensus should be sought and a politically neutral body should be formed to oversee and drive the movement forward.

It would be meaningless if there is no participation in this process by the people. And in the end, the people must be able to deliver what matters most for development: economic outputs and the promotion of social, political changes. People can always empower themselves through their actions without waiting to be empowered by the government.

Speaking of empowerment of the people, perhaps nothing is more relevant than instilling in the people the 'development-mindedness' that I have termed 'KPOP'. The components of KPOP, which are detailed in Chapter 5, are the basic ingredients that make people productive and successful as individuals. If an increasing proportion of the population, especially the youth, were to embody such traits, and the trend prevails, the nation will be on a promising path. From the perspective of individuals, these can be attained in the given order, but as I have explained, in Korea, 'reverse engineering' was successfully applied: rather than starting from the 'knowing (learning)' phase, working from the last phase of imbuing or motivating 'passion' proved to be very effective. When people feel passionate about something, then the rest (learning, practising and owning) comes naturally. Passion breeds actions and outcomes, and these lead to confidence. The benefits of such virtuous cycle are deemed to be immense.

In Korea, it was the Korean leaders, both civil and public, who taught, encouraged and mobilized the people to be empowered. It was not foreigners or aid organizations. Technical know-how can be learned or introduced from abroad and development partners can assist in training, but the promotion of the campaign to empower the people should come from African leaders themselves. Foreigners do not need to spell out to Africans that they need a mindset change to escape from poverty and achieve economic development. This should be the work of the African leaders, intellectuals and ordinary people, who will gain the most by undertaking such a campaign for change.

Without a noticeable enhancement in the development-mindedness of the people in general, the prospects for achieving successful national development will not be good. It is up to the African nations to aggressively take on the tasks and effect changes, as development-mindedness of the people can only be attained through their own efforts. Foreign partners can only show how it could be done in the preliminary stages; the real work itself has to be undertaken by the protagonists.

From 'Dualism' to a 'Medium-Bridging' Approach of Development

This book highlights the attitudinal factors and the 'missing links' that have long been forgotten, ignored or underestimated in the discourse and practice regarding Africa's development. However, I think there is another blind-spot that needs to be mentioned here, which is the failure to properly grasp the significance of the 'middle ground' between the 'traditional' sector and the 'modern' sector. For so long, the perception of 'economic dualism' appears to have dominated the minds of experts and ordinary people alike, especially when it comes to the issue of Africa's development. A dual economy refers to the state of two separate economic sectors existing within a country, divided by different development and technology levels. The concept was first conceived by Julius Herman Boeke to describe the coexistence of modern and traditional economic sectors in a colonial economy (social dualism).[1]

Later, Benjamin Higgins developed the idea into 'technological dualism', which proposes that resources and technological constraints in two sectors—modern and traditional—limit development in poor countries.[2] The most familiar dualist theory is Arthur Lewis' 'dual sector model', which postulates a rural low-productive, low-income subsistence sector with a surplus population and an expanding high-productive urban capitalist sector. He argued that developing economies could achieve substantial economic growth by encouraging labour to move from the agricultural sector to the manufacturing sector. The Lewis model is considered to have remained for more than 50 years as one of the dominant theories of development economics.[3]

All theories have their limitations, especially if they relate to social sciences, because they are inherently incapable of handling all the cases and variables of the complex reality of our world—that is why they are theories. Theoretical debates aside, what really matters is the possible negative impact that cursory interpretations of such ideas can have on developing nations. Economic theories should not be taken literally, but need to be understood each time in the different context that one is dealing with. As has already been pointed out, Africa's predicament continues because basically its problems are dealt with in a static context, in a rather superficial way without going through a sufficient thought process. Many African leaders and elites are seen to have harboured 'dualistic' thinking for a long time. In a desire to move out of backwardness and towards modernity, they have been drawn to the standards of rich countries and have sought the expertise and training that the advanced world has to offer, as well as promoting trade and investment. Terms like 'entrepreneurship', 'value-addition', 'agribusiness', 'innovation' have been frequently used in Africa. And almost always, there seem to be gaps between what is desired and what is achievable. For instance, some inexperienced leaders have unrealistic desires to have mammoth ultra-modern hospitals, new town complexes, etc. built with foreign assistance, without giving any thought to their cost and sustainability.

There is no such thing as making leaps and bounds when it comes to national development or transformation involving major structural changes. Nations cannot just move from one state of being to another in a routine fashion. Transformation cannot take place simply through making good policy choices, receiving good advice from donors or receiving investment and technology from foreign partners. Many Africans tend to take these as an end in themselves, but they are nothing more than a means and everything is dependent on how much the nation vigorously works towards development.

In Sub-Saharan Africa at least, a policy prescription based on the thinking of dual economy would not be very effective. Many countries must have at one point or another pursued such an approach, apparently with no or very little success. Lewis' dual-sector model does not apply well to Africa because there is such a big gap between the traditional and the modern sectors, and the modern sector is actually very small and weak. Furthermore, the modern sector, which is the manufacturing industrial sector, is mostly owned and run by multi-nationals, foreigners and the minority business community. In Africa, population growth is explosive, resulting in a youth-heavy population, which causes concern in view of the limited job opportunities for them. And, of course, there are the issues of attitudinal, cultural and social 'restraints' or limitations that have to be overcome.

The circumstances in Africa are that even with an open economy and business-friendly policies, the largely subsistence-oriented rural sector, to which most of the people belong, has not been impacted by or received much benefit from the modern sector. But the rural populace, especially the youth, flock to the cities, where they remain marginalized. Hence, it is not the growth of the manufacturing industrial sector (the modern sector) matched by a reduction in the traditional sector that we are witnessing, but an increase in the number of people at the 'periphery' of two sectors: relatively large rudimentary businesses or those linked to the 'informal' sector. The workers here do not really belong to the modern sector, though in a sense they might look entrepreneurial. This is due to a lack of skills/capacity, a lack of market demand or buying power, a lack of capital and investment, etc.

But the biggest consequence of this is the dearth of social capital, like trust, cooperation, bonds, reciprocity and sense of the common good. Probably the best way to close the gap between the traditional sector and the modern sector, or to move from the former to the latter, is to strengthen social capital so that it can serve as a mediatory force or a medium that facilitates the transition from the traditional sector to the modern sector. Social capital is deemed to be a very practical and effective means which can be created in any situation and is not dependent on foreign resources. On the other hand, financial capital is hard to come by and can be misused, as we see so frequently in the region. Another advantage of building social capital is that it can induce other positive values like good work ethics in addition to strengthening the social fabric of a nation.

The logical next step will be figuring out how to best foster social capital in Sub-Saharan Africa. One of the ways in which I think this could be done is by developing the 'medium'. This 'medium' I am talking about here can be defined as a 'sector' within the traditional sector that has potential 'developmental' elements which can be turned into a tool for the transition of the traditional sector into a modern sector. People would need to embody the necessary social, attitudinal qualities before they could be effectively incorporated into modern sector. The medium, as social capital or bond, can have a multitude of uses and could act as a powerful vehicle leading to the development of the modern sector. Therefore, identifying and promoting the medium should be actively carried out.

The 'medium-bridging approach' purports to explore and take advantage of positive elements inherent in developing nations' local practices, and reinvigorating them to expedite the transformation of the traditional sector into a modern sector. Since the potential elements of the medium are embedded in the local contents, it is easy to revive and resuscitate them.

In Korea, the 'medium' was successfully established and operated in the form of 'empowerment of the people', 'mindset change' and the *Saemaul Undong* (new village movement) campaigns. The contents of 'medium' can be found in traditional values or practices, or in the form of something that has been 'reinvented' and 'updated' to suit the current situation. Whether it is old or new is not important; what matters is whether or not it is initiated, 'owned' and subscribed to by the local populace.

As for the prospects of success of the 'medium' or 'home-grown solutions' in Africa, there are already promising signs to this effect in newly emerging countries like Rwanda. Of course, Botswana, a more established country in this respect, is in a class of its own. Rwanda provides an interesting case study as it is likened to South Korea. The two countries share many common traits. Both are small, resource-scarce, mountainous countries. The flat, habitable land is hard to find, so there is a high population density in the residential districts. But this contributes to a high rate of Internet connection. Both countries are surrounded by bigger neighbours and have faced major crises. The history of Korea is fraught with tribulations: harsh colonial rule, national division and the devastation of the Korean War. Rwanda suffered an unprecedented genocide in 1994 that still haunts the country. Korea turned the crisis into an opportunity, and so have Rwandans. When Korea had to rebuild from the ashes of war, it had nothing to rely on but its human resources. Korea is one of key benchmarking countries for Rwanda, along with Singapore.

Rwanda stands out all the more because in the region, such features as good governance that Rwanda displays are a rarity. Of course, there are issues in the political realm, but overall it is succeeding in winning the confidence of the international community. A number of the biggest international hotel chains have opened for business in Rwanda, the latest being the Kigali Marriott Hotel, which opened in September 2016. Now the meetings, incentives, conferences and exhibitions (MICE) business is flourishing in Rwanda.

What is the secret behind Rwanda's impressive turnaround in its governance, public services and business? According to President Kagame, it is the home-grown solutions that have improved citizens' participation and accountability: 'We have very high ambitions and scarce resources. Before we go out begging for things we may never get, we have to ask ourselves, "have we exhausted the resources around us?" This is how home grown solutions start.'[4] 'From our history as a nation, it became evident to us, in the hardest way possible, that we can only count on ourselves. Thus self-reliance became the rationale for life. Now, given the challenges that Rwanda is facing, and the ambitions and aspirations we have for the future, it is impossible that conventional approaches will get us there in the time-frame we want; hence, home-grown solutions.'[5]

This sounds strikingly similar to Korea's *Saemaul Undong*. Rwanda's home-grown solutions include *Abunzi* (mediation committees), *Gacaca* (speedy justice), *Umuganda* (communal self-help), *Umushyikirano* (citizen participation), *Itorero* (civic education) and *Umwhiherero* (national leadership retreat).[6] Similarly, Botswana has applied its own socio-cultural traditions like the system of chiefs—*Kgotla*—to enhance its development.

Many developing countries faltered in joining the ranks of the advanced economies because they succumbed to the challenge of 'dualism' and let the 'international economic tide' get the better of them. Besides the Asian Tigers, the reason why even the Southeast Asian countries have had much more economic success than African countries (in the 1960s and even the 1970s, the two regions were more or less at the same level) is that they were not tied to a 'dual-structure' mentality, but pursued pro-poor, pro-rural agricultural policies at an early stage of development. Perhaps less dramatic or successful than Korea's case but the 'medium' was in the works in these countries.

The lesson drawn from this is that African countries must find solutions for development from within. 'Internalizing' or taking ownership of development should be an integral part of the nation-building process, but African countries seem to have long forgotten about nation-building. As such, they prematurely 'exposed' themselves to the outside world before they got their own house in order and were prepared for this new venture. And just when the governments had the chance to duly take charge of their economy, they were quick to 'outsource', liberalize and privatize. This signified the abandonment, not the exercise, of the government's mandate.

It is during the nation-building phase that the government's grip and role need to be most robust. The political slogan 'small but efficient government' (although I do not hear it much these days) is premised on the 'overgrown' government bureaucracy. But it is doubtful that African countries have come near the threshold of strong, 'full-fledged' states. The size of the government itself is not so relevant, as the strength of government comes from its functionality, coherence and discipline, buttressed by good political leadership and the watchful eye of the public.

Figure 13.1 depicts the dual-economy structure and the medium-bridging approach used to deal with this. The top graph in the figure shows a typical underdeveloped economy with a very large traditional sector and a modest modern sector. The *y*-axis shows the scale of the population (number of people) and the *x*-axis the level of development, technology or productiveness. Apparently, there is a big gap between the two sectors so that the transition from a traditional sector to the modern sector is virtually at a standstill.

The middle and bottom graphs in the figure show how the medium-bridging approach works. The first thing to do in Phase 1 is to nurture the medium. Building the medium is critical for poor countries because this is the opportunity for the people to take ownership of development by internalizing it. In order for this endeavour to succeed, confidence, optimism and eagerness must be manifested, and the necessity of the campaign must be brought home to the people. In addition, the strong leadership of popular leaders will be required in this regard.

Once the medium is successfully formed through the participation and support of the public, it is important to keep the momentum

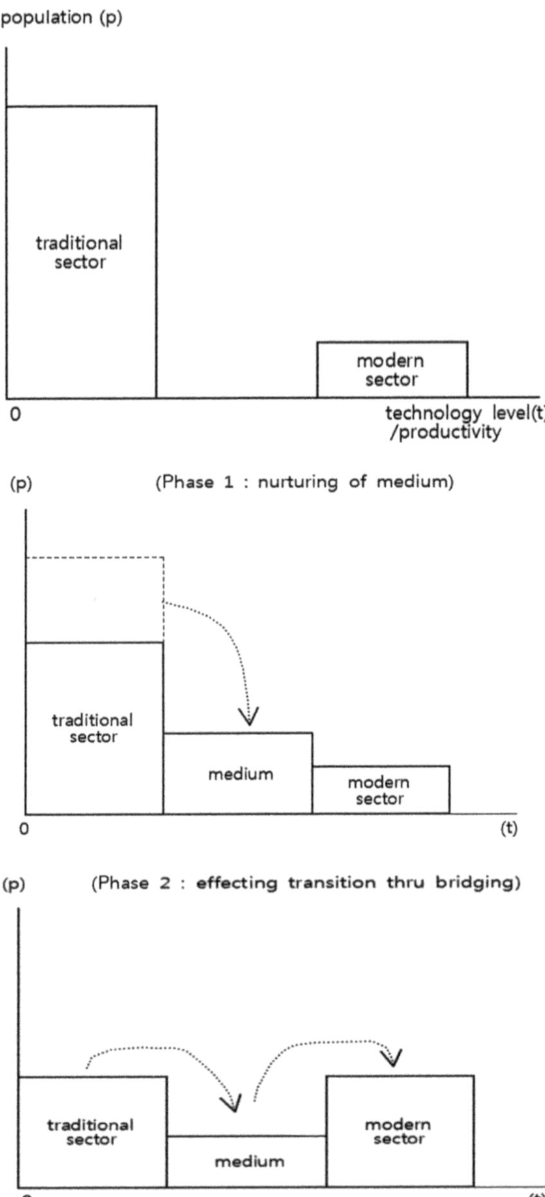

Fig. 13.1 The dual economic structure and the medium-bridging approach

going in order to expand the base of the medium and intensify its strength. For this, both the government and private engagement should ensue. The benefit of this initiative is that it promotes social capital, development-mindedness and local governance. Then, when the medium assumes a life of its own and is running, its positive impact on the economy can be substantial. The traditional sector is labour-intensive, while the modern sector is capital- and technology-intensive. The significance of the medium is that it is *social capital-intensive*, which the African nations sorely need.

We can see that the traditional sector is reduced with the growth of the medium which originates from the former. The traditional sector is being transformed into a modern sector through the vehicle of the medium. The end result is a transformed economic structure with a substantially enlarged modern sector and an equivalent decrease in the traditional sector. When the transition has run its full course, the medium, having exhausted its usefulness, will wither. A highly developed economy will have a very small traditional sector and a dominant modern sector, and will no longer need the medium. If the medium is not strong and large enough to have an impact on the economy, it can end up simply as 'peripheral'.

Aid Versus Business?

There has been a lot of talk about the worthiness of aid versus business in Sub-Saharan Africa. But discussions on this topic do not seem to have much merit. African development issues have continued for too long and have extended so widely that it is no longer a simple matter of 'aid versus business'. However, many people still seem to view the matter through such a lens, so there is a need to revisit this topic.

In Africa, aid and business are closely intertwined. Such a phenomenon is the outcome of natural forces at work rather than by design. In Africa, many drawbacks like weakness in management capability, work ethics and governance, as well as the prevalence of irregularities, persist. It will be difficult for Africa to extricate itself from poverty and other predicaments under such conditions. Foreign aid has not caused Africa's problems; it is the latter that has invited the former. Foreign assistance has flaws of its own for certain, but this is due to various limitations in reality, so it cannot be the central issue. When African countries start to get to grips with their fundamental challenges and do something about them, foreign aid will naturally dissipate.

Under such circumstances, business will not be business in strict terms. In other words, in many cases, some sort of development assistance has to be involved to support even private business activities. For example, because of various business risks posed by security issues, weak administration and governance, poor infrastructure, the lack of a productive local workforce, etc., foreign companies wanting to do serious business in Africa have to undertake activities well beyond the traditional scope of private business: offering technical support, capacity training, even governance and physical infrastructure, besides bringing in capital investment and management personnel. It is not the usual business partnerships between the 'equal' business collaborators that we see in other regions. 'Dependent partnership' is probably a better term to describe this.

Advocates of the neoliberal school of thought have been most critical of foreign aid while fervently supporting free trade and business. Their criticism of foreign aid to Africa is understandable as they have rightly pointed out that aid has had a limited impact on alleviating poverty and has aggravated the dependency syndrome in Africa. And I agree with the argument that entrepreneurship and the robustness of the private sector are what ultimately drive economic growth. Without question, the economic growth and strength of a nation hinges on the vitality of its private sector and businesses. But that is about as far as neoliberalism can go in terms of logical coherence; the rest is full of weaknesses. It neither describes the reality correctly nor offers persuasive and responsible policy prescriptions. It disregards so many factors that are in play, particularly in African countries.

The problems that make aid ineffective are also those that stymie business and the economy in general. These are not two different options that can be separated from each other, especially in the case of Sub-Saharan Africa. If more business and investment with less aid was the answer to Africa's predicament, then aid to Africa would not have been the problem in the first place. What makes aid ineffective and problematic is what also makes business and investments ineffective and problematic.

When there are few successful enterprises and industrial development virtually remains at a standstill in the region, there must be good reasons for this state of affairs. African countries need to work strenuously to overcome their shortcomings in the fundamentals, while also tackling the many negativities or 'leakages' that undercut their progress. In these circumstances, replacing foreign aid with business and investment will not work wonders, as some have suggested. South Africa is the most industrialized and advanced economy in the region, but the disparity and 'dependency' structure within it is all too evident.

There are many business elements in aid programmes and, equally, many business activities are closely linked with development in Sub-Saharan Africa. In this respect, the region's economic dependence on foreign partners and the international community in general has not diminished: Western countries continue to provide budgetary support to Africa; an increasing number of aid projects are undertaken in the form of public-private-partnerships (PPPs); African economies are heavily dependent on foreign companies and investments; direct foreign involvement, like foreign entrepreneurs' on-site management and the influx of foreign capital, is what supports the economies of many African countries; many major national projects like large-scale infrastructure building projects are carried out using foreign loans and technology. The trading of consumer goods, equipment and intermediary products is done by the private sector, but the limited purchasing power of locals poses an immediate challenge for business.

In terms of development assistance, foreign partners, the host government and other entities share the responsibility, and hence there is at the very least some level of governance exercised for the projects. But in private business, there is no assurance of such governance. As has been mentioned repeatedly, in the region, the nation-building task is largely unfinished and ongoing, and the social fabric and social capital are still weak. In these circumstances, foreign aid and business cannot be so clearly distinguished from each other, and both are needed. Aid indeed has its flaws and may not be the best thing for Africa, but the benefits that the whole array of foreign aid has brought to African countries, if these can be measured in real terms, would not be negligible. As I have pointed out, when the international community has given so much assistance for so many decades to a particular region, there must have been good reasons to make this happen.

And the people should reflect on what would have transpired had foreign aid not been provided to Africa. Here, foreign aid should not be considered as merely simple material or financial assistance, but a very wide range of means and activities, including management support and supervision, technical training and capacity-building, consulting, education, governance-enhancing measures, support for private businesses, the provision of various facilities and infrastructures, and even various donor 'pressure' on African governments to conform to universal norms and values. The actual value of these will be difficult to measure, but would African countries have fared better if there had been no such interventions and they were left entirely to the free market mechanism? By all accounts, it is likely that situation would have been much worse.

Basically, African countries remain poor and underdeveloped not because they lack resources and means, but because they have issues with respect to management from the very top to the very bottom across all sectors. This is the reflection of the countries' inability to take charge of their national development mission. Trade and investment do not come about simply by wishing it to be so; it has to make business sense. Business deals do not occur in a vacuum, but follow profitable markets while avoiding risks. For business in Africa to flourish, many things need to be enhanced or secured, like work ethics, the skills and capacity of the locals, accountability, good governance, active government support, better security, etc.

If aids and business both have limitations in Africa, then what is the alternative? Those who want to find a middle ground could fancy 'social entreprises' being a solution. Social entreprises look and work like regular, traditional enterprises because they are revenue-generating, but that have the goal of having a positive impact on society in terms of the well-being of the environment and human life.[7] But social entreprises that operate at the borderline between the for profit and non-profit domains can be even more difficult to manage successfully given the challenging conditions in Sub-Saharan Africa.

There is more to Africa's business model than meets the eye, and tackling relevant policy matters should begin with the understanding of more basic factors that lie beneath the surface. Having an overly rosy picture of the role of the private sector and business when the social fabric and the role of the government remain very weak is simply naive and detrimental: mismanagement, inefficiencies, shut-downs and corruption are the price to pay for this way of thinking.

The Last Word

Continued poverty and underdevelopment, not to mention various instabilities and conflicts, in the region can be attributed primarily to gross negligence on the part of the countries in terms of their task of nation-building. All African nations aspire to achieve economic prosperity and talk about transformation, but what they have not done is to actually put in place the things that allow such progress to occur. Because what is at stake and matters ultimately today is the most significant 'unit', the nation. When a nation becomes independent and forms a state, every effort should be made to make it worthwhile, otherwise there is no point in having a state to begin with.

Ethnical, racial and regional divides create a hurdle, but this is not uniquely an African issue. In fact, there are many developed and developing countries outside of Africa that have multi-ethnic, cultural features as well as regional divides. Therefore, such elements cannot serve as a good excuse for underdevelopment. Dealing with these matters is simply a part of the normal, everyday business of all nations. But what is intriguing is that many people want to treat Africa differently, forgetting the general rule applicable to all people in our history—no nations had all the right or favourable conditions (including doorstep or initial conditions for industrialization) to develop successfully when they emerged as nation states or territorial states. It is the process of consolidation, integration, harmonization and building the capacity to deal with various challenges that makes states viable. In this respect, nation-building, which is essential for national development, is not one-time event, but one which has to be worked on persistently in order to be achieved.

So the reason that Sub-Saharan African countries continue to struggle—despite their enormous riches in terms of natural endowments and external assistance, as well as the goodwill and opportunities provided to them by the international community at large—is because they have not done their part at their end. The worst thing that can happen is further 'internationalization of Africa's problems' or increasingly turning Africa's problems into the responsibility of the international community, thereby incapacitating African nations forever. Despite all the talk inside the African Union about Africa taking ownership of the Union, its members cannot agree to stop depending on outside assistance to finance its operations. In this regard, initiatives and progress to launch the African Continent Free Trade Area (AfCFTA) in 2018 are a positive development for the region. But the question remains how expediently and thoroughly will this be pursued and operated, and if it will not become another New Partnership for Africa's Development?

Improving basic living conditions and rights of the people, and achieving sustainable economic and social development should be the primary goals of African countries, and the role of the international donor community should be assist them in this respect. But in order to move in the direction of progress, efforts must be made to break the status quo and the elements that perpetuate the current state of poverty and underdevelopment. And it all comes down to people's mind and behaviour which determine how much and what kind of change can be brought about under the given circumstances.

Regarding work ethics, it is undeniable that when people become more diligent and disciplined in their work, things improve markedly. But people cannot simply be told to work harder or expected to behave in this way; they have to be 'motivated' to act differently. Among many things, what is probably more important is to have higher expectations or desires in life. People should be dissatisfied with their present lot and should be aspiring for a better life. Some African leaders implore their people to get out of a subsistence way of life and become more productive, but a perennial impediment is the *minimalist* tendency in the lifestyle of the people in general: exerting minimal effort while expecting minimal returns.

Mindful of this, a shift should be made from such a minimalist stance to a 'more-for-more' type of approach: people having greater desires and expectations in life, and exerting greater efforts to achieve them, while at the same time contributing in terms of economic value addition. A lesson from the Korean case is that during the emerging state of the economy at least, for the sake of rapid economic growth, it is vital to avoid the politicization of the economy; in other words, it is better to delink economic policies from political consideration as much as possible.

An interesting example in this respect is South Africa. Despite all its advantages compared to other Sub-Saharan African countries, South Africa suffers from an exceptionally low economic growth rate and a reduced credit standing. Mismanagement, corruption, inordinately politically oriented economic policies and uncertainties in politics, among other factors, are the challenges facing the new President Cyril Ramaphosa in the aftermath of Jacob Zuma's era of misrule and 'state capture'. The impending land expropriation without compensation is another potential 'dynamite' issue that may rock the country if it is not appropriately pursued. Besides its socio-economic ramifications, in purely technical terms, considering the lack of capacity and corruption in government circles, land reform poses another great hurdle for the nation.

Without a general change in people's mindset or their value system, and most importantly their 'motivational-behavioural system', it will be illogical to expect substantive progress to come about. The 'speed' of work is another thing that I have stressed, because development is essentially about how much change can be made over time. A most simple measurement of development could be represented as follows:

$$\text{Development} = \frac{\text{Change}}{\text{Time}}$$

Here 'change' means the extent of positive net change or improvement. So how can a society or nation manage to 'engineer' its people to become more actively oriented in a positive fashion? There can be a number of approaches at different levels and in order to be effective, they should be synchronized or pursued in unison. As explained, the basic economic principle or mechanism should be 'incentives and sanctions'. Here, a 'meritocracy' should be strictly observed, based on 'competition' and performance. And extra efforts need to be made to bring about positive attitudinal change on the part of the people, and a vigorous campaign to instil development-mindedness and KPOP in the populace may prove to be very useful.

There are clear limitations in terms of the extent to which a nation can develop in a transformational and sustainable way if the people are not increasingly empowered and if only a small number of people and companies remain productive and drive the economy forward. Foreign partners or companies can be brought into fill the gaps, but even this would not yield the expected outcomes in the end without the overall improvement in the conditions and capacity of the host nations. A national economy that is overdependent on foreign entities with the vast majority of its people remaining dependent and unproductive cannot be a sign of success. This is where Asian countries contrast with Sub-Saharan African countries, the former being able to empower and economically mobilize a large section of their population, while thus far, the latter has not able to do so.

The fastest way to transform for developing countries would be when there is both good governance and strong, effective mobilization of the people. But it could be considered as a given that poor countries lack such attributes and, as a consequence, they remain poor. In Africa, many things do not seem to work as they are supposed to, and some experts can claim to know more about the reasons why than others. However, coming to have a better understanding of an issue does not necessary mean that one will deal with it more proactively. Knowing is one thing, but taking action is quite another. It all depends on how, and with what objective, one approaches the issue.

Even governance and work ethic levels which people would think are more or less fixed should be regarded as variables that can altered. Experts can inadvertently promote the status quo rather than change with their 'this is how it works, so this is how it should be done' kind of attitude. I believe there is always a price to pay for choosing to remain in one's comfort zone, and catering to people's needs cannot be an end in itself for the sake of development.

Everything begins from the basics, and problems that are fundamental in nature call for equally fundamental responses. Whether it concerns daily business, construction works, technical training or institution-building, laying a solid foundation or embodying sound basics is the key to success. Development is a building-block process, and the quality as well as the quantity of inputs will determine the outputs. There is no silver bullet or shortcut to improving the state of the economy of a nation. It is not a simple matter of choice or timing like having the right things at the right time; it is a matter of how well and expeditiously things are actually *done*. So let us not be consumed by debates pitting 'aid vs. business', 'liberalization vs. protectionism' or 'private sector vs. government intervention' because these are peripheral topics that mask and divert our attention away from the central issues. We should also pay more attention to institutions; the indications are that the performance of institutions in Sub-Saharan Africa is weakening instead of improving, as noted by the World Bank.[8] Even in more advanced countries like South Africa, 'there had been a profound weakening of state institutions and a generalisation of criminality across the state and not only in national departments' (see Note 8).

Each person has different individual attributes, abilities and level of ambitions, and everyone can contribute to their society in different ways through the division of labour. The important thing is that individuals each play a part that matches their purported role. 'Small and steady progress' may not sound like a big deal, but means a lot. And it will take commitment and consistent efforts to achieve incremental progress on a sustained basis, including actions to prevent or minimize various 'leakages' that happen every so often across Africa. Small and steady improvement, on all fronts, can mean everything for the development of a nation. When improvements, even modest ones, add up, significant transformational changes can come about. Big achievements do not happen overnight, but must be worked on assiduously. The miraculous economic development of South Korea is the outcome of such a broad-based 'incremental and sustained' approach involving or mobilizing a large segment of the populace and driven by multiple actors.

But the voice of conscience has not died down. In South Africa, the Moral Regeneration Movement (MRM) emerged as early as 1997 with a sense of urgency in the midst of rising violence, intolerance and disregard for the wellbeing of others.[9] In 1994, the first post-apartheid government of Nelson Mandela was formed, but the legacy of apartheid manifested itself in an unexpected fashion, for example, in the rise of the black-on-black violence, despite the achievement of democracy. Hence, Mandela introduced the concept of the MDM, which he termed the RDP (Reconstruction and Development Programme) of the soul.[10] This movement goes on unabated in view of its apparent need, but there can be limits to such a campaign if it is confined to a moral-religious context. What is much needed alongside this is a different empowerment of the people, a social mobilization movement that drives people to become more positively oriented in their actions.

There should be some points to take away from this book that shed light on important things that were literally ignored. I will mention just two here. The first one is that, surprisingly, the development community, both international and local, has not identified and targeted human factors to any serious degree; that is, they have not gone straight to the heart of the matter. Development assistance has largely turned into diplomatic and political events that talk about the niceties on the surface, but avoid touching the innate, hard-to-deal-with subjects. If the intrinsic factors are not recognized and dealt with forcefully, then development efforts will continue to be a ritual or superficiality. The second point to take away is that the mainstream international development community and African countries have not heeded facts, truths and examples of economic development that history and the world have demonstrated for all to see and applied them in practice.

The best indicator of development is looking at it from the standard of 'way of life'. 'Has the way of life of people changed and become more developmental?' should be the central criterion. The measurement should not be how much funds or material wealth are transferred to the benefit of the recipients. So, various grant offering programmes that do not change people's behaviours but make them even more dependent are detrimental as they are anti-developmental and perpetuating poverty.

If the South Korean example is anything to go by, for a very poor country to emerge successfully in the way it did, improvements must be made in all aspects of nationhood and lives of the people: nation-building, national ideas and goals, work ethics, ambitions to lead better lives, civic-mindedness, adherence to norms, rules and regulations, democracy and universal values, etc. In fact, in the early stage of Korea's development, the focus was on nation-building, empowerment of the people and work ethics; in its latter phase, democracy, international standards, civic values and universal norms were increasingly pursued and valued.

I think these are all essential elements and features that characterize developed nations. But the established international community tends to place emphasis on democracy, the rule of law, human rights and good governance, while African states in general are seen to stress law and order, stability and security, or 'national interests' and unity above others. Meanwhile, in some African countries, the leaders or governments have launched moral campaigns or pleaded with the people to become more economically productive.

In any case, national objectives, international rules and global values are all necessary for African countries to espouse in their path to development. Thus far, the methods used to 'inculcate' the people with these values have not proven to be very effective. What then would be a more practical, effective and natural approach to use in this situation? I think one of the answers to this is the 'community approach', as explained earlier.

In Africa, people's attachment to their relatives and community is unmistakable. Inculcating values and ideas in the people, let alone changing their mindsets, may not come easily through public lecturing. Instead, it would require a mechanism of voluntarism and constraints that can be applied directly to the people. The advantage of the community approach is that 'community' is already embedded with certain elements of voluntarism and constraints, so there is already a mechanism in place that can be utilized. If worked on properly, this can turn out to be an effective 'medium' for development that can act as the bridge for converting a traditional sector into a modern one. The most prominent example of this presented in this book is Korea's *Saemaul Undong*.

To elaborate on the second point to take away from this book, developed countries, international organizations and African nations alike have long drifted away from the very fundamentals of economic development and have been looking for answers in the wrong places. The proper approach should have been to spell out the core elements or 'undeniable truth' in development and then, based on this, engineer implementation plans by making the necessary adjustments in their existing methods.

In hindsight, it is quite surprising that the examples and lessons of South Korea and other Asian countries that provide the latest and possibly the most valuable case studies for African countries have not been more seriously considered and applied. But it is never too late, even if the international economic environment has changed considerably over recent decades. As such, there needs to be fresh new thinking in both theory and practice when it comes to African development. In this regard, Sung-Hee Jwa mentions that: 'Under whatever circumstances, the Korean lessons of keeping to economic discrimination principle in building economic institutions and policies as well as in creating the self-help spirit should not be ignored for those seeking economic development because this principle is the key to economic as well as human development by helping to overcome the constraints of resource endowment and the international environment as well as developmental-unfriendly tradition and culture.'[11]

Development is about 'changing for the better'. The *Cambridge Dictionary* defines it as 'the process in which someone or something grows or changes and becomes more advanced'. So when nations want to achieve development without themselves making the necessary changes, it means that they either do not understand what development stands for or think that others can do the work for them. *Wanting change without changing*, which sounds like an oxymoron, is a deep-seated impediment to development in the region.

Turning to the private sector, the fact that Africa is open to the world for business, and that new and innovative technologies are increasingly being applied to its markets, while creative entrepreneurs are emerging in start-ups gives new hope for economic dynamism in Africa. But in order for these private initiatives to flourish, they will need an equally favourable environment and conducive support system, including administrative assistance, to facilitate their activities. In essence, it comes down to the management of state affairs and governance.

It is true that the current state of Sub-Saharan Africa requires many interventions in wide-ranging areas, and the various efforts made to this end by so many entities should not be overlooked. And we must go further in actively promoting development-mindedness, work ethics, social capital, civic values, etc. based on such spirit as voluntarism, ownership and 'harmonious change'. Although they are diverse, so we should always heed the call not to treat them as interchangeable, Sub-Saharan African countries can indeed all achieve successful economic transformation, under the present circumstances, should they espouse the key principles of development. And a more prosperous and stable Africa will be good for everybody and for the whole world.

In addition, the political stability and security that Africa's economic success will enhance will also greatly contribute to international peace and security. The best way to deal with the problem of refugees, illegal immigrants and modern-day slaves from Africa pouring into Europe and other parts of the world is by making Africa stable and prosperous. Hence, the global community should be more open-minded in its objectives and approach, and should work more in unison.

In this book, I have tried to make the case that a different approach is necessary for development in Sub-Saharan Africa. In laying out some ideas for 'reinventing Africa's development', I did not jump to the main points, but reviewed Africa's journey and its problems, the root causes of its underdevelopment; I then elaborated on South Korea's development model and experiences, and introduced relevant projects undertaken in Uganda as a main reference.

Certainly, there is room for improvement, and more cases in African countries could have been reviewed. While admitting limitations, I will leave the task to be further pursued in the near future. In any case, this endeavour was a challenging task, and my objective was to highlight the significance of the 'missing links' in Africa's development, and to bring the focus back to the 'basics' of social, economic and political development that the South Korean case very forcefully demonstrates. The grand theme of reinventing Africa's development is 'mindset change', and under this proposition, I have attempted to link Africa's development to the Korean model of development, highlighting the mindset change approach and focusing on Korea's ingredients of success that are applicable to Africa. In order to do so, I had to newly construct the conceptual model of Korea's development to make sense of Korea's experience by accommodating socio-political alongside economic factors. The results are the derivation of a set of policy implications and recommendations for Africa.

Let me end by citing Nelson Mandela: 'The first thing is to be honest with yourself. You can never have an impact on society if you have not changed yourself.' These priceless words are displayed for everyone to see in Johannesburg's Apartheid Museum.

Notes

1. 'Dualistic Theories', *Theories of Underdevelopment*, http://economicsconcepts.com/dualistic_theories.htm. See also Sanket Suman, 'Social Dualism: Meaning, Characteristics and Critical Appraisal', *Economics Discussion*, http://www.economicsdiscussion.net.
2. Ibid.
3. Douglas Gollin, 'The Lewis Model: A 60-Year Retrospective', *Journal of Economic Perspectives* 28, no. 3 (Summer 2014), pp. 71–88.
4. Rwandan President Paul Kagame's speech delivered to a delegation from St Andrew's University in March 2015, quoted from the article 'Rwanda's Homegrown Solutions: Nation Harnesses Its Traditions for Success Today', *The Independent* (Uganda), supplement section, 23–29 December 2016.
5. Professor Anastase Shyaka, CEO of the Rwanda Governance Board, was elaborating on the Homegrown Solutions (quoted from the above article in *The Independent*).
6. Rwanda Governance Board, http://www.rgb.rw/index.php?id=134.
7. Social Enterprise Alliance, https://socialenterprise.us/about/social-enterprise; BC Centre for Social Enterprise, http://www.centreforsocialenterprise.com/what-is-social-enterprise.
8. 'World Bank Reveals a Weakening of Policy and Institutional Performance in Africa', World Bank press release, 24 July 2017.

9. 'Weakening of State Institutions "Boosts Private Sector Corruption"', *Business Day*, 27 July 2017, https://www.businesslive.co.za/bd/national/2017-07-27-weakening-of-state-institutions-boosts-private–sector-corruption.
10. See http://www.satyagraha.org.za/word/the-moral-regeneration-movement, http://mrm.org.za/about-us/history.
11. Sung-Hee Jwa, *The Rise and Fall of Korea's Economic Development: Lessons for Developing and Developed Economies* (London: Palgrave Pivot, 2017), p. 132.

Bibliography

Acemoglu, Daron, and James Robinson. 2012. *Why Nations Fail*. New York: Crown Business.

Acemoglu, Daron, and James Robinson. 2014. 'Why Foreign Aid Fails—And How to Really Help Africa.' *The Spectator*, 25 January. http://www.spectator.co.uk/2014/01/why-aid-fails/.

Acemoglu, Daron, Simon Johnson, and James Robinson. 2001. 'The Colonial Origins of Comparative Development: An Empirical Investigation.' *American Economic Review* 91(5): 1369–1401.

Adejo, Armstrong. 2001. 'From OAU to AU: New Wine in Old Bottles?' *African Journal of International Affairs* 4(1–2): 119–141.

Adejumobi, Said. 2001. 'Citizenship, Rights, and the Problem of Conflict and Civil Wars in Africa.' *Human Rights Quarterly* 23(1): 103–170.

Adelman, Irma. 2000. 'The Role of Government in Economic Development.' In Finn Tarp (ed.), *Foreign Aid and Development-Lessons Learnt and Directions for the Future*. London: Routledge.

Africa Development Bank, OECD Development Centre, UNDP. 2007. *African Economic Outlook 2017, Special Theme: Entrepreneurship and Industrialization*. Paris: OECD Publishing.

Africa Progress Panel. 2012. *Africa Progress Report 2012: Jobs, Justice and Equality: Seizing Opportunities in Times of Global Change*. Geneva: Africa Progress Panel.

J.-D. Park, *Re-Inventing Africa's Development*,
https://doi.org/10.1007/978-3-030-03946-2

African Union. 2011. New Partnership for Africa's Development. *African Peer Review Mechanism*. Midrand, South Africa: NEPAD Secretariat.

Aghion, Philippe. 2012. 'Industrial Policy, Entrepreneurship, and Growth.' In David Audretsch, Oliver Falck, Stephan Heblich, and Adam Lederer (eds), *Handbook of Research on Innovation and Entrepreneurship*. Cheltenham: Edward Elgar, 45–54.

Aiginger, Karl. 2007. 'Industrial Policy: Past Diversity and Future; Introduction to the Special Issue on the Future of Industrial Policy.' *Journal of Industry, Competition and Trade* 7(3&4): 143–146.

Ajakaiye, Olu. 2007. 'Levelling the Playing Field: Strengthening the Role of African Research in Policy Making in and for Sub-Saharan Africa.' In Elian T. Ayuk and Mohammed Ali Marouani (eds), *The Policy Paradox in Africa: Strengthening Links Between Economic Research and Policy Making*. Trenton, NJ and Ottawa: Africa World Press and International Development Research Centre (IDRC), Chapter 1.

Ajakaiye, Olu, and Afeikhena Jerome. 2014. 'Economic Development.' In Bruce Currie-Alder, Ravi Kanbur, David M. Malone, and Rohinton Medhorae (eds), *International Development-Ideas, Experience, and Prospects*. Oxford: Oxford University Press.

Ake, Claude. 1996. *Democracy and Development in Africa*. Washington, DC: The Brookings Institution.

Akyeampong, Emmanuel, Robert H. Bates, Nathan Nunn, and James A. Robinson (eds). 2014. *Africa's Development in Historical Perspective*. New York: Cambridge University Press.

Alden, Chris. 2007. *China in Africa*. London: Zed Books.

Alemazung, Asongazoh. 2011. 'Leadership Flaws and Fallibilities Impacting Democratization Processes, Governance and Functional Statehood in Africa.' *African Journal of Political Science and International Relations* 5(1) (January): 30–41.

Alesina, Alberto, and David Dollar. 2000. 'Who Gives Foreign Aid to Whom and Why?' *Journal of Economic Growth* 5(1): 33–63.

Amsden, Alice H. 1989. *Asia's Next Giant: South Korea and Late Industrialization*. New York and Oxford: Oxford University Press.

———. 2001. *The Rise of the Rest: Challenges to the West from Late-Industrializing Economies*. Oxford: Oxford University Press.

Andrews, Matt. 2008. 'The Good Governance Agenda: Beyond Indicators Without Theory.' *Oxford Development Studies* 36(3): 379–407.

———. 2013. *The Limits of Institutional Reform in Development*. New York: Cambridge University Press.

Annen, Kurt, and Luc Moers. 2012. 'Donor Competition for Aid Impact, and Aid Fragmentation.' IMF Working Paper (WP/12/204), August.

Ansoms, An. 2009. 'Re-engineering Rural Society: The Visions and Ambitions of the Rwandan Elite.' *Foreign Affairs* 108(431): 289–309.

Arndt, Channing, Sam Jones, and Finn Tarp. 2009. 'Who Gives Foreign Aid to Whom and Why?' *Journal of Economic Growth* 5(1): 33–63.

Aryeetey, Ernest, Julius Court, Machiko Nissanke, and Beatrice Weber (eds). 2003. *Africa and Asia in the Global Economy*. Tokyo: United Nations Press.

Asia Development Bank. 2014. *Global Partnership for Effective Economic Development- What It Means for ADB*. Manila: ADB. https://www.adb.org/sites/default/files/publication/42585/global–partnership-effective-development-cooperation.pdf.

Austin, Gareth. 2008. 'The "Reversal of Fortune" Thesis and the Compression of History: Perspective from African and Comparative Economic History.' *Journal of International Development* 20(8): 996–1027.

———. 2013. 'African Economic Development and Colonial Legacies.' In Pierre Englebert and Kevin C. Dunn (eds), *Inside African Politics*. Boulder: Lynne Rienner.

Auty, Richard M. 1999. *Sustaining Development in Mineral Economics: The Resource Curse Thesis*. London and New York: Routledge.

Ayodele, Thompson, Franklin Cudjoe, Temba Nolutshungu, and Charle Sunawabe. 2005. 'African Perspective on Aid: Foreign Assistance Will Not Pull Africa Out of Poverty.' *Cato Institute Economic Development Bulletin*, No. 2, 14 September, p. 1. https://object.cato.org/sites/cato.org/files/pubs/pdf/edb2.pdf.

Azarya, Victor. 1994. 'Civil Society and Disengagement in Africa.' In John Harbeson, Donald Rothchild, and Naomi Chazan (eds), *Civil Society and the State in Africa*. Boulder: Lynne, 83–101.

Bach, Daniel C., and Mamoudou Gazibo (eds). 2012. *Neopatrimonialism in Africa and Beyond*. New York: Routledge.

Badie, Bertrand. 1992. *L'État importé: l'occidentalisation de l'ordre politique*. Paris: Fayard.

Baek, Suk-ki. 2007. *Koreans' Success DNA*. Seoul: Maekyung Publications.

Bailey, Tom. 2016. 'Africa Comes to the End of Its Commodities Boom.' *World Finance*, 15 March.

Baldwin, David. 1989. *Paradoxes of Power*. New York: Basil Blackwell.

———. 1993. *Neorealism and Neoliberalism*. New York: Columbia University Press.

Barkey, Karen, and Sunita Karen. 1991. 'Comparative Perspectives on the State.' *Annual Review of Sociology* 17: 523–549.

Barnett, Michael, and Martha Finnemore. 2004. *Rules for the World: International Organization in Global Politics*. Ithaca and London: Cornell University Press.

Belle, Douglas A. Van, and Jean-Sebastien Rioux, et al. 2004. *Media, Bureaucracies and Foreign Aid: A Comparative Analysis of the United States, the United Kingdom, Canada, France and Japan*. New York: Palgrave Macmillan.

Berendsen, Bernard, Ton Dietz, Henk Schulte Northolt, and Roel van der Veen (eds). 2013. *Asian Tigers, African Lions: Comparing the Development Performance of Southeast Asia and Africa*. Leiden: Brill.

Berenskoetter, Felix, and M.J. Williams (eds). 2007. *Power in World Politics*. London and New York: Routledge.

Berman, John. 2013. *Success in Africa: CEO Insights from a Continent of the Rise*. Brookline: Bibliomotion.

Bertucci, Guido, and Adriana Alberti. 2001. 'Globalization and the Role of the State: Challenges and Perspective.' United Nations World Public Sector Report.

Bezemer, Dirk, and Derek Headey. 2008. 'Agriculture, Development, and Urban Bias.' *World Development* 36(8): 1342–1364.

Bhorat, H., R. Kanbur, C. Rooney, and F. Steenkamp. 2017. 'Sub-Saharan Africa's Manufacturing Sector: Building Complexity.' Working Paper Series No. 256, May. African Development Bank.

Bierwith, Chris. 2011. 'The Lebanese Communities of Cote d'Ivoire.' *African Affairs* 98(290): 79–99.

Bjorkman, Martina, and Jakob Svensson. 2009. 'Power to the People: Evidence from a Randomized Field Experiment of a Community-based Monitoring Project in Uganda.' *Quarterly Journal of Economics* 124(2): 735–769.

Blatt, Daniel. 2004. 'Book Review-Soft Power by Joseph Nye.' *FUTURECAST Online Magazine* 6(9), 1 September.

Bloom, David E., and Jeffrey D. Sachs. 1998. 'Geography, Demography, and Economic Growth in Africa.' *Brookings Papers on Economic Activity* 2: 207–273.

Blyth, M. 2002. *Great Transformations*. Cambridge: Cambridge University Press.

Booth, Anne. 1999. 'Initial Conditions and Miraculous Growth: Why Is South East Asia Different from Taiwan and South Korea?' *World Development* 27(2): 301–321.

Booth, David. 2012. *Development as a Collective Action Problem: Addressing the Real Challenges of African Governance*. London: Overseas Development Institute.

Booth, David, and Diana Gammack. 2013. *Governance for Development in Africa*. London: Zed Books.

Booth, David, and Frederick Golooba-Mutebi. 2011. 'Developmental Patrimonialism? The Case of Rwanda.' African Power and Politics Program Working Paper 16. London: Overseas Development Institute.

Bosker, E. Martin, and Harry Garretsen. 2008. 'Economic Geography and Economic Development in Sub-Saharan Africa.' CESifo Working Paper 2490. Munich: Centre for Economic Studies/ifo Institute.

Bovard, James. 1986. 'The Continuing Failure of Foreign Aid.' CATO Institute Policy Analysis No. 65, 31 January.

Bratton, Michael, and Nicolas van de Walle. 1997. *Democratic Experiments in Africa: Regime Transitions in Comparative Perspective*. Cambridge: Cambridge University Press.

Brautigam, Deborah. 1995. 'The State as an Agent: Industrial Development in Taiwan, 1957–1972.' In Howard Stein (ed.), *Asian Industrialization and Africa*. New York: St. Martin's Press, 145–181.

———. 2001. *Aid Dependence and Governance* (Expert Group on Development Issues 2000, 1). Stockholm: Almquiest & Wiksell Intl.

———. 2005. 'Local Entrepreneurship in Southeast Asia and Sub-Saharan Africa: Networks and Linkages to the Global Economy.' In Ernest Aryeetey, Julius Court, Machiko Nissanke, and Beatrice Weber (eds), *Africa and Asia in the Global Economy*. Tokyo: United Nations University Press, 106–127.

———. 2009. *The Dragon's Gift: The Real Story of China in Africa*. Oxford: Oxford University Press.

Buchanan, James M. 1975, 'The Samaritan's Dilemma.' In E.S. Phelps (ed.), *Altruism, Morality and Economic Theory*. New York: Russell Sage Foundation.

Bukenya, Badru, Sam Hickey, and Sophie King. 2012. 'Making Schools Work: New Evidence on Accountability Interventions: Towards and Evidence-Based Approach.' Report Commissioned by the World Bank's Social Accountability and Demand for Good Governance Team, June.

Burnside, Craig, and David Dollar. 2000. 'Aid, Growth, the Incentive Regime and Poverty Reduction.' In Christopher L. Gilbert and David Vines (eds), *The World Bank Structure and Policies*. Cambridge: Cambridge University Press.

Callaghy, Thomas. 1988. 'The State and the Development of Capitalism in Africa: Theoretical, Historical, and Comparative Reflections.' In Donald Rothschild (ed.), *The Precarious Balance*. Boulder: Westview, 67–99.

Car mody, Padraig. 2010. *Globalization in Africa: Recolonization or Renaissance?* Boulder: Lynne Rienner.

Carothers, T., and D. de Gramont. 2013. *Development Aid Confronts Politics: The Almost Revolution*. Washington, DC: Carnegie Endowment.

Chabal, Patrick. 2009. *Africa: The Politics of Suffering and Smiling*. London: Zed Books.

Chabal, Patrick, and Jean-Pascal Daloz. 1999. *Africa Works: Disorder as Political Instrument*. Oxford: James Currey.

Chambers, Robert, et al. 2001. 'The New Dynamics of Aid: Power, Procedures and Relationships.' IDS Policy Briefing Issue 11, August.

Chang, Ha Joon. 2002. *Globalisation, Economic Development & the Role of the State*. London: Zed Books.

———. 2003. *Kicking Away the Ladder: Development Strategy in Historical Perspective*. London: Anthem Press.

———. 2007. *The East Asian Development Experience*. London: Zed Books.

———. 2008. *Bad Samaritans: The Myth of Free Trade and the Secret History of Capitalism*. New York: Bloomsbury Press.

———. 2010. *23 Things They Don't Tell You About Capitalism*. London: Penguin Books.

———. 2016. 'Transformative Industrial Policy for Africa: Put Manufacturing at the Centre of Development.' A lecture at the Second Annual Adebayo Adedeji Lecture, 3 April 2016, Addids Abbaba. Provided by UNECA.

Chase, Susan, and Elisa Wilkinson. 2015. 'What Happened to Integrated Rural Development?' *The Hunger Project*, 10 August.

Chege, Michael. 1995. 'Sub-Saharan Africa: Underdevelopment's Last Stand.' In Barbara Stallings (ed.), *Global Change, Regional Response: The New International Context of Development*. Cambridge: Cambridge University Press, 309–348.

Choi, Hae-Suk. 2006. *Study of Canaan Farmers School from the Perspective of Life Time Education*. Seoul: Ajou University (Korean).

Choi, Joon-Kyung. 2013. *Upside-Down Success Story of Korea's Economic Development*. Seoul: Daewon Publishing. Translated by Christy Hyun-Joo Lee.

Choi, Sung-Ho. 2016. 'The Future Path of Korea-Africa Partnership in Development Cooperation.' A paper presented at the International Conference on Korea-Africa Partnership II hosted by Korea-Africa Center and MOFA, 22 September 2016, Plaza Hotel, Seoul.

Cilliers, Jakkie. 2018. 'Made in Africa-Manufacturing and the Fourth Industrial Revolution.' *Africa in the World Report 8*, Institute for Security Studies, April.

Clarence-Smithm, William G. 2014. 'The Textile Industry of Eastern Africa in the Long Duree.' In Emmanuel Akyeampong, Robert H. Bates, Nathan Nunn, and James A. Robinson (eds), *Africa's Development in Historical Perspective*. New York: Cambridge University Press.

Clarke, Ian. 2010. *How Deep Is This Pothole?* London: New Wine Press.

Collier, Paul. 2000. 'Ethnicity, Politics and Economic Performance.' *Economics and Politics* 12(3) (November): 225–245.

———. 2001. 'Implications of Ethnic Diversity.' World Bank Working Paper Report No. 28127, vol. 1, December 17. World Bank, 1–55.

———. 2006. 'Is Aid Oil?' An Analysis of Whether Africa Can Absorb More Aid.' *World Development* 34(9): 1482–1497.

———. 2007. *The Bottom Billion: Why the Poorest Countries Are Failing and What Can Be Done About It*. New York: Oxford University Press.

———. 2010. *The Plundered Planet*. Oxford: Oxford University Press.

Collier, Paul, and Jan Willem Gunning. 2008. 'Sacrificing the Future: Intertemporal Strategies and Their Implications for Growth.' In Benno J. Ndulu, Stephen A. O'Connell, Robert H. Bates, Paul Collier, and Chukwuma C. Solubo (eds), *The Politcal Economy of Growth in Africa 1960–2000*, vol. 1. Cambridge: Cambridge University Press, 202–224.

Collins, Robert O., and James M. Burns. 2014. *A History of Sub-Saharan* Africa, 2nd ed. New York: Cambridge University Press.

Committee for International Development Cooperation (ROK). 2014. *2014 Korea's Official Development Assistance White Paper*. Seoul: CIDC.

———. 2017a. *2017 Korea's Official Development Assistance White Paper*. Seoul: CIDC (Korean).

———. 2017b. *A Time Traveller's Guide to South Africa in 2030*. Cape Town: Tafelberg.

Cronje, Francis. 2014. *A Time Traveller's Guide to Our Next Ten Years*. Cape Town: Tafelberg.

Currie-Alder, Bruce, Ravi Kanbur, David M. Malone, and Rohinton Medhora (eds). 2014. *International Development-Ideas, Experience, and Prospects*. Oxford: Oxford University Press.

Dasgupta, Dipak. 1998. 'Poverty Reduction in Indonesia.' In Henry S. Rowen (ed.). *Behind East Asian Growth: The Political and Social Foundations of Prosperity*. London: Routledge, 209–233.

Davidson, Basil. 1992. *The Black Man's Burden: Africa and the Curse of the Nation-State*. New York: Times Books.

Davis, Diane E. 2004. *Discipline and Development: Middle Class and Prosperity in East Asia and Latin America*. Cambridge: Cambridge University Press.

Davis, Melissa. 2007. 'Is Africa Misbranded?' *Brand Channel*, 13 August. http://www.brandchannel.com.

Debrah, Isaac Ofosu, Thomas Yeboah, and James Boafo. 2015. 'Development for Whom? Emerging Donors and Africa's Future.' *African Journal of Economic and Sustainable Development* 4(4): 308–328.

Degen, Robert A. 2011. *The Triumph of Capitalism*. New Brunswick: Transaction Publishers.

Degnbol-Martinussen, John, and Poul Engberg-Pedersen. 2005. *AID-Understanding International Development Cooperation*. London: Zed Books. Translated by Marie Bille.

DeGrassi, Aaron. 2008. 'Neopatrimonialism and Agricultural Development in Africa: Contributions and Limitations of a Contested Concept.' *African Studies Review* 51(3): 107–133.

Deutscher, Eckhard, and Sara Fyson. 2008. 'Improving the Effectiveness of Aid.' *Finance & Development, IMF* 45(3) (September): 15–19.

Devarajan, Shantayanan, Stuti Khemani, and Michael Walton. 2011. 'Civil Society, Public Action and Accountability in Africa.' World Bank Policy Research Working Paper 5733. Washington, DC: World Bank.

Diamond, Jared. 2006. *Collapse: How Societies Choose to Fail or Survive*. London: Penguin.

Dinh, Hinh, Vincent Palmade, Vandana Chandra, and Frances Cossar. 2012. *Light Manufacturing in Africa*. Washington, DC: Agence Francaise de Development and World Bank.

Djankov, Simeon, José García Montalvo, and Marta Reynal-Querol. 2008. 'The Curse of Aid.' *Journal of Economic Growth* 13:169–194, the World Bank.

Donor, Richard F., Bryan K. Ritchie, and Dan Slater. 2005. 'Systemic Vulnerability and the Origins of Developmental States: Northeast and Southeast Asia in Comparative Perspective.' *International Organization* 59(2): 327–361.

Doran, Charles F. 2000. 'Globalization and Statecraft.' *SAISphere* (Winter). Paul H. Nitze School of Advanced International Studies.

Dorward, Andrew, Jonathan Kydd, Jamie Morrison, and Ian Urey. 2004. 'A Policy Agenda for Pro-Poor Agricultural Growth.' *World Development* 32(1): 73–89.

Drezner, Dan. 2007. 'Persistent Power of State in the Global Economy,' 7 June. economistview.typepad.com.

Easterly, William. 2001. *The Elusive Quest for Growth-Economists' Adventures and Misadventures in the Tropics*. Cambridge: MIT Press.

———. 2006. *The White Man's Burden: Why the West's Efforts to Aid the Rest Have Done So Much Ill and So Little Good*. New York: Oxford University Press.

———. 2013. *The Tyranny of Experts: Economists, Dictators, and the Forgotten Rights of the Poor*. New York: Basic Books.

The Economist. 2000. 'The Hopeless Continent,' 11 May.

———. 2011. 'Africa Rising: The Hopeful Continent,' 3 December.

EDCF. 2016. *EDCF Annual Report*. Korea EXIM Bank.

Edwards, Sebastian. 2014. 'Economic Development and the Effectiveness of Foreign Aid: A Historical Perspective.' *VOX, CEPR's Policy Portal*, 28 November.

Eisenstadt, Samuel. 1973. *Traditional Patrimonialism and Modern Neo-Patrimonialism*. Beverly Hills: Sage.

Elbadaw, Ibrahim A., Benno J. Ndulu, and Njuguna S. Ndung'u. 2003. 'Macroeconomic Performance in Sub-Saharan Africa in a Comparative Setting.' In Machiko Nissanke and Ernest Aryeetey (eds), *Comparative Development Experiences of Sub-Saharan Africa and East Asia*. Aldershot: Ashgate, 72–112.

Ellis, Stephen. 2005. 'How to Rebuild Africa.' *Foreign Affairs* 84(5): 135–148.

Englebert, Pierre. 2000. 'Pre-colonial Institutions, Post-colonial States, and Economic Development in Tropical Africa.' *Political Research Quarterly* 53(1): 7–36.

———. 2009. *Africa: Unity, Sovereignty, Globalization, and Sorrow*. Boulder: Lynne Rienner.

Englebert, Pierre, and Kevin C. Dunn. 2013. *Inside African Politics*. Boulder: Lynne Rienner.

Erdmann, Gero, and Ulf Engel. 2007. 'Neopatrimonialism Reconsidered: Critical Review and Elaboration of an Elusive Concept.' *Commonwealth and Comparative Politics* 45(1): 5–119.

Evans, Peter B. 1996. *Embedded Autonomy: States and Industrial Transformation*. Princeton: Princeton University Press.

———. 1999. 'Transferable Lessons? Re-examining the Institutional Prerequisite of East Asian Economic Policies.' In Yilmaz Akÿuz (ed.), *East Asian Development: New Perspectives*. London: Frank Cass.

Evans, Peter B., and Patrick Heller. 2012. 'Human Development, State Transformation and the Politics of Development State.' In Stephan Leibfried, Frank Nullmeier, Evelyn Huber, Matthew Lange, Jonah Levy, and John D. Stephens (eds), *The Oxford Handbook of Transformations of the State*. Oxford: Oxford University Press.

Fan, Shenggen (ed.). 2008. *Public Expenditures, Growth, and Poverty: Lessons from Developing Countries*. Baltimore: Johns Hopkins University Press.

Fatton, Robert. 1992. *Predatory Rule: State and Civil Society in Africa*. Boulder, CO: Lynne Rienner.

Fieldhouse, David K. 1983. *Colonialism, 1870–1945: An Introduction*. New York: St. Martin's Press.

Fishlow, Albert. 2012. 'Review Essay on Gerschenkron's *Economic Backwardness in Historical Perspective*.' *The Economic History Network*. www.eh.net/node/276, accessed March 2012.

Frank, André Gunder. 1998. *ReOrient: Global Economy in the Asian Age*. Berkeley: University of California Press.

Friedman, George. 2013. 'The PC 16: Identifying China's Successors.' *Stratfor World View on Geopolitics*, 30 July. https://www.stratfor.com/weekly/pc16-identifying-chinas-successors.

Friedman, Thomas L. 2006. 'The New System.' In Joel Krieger (ed.), *Globalization and State Power*. New York: Pearson Longman.

Fritz, Verna, Brian Levy, and Rachel Ort (eds). 2014. *Problem Driven Political Economy Analysis: The World Bank Experience*. Washington, DC: World Bank.

Fukuyama, Francis. 2004. *Statebuilding*. Ithaca: Cornell University Press.

———. 2012. *The Origins of Political Order*. New York: Farrar, Straus and Giroux.

Fyle, C. Magbaily. 2002. 'Indigenous Values and the Organization of Informal Sector Business in West Africa.' In Allusine Jalloh and Toyin Falola (ed.), *Black Businesses and Economic Power*. Rochester, NY: University of Rochester Press, 29–40.

Gallup, John Luke, Jeffrey D. Sachs, and Andrew D. Mellinger. 1998. 'Geography and Economic Development.' NBER Working Paper 6849. Cambridge, MA: National Bureau of Economic Research.

Gelb, Stephen. 2005. 'South-South Investment: The Case of Africa.' In *Africa in the World Economy: The National, Regional and International Challenges*. Hague: Fondad. http://www.fondad.org.

Gemandze, GeBobuin John. 2006. 'Transcending the Impasse: Rethinking the State' and "Development" in Africa.' *African Journal of International Affairs* 9(1): 75–90.

Gennaioli, Nicola, and Ilia Rainer. 2007. 'The Modern Impact of Precolonial Centralization in Africa.' *Journal of Economic Growth* 12: 185–234.

Gerschenkron, Alexander. 1962. *Economic Backwardness in Historical Perspective: A Book of Essays*. Cambridge, MA: Belknap Press.

Geschiere, Peter, and Josef Gugler. 1998. 'The Urban-rural Connection: Changing Issues of Belonging and Identification.' *Africa: Journal of the International African Institute* 68(3): 309–319.

Gibbon, Peter. 2002. 'Present-day Capitalism, the New International Trade Regime and Africa.' *Review of African Political Economy* 29(91): 95–112.

Goldin, Ian, and Kenneth A. Reinert. 2007. *Globalization for Development*. New York: World Bank Publications.

Goldman, Michael. 2005. *Imperial Nature: The World Bank and Struggles for Social Justice in the Age of Globalization*. New Haven and London: Yale University Press.

Gollin, Douglas. 2014. 'The Lewis Model: A 60-Year Retrospective.' *Journal of Economic Perspectives* 28(3) (Summer): 71–88.

Gong, Byeong Ho. 2016. *There Is No Korea After 3 Years*. Seoul: Ishipilsegibooks (Korean).

Green, Elliot. 2010. 'Patronage, District Creation, and Reform in Uganda.' *Studies in International Comparative Development* 45(1): 83–103.

———. 2012. 'On the Size and Shape of African States.' *International Studies Quarterly* 56(2) (June): 229–244.

Grief, Avner. 2005. *Institutions and the Path to the Modern Economy*. New York: Cambridge University Press.

Grindle, Merilee. 2004. 'Good Enough Governance: Poverty Reduction and Reform in Developing Countries.' *Governance* 17(4): 525–548.

Gruzd, Steven, and Yarik Turainskyi (eds). 2015. *African Accountability: What Works and What Doesn't*. Johannesburg: SAIIA.

Gyimah-Brempong, Kwabena. 2002. 'Corruption, Economic Growth, and Income Inequality in Africa.' *Economics of Governance* 3:183–209.

Haggard, Stephen, Andrew MacIntyre, and Lydia Tiede. 2008. 'The Rule of Law and Economic Development.' *Annual Review of Political Science* 11: 205–234.

Hahn, Chin Hee, and Shin Sukha. 2010. 'Understanding the Post-crisis Growth of the Korean Economy: Growth Accounting and Cross-country Regressions.' In Takatoshi Ito and Chin Hee Hahn (eds), *The Rise of Asia and Structural Changes in Korea and Asia*. Cheltenham: Edward Elgar, 97–110.

Hanson, Stephanie. 2009. 'Corruption in Sub-Saharan Africa' for the Council on Foreign Relations, 6 August.

Hardt, Michael, and Antonio Negri. 2000. *Empire*. Cambridge: Harvard University Press.

Harris, John. 2014. 'Development Theories.' In Bruce Currie-Alder, Ravi Kanbur, David M. Malone, and Rohinton Medhora (eds), *International Development-Ideas, Experience, and Prospects*. Oxford: Oxford University Press.

Headrick, Daniel R. 1981. *The Tools of Empire: Technology and European Imperialism in the Nineteenth Century*. New York: Oxford University Press.

Henley, David. 2012. 'Agrarian Roots of Industrial Growth: Rural Development in South-east Asia and Sub-Saharan Africa.' *Development Policy Review* 30(S1): 25–47.

———. 2015. *Asia-Pacific Development Divergence—A Question of Intent*. London: Zed Books.

Henley, David, and Ahmad Helm Fuady. 2014. 'Sources of Developmental Ambition in Southeast Asia and Sub-Saharan Africa.' *Developmental Regimes in Africa*—A Joint Initiative Between *Africa Power and Politics* (APPP) and *Tracking Development*—Policy Brief No. 4, January.

Henderson, Jeffrey, David Hume, Richard Philips, and Eun Mee Kim. 2002. 'Economic Governance and Poverty Reduction in South Korea.' *Globalization and Poverty Report to the DFID*. London: Department for International Development.

Hope, Kempe Ronald. 2002. 'From Crisis to Renewal: Towards a Successful Implementation of the New Partnership for Africa's Development.' *African Affairs* 101: 387–402.

———. 2017. *Corruption and Governance in Africa: Swaziland, Kenya, Nigeria*. Cham: Palgrave Macmillan.

Hubbard, Paul. 2007. 'Putting the Power of Transparency in Context: Information's Role in Reducing Corruption in Uganda's Education Sector.' Center for Global Development Working Paper 136. Washington, DC: Center for Global Development.

Hyden, Goran. 1980. *Beyond Ujamaa in Tanzania: Underdevelopment and Uncaptured Peasantry*. Berkeley: University of California Press.

———. 1983. *No Shortcuts to Progress: African Development Management in Perspective*. London: Heinemann.

Ingelhart, Ronald. 1997. *Modernization and Postmodernization: Cultural, Economic, and Political Change in 43 Societies*. Princeton: Princeton University Press.

Ingelhart, Ronald, and Christian Welzel. 2005. *Modernization, Cultural Change, and Democracy: The Human Development Sequence*. New York: Cambridge University Press.

International Monetary Fund. 2017. *Regional Economic Outlook—Sub-Saharan Africa Restarting the Growth Engine*. Washington, DC: IMF (April).

Jackson, Robert. 1985. 'The Marginality of African States.' In Gwendolen Carter and Patrick O'Meara (eds), *African Independence: The First Twenty-Five Years*. Bloomington: Indiana University Press, 45–70.

Jacobs, Norman. 1985. *The Korean Road to Modernization and Development*. Urbana and Chicago: University of Illinois Press.

Jager, Sheila Miyoshi. 2003. *Narratives of Nation Building in Korea: A Genealogy of Patriotism*. Armonk, NY: M.E. Sharp.

Jeong, U-jin. 2010. 'Successful Asian Recipient Countries: Case Studies of Korea and Vietnam.' *International Development Cooperation, KOICA* (March).

Joh, Jung Jay, Young-Pyo Kim, and Youngsun Koh. 2010. 'Territorial Development Policy.' In Il Sakong and Youngsun Koh (eds), *The Korean Economy: Six Decades of Growth and Development*. Seoul: Korea Development Institute, 177–224.

Joh, Sung Wook, and Euysung Kim. 2003. 'Corporate Governance and Performance of Korean Firms the 1990s.' In Stephen Haggard, Wonhyuk Lim, and Euysung Kim (eds), *Economic Crisis and Corporate Restructuring in Korea: Reforming the Chaebol*. Cambridge: Cambridge University Press, 102–126.

Johnson, Simon, Jonathan D. Ostry, and Arvind Subramaniam. 2007. 'The Prospects for Sustained Growth in Africa: Benchmarking the Constraints.' IMF Working Paper 07/52. Washington, DC: International Monetary Fund.

Jones, Catherine. 1993. 'The Pacific Challenge: Confucian Welfare States.' In Catherine Jones (ed.), *New Perspectives on the Welfare State in Europe*. London: Routledge, 198–217.

Jones, Leroy P., and Il Sakong. 1980. *Business, Government and Entrepreneurship: The Korean Case*. Cambridge, MA: Harvard University Press.

Jwa, Sung-Hee. 2002. *A New Paradigm for Korea's Economic Development: From Government Control to Market Economy*. New York: Palgrave.

———. 2015a. 'Korean Economic Development and Saemaul Undong: Experience and Lessons.' Presentation paper for Uganda, 8 September.

———. 2015b. 'Success Factors of Saemaul Undong' (Korean). Presentation paper for the Korea Forum for Progress, 1 September.

———. 2016. 'Korea in Crisis Asking Park Chung-Hee for Answers' (Korean). Presentation made at the symposium held by Park Chung-Hee Foundation, 15 June.

———. 2017a. *A General Theory of Economic Development: Towards a Capitalistic Manifesto*. Cheltenham: Edward Elgar.

———. 2017b. *The Rise and Fall of Korea's Economy: Lessons for Development and Developed Economies*. New York: Palgrave Macmillan.

Kagame, Paul. 2009. 'The Backbone of a New Rwanda.' In Michael Fairbanks, Malik Fal, Marcela Escobari-Rose, and Elizabeth Hooper (eds), *In the River They Swim: Essays from Around the World on Enterprise Solutions to Poverty*. West Conschohocken, PA: Templeton Press, 11–14.

Kanbur, Ravi. 2000. 'Aid, Conditionality and Debt in Africa.' In Finn Tarp (ed.), *Foreign Aid and Development-Lessons Learnt and Directions for the Future*. Routledge: London, 409–422.

Kang, David. 2002. *Crony Capitalism: Corruption and Development in South Korea and the Philippines*. New York: Cambridge University Press.

Kang, Seonjou. 2015. 'Adoption of Post–2015 Sustainable Development Goals (SDGs) and Its Implications for Development Cooperation Diplomacy.' *International Analysis*, No. 2015–29, 23 October. Institute of Foreign Affairs and National Security, Republic of Korea (Korean).

Karshenas, Massoud. 1995. *Industrialization and Agricultural Surplus: A Comparative Study of Economic Development in Asia*. Oxford: Oxford University Press.

Kaufmann, Daniel, Aart Kraai, and Massimo Mastruzi. 2010. 'The World Wide Governance Indicators: Methodology and Analytical Issues.' Policy/Research Paper No. 5430, Washington, DC: World Bank.

Keim, Curtis. 2010. *Mistaking Africa: Curiosities and Inventions of the American Mind*, 2nd ed. Boulder: Westview.

Keller, Edmond. 2014. *Identity, Citizenship, and Political Conflict in Africa*. Bloomington: Indiana University Press.

Kelsell, Tim. 2005. 'History, Identity, and Collective Action: Difficulties of Accountability.' In Ulf Engel and Gorm Rye Olsen (eds), *The African Exception*. London: Ashgate, 53–68.

———. 2011. 'Rethinking the Relationship Between Neo-Patrimonialism and Economic Development in Africa.' *IDS Bulletin* 42(2) (2 March): 76–87.

———. 2013. *Business, Politics and the State in Africa*. London: Zed Press.

Kelsell, Tim, and David Booth. 2010. 'Developmental Patrimonialism?' Africa Power and Politics Series, Working Paper. London: Overseas Development Institute.

Khan, Mushtaq H, and Jomo Kwame Sundaram (eds). 2000. *Rents, Rent-seeking and Economic Development: Theory and Evidence in Asia*. Cambridge: Cambridge University Press.

———. 2007. 'Governance, Economic Growth and Development Since the 1960s.' DESA Working Paper 54. New York: United Nations Department of Economic and Social Affairs.

Kharas, Homi. 2014. *'Development Assistance.'* In Bruce Currie-Alder, Ravi Kanbur, David M. Malone, and Rohinton Medhora (eds), *International Development: Ideas, Experience, and Prospects*. Oxford: Oxford University Press, 847–865.

Killick, Tony. 1998. *Aid and the Political Economy of Policy Reform*. London and New York: Routledge.

Kim, Byung-Kook, and Ezra Vogel (eds). 2011. *The Park Chung Hee Era: The Transformation of South Korea*. Cambridge, MA: Harvard University Press.

Kim, Chuk Kyo. 2016. *Korean Economic Development*, 2nd ed. Seoul: Parkyoungsa (Korean).

Kim, Chung-yum. 2006. *From the Poorest Country to an Advanced Country: Thirty Year History of Korean Economic Policy*. Random House Joong-ang (Korean).

Kim, DoHoon, and Youngsun Koh. 2010. 'Korea's Industrial Development.' In Il Sakong and Youngsun Koh (eds), *The Korean Economy—Six Decades of Growth and Development*. Seoul: Korea Development Institute, 83–122.

Kim, Kwang Suk. 2001. *Korea's Industrial and Trade Policies*. Seoul: Institute for Global Economics (Korean).

Kim, Eun Mee, and Ho Kim (eds). 2014. *The South Korean Development Experience: Beyond Aid*. New York: Palgrave Macmillan.

Kim, Kyong Ju. 2006. *The Development of Modern South Korea—State Formation, Capitalist Development and National Identity*. London: Routledge.

Kim Pyung-joo. 1995. 'Financial Institutions and Economic Policies.' In Dong-Se Cha and Kwang Suk Kim (eds), *The Korean Economy 1945–1995: Performance and Vision for 21st Century*. Seoul: Korea Development Institute, 179–254 (Korean).

Kim, Sung-Taek. 2016. 'EDCF's Development Strategy for Africa.' A presentation made at the International Conference on Korea-Africa Partnership II, 22 September, Seoul.

Kimura, Fukunari. 2004. 'New Development Strategies Under Globalization: Foreign Direct Investment and International Commercial Policy in Southeast Asia.' In Akira Kohsaka (ed.), *New Development Strategies: Beyond the Washington Consensus*. Basingstoke: Palgrave Macmillan, 115–133.

Kohli, Atul. 2004. *State-Directed Development: Political Power and Industrialization in the Global Periphery*. New York: Cambridge University Press.

KOICA. 2014. *Opening a New Era of Happiness for All Humanity*. 2014 Korea's Official Development Assistance White Paper. Committee for International Development Cooperation, Republic of Korea.

KOICA. 2015. 'Korea's ODA for Africa-Current Status and Tasks.' KOICA's presentation paper, 22 September.

Krugman, Paul. 1999. *Geography and Trade*. Cambridge, MA: MIT Press.

Kyle, Jordan. 2017. 'Perspectives on the Role of the State in Economic Development—Taking Stock of the "Developmental State" After 35 Years.' *IFPRI Discussion Paper* 01597, January.

Labelle, Huguette. 2014. 'Corruption'. In Bruce Currie-Alder, Ravi Kanbur, David M. Malone, and Rohinton Medhora (eds), *International Development-Ideas, Experience, and Prospects*. Oxford: Oxford University Press, 239–255.

Lancaster, Carol. 2007. *Foreign Aid: Diplomacy, Development, Domestic Politics*. London: University of Chicago Press.

Lawrence, Peter, and Colin Thirtie (eds). 2001. *Africa and Asia in Comparative Economic Perspective*. Basingstoke: Palgrave.

Lee, Dae Geun. 2002. *Korean Economy in the Post War 1950s*. Seoul: Samsung Economic Institute (Korean).

Lee, Jaewoo. 2014. 'The Effect of Aid Allocation: An Econometric Analysis of Grant Aid and Concessional Loans to South Korea, 1953–1978.' In Eun Mee Kim and Pil Ho Kim (eds), *The South Korean Development Experience—Beyond Aid*. New York: Palgrave Macmillan, 26–46.

Lee, Je-min. 2001. 'Korea's Industrialization and the Industrialization Policy.' In Byeong-jik Ahn (ed.), *The Korean Economic History: A Preliminary Study*. Seoul: Seoul National University Press (Korean), 483–524.

Lee, Keun. 2016. *Economic Catch-up and Technological Leapfrogging—The Path to Development and Macroeconomic Stability in Korea*. Cheltenham: Edward Elgar.

Lee, Sang-cheol. 2005. 'Switching to an Export-led Industrialization Strategy and Its Outcome.' In Dae-geun Lee (ed.), *New Korean Economic History:*

From the Late Joseon Period to the High-Growth Period of the 20th Century. Seoul, Na-nam (Korean), 377–401.

Levinsohn, Jim. 2003. 'The World Bank's Poverty Reduction Strategy Paper Approach: Good Marketing or Good Policy?' G–24 Discussion Paper Series 21, April. UNCTAD.

Levitsky, Steven, and Lucan Way. 2010. *Competitive Authoritarianism*. New York: Cambridge University Press.

Levy, Brian. 2007. *Governance Reform: Bridging Monitoring and Action*. Washington, DC: World Bank.

———. 2010. 'Democracy Support and Development Aid: The Case for Principled Agnosticism.' *Journal of Democracy* 21(4): 27–34.

———. 2014. *Working with the Grain—Integrating Governance and Growth in Development Strategies*. New York: Oxford University Press.

Levy, Brian, and Francis Fukuyama. 2010. 'Development Strategies: Bridging Governance and Growth.' World Bank Policy Research Working Paper 5196. Washington, DC: World Bank.

Levy, Brian, and Sahr Kpundeh. 2004. *Building State Capacity in Africa*. World Bank Institute Development Studies. Washington, DC: World Bank.

Lewis, W. Arthur. 1954. 'Economic Development with Unlimited Supplies of Labour.' *The Manchester School* 22: 139–191.

Lim, Justin Yifu. 2011. 'New Structural Economics: A Framework for Rethinking Development.' *World Bank Research Observer* 26(2) (July): 193–221.

Lim, Philip Wonhyuk. 2001. 'The Evolution of Korea's Development Paradigm: Old Legacies and Emerging Trends in the Post-crisis Era.' ADB Institute Working Paper No. 21, July.

Lindauer, David L., and Michael Roemer (eds). 1994. *Asia and Africa: Legacies and Opportunities in Development*. California: Institute for Contemporary Studies Press.

Lipton, Michael. 1977. *Why Poor People Stay Poor: A Study of Urban Bias in World Development*. London: Temple Smith.

———. 2010. *Land Reform in Developing Countries: Property Rights and Property Wrongs*. London and New York: Routledge.

Losch, Bruno. 2012. *Agriculture: The Key to the Employment Challenge*. Development Strategies Perspective 19, October, Paris: CIRAD Agricultural Research for Development.

Mamdani, Mahmood. 1996. *Citizen and Subject: Contemporary Africa and the Legacy of Late Colonialism*. Princeton: Princeton University Press.

———. 2001. 'Beyond Settler and Native as Political Identities: Overcoming the Political Legacy of Colonialism.' *Comparative Studies in Society and History* 43(4): 651–664.

———. 2012. *Define and Rule: Native as Political Identity* (The W. E. B. Du Bois Lectures Book 12). Cambridge, MA: Harvard University Press.

Marks, Robert B. 2006. *The Origins of the Modern World*, 2nd ed. Lanham: Rowman & Littlefield. Korean Translation by Sa-I Publishing, 2014.

Marshall, Thomas Humphrey. 1950. *Citizenship and Social Class: And Other Essays*. Cambridge: Cambridge University Press.

Marshall, Tim. 2015. *Prisoners of Geography: Ten Maps That Tell You Everything You Need to Know About Global Politics*. London: Elliot and Thompson.

Maslow, Abraham. 1971. *The Farther Reaches of Human Nature*. New York: The Viking Press.

Mason, Edward S., et al. 1980. *The Economic and Social Modernization of the Republic of Korea*. Cambridge, MA: Harvard University Press.

Mataen, David. 2012. *Africa the Ultimate Frontier Market: A Guide to the Business and Investment Opportunities in Emerging Africa*. Hampshire: Harriman House.

Mawji, Amin. 2017. *Poverty to Prosperity-Empowering the Future, Best Practice Ideas from Civil Society*. Kampala: Graphic Systems Uganda.

Mbeki, Moeletsi. 2011. *Advocates for Change: How to Overcome Africa's Challenges*. Johannesburg: Picardo Africa.

McNeil, Mary, and Carmen Malena (eds). 2010. *Demanding Good Governance: Lessons from Social Accountability Initiative in Africa*. Washington, DC: World Bank.

Mellor, John W. (ed.). 1995. *Agriculture on the Road to Industrialization*. Baltimore: Johns Hopkins University Press.

Meredith, Martin. 2011. *The State of Africa: A History of the Continent Since Independence*. London: Simon & Schuster UK.

Mills, Greg. 2010. *Why Africa Is Poor: And What Africans Can Do About It*. Cape Town: Penguin Books.

Millis, Greg, Olusegun Obasanjo, Jeffrey Herbst, and Dickie Davis. 2017. *Making Africa Work: A Handbook for Economic Success*. Cape Town: Tafelberg.

Mkandawire, Thandika. 2001. 'Thinking About Developmental States in Africa.' *Cambridge Journal of Economics* 25 (May): 289–313.

Mo, Jongryn, and Barry R. Weingast. 2013. *Korean Political and Economic Development: Crisis, Security and Institutional Rebalancing*. Cambridge, MA: Harvard University Press.

Moghalu, Kingsley Chiedu. 2014. *Emerging Africa*. London: Penguin Books.

Montalvo, Jose G., and Marta Reynal-Querol. 2005. 'Ethnic Diversity and Economic Development.' *Journal of Development Economics* 76: 293–323.

Morrissey, Oliver. 2001. 'Lessons for Africa from East Asian Economic Policy.' In Peter Lawrence and Colin Thirtle (eds), *Africa and Asia in Comparative Economic Perspective*. Basingstoke: Palgrave, 34–48.

Mosely, Paul. 2002. 'The African Green Revolution as a Pro-Poor Policy Instrument.' *Journal of International Development* 14(6): 695–724.

Moss, Todd. 2011. *African Development: Making Sense of the Issues and Actors*, 2nd ed. Boulder: Lynne Rienner.

Moyo, Dambisa. 2009. *Dead Aid: Why Aid Is Not Working and How There Is a Better Way for Africa*. New York: Farrar, Strauss and Giroux.

Mpofu, Thomas P.Z. 2013. 'Urbanization and Urban Environmental Challenges in Sub-Saharan Africa.' *Research Journal of Agricultural and Environmental Management* 2(6) (June): 127–134.

Muchie, Mammo, Visi Gumede, Samuel Oloruntoba, and Nicasius Achu Check (eds). 2016. *Regenerating Africa: Bringing African Solutions to African Problems*. Pretoria: Africa Institute of South Africa.

Muriaas, Ragnhild L. 2011. 'Traditional Institutions and Decentralization: A Typology of Co-Existence in Sub-Saharan Africa.' *Forum for Development Studies* 38(1): 87–107.

Mwabu, Germano, and Eric Thorbecke. 2004. 'Rural Development, Growth and Poverty in Africa.' *Journal of African Economies* 13, AERC Supplement 1: i16–i65.

Na, Jong-seok. 2017. *Daedong Democratic Confucianism and 21st Shilhak*. Seoul: Dosochulpan b (Korean).

Ndulu, Benno J., Lopamudra Chakraborti, Lebohang Lijane, Vijaya Ramachandran, and Jerome Wolgin. 2007. *Challenges of African Growth: Opportunities, Constraints and Strategic Directions*. Washington, DC: World Bank.

Ndulu, Benno J., Stephen A. O'Connell, Robert H. Bates, Paul Collier, Chukwuma C. Soludo, Jean-Paul Azam, Augustin K. Fosu, Jan Willem Gunning, and Dominique Njinkeu (eds). 2008. *The Political Economy of Economic Growth in Africa, 1960–2000*, 2 vols. Cambridge: Cambridge University Press.

New Partnership for Africa's Development (NEPAD). 2000. *The New Partnership for Africa's Development*. Durban: Heather Botha, Natal Press.

———. 2010. 'Implementing CAADP for Africa's Food Security Needs: A Progress Report on Selected Activities.' New Partnership for Africa's Development (AU) Briefing Paper, July.

Nhamo, Godwell, and Caiphas Chekwoti (eds). 2014. *Land Grabs in a Green African Economy*. Pretoria: Africa Institute of South Africa.

Nissanke, Machiko, and Ernest Aryeetey (eds). 2003. *Comparative Development Experiences of Sub-Saharan Africa and East Asia: An Institutional Approach*. Aldershot: Ashgate.

Nkrumah, Kwame. 1965. *Neo-Colonialism, the Last Stage of Imperialism*. London: Thomas, Nelson.

Noman, Akbar, Kwesi Botchwey, Howard Stein, and Joseph E. Stiglitz. 2011. *Good Growth and Governance in Africa: Rethinking Development Strategies*. Oxford: Oxford University Press.

North, Douglass C. 1982. *Structure and Change in Economic History*. New York: W.W. Norton.

———. 1990. *Institutions, Institutional Change and Economic Performance*. New York: Cambridge University Press.

North, Douglass C., John Wallis, Barry Weingast, and Stephen Webb (eds). 2013. *In The Shadow of Violence: The Problem of Development in Limited Access Order Societies*. New York: Cambridge University Press.

Nye, Joseph. 2004. *Soft Power: The Means to Success in World Politics*. New York: Public Affairs.

OECD. 2011. *African Economic Outlook 2011: Special Theme: Africa and Its Emerging Partners*. Paris: OECD Publishing.

Olivier de Sardan, Jean-Pierre. 2009. 'State Bureaucracy and Governance in West Africa: An Empirical Diagnosis and Historical Perspective.' In Giorgio Blundo and Pierre-Yves le Meur (eds), *The Governance of Daily Life in Africa*. Leiden: Koninklijke Brill NV, 39–72.

Olowu, Dele, and James S. Wunsch (eds). 2004. *Local Governance in Africa: The Challenges of Democratic Decentrialization*. Boulder: Lynee Rienner.

Olson, M. 1982. *The Rise and Decline of Nations: Economic Growth, Stagflation, and Social Rigidities*. New Haven, CT: Yale University Press.

Onis, Ziya, and Ahmet Aysan. 2000. 'Neoliberal Globalization, the Nation State and Financial Crises in the Semi-Periphery: A Comparative Analysis.' *Third World Quarterly* 21(1): 119–139.

Onyeiwu, Steve, and Hemanta Shrestha. 2004. 'Determinants of Foreign Direct Investment in Africa.' *Journal of Developing Societies* 20(1/2): 89–106.

Osterhammel, Jürgen. 2003. *Kolonialismus: Geschichte, Formen, Folgne*. Munchen: Verlag C.H. Beck oHG. Korean Translation by Yuksa Bipyongsa, 2006.

Ostrom, Elinor. 2005. *Understanding Institutional Diversity*. Princeton, NJ: Princeton University Press.

———. 2009. 'Beyond Markets and States: Polycentric Governance of Complex Economic Systems.' 2009 Nobel Prize Lecture, *American Economic Review* 100(3): 641–672.

Ottaway, Marina. 2003. *Democracy Challenged: The Rise of Semi-Authoritarianism*. Washington, DC: Carnegie Endowment for International Peace.

Oxfam. 2011. 'Land and Power. The Growing Scandal Surrounding the New Wave of Investment in Land.' Oxfam Briefing Paper No. 151. Oxford: Oxfam.

Park, Hyung Ho. 2013. *2012 Modulation of Korea's Development Experience: Land Reform in Korea*. Seoul: Ministry of Strategy and Finance.

Park, Jong-Dae. 2009. *Korea's Soft Power Foreign Policy Towards Developing Countries* (PhD thesis). Seoul: Kyungnam University (Korean).

Parpart, Jane. 1989. *Women and Development in Africa*. Lanham: University Press of America.

Pitcher, Anne, Mary Moran, and Michael Johnston. 2009. 'Rethinking Patrimonialism and Neopatrimonialism in Africa.' *African Studies Review* 51(1) (April): 125–156.

Posner, Daniel. 2004. 'Measuring Ethnic Fractionalism in Africa.' *American Journal of Political Science* 48(4): 849–863.

Posner, Daniel, and Daniel Young. 2007. 'The Institutionalization of Political Power in Africa.' *Journal of Democracy* 18(3): 126–140.

Poulton, Colin. 2012. 'Democratisation and the Political Economy of Agricultural Policy in Africa.' Future Agricultures Working Paper 43, Africa Power and Politics Programme. London: Future Agricultures Consortium.

Pritchett, Lant, Michael Woolcock, and Matt Andrews. 2010. 'Capability Traps? The Mechanism of Persistent Implementation Failure.' Center for Global Development Working Paper 234. Washington, DC: Center for Global Development.

Przeworski, Adam, Michael Alvarez, Jose A. Cheibub, and Fernando Limongi. 2000. *Democracy and Development: Political Institutions and Material Well-being in the World, 1950–1990*. Cambridge: Cambridge University Press.

Radcliffe, Sarah A. (ed.). 2006. *Culture and Development in a Globalizing World*. London and New York: Routledge.

Radelet, Steven. 2003. 'Bush and Foreign Aid.' *Foreign Affairs* 82(5): 104–117.

———. 2010. *Emerging Africa: How 17 Countries Are Leading the Way*. Washington, DC: Center for Global Development.

———. 2015. 'Angus Deaton, His Nobel Prize and Foreign Aid.' *Future Development* Blog, Brookings. 20 October.

Radelet, Steven, and Jeffrey D. Sachs. 1998. 'The East Asian Financial Crisis: Diagnosis, Remedies, Prospects.' *Brookings Papers on Economic Activity* 1998(1): 1–90.

Ramachandran, Vijaya, Alan Gelb, and Manju Kedia Shah. 2009. *Africa's Private Sector: What's Wrong with the Business Environment and What to Do About It.* Washington, DC: Center for Global Development.

Raskin, Paul, and T. Banuri, et al. 2002. *The Great Transition: The Promise and the Lure of the Times Ahead.* Boston: Tellus Institute.

Rhee, Younghoon. 2007. *A Story of the Republic of Korea: Re-understanding the Post-liberation Period.* Seoul: Ki-pa-rang (Korean).

Robinson, James A. 2009. 'Industrial Policy and Development: A Political Economy and Perspective.' Paper presented at the World Bank ABCDE conference in Seoul, Korea, June 22–24, 2009.

Rodrik, Dani. 1997. *Has Globalization Gone Too Far?* Washington, DC: Institute for International Economics.

———. 2004. 'Industrial Policy for the Twenty-first Century.' CEPR Discussion Paper No. 4767. Center for Economic Policy Research.

———. 2006. 'Goodbye Washington Consensus, Hello Washington Confusion.' *Journal of Economic Literature* 44(4): 973–987.

———. 2007. 'Normalizing Industrial Policy.' CDG Working Paper No. 3. Washington, DC: Center for Global Development.

———. 2011. *The Globalization Paradox—Democracy and the Future of the World Economy.* New York: W.W. Norton.

———. 2015. *Economics Rules: The Rights and Wrongs of the Dismal Science.* New York: W.W. Norton.

———. 2016. 'Premature Deindustrialization.' *Journal of Economic Growth* 21(1): 1–33.

Rodrick, Dani, Arvind Subramaniam, and Francesco Trebbi. 2004. 'Institutions Rule: The Primacy of Institutions Over Geography and Integration in Economic Development.' *Journal of Economic Growth* 9(2): 131–165.

Roemer, Michael. 1994. 'Industrial Strategies: Outward Bound.' In David L. Lindauer and Michael Roemer (eds), *Asia and Africa: Legacies and Opportunities in Development.* San Francisco: Institute for Contemporary Studies Press, 233–268.

Ross, Michael L. 2012. *The Oil Curse: How Petroleum Wealth Shapes the Development of Nations.* Princeton: Princeton University Press.

Rostow, W.W. 1960. *The Stages of Economic Growth: A Non-communist Manifesto*. Cambridge: Cambridge University Press.

Rowden, H.S. 1998. *Behind East Asian Growth: The Political and Social Foundation of Prosperity*. London: Routledge.

Rowden, Rick. 2015. 'Africa's Boom Is Over.' *Foreign Policy*, 31 December. http://foreignpolicy.com/2015/12/31/africas-boom-is-over/.

———. 2016. 'Here Is Why 'Africa Rising' Is Just a Myth.' Article in *The Observer* (Uganda). 6 January 24.

Rozman, G. 1991. *The East Asian Region: Confucian Heritage and Its Modern Adaptation*. Princeton, NJ: Princeton University Press.

Sacks, Jeffrey. 2005. *End of Poverty*. New York: The Pengiun Press.

———. 2008. *Commonwealth: Economics for a Crowded Planet*. New York: Penguin Press.

———. 2015. *The Age of Sustainable Development*. New York: Columbia University Press.

Sakong, Il, and Youngsun Koh (eds). 2010. *The Korean Economy: Six Decades of Growth and Development*. Seoul: Korea Development Institute.

Sardanis, Andrew. 2007. *A Venture in Africa: The Challenges of African Business*. New York: I.B. Tauris.

Sassen, Saskia. 2001. *The Global City: New York, London, Tokyo*, 2nd ed. Princeton: Princeton University Press.

Schleifer, Andrei. 2009. 'Peter Bauer and the Failure of Foreign Aid.' *Cato Journal* 29(3) (Fall): 379–390.

Schmid, Andre. 2002. *Korea Between Empires, 1895–1919*. New York: Columbia University Press.

Schulpen, L., and P. Gibbon. 2001. *Private Sector Development: Politics, Practices and Problems*. CDR Policy Paper. Copenhagen: Centre for Development Research.

Seth, Michael J. 2006. *A Concise History of Korea*. Maryland: Rowman & Littlefield.

Shin, Gwang-chul. 2013. *Extremist Koreans, Extreme Creativity*. Seoul. Sam & Parkers.

Shin, Gi-wook, and M. Robinson (eds). 1999. *Colonial Modernity in Korea*. Cambridge and London: Harvard University Asia Center.

Shin, Gi-wook, James Freda, and Gihong Yi. 1999. 'The Politics of Ethnic Nationalism in Divided Korea.' *Nation and Nationalism* 5(4): 465–484.

Slaughter, Anne-Marie. 2005. *The New World Order*. Princeton, NJ: Princeton University Press.

Sobhan, Rehman. 1993. *Agrarian Reform and Social Transformation*. London: Zed Books.

Soludo, Charles Chukwuma. 2003. 'Export-Oriented Industrialisation and Foreign Direct Investment in Africa.' In Ernest Aryeetey, Julius Court, Machiko Nissante, and Beartrice Weber (eds), *Africa and Asia in the Global Economy*. Tokyo: United Nations University Press, 246–281.

Spring, Anita, and Barbara E. McDade (eds). 1998. *African Entrepreneurship: Theory, and Reality*. Gainsville: University of Florida Press.

Stein, Howard (ed.). 1996. *Asian Industrialization and Africa*. New York: St. Martin's.

Stiglitz, Joseph. 2005. 'Finance for Development.' In Melvin Ayogu and Don Ross (eds), *Development Dilemmas: The Methods and Political Ethics of Growth Policy*. Abingdon: Routledge, 15–29.

Stiglitz, Joseph E. 2000. *Globalization and Its Discontents*. New York: W.W. Norton.

———. 2006. *Making Globalization Work*. New York: W.W Norton.

Stein, Howard. 1995. *Asian Industrialization and Africa: Studies in Policy Alternatives to Structural Adjustment*. New York: St. Martin's Press.

———. 2008. *Beyond the World Bank Agenda: An Institutional Approach to Development*. Chicago: University of Chicago Press.

———. 2015a. *Rewriting the Rules of the American Economy: An Agenda for Growth and Shared Prosperity*. New York: W.W. Norton.

———. 2015b. 'Industrial Policy, Learning and Development.' In John Page and Finn Tarp (eds), *The Practice of Industrial Policy: Government-Business Coordination in Africa and East Asia*, Oxford: Oxford University Press, pp. 23–39 and WIDER Working Paper 2015/149, published by UNU-WIDER and the Korean International Cooperation Agency, Helsinki, Finland, December 2015.

Stubbs, Richard. 2005. *Rethinking Asia's Economic Miracle*. Basingstoke: Palgrave Macmillan.

Studwell, Joe. 2013. *How Asia Works: Success and Failure in the World's Most Dynamic Region*. London: Profile Books.

Sugema, Iman, and Anis Chowdhury. 2007. 'Has Aid Made the Government of Indonesia Lazy?' *Asia-Pacific Development Journal* 14(1): 105–124.

Sun, Yun. 2015. 'How the International Community Changed China's Asian Infrastructure Investment Bank.' *The Diplomat*, 31 July. //thediplomat.com.

Swindler, A., and S. Cotts Watkins. 2009. 'Teach a Man to Fish: Sustainability Doctrine and Its Social Consequences.' *World Development* 37(7): 1182–1196.

Taylor, Ian. 2005. *NEPAD and the Global Economy: Towards the Africa's Development or Another False Start?* Boulder: Lynne Rienner.

———. 2010. *The International Relations of Sub-Saharan Africa*. New York: Continuum.

Taylor, Scott D. 2007. *Business and the State I Southern Africa: The Politics of Economic Reform*. Boulder: Lynne Rienner.

———. 2012. *Globalization and the Cultures of Business in Africa*. Bloomington: Indiana University Press.

Thomas, Melissa. 2009. 'What Do the Worldwide Governance Indicators Measure?' *European Journal of Development Research* 22: 31–54.

Thompson, M. 1996. 'Late Industrialization, Late Democratisers: Developmental States in the Asia-Pacific.' *Third World Quarterly* 17(4): 625–647.

Thorbecke, Erik. 2000. 'The Evolution of the Development Doctrine and the Role of Foreign Aid.' In Finn Tarp (ed.), *Foreign Aid and Development: Lessons Learnt and Directions for the Future*. London: Routledge, 16–47.

Thornton, W. 1994. 'The Korean Road to Postmoderniszation and Development.' *Asian Pacific Quarterly* 26(1): 1–11.

———. 1998. 'Korea and East Asian Exceptionalism.' *Theory, Culture and Society* 15(2): 137–154.

Tilly, Charles. 1985. *War Making and State Making as an Organized Crime*. In Peter Evans, et al. (eds), *Bringing the State Back In*. Cambridge, UK: Cambridge University Press, 169–187.

———. 1990. *Coercion, Capital and European States. A.D. 990–1990*. Oxford and New York: Basil Blackwell.

Timmer, C. Peter. 2007. 'How Indonesia Connected the Poor to Rapid Economic Growth.' In Timothy Besley and Louise J. Cord (eds), *Delivering on the Promise of Pro-Poor Growth: Insights and Lessons from Country Experiences*. Washington, DC: World Bank (with Palgrave Macmillan), 29–57.

Trip, Aili Mary. 2001. 'The Politics of Autonomy and Cooperation in Africa: The Case of the Ugandan Women's Movement.' *Journal of Modern African Studies* 39(1): 101–128.

———. 2010. *Museveni's Uganda: Paradoxes of Power in a Hybrid Regime*. Boulder: Lynne Rienner.

UNDP. 2008. *Climate Change and Human Development in Africa: Assessing the Risks and Vulnerability of Climate Change in Kenya, Malawi and Ethiopia*. New York: UNDP.

———. 2010. *Human Development in Africa*. New York: UNDP.

———. 2016. *Regional Human Development Report 2016: Africa*. New York: UNDP.

UNECA. 2015. *Macroeconomic Policy and Structural Transformation of African Economies*. Addis Ababa: UNECA.

———. 2016a. *Economic Report on Africa 2016: Greening Africa's Industrialization*. Addis Ababa: UNECA.

———. 2016b. *African Governance Report IV: Measuring Corruption in Africa—The International Dimension Matters*. Addis Ababa: UNECA.

———. 2017. *Economic Report on Africa 2017: Urbanization and Industrialization for Africa's Transformation*. Addis Ababa: UNECA.

Unsworth, S. 2009. 'What's Politics Got to Do with It? Why Donors Find It so Hard to Come to Terms with Politics, and Why This Matters.' *Journal of International Development* 21(6): 883–894.

USAID. 2016. *USAID Uganda Country Development Cooperation Strategy 2016–2021*. USAID Uganda, 6 December.

US Embassy in Uganda. 2016. *Report to the Ugandan People*. US Embassy in Uganda, 30 September.

Van de Walle, Nicola. 2001. *African Economies and the Politics of Permanent Crisis, 1979–1999*. Cambridge: Cambridge University Press.

———. 2007. 'Meet the New Boss, Sam as the Old Boss? Evolution of Political Clientelism in Africa.' In H. Kitschelt and S. I. Wilkinson (eds), *Patrons, Clients, and Policies: Pattern of Democratic Accountability and Political Competition*. Cambridge: Cambridge University Press, 50–67.

Van der Veen, Roel. 2004. *What Went Wrong with Africa: A Contemporary History*. Amsterdam: KIT Publishers.

Van Dijk, Meine Pieter (ed.). 2009. *The New Presence of China in Africa*. Amsterdam: Amsterdam University Press.

Van Donge, Jan Kees. 2012. 'Governance and Access to Finance for Development: An Explanation of Divergent Development Trajectories in Kenya and Malaysia.' *Commonwealth and Comparative Politics* 50(1): 53–74.

Van Donge, Jan Kees, David Henley, and Peter Lewis. 2012. 'Tracking Development in Southeast Asia and Sub-Saharan Africa: The Primacy of Policy.' *Development Policy Review* 30(S1): 5–24.

Vlasblom, D. 2013. *The Richer Harvest: The Tracking Development Study 2006–2011*. Leiden: African Studies Centre.

Wade, Robert. 2003. *Governing the Market: Economic Theory and the Role of the Government in East Asian Industrialization*. Princeton: Princeton University Press.

Wade, Robert, and Frank Veneroso. 1998. 'The Asian Crisis: The High Debt Model Versus the Wall Street-Treasury-IMF Complex.' *New Left Review* 228: 1–22.

Weaver, Catherine. 2008. *Hypocrisy Trap: The World Bank and the Poverty of Reform.* Princeton, NJ: Princeton University Press.

Welz, Martin. 2013. *Integrating Africa: Decolonization's Legacies, Sovereignty, and the African Union*. London: Routledge.

Williamson, John. 2000. 'What Should the World Bank Think About the Washington Consensus?' *World Bank Research Observer* 15(2): 251–264.

Williamson, Olivier. 2000. 'The New Institutional Economics: Taking Stock, Looking Ahead.' *Journal of Economic Literature* 38: 593–613.

Wood, Ellen Meiksins. 1998. 'The Agrarian Origins of Capitalism.' *Monthly Review* 50(3) (July–August): 14.

Wong, Susan. 2012. *What Have Been the Impacts of World Bank Community-Driven Development Programs?* Washington, DC: World Bank Social Development Department.

World Bank. 1993. *The East Asian Miracle*. New York: Oxford University Press for the World Bank.

———. 1997. *World Development Report 1997: The State in a Changing World.* Washington, DC: Oxford University Press/World Bank.

———. 2001. *Aid and Reform in Africa: Lessons from Ten Case Studies.* Washington, DC: The World Bank.

———. 2007. *World Development Report 2008: Agriculture for Development.* Washington, DC: The World Bank.

———. 2009. *Governance and Anticorruption in Projects: Benchmarking and Learning Review*. Washington, DC: The World Bank.

———. 2016. *Poverty in a Rising Africa*. Washington, DC: The World Bank.

———. 2017a. *Atlas of Sustainable Development Goals 2017: From World Development Indicators*. Washington, DC: The World Bank.

———. 2017b. *Global Economic Prospects: A Fragile Economy*. Washington, DC: The World Bank.

Wunsch, James S., and Dan Ottemoeller. 2004. 'Uganda: Multiple Levels of Local Governance.' In Dele Olowu and James S. Wunsch (eds), *Local Governance in Africa: The Challenges of Democratic Decentralization*. Boulder: Lynne Rienner, 101–210.

Young, Crawford. 2007. 'Nation, Ethnicity, and Citizenship: Dilemmas of Democracy and Civil Order in Africa.' In Sara Dorman, Daniel Hammett, and Paul Nugent (eds), *Making Nations, Creating Strangers: States and Citizenship in Africa*. Leiden: Brill, 241–264.

———. 2012. *The Postcolonial State in Africa*. Madison: The University of Wisconsin Press.

Zadek, Simon. 2006. 'The Logic of Collaborative Governance.' Corporate Social Responsibility Initiative Working Paper 17. Kennedy School of Government, Harvard University.

Index

J.-D. Park, *Re-Inventing Africa's Development*,
https://doi.org/10.1007/978-3-030-03946-2

M

N

CPSIA information can be obtained
at www.ICGtesting.com
Printed in the USA
LVHW011430030119
602637LV00003B/3/P